Practitioner's Complete Guide to M&As

Founded in 1807, John Wiley & Sons is the oldest independent publishing company in the United States. With offices in North America, Europe, Australia, and Asia, Wiley is globally committed to developing and marketing print and electronic products and services for our customers' professional and personal knowledge and understanding.

The Wiley Finance series contains books written specifically for finance and investment professionals as well as sophisticated individual investors and their financial advisors. Book topics range from portfolio management to e-commerce, risk management, financial engineering, valuation, and financial instrument analysis, as well as much more.

For a list of available titles, visit our Web site at www.WileyFinance.com.

Practitioner's Complete Guide to M&As

An All-Inclusive Reference

DAVID T. EMOTT

John Wiley & Sons, Inc.

Copyright © 2011 by David T. Emott. All rights reserved.

Published by John Wiley & Sons, Inc., Hoboken, New Jersey.
Published simultaneously in Canada.

No part of this publication may be reproduced, stored in a retrieval system, or transmitted in any form or by any means, electronic, mechanical, photocopying, recording, scanning, or otherwise, except as permitted under Section 107 or 108 of the 1976 United States Copyright Act, without either the prior written permission of the Publisher, or authorization through payment of the appropriate per-copy fee to the Copyright Clearance Center, Inc., 222 Rosewood Drive, Danvers, MA 01923, (978) 750-8400, fax (978) 646-8600, or on the Web at www.copyright.com. Requests to the Publisher for permission should be addressed to the Permissions Department, John Wiley & Sons, Inc., 111 River Street, Hoboken, NJ 07030, (201) 748-6011, fax (201) 748-6008, or online at http://www.wiley.com/go/permissions.

Limit of Liability/Disclaimer of Warranty: While the publisher and author have used their best efforts in preparing this book, they make no representations or warranties with respect to the accuracy or completeness of the contents of this book and specifically disclaim any implied warranties of merchantability or fitness for a particular purpose. No warranty may be created or extended by sales representatives or written sales materials. The advice and strategies contained herein may not be suitable for your situation. You should consult with a professional where appropriate. Neither the publisher nor author shall be liable for any loss of profit or any other commercial damages, including but not limited to special, incidental, consequential, or other damages.

For general information on our other products and services or for technical support, please contact our Customer Care Department within the United States at (800) 762-2974, outside the United States at (317) 572-3993 or fax (317) 572-4002.

Wiley also publishes its books in a variety of electronic formats. Some content that appears in print may not be available in electronic books. For more information about Wiley products, visit our Web site at www.wiley.com

Library of Congress Cataloging-in-Publication Data:

Emott, David T., 1944–
Practitioner's complete guide to M&As : an all-inclusive reference / David T. Emott.
p. cm. – (Wiley finance ; 635)
Includes index.
ISBN 978-0-470-92044-2 (pbk.); ISBN 978-1-118-01589-6 (ebk);
ISBN 978-1-118-01590-2 (ebk); ISBN 978-1-118-01591-9 (ebk)
1. Consolidation and merger of corporations. I. Title.
HD2746.5.E46 2011
658.1′62–dc22

2010045218

Printed in the United States of America

10 9 8 7 6 5 4 3 2 1

Contents

Preface xi

Acknowledgments xiii

TOPIC 1
Strategy Development, Then M&A 1

TOPIC 2
M&A Process: Front to Back 13

TOPIC 3
Why M&A? 17

TOPIC 4
Deal Criteria 19

TOPIC 5
Deal Sourcing 26

TOPIC 6
Fees for Services 29

TOPIC 7
Financial and Strategic Buyers 36

TOPIC 8
How Long Will It Take to Complete the Deal? 38

TOPIC 9
Confidentiality Agreements 39

TOPIC 10
"Concern Capture" Due Diligence 44

TOPIC 11
Keep Deal Conversations Quiet 53

TOPIC 12
Auctions 54

TOPIC 13
Seller's Prospectus 62

TOPIC 14
Pay for Inherent Capabilities Only 65

TOPIC 15
Platform Value 68

TOPIC 16
Buyer and Seller Value Perspectives 70

TOPIC 17
Integration Initiatives Will Determine Deal Value 73

TOPIC 18
Unlock Hidden Value: The Lean Enterprise 75

TOPIC 19
The Real Deal: Lean 78

TOPIC 20
Valuation: An Introduction 82

TOPIC 21
Discounted Cash Flow: An Introduction 86

TOPIC 22
Free Cash Flow 90

TOPIC 23
Fair Return on a Deal 95

TOPIC 24
Risk-Free Rates 104

TOPIC 25
Equity Risk Premiums 105

TOPIC 26
What Is Business Risk? 106

TOPIC 27
Entropy: Tendency toward Negative Variation 110

TOPIC 28
Equity Investor Risk 112

TOPIC 29
Beta 113

TOPIC 30
Systematic Risk 116

TOPIC 31
Unsystematic Risk 118

TOPIC 32
Beta with or without Debt 119

TOPIC 33
Beta: Levered or Unlevered 120

TOPIC 34
Beta Application in Determination of C_U 123

TOPIC 35
Levered Beta Moves as Debt to Equity Moves 125

TOPIC 36
Size Premium 127

TOPIC 37
Weighted Average Cost of Capital 130

TOPIC 38
Terminal Values, Terminal Value Multiples, and Terminal Value DCFs 137

TOPIC 39
Discounted Cash Flow Valuation Illustrated 142

TOPIC 40
Leverage: The Real Deal 147

TOPIC 41
Debt Limits 149

TOPIC 42
Debt Adds Value: Derivation of Dt 151

TOPIC 43
The Leveraged Buyout; Definition and Valuation 155

TOPIC 44
Valuing the Leveraged Buyout 160

TOPIC 45
Real Option Valuation: An Introduction 169

TOPIC 46
Real Option Valuation: Application and Illustration 173

TOPIC 47
M&A Values Are Not All the Same 179

TOPIC 48
Discounts and Premiums 183

TOPIC 49
Discounted Cash Flow Valuations: Minority or Control 192

TOPIC 50
Inflation in DCF Valuations 194

TOPIC 51
Integration, Alignment, and Synergy Benefits: Plan It Out 195

TOPIC 52
Integration, Alignment, and Valuing Synergy Benefits 197

TOPIC 53
Venture Capital Valuation 208

TOPIC 54
Discount Rates and Valuing Free Cash Flow 211

TOPIC 55
Growth, C*, and Return: The Engine to Increased Valuations and Deferred Tax Advantage 222

TOPIC 56
How Fast Can the Target Grow? 225

TOPIC 57
Cash Flow Multiples, Growth Rates, and Discount Rates 227

TOPIC 58
Comparable Multiples 239

TOPIC 59
Converting FCF_M to P/Es and Other Valuation Multiples and Deriving Slot Multiples for Public Companies 247

TOPIC 60
EBITDA Valuation Engine 264

TOPIC 61
Free Cash Flow Equivalent Impacts for Arbitrary Adjustments to Discount Rates 276

TOPIC 62
Transferring Defined Benefit Pension Plan Liability Issues 278

TOPIC 63
Environmental Remediation Expenses 282

TOPIC 64
Environmental Insurance 283

TOPIC 65
Management Warrant Incentive Plans 285

TOPIC 66
Negotiation: Introduction and Overview 290

TOPIC 67
Negotiation: Values, Offers, Prices, and Risk Assumption 292

TOPIC 68
Negotiation: Offer Content 296

TOPIC 69
Negotiation: Create Space in Your Ideas 298

TOPIC 70
Negotiation: Beware of the Emotions of Private Sellers 299

TOPIC 71
Negotiation: Imprint; Do Not Lecture 301

TOPIC 72
Negotiation: Handling Tight Spots 303

TOPIC 73
Negotiation: Closing the Bid-Ask Negotiating Gap 305

TOPIC 74
Negotiation: Be Aware of Leverage and Deal Momentum Shift 308

TOPIC 75
Negotiation in the Final Stages 311

TOPIC 76
Negotiation: Use Earn-Outs or Noncompete Agreements to Close a Bid-Ask Gap 313

TOPIC 77
Negotiation: After the Deal Is Agreed 318

TOPIC 78
Negotiation: Bluffing and How to Handle It 321

TOPIC 79
Negotiation: When Do You Step Away? 324

TOPIC 80
Negotiation: When Do You Proceed? 326

TOPIC 81
Negotiation: Do a Time Capsule 328

TOPIC 82
Negotiation: Build Trust to Get Closed 329

TOPIC 83
Exits under Duress: Have a Plan if the Deal Does Not Work 333

TOPIC 84
Structuring the Deal: An Overview 334

TOPIC 85
Structuring the Deal: Asset Step-Ups, Noncompete, and Synergy Valuation Engines 341

TOPIC 86
Total Shareholder Return 346

TOPIC 87
Stakeholder Value Creation 349

TOPIC 88
EVAquity: Align Shareholder and Management Interests 353

TOPIC 89
Letter of Intent 358

TOPIC 90
Purchase and Sale Agreement 359

TOPIC 91
Purchase and Sale Agreement: Explanation by Section 361

TOPIC 92
Purchase Price Adjustments for Working Capital 370

TOPIC 93
Indemnification and Survival Provisions 374

TOPIC 94
Escrows 379

TOPIC 95
Joint Venture Transaction: Valuation and Structuring Overview 381

TOPIC 96
Why Deals Go Bad 389

TOPIC 97
After the Deal: Do a Deal Bible 391

TOPIC 98
Do the Audits of the Integration and Deal Value Creation Plan 393

About the Web Site 395

Index 397

Preface

This book is a hands-on, practical guide and reference to the key topics, issues, and methodologies buyers and sellers face and employ in doing M&A (business mergers, acquisitions, divestitures, stock buybacks, equity investments, and joint venture transactions). It is a quick, easy-to-use reference for those new to the process of M&A (private business owners, students, associates, trainees). In addition, it will refresh and reacquaint those already familiar with deal making (CEOs, CFOs, lawyers, accountants, tax and finance, and insurance and deal professionals) with what happens, when, who is doing it, and why, and answer the question: What do we need to know and do at this phase of the process?

The book is written as a quick-read reference of ideas, approaches, and don't-forgets for use during live transactions and as a self-study guide to enable fast transfer of essential M&A knowledge.

The topics in the book are laid out sequentially to enable the reader to build the highly relevant knowledge base necessary for pursuing and understanding corporate development via M&A. Topics covered including strategy development, acquisition criteria, deal sources, deal fee arrangements, due diligence, conducting auctions, lean enterprise, cost of capital, risk premiums, size premiums, leveraged and unleveraged beta, systematic and unsystematic risk, discount rate construction, valuation, pricing leveraged buyouts, the real deal about using debt, terminal values, real options in valuation, platform value, joint venture valuation and structuring, values, offers and deal pricing, discounts and premiums, venture capital valuation, growth, comparable pricing multiples, transferring pension obligations, deal integration, negotiation, risk and entropy, taxable and tax deferred deal structures, warrant- and economic value added– (EVA) based incentive plans, contracts and papering the deal, earn-outs, valuing synergies and tax step-ups, tax treatment of deal fees, escrows, caps, baskets, indemnity duration, why deals go bad, and much more.

Although some of the topics are longer than others, they all provide a succinct, pragmatic, and understandable view of each topic. The appendices referred to in each topic provide illustrations and visual guides that will prompt the reader to ask: How can this be adapted to work for us?

One of my goals when writing this book was to demonstrate the application of pertinent academic theory to the practical process of getting deals done. Sources in the footnotes and in the reference list direct the reader to additional information on the subjects discussed. It is my hope that the reader will view the book as a key reference when preparing for and undertaking the heady challenge of doing M&A. My aim is for the reader to finish a topic or the entire text with the feeling of "I get it."

David T. Emott

Acknowledgments

I would like to thank many friends and associates who have contributed to the writing of this book.

Attorneys Lawrence Coassin, Mathew Guanci, John Lynch, and Richard Tomeo of Robinson & Cole, Hartford, Connecticut, provided invaluable assistance with the tax, deal structuring, negotiating, and contractual overview topics. This assistance was provided in the context of working many acquisitions and joint ventures together over the years as well as discussing and reviewing drafts of textual material. Working with John Stempeck, Partner, Avalon Associates, Boston, Massachusetts, provided valuable insight into the strategy and business development process.

I would also like to acknowledge the many individuals who encouraged me and allowed me to engage in the corporate development process while at The Dexter Corporation, where I cut my teeth on M&A transactions: David Coffin, Worth Loomis, Harold Fleming, and Bob McGill; and my associates in the trenches at The Dexter Corporation, John Vrabel, Dick Hurley, and Stiles Twitchell. Thanks also to my associates at Ensign Bickford Industries, who worked with me on many transactions and whose comments, work product, and insights contributed to and have found their way into the contents of this book: Herman Fonteyne, Joe Lovejoy, Ray Tremaglio, Dave Edwards, Tony Cicchetti, Jackie Levin, Bob Pallanck, Rick Roberts, Denise Grant, and Mike Long. Special thanks to my assistant while at Ensign Bickford Industries, Sue Mazurski, who prepared the first working draft of my manuscript from many handwritten pages prepared on my many flights to and from cities here and abroad as deals ran their course.

Thanks also to John Brzezenski, Partner, Avalon Associates, Boston, Massachusetts, who introduced me to Michael Frankel, Vice President Business Development and M&A, LexisNexis, New York City, who provided me with an introduction to Sheck Cho, my eventual Executive Editor at John Wiley & Sons. Thanks to Sheck and to Dexter Gasque, Senior Production Editor, at John Wiley & Sons for their encouragement and attention to detail as this book was prepared.

I should also acknowledge the many unnamed persons who sat across the table from me on many transactions here and abroad for their insights, offerings, and constant reminder that there is always a faster gun in town.

Lastly, thanks to my wife, Karen, who put up with me during the years of development of this book.

D. T. E.

Practitioner's Complete Guide to M&As

TOPIC 1

Strategy Development, Then M&A

Topic 1 presents an overview of the fundamental elements typically addressed in the strategic planning process; explores a number of work activities, approaches, and ideas pertinent to the process of developing strategy; and explores where mergers and acquisitions (M&A) fit in the strategy development and execution process.

The reader is encouraged to take the time to read through the Appendices referenced in the text of this and all remaining Topics in conjunction with the narrative to gain the appropriate level of understanding of the subject matter discussed. Appendices are either presented at the end of this and each remaining Topic or are available for review and download on this book's companion Web site (see the About the Web Site page for login information).

M&A IS ONE OF MANY BUSINESS DEVELOPMENT OPTIONS

- M&A in an operating business is one of a number of means to accomplish a strategic goal and generally results from a strategic planning and strategy development process.
- M&A activity is the strategic activity of investor groups (equity funds, venture capital funds, etc.).
- The work involved in strategy development in manufacturing or service firms is often found to be frustrating and difficult.
- The questions, introspective search, dialog, and answers often are time consuming and unclear, particularly to the operating executives doing this work who are used to dealing with issues and process refinements of running a business and making decisions.
- The operating executives include chief executive officers, chief financial officers, chief operating officers, operations directors, plant managers, manufacturing managers, chief marketing executives, or sales officers.
- The operating executives, however, are the source of the knowledge gained over years in the business that matters most in developing strategy.

- The work agenda must acknowledge early on that strategy development deals with issues and questions that do not have great clarity. The answers to these questions usually surrender not to analysis but to participants' best thinking and judgment.
- The strategy development team should move along as fast as the pace of capturing and quantifying judgment allows and determine where complementary off-line research and analysis by the team and or team analysts is needed to enhance the judgment.
- Avoid a heavily research-driven process.

STAGES INVOLVED IN THE STRATEGIC PLANNING PROCESS

- *This section provides a general overview of the key elements of the strategic planning process* usually employed in an operating company and indicates where M&A fits in. The information is presented in the Strategy Planning Process Engine in Appendix 1.1.
  - *Corporate vision* embodies a brief, understandable, timeless statement of the rationale for why the firm exists (not what it does or wants to be) and the core principles that govern how the firm and its employees will conduct business and themselves during its existence.
  - *Corporate mission* embodies a brief, understandable, realistic statement of what the firm wants to be (and be seen as) in the medium term, say 15 to 20 years.
  - *Corporate strategies* are brief, understandable, achievable action statements of intent, direction, and desired result that are necessary to achieve and that, if achieved, will move the firm toward its mission (if not achieved, they will prevent achievement of the mission). These strategies are intended to create sustainable competitive advantage in the organization's market space. These strategies emanate from the strategy development process discussed later in this topic.
  - *Initiatives* are big, achievable activities and programs that individuals and teams rally around and participate and take ownership in. Initiatives are necessary to complete and, if completed, will move the firm toward realization of the desired results embodied in each strategy. They are usually multiyear in duration. M&A is potentially one of a number of business development initiatives.
  - *Key performance indicators (KPIs)* are descriptions of relevant, timeless indicators of performance in operating and functional support processes and initiative realization.
  - *Metrics* are relevant, preferably quantitative measures by which to gauge performance toward and achievement of initiatives and of KPIs.
  - *Goals* are brief statements of this year's (perhaps part of a multiyear goal) expected achievements and related metrics of achievement for each initiative or KPI. Goals are owned by individuals and teams and provide a clear measure of personal and team performance.

- *Results* are measurement based, integrate with incentive plan design and rewards, and provide the basis for measuring goal achievement and making cyclical, periodic adjustments to strategy, initiatives, metric targets, and goals.

STRATEGY DEVELOPMENT—WHERE AND HOW TO CREATE VALUE

- *The essential thrust of strategy development* is identifying *where to create value* (attractive market spaces to enter or maintain and defend) and *how to create value* in the spaces selected. (What are the enabling capabilities and strategies required to close the capability gaps that exist for the firm to compete in the identified spaces and create enduring stakeholder value?)
- M&A is one of a number of means of closing the capability gaps. Other methods include organic development, in-house start-up, licensing, joint ventures, and other contractual arrangements.
- The process involved in detail strategy development usually includes the two steps noted above, which are shown in the Strategy Development and Gap Closure Engine in Appendix 1.2.
- Many of the process steps presented on Appendix 1.2 may not be carried out explicitly in reaching strategy conclusions in businesses that prefer a more intuitive strategy development approach, but they probably reflect the thought processes and trade-offs made by intuitive strategy developers.
- Do not underestimate what a highly skilled and experienced strategy development consultant can offer to drive the strategy development process. Experienced experts will, at the very least, provide a voice of reason, contrast, and clarity to the process. More often they will provide the results of external research and insights, options, points of focus, and direction, which are all of timeless value to the user.
- There is also great benefit to focus the due diligence process (normally applied to acquisition targets as discussed in Topic 10) internally (the firm's due diligence self-assessment) as part of the firm's strategic planning process. Doing so captures much of the knowledge of the firm's capabilities discussed later in this topic, as well as the business and valuation drivers discussed in Topic 10 and attractive market criteria discussed in Topic 4.

WHERE—IDENTIFY CUSTOMER'S INITIATIVES AND ATTRACTIVE MARKET SPACES

- *Identify your customer's (and your customer's customers) strategic initiatives* in the market spaces you are now engaged in (See Appendix 1.2). Also identify their current and future product and service needs and requirements that will fulfill their initiatives (B, Appendix 1.2):

- By doing so, you can identify where are they going, what will they need to get there, and what is most important to them to enable them to succeed. You will also identify what capabilities will be necessary for vendors to excel at to meet their customers' product and service requirements (B1, Appendix 1.2). Consider the following:
  - Closely follow industry trends.
  - Hold "customer futures" conferences for your industry and its future.
  - Talk to your customers: How can you be in their future?
  - Attend customer industry conferences and trade shows.
- *Identify new attractive market spaces* (B2, B3, Appendix 1.2) and the future product and service requirements of those spaces worthy of developing, entering, and defending (B, Appendix 1.2). Identify the capabilities necessary to meet those product and service requirements (B1, Appendix 1.2).
- *Use brainstorming techniques* to identify adjacent and new market space ideas. Cross-reference them to the results from these idea-generating methods:
  - Search Web databases for ideas on where others are placing investments.
  - Interview pension advisors and venture capital and equity investors for investment trends and developing sectors.
  - Interview "blue sky" thinkers for megatrends and implications on business sectors.
  - Perform top-down growth segment identification methods using macro, segment-oriented databases. Where is growth and investment occurring?
  - Examine the value chains in growth sectors to identify the key value-creating enablers and inputs to the identified attractive macro sectors: What is the key ingredient, enabler, or activity in the value chain that adds the critical function to the end products and services within the sector?
  - Identify the key value-added ingredient sector of the value chain that becomes the target market space in the attractive sector.
  - Question industry experts to identify the value chain and enhance the analysis.
  - Cross-correlate the findings from each method.
  - Perform activity and capability extension analysis as discussed later in this topic.

HOW—IDENTIFY YOUR ACTIVITIES AND CAPABILITIES—EXTEND THEM

- *Identify your business's internal activity and capability strengths* (Activities, Capabilities, and possibly Competencies) (C, Appendix 1.2).[1]
  - Activities and capabilities are all the relevant things done in the business to serve customers in one way or another.

[1] This activity and capability extension analysis is grounded in the excellent work of John Stempeck, of Avalon Associates, Boston, MA, a strategy development consulting firm.

- Activities and capabilities as illustrated in Appendix 1.3 are evaluated in terms of how well they are done and the relative state of evolution of the activity within the company versus the requirements in targeted market spaces and as practiced by principal competitors. They are described as follows:

  How Well the Activity Is Practiced in the Company

  - Leader or cutting edge; equal to or just okay; follower or lagging behind

  State of Evolution of the Activity as Practiced in the Marketplace and as Required to Meet Future Market Requirements

  - Emerging, recently developed, gaining traction
  - Required and undergoing change
  - Mature, subject to competitive replacement

  Activities and Capabilities Might Include, for Example

  - Conceiving, designing, assembling, fabricating, engineering
  - Proposal preparation, selling, order taking, chemical synthesis
  - Milling, cutting, folding, drawing, welding, bending, preparing, polishing
  - Field service, customer inventory management, distributing, delivering
  - Some activities may be competencies (see below)

  Competencies Are the Reason(s) Customers Come Back

  - Competencies are the conjoint result of excellent business process execution (combinations of activities performed at a cutting-edge level) and deep capabilities described in terms of years of know-how, education, and unique learned and applied skills that are utilized in work activities.
  - Competencies are observable and identifiable by customers as activities performed that they rely on most heavily and are not easily replicated by the competition.
  - Bain & Company defines a core competency as a deep proficiency that enables a company to deliver unique value to customers. It embodies an organization's collective learning, particularly of how to coordinate diverse production skills and integrate multiple technologies.[2]
  - Customer interviews asking why customers rely on you, buy from you, and keep coming back rather than going to the competition are often the most productive way to identify competence. Customers may say:
    - "They always deliver on time in full quantities needed."
    - "Their product always functions to spec under the harshest use conditions."
    - "They can solve any technical design and application problem we throw at them and do it quickly."
    - "Their technical and delivery proposals to our conceptual requirements leave no questions unanswered—we know what we are going to get."

[2] www.bain.com/management_tools/tools_competencies.asp?groupcode=2.

- A company's competence is the conjoint process/capability set that leads to the end result desired and identified by the customer.
- Competencies allow a company to stay in business.
- There are many capabilities, business processes, activities, and skills; they are not necessarily competencies.
- There is usually only one competency in an organization, if any at all.

Activity and Capability Extension Analysis

- Perform activity and capability extension analysis (D in Appendix 1.2) to identify adjacent market application potentials.[3] Once you understand your key activity and capability strengths (perhaps competencies) as practiced in your segment, extend these activities into other potentially attractive segments.
- Ask key staff to examine where else (other served markets segments, other product or technical applications) your key activities and capabilities can be practiced, as illustrated in Appendix 1.4.
- Perform key word searches of your activities descriptors on databases to identify other "where used" potential market segments. Then analyze the segments to determine how attractive they are, who plays there, and how deep and how profitable the value chain in the sectors are (B2, B3, Appendix 1.2).

HOW—IDENTIFY YOUR CAPABILITY GAPS VS. MARKET AND PRODUCT REQUIREMENTS

- *Compare your existing company activities and capabilities (C, Appendix 1.2) with those required to defend present or develop or enter new attractive market spaces* (B1).
  - Identify your capability gaps (G) and consider alternative ways to close the gaps: M&A, joint venture, acquire or license technology, build a capability organically, etc. (see the Attractive Market Composite Assessment Engine in Appendix 1.5 for an illustration).
  - Do you have what it takes to compete there? What capabilities do you need?

HOW—IDENTIFY YOUR CAPABILITY GAPS VS. COMPETITION

- *Compare your existing product and service offering strengths* (E, Appendix 1.2) with existing competitor product and service offering strengths (E1) by conducting customer interviews and internal assessments. Identify product and service gaps (F) and possible gap closure approaches.

[3] This activity and capability extension analysis is grounded in the excellent work of John Stempeck, of Avalon Associates, Boston, MA, a strategy development consulting firm.

- *Compare your existing company activities and capabilities* (C, Appendix 1.2) with those of your competition (C1) in present and new attractive market spaces.
  - Identify the competitive gaps (H): What does it take to meet or beat the competition and close the gaps? Identify possible gap closure approaches (see the Capabilities versus Competitive Assessment Engine in Appendix 1.6 for an illustration of this process). Are you better or worse than the competition? What capabilities do you need to improve?

HOW—DEFINE ATTRACTIVE MARKET CRITERIA, RATE MARKETS, CLOSE GAPS

- *Define attractive market criteria (I, Appendix 1.2), and measure and rate each market space identified against the criteria* (see Topic 4 for an illustration of attractive market criteria). How well does each potential market stack up against your criteria for an attractive place to compete: well or not well? Do you want to be there or not?
- *Perform a strategic option assessment* (J, Appendix 1.2) of the capabilities that are required to defend, develop, enter, and exploit success and close gaps in each attractive market space.
- *Identify the likely mode of closing the capabilities gap* or achieving market penetration, such as in house start-up, acquisition, joint venture, technology license, and so forth (J1, appendix 1.2).
- *Rate the expected effectiveness of successful penetration* into each new attractive market space, given each likely entry mode considered (K, Appendix 1.2) against the firm's key business investment success criteria, including, for example:
  - Extent of activity overlap (Appendix 1.5)
  - Level of difficulty (to enter, develop, defend) given the likely entry mode
  - Level of competitive risk (Appendix 1.6)
  - Level of likely realization of opportunity potential given the likely entry mode
  - Amount of time required to succeed given the likely entry mode
  - Level of human resources required to succeed given the likely entry mode
  - Level of dollar investment required given the likely entry mode
  - Level of impact if risk cannot be managed given the likely entry mode
  - Level of confidence in the size of the opportunity as described given the likely entry mode
- *Establish a* composite *rating for each market space* (K, Appendix 1.2) of the attractive market criteria rating (see Topic 4) combined with the composite assessment of penetration success (see the Attractive Market Composite Assessment Engine in Appendix 1.7).
  - In this way, identify the most attractive markets with the highest likelihood of meeting the success criteria threshold given the mode of entry (see the Attractive Market Composite Assessment Engine in Appendix 1.7). In the illustration in Appendix 1.7, Market F has the highest composite score for

attractiveness and the highest likelihood of meeting the market penetration success threshold given the mode of entry.

- *Rank order and prioritize the market spaces* (K, Appendix 1.2) by the composite result, and identify the cumulative resource (financial or otherwise) requirement.
- *By synthesizing the output from the prior steps, identify the selected initiatives* (L, Appendix 1.2) to enter and develop the new or existing market space and/or close the market, capability, and competitive gaps such as:
  - In-house start-up initiatives: new product development, hire new staff and technical resources (sales, marketing, research and development, etc.), license technology, training, and so forth.
  - M&A initiative: acquire, merge, joint venture, alliance (L1, Appendix 1.2).
- *Perform a strengths, weaknesses, opportunities, and threats (SWOT) analysis*[4] (J2, Appendix 1.2) for the company as a whole, as illustrated in Appendix 1.8. Identify your key company-level SWOTs and isolate active strategies or steps that will:
  - Optimize each strength in your markets and close gaps.
  - Correct or minimize the impact of your weaknesses and close gaps.
  - Take advantage of each key opportunity available to you and close gaps.
  - Minimize the impact of each imminent threat. And close gaps.

HOW—IF M&A IS VEHICLE TO CLOSE GAPS, IDENTIFY TARGETS

- *Where M&A is the likely or chosen entry mode, identify M&A target opportunities* (L1, M, Appendix 1.2) to close the gaps in the most attractive and highly rated new or existing market spaces and engage in the M&A process (see Topic 2). Consider these approaches to identify acquisition targets:
  - Develop a search mandate identifying the sought-after industry, market space, capabilities, technologies, products sought, and so on (see Topic 4).
  - Provide the search mandate to finders, search firms, investment banks, and the like (see Topic 4).
  - Interview large companies and universities that may be interested in dispositions of technologies or nonstrategic fit businesses in the market spaces identified.
  - Conduct data mining to identify the producers of the critical value-added input in the market spaces identified. For example, search Thomas Register, Compustat, Standard & Poor's, One Source, and Hoovers, among other sources.

[4] SWOT analysis is credited to Albert Humphry of Stanford University, but its origin is not entirely clear. See www.marketingteacher.com/swot/history-of-swot.html for a survey of the origins of SWOT analysis.

- *After target identification and preliminary fact finding and evaluation, measure the fit* (M, Appendix 1.2) of each target's capabilities combined with the buyer's capabilities (as if the entities were combined) versus the requirements of each market, as illustrated in Appendix 1.9, to determine which acquisition candidates in which market provide the most improved gap closure, on a pro-forma post acquisition combined basis.

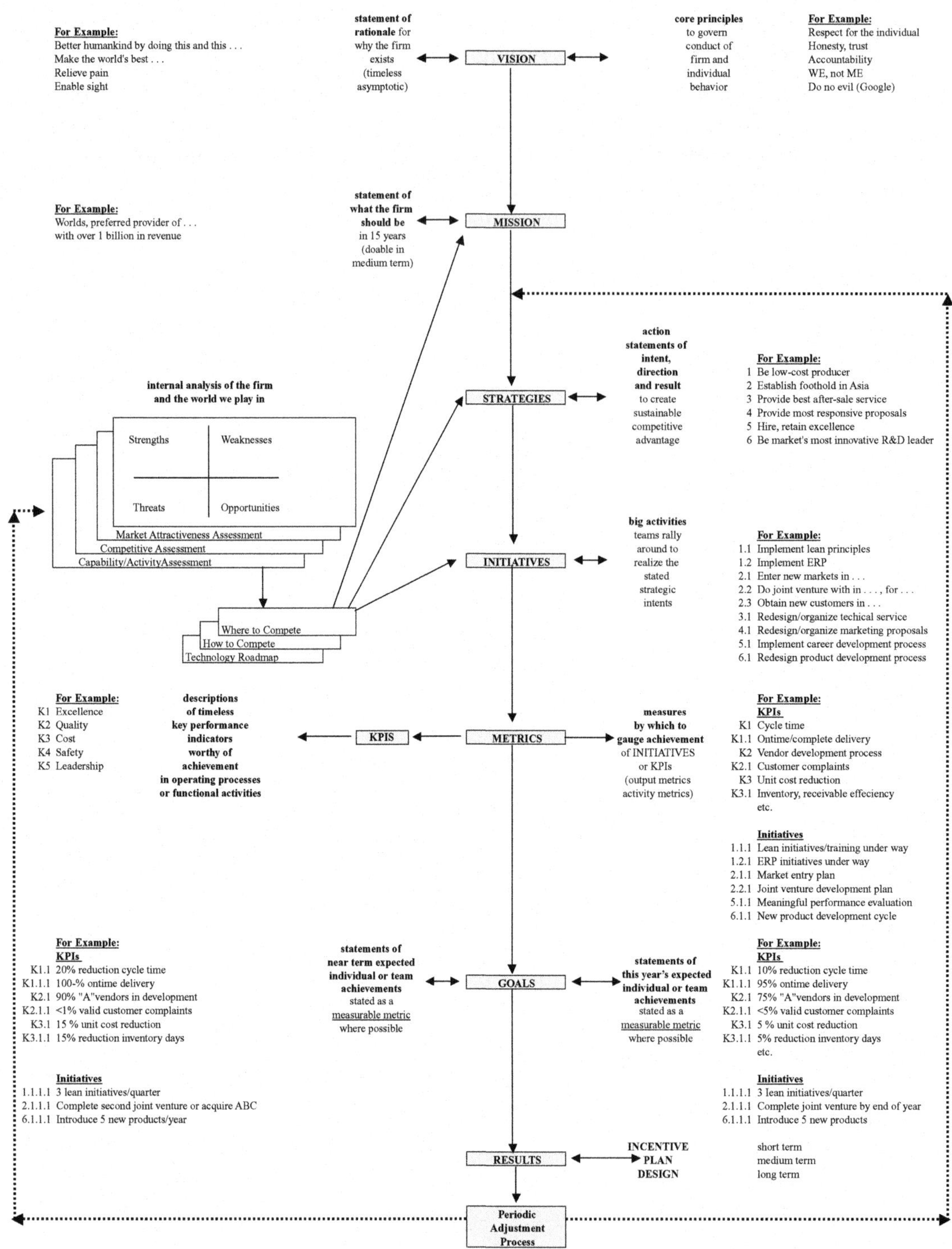

APPENDIX 1.1 Strategic Planning Process Engine: Core Essentials

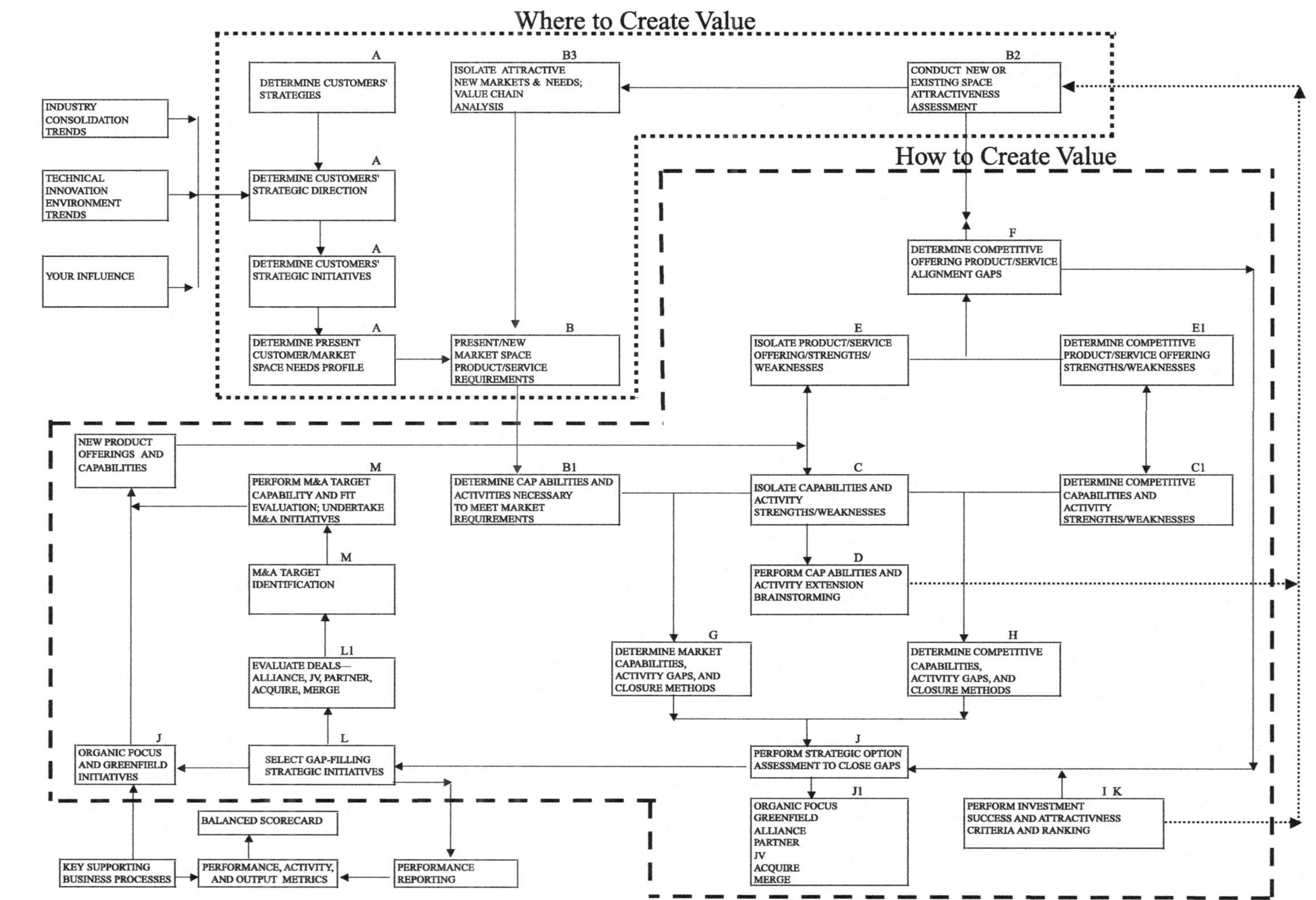

APPENDIX 1.2 Key Process Steps to Identify Where and How to Create Value and Close Strategic Gaps

The following Appendices, as well as those presented earlier, are available for viewing or download on the Web site for this book at: www.wiley.com/go/emott. Please see the About the Web Site page at the back of this book for login information.

APPENDIX 1.3 Activity/Capability Analysis: Us versus the Market

APPENDIX 1.4 Activity/Capability Extension Analysis: Where Else Used Brainstorming Example

APPENDIX 1.5 Our Capabilities versus Market Requirements Assessment Engine

APPENDIX 1.6 Our Capabilities versus Competition Assessment Engine for Market A

APPENDIX 1.7 Attractive Market Composition Assignment Engine: Composite Assessment of Likely Penetration Success in Each Target Market

APPENDIX 1.8 SWOT Analysis Chart

APPENDIX 1.9 Competence Alignment Engine of Acquisition Targets in Markets F, A, J

TOPIC 2

M&A Process: Front to Back

This topic and Appendix 2.1 present an overview of the M&A process activity and stages typical of most corporate development processes. Auction M&A transactions, which share most of the activities presented but on a more compressed timeline, are covered in Topic 12.

The reader is encouraged to take the time to read through the sequential time line of activities on Appendix 2.1 to gain a feel of the flow of events. Topic numbers are listed in parentheses next to each activity that is expanded on in the text that follows.

DEFINITION OF THE M&A PROCESS

- *Preparation.* Deal flow starts with strategy development and development of target acquisition criteria (see Topic 4) and runs through creation of deal flow.
  - Acquisition criteria are developed in a collaborative process that attempts to capture the qualitative and quantitative attributes of attractive target markets and target companies. They are used as a screen to rule target candidates out or in.
  - Deal flow can emanate from internal sources, including research and development, sales and marketing, corporate development efforts, and programs such as activity extension and brainstorming and external efforts, such as mandated investment banks, targeted searches, over-the-transom offerings, or competition.
- *Activity and Contact.* This activity starts with market and target evaluation including preliminary intelligence gathering, criteria screening, and a target prospect report.
  - If not rejected at this stage, contact with the target and potential establishment of common, complementary interest between buyer and seller follows.
- *Come to Terms.* This stage encompasses expanded preliminary due diligence, deal valuation and offer structuring, deal financing and value creation, synergies realization, and integration plan development. A preliminary letter of intent (LOI), offer term sheet, and acquisition proposal are presented internally for go-forward approval and degrees of negotiation freedom.
  - If not rejected at this stage, target contact, negotiation of deal elements, and a conditional offer ensue.

- *Close It.* This phase encompasses expanded final due diligence, final deal valuation and offer structuring, deal financing and a value creation, synergies realization, and integration plan. A final offer term sheet (LOI) and acquisition proposal are presented internally for go-forward approval and degrees of negotiation freedom.
  - If not rejected at this stage, target contact, final LOI is agreed and negotiation of deal and principal contract terms ensues.
- *Create Value.* This stage includes the execution of integration plans and realization and measurement of deal synergy and market, product, and customer, objectives.
- Appendix 2.2 illustrates the typical level of involvement of various business functions pertinent to the each stage of the process on the Matrix of Responsibility and Authority in M&A Transaction Flow.

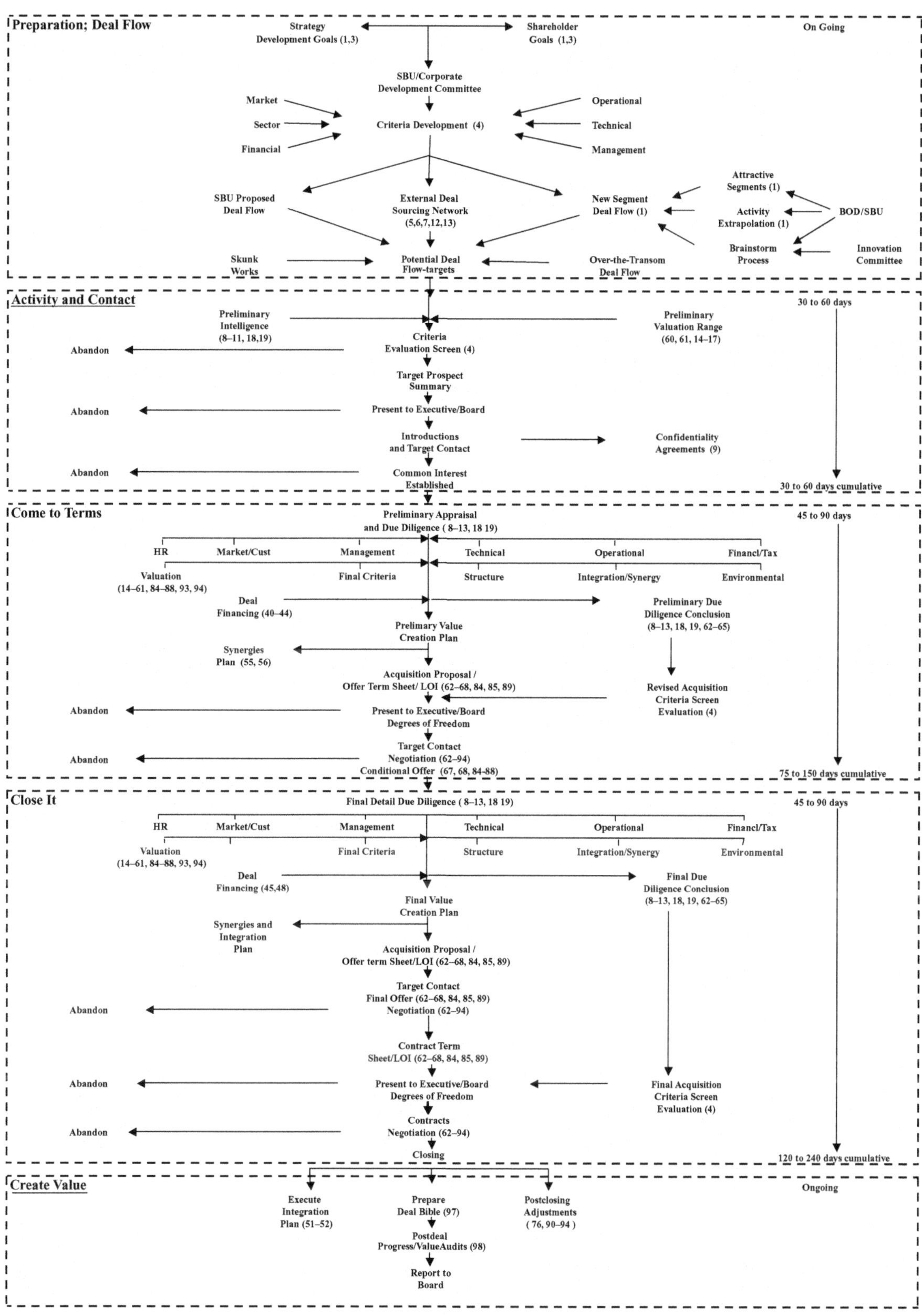

APPENDIX 2.1 M&A Process Activity and Stages Map (Topic Reference)

A REVIEW, APPROVAL DECISION ROLE
L SOLE LEADERSHIP RECOMMENDATION DECISION ROLE
JL JOINT LEADERSHIP RECOMMENDATION DECISION ROLE
DS DATA SUPPORT ROLE
C CONSULTATIVE INPUT

	M&A ACTIVITY	BOD	CEO	C.DEVEL	FINCL	LEGAL	HR	OUTSIDERS	SBU BDEV / EXEC	SBU FINCL	SBU OPNS	SBU TECH	SBU R&D	SBU MKTG	SBU HR
Preparation; Deal Flow	STRATEGY DEVELOPMENT, PROCESS COORDINATION	A	A	JL	DS	C	C		JL	DS	C	C	C	C	C
	SBUSTRATEGY DEVELOPMENT	A	A	C	DS	C	C		L	DS	C	C	C	C	C
	DRIVES EBI PROCESS FORWARD—AGENDAS, TIMELINES, BOD COORD		C	L	C	C	C		C						
	CRITERIA DEVELOPMENT	A	A	JL	C	C	C		JL	DS	C	C	C	C	
	CRITERIA DISBURSEMENT TO SBU/NETWORK			JL					JL						
	I BANKER RELATIONSHIP CONTACT		JL	JL	C	C									
	FINDER RELATIONSHIP CONTACT		C	L					C						
	SBU PROPOSED DEALS			C					L	DS					
	MANAGE NEW OPPORTUNITY PROCESS	C	JL	JL				C	C						
	MANAGE INNOVATION COMMITTEE / RESULTS	C	JL	C	DS			C	JL			DS			
	OVERSEE BRAINSTORM PROCESS		JL	C	DS			C	JL			DS			
Activity and Contact	CONDUCT CRITERIA EVALUATION SCREEN			JL	DS				JL	DS	C	C	C	C	
	GATHER PRELIMINARY MARKET, COMPETITIVE INTELLIGENCE			JL		C		C	JL						
	PREPARE PRELIMINARY PROSPECT REPORT			JL	DS				JL	DS					
	PRESENT TO EXECUTIVES/BOARD DECIDES DEGREES OF NEGOTIATION FREEDOM	A	A	JL					JL						
	TARGET CONTACT		C	JL					JL						
	INTRODUCTIONS TARGET CONTACT / PRELIMINARY NEGOTIATIONS		C	JL					JL	C					
Come to Terms	PRELIMINARY DUE DILIGENCE — HR APPRAISAL			C			L		JL						L
	MARKET APPRAISAL			C				C	JL					JL	
	MANAGEMENT APPRAISAL		JL	C			C		JL						
	TECHNICAL APPRAISAL			C					JL			JL			
	OPERATIONAL APPRAISAL			C	C			C	JL	C	JL				
	FINCL APPRAISAL			C	JL				JL	DS					
	TAX APPRAISAL			C	L				C	DS					
	CRITERIA SCREEN APPRAISAL			JL	DS				JL	DS					
	VALUATION APPRAISAL		A	L	DS				C	DS					
	DEAL STRUCTURE APPRAISAL		A	C	JL	JL				C					
	OPERATIONAL INTEGRATION PLAN APPRAISAL		A	C	DS				L	DS	C	C	C	C	
	IT, FINANCIAL INTEGRATION PLAN APPRAISAL		A	C	JL				JL	DS	C	C	C	C	
	ENVIRONMENTAL APPRAISAL		A	C	DS	JL			JL		C				
	PREPARE PRELIMINARY DUE DILIGENCE REPORT		C	JL	DS	C			JL	DS					
	PRELIMINARY VALUE CREATION/ACQUISITION PLAN		A	JL	DS				JL	DS					
	DEAL FINANCING		A	C	L	C									
	ACQUISITION PROPOSAL TERM SHEET		A	L	C	C			C	C					
	PRESENT TO EXECUTIVE/BOARD DECIDES DEGREES OF NEGOTIATION FREEDOM	A	A	JL					JL						
	CONDITIONAL OFFER NEGOTIATION		C	L	C	C			C	C					
	DEALTERM SHEET PREPARATION		C	L	DS				C	DS	C	C	C	C	
Close It	DETAIL DUE DILIGENCE — HR APPRAISAL			C			L		JL						
	MARKET APPRAISAL			C				C	JL					JL	
	MANAGEMENT APPRAISAL		JL	C			C		JL						
	TECHNICAL APPRAISAL			C					JL			JL			
	OPERATIONAL APPRAISAL			C	C			C	JL	C	JL				
	FINANCIAL/TAX APPRAISAL			C	JL				JL	DS					
	FINANCIAL/TAX APPRAISAL			C	L				C	DS					
	CRITERIA SCREEN APPRAISAL			JL	DS				JL	DS					
	VALUATION APPRAISAL		A	L	DS				C	DS					
	DEAL STRUCTURE APPRAISAL		A	C	JL	JL				C					
	OPERATIONAL INTEGRATION PLAN APPRAISAL		A	C	DS				L	DS	C	C	C	C	
	IT, FINANCIAL INTEGRATION PLAN APPRAISAL		A	C	JL				JL	DS	C	C	C	C	
	ENVIRONMENTAL APPRAISAL		A	C	DS	JL			JL		C				
	PREPARE FINAL DUE DILIGENCE REPORT		C	JL	DS	C			JL	DS					
	VALUE CREATION / ACQUISITION PLAN		A	JL	DS				JL	DS					
	DEAL FINANCING PLAN		A	C	L	C									
	ACQUISITION PROPOSAL, LOI, OFFER TERM SHEET		A	L	C	C			C	C	C	C	C	C	
	PRESENT TO EXECUTIVE/BOARD SETS DEGREES OF FREEDOM	A	A	JL					JL						
	FINAL OFFER NEGOTIATION		C	L	C	C			C	C					
	CONTRACT TERM SHEET		C	JL	C	JL			C	C					
	CONTRACT PREPARATION/COORDINATION		C	C	C	L			C	C					
	CONTRACT NEGOTIATION		C	JL	C	JL			C	C					
	CLOSING COORDINATION			JL	C	JL			C	C					
Create Value	EXECUTE INTEGRATION PLAN			C	C				L	DS	C	C	C	C	
	PREPARE DEAL BIBLE			L	DS				C	DS					
	POSTDEAL VALUE CREATION AUDIT	C	C	JL	DS				JL	DS					

APPENDIX 2.2 Matrix of Responsibility and Authority in M&A Transaction Flow

TOPIC 3

Why M&A?

Topic 3 summarizes the rationale for undertaking M&A. Acquirers should have specific reasons that target their M&A effort to fill a strategic void (see Topic 1). M&A is not without risk. Having operational overlaps with potential targets is a reasoned way to mitigate potential risk impacts. Additionally, acquisition risk is mitigated by building your M&A capabilities with smaller, digestible deals before taking on a large one.

DEFINE THE ROLE AND GOAL FOR M&A

- Based on your strategic planning process, know the role you want an acquisition to play (see Topics 1 and 2).
- What do you want out of M&A? Consider these choices:
  - Improve market or channel access position
  - Improve product line or served market extension
  - Fill a technology or other operational capability gap
  - Achieve a targeted competitive advantage
  - Promote growth or geographic expansion
  - Eliminate redundant costs (plants and overhead consolidation)
  - Consolidate or exploit excess capacity
  - Improve long-term return on investment (ROI)
  - Do a roll-up or consolidation leading to an initial public offering (IPO) or strategic sale
  - Achieve incremental size and volume
  - Do it just for the adventure (not a good idea)
- Deals are not about taking risk; they are about taking on and managing risk to achieve a desired end.
- The closer the capabilities and activities of the target company are to what the buyer knows and does well, the better the buyer can manage the risk of what can (and generally does) go wrong. (See Topics 26 and 27.)
- Having said that, many buyers enter into deals to fill certain buyer capability gaps with those possessed by the target.

LOOK FOR CAPABILITY OVERLAPS WITH TARGETS TO BALANCE ACQUISITION RISK

- Strategic buyers should look for three or four overlaps between their own key characteristics and capabilities and those of the acquisition target to increase the likelihood of a successful acquisition and integration. Important overlaps can include:
  - Served customer base
  - Distribution channel and selling process
  - Marketing and product positioning process
  - Technology base employed and technology development process
  - R&D project management process
  - New product development and deployment process
  - Lean manufacturing method and process expertise
  - Procurement process, vendor base, and vendor development process
  - Management processes and practices
  - Company culture
- Deals motivated to fill certain buyer capability gaps with those possessed by the target, which is often the case in strategic deals, are not unusual. In such deals, the buyer should have some overlap knowledge of the acquired capabilities. Elimination or enhancement of certain redundant capability overlaps and overhead expense is also often a motivator.
- The likelihood of post-closing deal success declines quickly where buyer knowledge of acquired capabilities is very limited, unless a highly effective integration planning process that executes well mitigates the lack of capability overlap.
- Things that can go wrong generally do; acquirers must remedy the problems quickly and a lack of acquired capability knowledge can be a problem if, for example, the acquired capabilities are found to be deficient or a key acquired employee leaves. (See Topics 51 and 52.) Buyers must be able to fix things that go wrong.
- The buyer must balance risk mitigation of overlaps with the need to expand the capability base.
- New entrants to M&A activity should start with smaller deals and build a set of acquisition and integration capabilities before tackling larger, more complex transactions.

TOPIC 4

Deal Criteria

Topic 4 discusses in depth the need for well-thought-out criteria to guide the acquisition search and candidate evaluation. Acquisition criteria capture the essence of what the acquirer is after and provide a basis for measuring both how close a target is to the ideal fit and helps identify the target's strengths and weaknesses. Criteria development allows the chief executive officer (CEO) and board of directors to emphasize what matters most to them. It must be emphasized during acquisition search and evaluation. This topic illustrates acquisition criteria and criteria rating.

DEAL CRITERIA DEVELOPMENT

- Having clear acquisition criteria helps narrow your search, develop the search mandate, and eventually make choices between candidates. Illustration 4.1 provides an example of acquisition criteria.[1] Readers should consider all and select those most relevant to their merger and acquisition goals.

ILLUSTRATION 4.1 POSSIBLE ACQUISITION CRITERIA

Strategy Output Criteria for Target Identification (see Topic 1)

- Industry/business/product/service area sought to close identified gaps
- Technology/know-how/enabling competency sought to close identified gaps
- Geographic dispersion sought to close identified gaps

Qualitative Criteria for Target Consideration and Evaluation

Market Attractiveness Attributes of Target Served Market

Value Chain	Clearly defined chain of value-added steps from producer to customer to end consumer

(*Continued*)

[1] Acquisition criteria are drawn from acquisition criteria development work while the author was employed at The Dexter Corporation in the early 1980s. They remain viable and pertinent.

Growth Forces	Positive; intrinsic mega-trend forces drive market growth at each stage of the value chain
Barriers to Entry	High technical know-how, client-critical function, and difficulty-level barriers exist for new competition; a performance legacy exists
Quality Clients	Solid, stable, profitable client base
Quality End	Performance-critical end of the served market
Stability	Inherently resistant to other than major economic dislocation
Technical/Industrial	Technology-driven producers or service providers
Domestic	Predominantly domestic-served market and customers
Specialty Franchise	Proprietary niche positions predominate to serve market needs
Concentration	Competitive landscape broad; many competitors and offerings create ability to differentiate.

Product/Business Attractiveness Attributes of Target Company That Can Create Significant Barriers to Entry if Not Easily Replicated by Competition

Critical Function	Delivery of solutions that provide a clear customer-determined critical function (technical impact, cost reduction, enabler) grounded in proprietary technology and know-how that drives the client purchasing decision for the target's product or service
Problem Solving	High client problem solving is required through applications engineering directly with consumer/client/user
Breedable Technology	Know-how must be growable and breedable into adjacent applications and client-critical function solutions
Low Relative Cost	Product or service cost is small percentage of customer total product or service cost
Innovation	Products are subject to in-house and customer-driven technical improvement
Low Obsolescence Risk	Replacement technologies are not readily apparent
Long Life Cycle	Target products are at growth stage of long S curve
Difficulty	Inherent product difficulty (handling, use, application) drives client need for solution relationships with target
Expertise Relationship	Client must have need to turn to differentiated expertise
Repeat Business	Consumable, disposable process, product, or service
Low Investment Intensity	Low capital employed per dollar of sales
High Switching Cost	Costly for customer to switch product once employed
Multifunction	Base technology can be utilized in various applications
Technical Service	High level of technical service, selling, and after-sales service required
Regulatory Driven	Product application environment may be driven by need to meet high regulatory thresholds
Applied R&D Driven	High degree of market requirement-driven applied research and development (R&D) is required (e.g., not new molecules; new innovative application of existing molecules).

Proprietary Position	Measurable, sustainable, differentiated in specialty market.
Leadership Position	One of top three competitors in served market or emerging leader in new market
Effective Marketing Process	Thoughtful, creative, focused, disciplined, customer focused
Sound Management Team	Practical hands-on leadership, motivators, empowerment, lean enterprise execution and practice, innovative, strategic focus
Sound Management Process	Accountable, effective metrics measurement, empowered employees, effective incentives, cross-dependence, no isolated silos, process thinkers and improvers
Integration Synergy Potential	Significant economic benefit possible from elimination or consolidation of duplicate activities and facilities
Capability Complements	Needed capability complements exist
Key Characteristic Overlaps	Buyer overlaps with key target characteristics and capabilities.
Quantitative Fundamental Criteria for Target Evaluation	
Sustainable Potential Gross Margin as a Percentage of Sales	Exceed 45% of sales
Sustainable Potential Earnings before Interest, Taxes Depreciation, and Amortization (EBITDA) as a Percentage of Sales	Exceed 25% of sales
Capital-Intensity as a Percentage of Sales	Operating capital to sales is less than 40% of sales
Served Market Size	Exceed $250 million
Market Growth Rate	Exceed 4 times real gross national product (GNP) plus inflation
EBITDA Potential Growth Rate	Exceeds market growth rate

- Have a clearly stated description of the characteristics of the industry, technology, market segment, and product or service line sought, and include it in your criteria.
- Ensure that the criteria against which target candidates are measured also reflects the critical capability overlaps desired (see Topic 3).
- Acquisition candidates should compare favorably in their current state with most of the general, qualitative, and quantitative criteria or have the potential to get there under new owners.
- Develop criteria for a potential buyer that reflect the specific factors that result from its strategy development and strategic gap identification process (see Topic 1).

- Identify critical knock-out criteria that must be met by a potential target as it is or shortly after a change in ownership.
- Ensure that criteria developed for a given target also provide the framework to focus the due diligence process work (see Topic 10).
- Develop a quantitative rating for each potential candidate against the general and specific criteria to assist in completing the relative target attractiveness evaluation. Does the target meet the criteria or not? If not, where does it fall short? This observation can help you evaluate why and whether the target has the potential to meet the criteria post acquisition. A criteria rating approach is presented next.

CRITERIA RATING ENGINE

- Appendix 4.1 presents an example of a criteria rating engine. Follow the numbered elements discussed next and in Appendix 4.1.
- *Weight the criteria* as to the relative importance of each to achieving strategic goals: what really matters to sustaining value growth in the judgment of the CEO and the board of directors (column 1). In Appendix 4.1 the weights range from 1 (least important) to 5 (most important).
- *Minimum required rating* (column 2) is based on the relative weight (column 1) times the desired overall minimum fit target (85% in column 8 of Appendix 4.1) as determined by the CEO and/or the board.
- *Target criteria score* (column 3) should be scored based on the ratings provided by the due diligence process team. Care must be taken to ensure an independent consensus rating based on factual observation and reasoned judgment, given that the desired weighted ratings are known.
- The *minimum required* weighted *rating* (column 4) is based on the relative weight (column 1) times the minimum required rating (column 2).
- The *target weighted score* (column 5) is based on the relative weight (column 1) times the target rating (column 3). The due diligence process must be focused on obtaining the knowledge required to make reasoned judgments of the target's attributes versus the criteria.
- *The target score over (under) minimum rating* (column 6) is the target's weighted score (column 5) less the minimum required weighted rating (column 4).
- *The target weighted fit %* (column 7) is an indication of how closely the target fits the established weighted criteria. Scores exceeding 100% indicate the target exceeds the criteria; scores less than 100% indicate the target does not meet the criteria. The weighted fit % equals column 5 divided by column 4 for all criteria groups other than the qualitative criteria. For the qualitative group criteria, the weighted fit % is the expected qualitative result (column 3), divided by the target result (column 2), times the CEO's importance factor for each item (column B).
- *The deviation of the target fit %* with the CEO's desired target fit % (85% in column 8 of Appendix 4.1) is shown in column 8 (column 7 less 85%).

- *The target composite weighted fit %*—75.2% in the illustration (column 9)—is the sum of the weighted fits for each criteria group subtotal (general, market attractiveness, product and target attractiveness, qualitative) in column 9. The criteria group subtotals equals the sum of the target fit % for each criteria line item in the criteria group (column 7) times the subtotal percentage for each criteria group that each importance weight is to the total of all importance weights (column A).
- A secondary criteria rating evaluation should be made if the target composite weighted fit (column 9) falls below the desired fit (column 8) *as it is predeal* to evaluate whether the target fit is *achievable* in the hands of the buyer postdeal, after buyer improvements.
- The prospective postdeal evaluation will require estimating the impact of buyer initiatives within the target after the closing.
- *The target composite weighted fit over (under) the minimum fit*—9.8% in the illustration—is presented in total in column 10. It is the sum of the weighted over (under) fits for each criteria group subtotal (general, market attractiveness, product and target attractiveness, qualitative) in column 10. The subtotal weighted over (under) fits for each criteria group equals the sum of the target fit % for each criteria line item in the criteria group (column 8) times the subtotal percentage for each criteria group that each importance weight is to the total of all importance weights (column A).

CONCLUSION TO THE CRITERIA RATING ENGINE

- The target composite weighted fit over (under) the minimum fit is a measure of how far the target's fit rating is—below the CEO's overall desired fit of 85% (9.8% below in the illustration) against all criteria and which criteria group is lacking most fit. On a weighted basis, the qualitative market attractiveness and quantitative measures exceed the CEO's expectations by 6%, but the general product and target attractiveness ratings are well below the CEO's weighted expectations by 15.8% for a net fit of –9.8% below.
- The takeaway may be that the team needs to reassess the attractiveness of the product and the business attributes of the target. While the target scores well on capital intensity, regulatory-driven barriers, and low-cost producer, it does not score well on technology, innovation, and related attributes, which might indicate lower barriers to entry and a weaker franchise position than the CEO hopes for.

WHERE DOES TARGET FALL ON COMPETITIVE CONTINUUM?

- It is critical to have a meaningful understanding of the target and its served market in terms of the acquisition criteria. This understanding defines where the company falls on the competitive continuum and therefore how it competes (or should compete) and therefore what its strategic thrusts and initiatives are (or should be) in support of how it should compete.

- This understanding allows the buyer to test the consistency of the targets practices and the target's understanding of its position in its market place.
- Appendix 4.2 presents an illustration of the potential general end points of the competitive continuum: "Proprietary, specialty franchise niche provider" at one end and "Non proprietary OEM provider, distributor" at the other end recognizing that there are many variations on these themes.
- The end points are defined in terms of:
  - apparent served market attributes,
  - apparent product and business attributes,
  - basis of competition characteristics and practices typically associated with the demonstrated attributes,
  - indicative business strategic thrusts and initiatives associated with the competitive practices, and
  - the business value proposition that might typically be associated with the continuum end points.

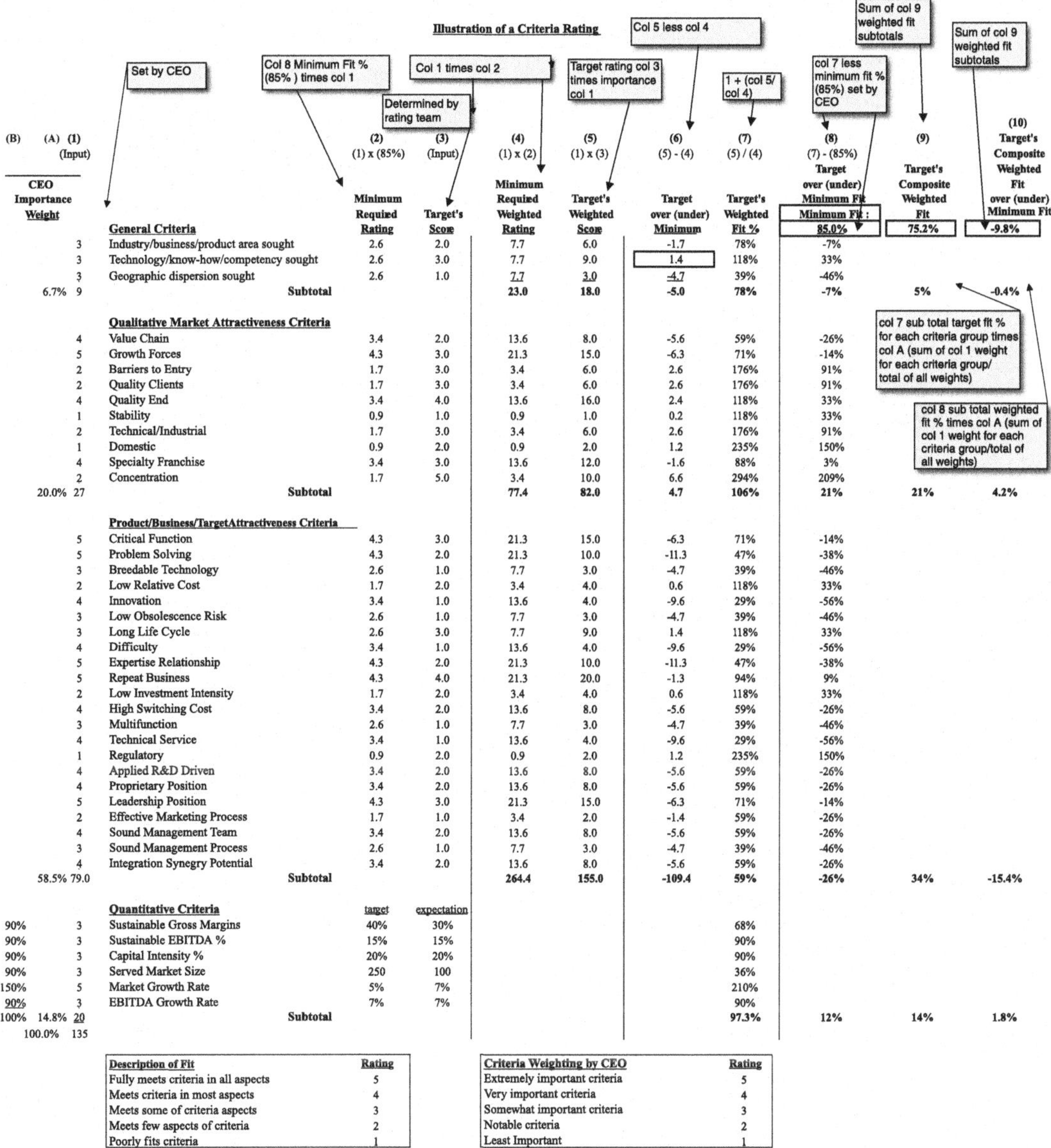

Illustration of a Criteria Rating

(B)	(A)	(1) (Input) CEO Importance Weight		(2) (1) x (85%) Minimum Required Rating	(3) (Input) Target's Score	(4) (1) x (2) Minimum Required Weighted Rating	(5) (1) x (3) Target's Weighted Score	(6) (5) - (4) Target over (under) Minimum	(7) (5) / (4) Target's Weighted Fit %	(8) (7) - (85%) Target over (under) Minimum Fit Minimum Fit:	(9) Target's Composite Weighted Fit	(10) Target's Composite Weighted Fit over (under) Minimum Fit
			General Criteria							85.0%	75.2%	-9.8%
		3	Industry/business/product area sought	2.6	2.0	7.7	6.0	-1.7	78%	-7%		
		3	Technology/know-how/competency sought	2.6	3.0	7.7	9.0	1.4	118%	33%		
		3	Geographic dispersion sought	2.6	1.0	7.7	3.0	-4.7	39%	-46%		
	6.7%	9	**Subtotal**			**23.0**	**18.0**	**-5.0**	**78%**	**-7%**	**5%**	**-0.4%**
			Qualitative Market Attractiveness Criteria									
		4	Value Chain	3.4	2.0	13.6	8.0	-5.6	59%	-26%		
		5	Growth Forces	4.3	3.0	21.3	15.0	-6.3	71%	-14%		
		2	Barriers to Entry	1.7	3.0	3.4	6.0	2.6	176%	91%		
		2	Quality Clients	1.7	3.0	3.4	6.0	2.6	176%	91%		
		4	Quality End	3.4	4.0	13.6	16.0	2.4	118%	33%		
		1	Stability	0.9	1.0	0.9	1.0	0.2	118%	33%		
		2	Technical/Industrial	1.7	3.0	3.4	6.0	2.6	176%	91%		
		1	Domestic	0.9	2.0	0.9	2.0	1.2	235%	150%		
		4	Specialty Franchise	3.4	3.0	13.6	12.0	-1.6	88%	3%		
		2	Concentration	1.7	5.0	3.4	10.0	6.6	294%	209%		
	20.0%	27	**Subtotal**			**77.4**	**82.0**	**4.7**	**106%**	**21%**	**21%**	**4.2%**
			Product/Business/TargetAttractiveness Criteria									
		5	Critical Function	4.3	3.0	21.3	15.0	-6.3	71%	-14%		
		5	Problem Solving	4.3	2.0	21.3	10.0	-11.3	47%	-38%		
		3	Breedable Technology	2.6	1.0	7.7	3.0	-4.7	39%	-46%		
		2	Low Relative Cost	1.7	2.0	3.4	4.0	0.6	118%	33%		
		4	Innovation	3.4	1.0	13.6	4.0	-9.6	29%	-56%		
		3	Low Obsolescence Risk	2.6	1.0	7.7	3.0	-4.7	39%	-46%		
		3	Long Life Cycle	2.6	3.0	7.7	9.0	1.4	118%	33%		
		4	Difficulty	3.4	1.0	13.6	4.0	-9.6	29%	-56%		
		5	Expertise Relationship	4.3	2.0	21.3	10.0	-11.3	47%	-38%		
		5	Repeat Business	4.3	4.0	21.3	20.0	-1.3	94%	9%		
		2	Low Investment Intensity	1.7	2.0	3.4	4.0	0.6	118%	33%		
		4	High Switching Cost	3.4	2.0	13.6	8.0	-5.6	59%	-26%		
		3	Multifunction	2.6	1.0	7.7	3.0	-4.7	39%	-46%		
		4	Technical Service	3.4	1.0	13.6	4.0	-9.6	29%	-56%		
		1	Regulatory	0.9	2.0	0.9	2.0	1.2	235%	150%		
		4	Applied R&D Driven	3.4	2.0	13.6	8.0	-5.6	59%	-26%		
		4	Proprietary Position	3.4	2.0	13.6	8.0	-5.6	59%	-26%		
		5	Leadership Position	4.3	3.0	21.3	15.0	-6.3	71%	-14%		
		2	Effective Marketing Process	1.7	1.0	3.4	2.0	-1.4	59%	-26%		
		4	Sound Management Team	3.4	2.0	13.6	8.0	-5.6	59%	-26%		
		3	Sound Management Process	2.6	1.0	7.7	3.0	-4.7	39%	-46%		
		4	Integration Synegry Potential	3.4	2.0	13.6	8.0	-5.6	59%	-26%		
	58.5%	79.0	**Subtotal**			**264.4**	**155.0**	**-109.4**	**59%**	**-26%**	**34%**	**-15.4%**
			Quantitative Criteria	target	expectation							
90%		3	Sustainable Gross Margins	40%	30%				68%			
90%		3	Sustainable EBITDA %	15%	15%				90%			
90%		3	Capital Intensity %	20%	20%				90%			
90%		3	Served Market Size	250	100				36%			
150%		5	Market Growth Rate	5%	7%				210%			
90%		3	EBITDA Growth Rate	7%	7%				90%			
100%	14.8%	20	**Subtotal**						**97.3%**	**12%**	**14%**	**1.8%**
	100.0%	135										

Description of Fit	Rating
Fully meets criteria in all aspects	5
Meets criteria in most aspects	4
Meets some of criteria aspects	3
Meets few aspects of criteria	2
Poorly fits criteria	1

Criteria Weighting by CEO	Rating
Extremely important criteria	5
Very important criteria	4
Somewhat important criteria	3
Notable criteria	2
Least Important	1

APPENDIX 4.1 Criteria Rating Engine

The following Appendix, as well as Appendix 4.1 is available for viewing or download on the Web site for this book at: www.wiley.com/go/emott. Please see the About the Web Site page at the back of this book for login information.

Appendix 4.2 Basis of Competition and Strategic Thrust Is a Function of Served Market, Product, Business Attributes

TOPIC 5
Deal Sourcing

Deals can be sourced from formal or informal solicitation activity on your part or from unsolicited approaches from a variety of outside sources. Like most things, however, you get what you pay for.

POTENTIAL SOURCES, PROS AND CONS

- Potential deal opportunities can arise from targeted corporate development initiatives and mandates, research and development (R&D) efforts, internal skunk works, or unsolicited approaches from:
  - Employees
  - Commercial banks
  - Investment banks
  - Venture capital firms
  - Investment management funds
  - Lawyers
  - Customers
  - Accountants
  - Competitors
  - Search firms and brokers
  - Contacts made from attending deal seminars and conferences
  - Strategy, segment, and target identification work (see Topic 1)
- Third-party targeted deal sourcing–related engagement services are provided by investment banks; acquisition intermediaries, search firms and agents and brokers; accounting firms, and others. Services can range from and include:
  - Assistance in developing acquisition criteria and strategic rationale
  - Names of sellers or buyers that appear to meet a specific or general criteria
  - Targeted searches and qualified contacts of sellers or buyers that meet a specific or general criteria
  - Valuations and/or due diligence
  - Full-service representation from criteria development, target search and qualification through valuation, conducting an auction, negotiation, and closing
- Determine the services you need based on your resources and deal flow interests.

- Often, it is less expensive but slower to search out, contact, and cultivate targets on your own.
- An opportunistic approach is to provide your deal criteria, including targeted attractive market sectors, to the network of "sell-side" deal brokers or investment bankers that represent potential sellers to stimulate deal flow within the context of the search mandate. See Appendix 5.1 for an example of a search mandate.
  - This approach generally produces a wide variety of offerings that may or may not resonate with your search mandate.
- A similar approach opportunistic is to attend seminars designed to bring sellers in front of potential buyers. Brief seller presentations to the group are followed by the possibility of one-on-one time with interested listeners.
  - Local chapters of The Association for Corporate Growth often provide deal exchange seminars (see ACG.org).
- A more expensive approach that yields targeted deal flow (not necessarily deals) is to enter into a "buy-side" assignment with an investment bank or search firm engaged to find potential deals based on your specific search mandate.

ABC Company seeks to acquire unique manufacturing capability in the fabrication of specialty engineered metal or composite products business serving aerospace and defense, propulsion, automotive racing, earth-moving equipment, and or yacht- and ship-building component or manufacturing industries.

Manufacturer business models should be based on demonstrated high-value customer problem-solving and service relationships resulting in highly engineered solution-oriented products designed to meet demanding, critical-function performance requirements such as:

Airfoil structures

Rigging components

Landing gear or door components

Brake components and materials

Containment and housing structures

Seat components and structures

Aerospace and marine jet engine propulsion components

Steering, power transmission and gearing components

Manufacturer should possess a stable of unique engineering and manufacturing capabilities and activities such as:

Composite resin handling and matrix development

Milling

Forming

Metallurgy

Turning

Casting

Proposal development

Materials research and development and testing

Manufacturer should be recognized as the premier and preferred supplier to a broad base of demanding, high-quality repeat customers in its served client and industry base.

Manufacturer should have:

Sales of $150 to $250 million +

Sales growth of 8% last five years

Sales growth potential of 8% next five years

Ebitda of 10%+; 15–20% potential

RONA of 15%+; 15–20% potential

APPENDIX 5.1 General Search Mandate

TOPIC 6

Fees for Services

Targeted acquisition services by qualified intermediaries will vary depending on the scope of services provided and the reputation and quality of the provider. Topic 6 presents and overview of the nature of the services typically rendered and representative fee structures. It also presents a "buy-side" fee structure designed to align the interests of the buyer and the buyer's banker.

The reader is encouraged to take the time to read the text in conjunction with the referenced Appendices to gain the appropriate level of understanding of the subject matter discussed in the narrative. Appendices are either presented at the end of this Topic or are available for review and download on the companion Web site noted at the end of this Topic.

OVERVIEW

- Fees for service vary greatly, depending on the services and the scope and quality provided.
- Project scope and fee basis should be agreed on and documented in an engagement letter between the vendor and the seller or buyer.
- Finders retained by sellers (sell-side arrangement) occasionally attempt to collect their fees from buyers:
  - Buyers who are approached by unsolicited finders should resist accepting a potential target's name and contact until the question of liability for the finder's fee is clarified.
  - Buyers who are approached should ask unsolicited finders: "Who pays your fees?"
  - Buyers should consider taking the position that sellers should pay finder's fees and build such fees into target price expectations.
  - Buyers should negotiate the purchase price without the encumbrance of finder fee liabilities.
- Generally, as a matter of good practice, each party should pay for its own retained experts fees (e.g., finders, legal, advisory, accounting, and tax). Certain fees of benefit to both parties are shared.
- Sell-side deal advisory services (and often buy-side arrangements where a banker is retained to sell a property) and fee expectations can be expected to be similar to those in Illustration 6.1, depending on the scope of the effort.

ILLUSTRATION 6.1 OVERVIEW OF SELL-SIDE ADVISORY SERVICES AND BASIS OF FEES

Scope of Engagement	Fee Basis
Names of interested potential buyers	A one-time finder's fee if deal closes with named party (plus or minus $50,000 on smaller deals)
Targeted searches; identify potential buyers, preliminary valuations plus screen buyers, make contacts, make introductions	Hourly fee based, or fixed project price plus retainer. Sometimes retainers are creditable against success fees if a broader assignment is granted.
Full-service representation (e.g., search, contacts, valuation, auction, negotiate, and close)	Generally a retainer plus a success fee equal to a minimum fee plus a fixed or stepped percentage of purchase price over a set level, depending on deal size. Retainers are generally creditable against total success fee.

FEE STRUCTURES: AN OVERVIEW

- Fee structures vary in complexity, incentive levels, and deal size,[1] as shown in Appendix 6.1.
- Lehman scale fees, originally used for initial public offering (IPO) fee determination and sometimes used as a deal fee basis, are expressed as a percent of deal value:
  - 5% of first million of purchase price
  - 4% of next million of purchase price
  - 3% of next million of purchase price
  - 2% of next million of purchase price
  - 1% on remainder of purchase price
- Occasionally sell-side deal fees are based on twice the Lehman scale, a stuttering Lehman scale, or a minimum fee plus a sliding scale, depending on the service provider and deal size (see Appendix 6.1).
- *On very small deals of, say, $5 to $10 million in total transaction value,* all-in sell-side full-service representation success fees might range from plus or minus 5% to 8% of the deal value. As illustrated in Appendix 6.1, a deal fee might approximate a minimum of $150,000 plus 4% of the first $5 million, 2% of the next $5 million, and 0.75% of the remainder. For a $10 million deal value, this results in a fee of $450,000, or 4.5% of deal value. A retainer of $50,000

[1] See also www.angelblog.net/M&A_Advisor_Fees.html for an excerpt from a book titled *Early Exits, Exit Strategies for Entrepreneurs and Angel Investors (But Maybe Not Venture Capitalists)* by Dr. Basil Peters for insight on the subject of deal fees.

to $75,000 up front (or a monthly arrangement of $5,000 to $15,000) that generally is creditable against the success fee would not be unusual.

  - Very small deals are typically done by individuals or very small brokers. The fees are simply not large enough to attract investment banks of reasonable size.[2] Individuals and small brokers operate with much lower overheads so their fees typically are lower.

- *On small deals, say, $10 to $50 million in total transaction value,* all-in sell-side full-service representation success fees might range from plus or minus 2% to 6% of the deal value. As illustrated in Appendix 6.1, a deal fee might approximate a minimum of $450,000 plus 3% of the first $5 million and 1% of the remainder. For a $50 million deal value, this results in a fee of $1.05 million, or 2.1% of deal value. A retainer of $75,000 to $100,000 up front (or a monthly arrangement of $5,000 to $15,000) that generally is creditable against the success fee would not be unusual.
  - Small deals typically are done by individuals or small to midsize investment banks.[3]
- *On deals between $50 million to $100 million in total transaction value,* all-in sell-side full-service representation success fees might range from plus or minus 1.5% to 2% of the deal value. As illustrated in Appendix 6.1, a deal fee might approximate a minimum of $450,000 plus 3% of the first $5 million and 1% of the remainder. For a $100 million deal value, this results in a fee of $1.550 million, or 1.6% of deal value. A retainer of $75,000 to $100,000 up front (or a monthly arrangement of $5,000 to $15,000) that generally is creditable against the success fee would not be unusual.
  - Smaller deals under $100 million typically are done by small to midsize investment banks and brokers. The fees are simply not large enough to attract larger tier 1investment banks.[4]
- *On larger deals of over $1 billion in total transaction value,* all-in sell-side full-service representation success fees might range from plus or minus 0.75% to 1%, perhaps higher. Full-service sell-side representation success fees can be structured around the likely ranges of deal value with incentive fee percentages escalating with higher levels of deal value. An illustration might approximate a minimum fee of, say, $6 million at $1 billion in value plus scaled incentive fees of 1% of the next $400 million, plus 1.5% of the amount over $1.4 billion. At a $1.5 billion deal value, this results in a deal fee approaching $11.5 million, or approximately 0.77% of deal value. Lehman arrangements would approach 1% to 2% of a $1.5 billion deal value (see Appendix 6.1).
  - Very large deals are typically done by the first tier, big-city investment banks.[5]
- In determining deal fees, components of deal value should be defined carefully.

---

[2] Ibid.

[3] Ibid.

[4] Ibid.

[5] Ibid.

- Considerations should include how deferred payments, real estate, postclosing purchase price adjustments, earn-outs, escrows, and subsequent disposal of seller-retained assets not part of the deal are to be treated in determination of deal fee consideration and payment. An example of a sell-side engagement letter is presented in Appendix 6.2.

BUY-SIDE BANKER FEE ARRANGEMENTS

- Sell-side–based fee arrangements are often employed in buy-side banker assignments (a banker is retained to find a property).
- This creates a situation where the higher the price paid by the buyer, the higher the fee paid to the buyer's banker, who has been retained to find and negotiate the best deal for the buyer, presumably at the lowest price possible.
- This apparent conflict of interest may be based on the premise that the higher the value finally paid, the greater the inherent real value of the property (to the buyer). Hence, as the buyer's value is enhanced, a higher fee is earned.
- An alternative fee structure that potentially better aligns the interests of the buyer and the buy-side banker is to compensate the banker based on the best deal for the buyer—the lower the consideration paid, the higher the fee paid to the banker.

BUY-SIDE BANKER FEE ILLUSTRATION

- Appendices 6.3 and 6.4 illustrate a model for a buy-side fee structure where the banker's fee is based on a reverse incentive structure called the buy-side finder fee engine, which can be described as:
  - The target selling price ($20,000) (1) is based on a midpoint (or other value agreed between the deal banker and the buyer) between the seller's actual offer ($21,250) (8) and the buyer's initial bid ($17,000) (9).
  - The nominal target fee ($300) at the target selling price is based on a typical and appropriate (Lehman scale or other) sell-side fee arrangement (2).
  - The maximum fee ($390), payable at the lowest agreed price, is a stretch target fee for the banker and is based on the nominal target fee times 1 plus a premium of, say, 30% in the illustration (3).
  - The minimum floor fee ($280 in the illustration, (4)), payable at the seller's offer price or higher, must be attractive enough to the banker to make the effort to find and negotiate a deal but fair to the buyer if the price cannot be negotiated below the seller's asking offer price ($21,250) (8).
  - The minimum floor fee can be based on the nominal target fee less a discount—7% in the illustration—resulting in a mutually agreed amount of $280 (4), or can be set at the bid price ($17,000) (9) based on a typical and appropriate sell-side fee arrangement ($270) (4).
  - The fee range of ($110) (5) is the maximum fee ($390) (2) less the floor fee ($280) (4).

- The slope of the reverse fee incentive payment arrangement (2.59%) (6) is the fee range ($110) (5) divided by the negotiation price range ($4,250) (7), which is the difference between the seller's offer ($21,250) (8) and the buyer's bid ($17,000) (9). The slope is the instantaneous rate of increase in the banker's fee for every dollar that the final selling price is below the seller's offer price.
- The fee structure (10) runs from the floor fee ($280) (at the seller's offer of $21,250) up to the maximum fee ($390) (at the buyer's bid, $17,000) (9).
- The fee at any step in the structure (10) equals the floor fee plus the difference between the seller's offer and the actual price times the slope but not less than the floor fee.
- The closer the final price is to the buyer's offer, the higher the fee to the banker. If the fee arrangement is properly structured, the additional banker's fee is more than paid for by the reduction in the selling price. Interests are aligned between the buyer and his or her banker.

- Put the deal fee terms in the engagement letter.

Larger Deals — over $100 million — First-Tier Big-City Invesment Banks

Smaller Deals — $50 million to under $100 million — Smaller to Midsize Banks/Brokers

Very Small Deals — under $50 million — Individuals/Small Brokers

LEHMAN FORMULA SCHEDULE	OF FEES
1ST MIL	5.0%
2ND MIL	4.0%
3RD MIL	3.0%
4TH MIL	2.0%
THEREAFTER	1.0%

TWICE LEHMAN FORMULA SCHEDULE	OF FEES
1ST MIL	10.0%
2ND MIL	8.0%
3RD MIL	6.0%
4TH MIL	4.0%
THEREAFTER	2.0%

STUTTERING LEHMAN FORMULA SCHEDULE	OF FEES
1ST MIL	5.0%
2ND MIL	5.0%
3RD MIL	4.0%
4TH MIL	4.0%
5TH MIL	3.0%
6TH MIL	3.0%
7TH MIL	2.0%
8TH MIL	2.0%
THEREAFTER	1.0%

LEHMAN VARIATION FORMULA SCHEDULE	OF FEES
1ST 5 MIL	5.0%
2ND 5 MIL	3.0%
THEREAFTER	1.0%

MINIMUM PLUS % FORMULA SCHEDULE	OF FEES
MINIMUM	450000
1ST 5 MIL	3.0%
THEREAFTER	1.00%

MINIMUM PLUS % FORMULA SCHEDULE	OF FEES
MINIMUM	150000
1ST 5 MIL	4.0%
2ND 5 MIL	2.0%
THEREAFTER	0.75%

DEAL SIZE	INCREMENTAL LEHMAN FORMULA FEES	TOTAL FEES	% OF DEAL	INCREMENTAL TWICE LEHMAN FORMULA FEES	TOTAL FEES	% OF DEAL	INCREMENTAL STUTTERING LEHMAN FORMULA FEES	TOTAL FEES	% OF DEAL
1,000,000	50,000	50,000	5.0%	100,000	100,000	10.0%	50,000	50,000	5.0%
2,000,000	40,000	90,000	4.5%	80,000	180,000	9.0%	50,000	100,000	5.0%
3,000,000	30,000	120,000	4.0%	60,000	240,000	8.0%	40,000	140,000	4.7%
4,000,000	20,000	140,000	3.5%	40,000	280,000	7.0%	40,000	180,000	4.5%
5,000,000	10,000	150,000	3.0%	20,000	300,000	6.0%	30,000	210,000	4.2%
6,000,000	10,000	160,000	2.7%	20,000	320,000	5.3%	30,000	240,000	4.0%
7,000,000	10,000	170,000	2.4%	20,000	340,000	4.9%	20,000	260,000	3.7%
8,000,000	10,000	180,000	2.3%	20,000	360,000	4.5%	20,000	280,000	3.5%
9,000,000	10,000	190,000	2.1%	20,000	380,000	4.2%	10,000	290,000	3.2%
10,000,000	10,000	200,000	2.0%	20,000	400,000	4.0%	10,000	300,000	3.0%
15,000,000	50,000	250,000	1.7%	100,000	500,000	3.3%	50,000	350,000	2.3%
20,000,000	50,000	300,000	1.5%	100,000	600,000	3.0%	50,000	400,000	2.0%
25,000,000	50,000	350,000	1.4%	100,000	700,000	2.8%	50,000	450,000	1.8%
30,000,000	50,000	400,000	1.3%	100,000	800,000	2.7%	50,000	500,000	1.7%
35,000,000	50,000	450,000	1.3%	100,000	900,000	2.6%	50,000	550,000	1.6%
40,000,000	50,000	500,000	1.3%	100,000	1,000,000	2.5%	50,000	600,000	1.5%
45,000,000	50,000	550,000	1.2%	100,000	1,100,000	2.4%	50,000	650,000	1.4%
50,000,000	50,000	600,000	1.2%	100,000	1,200,000	2.4%	50,000	700,000	1.4%
55,000,000	50,000	650,000	1.2%	100,000	1,300,000	2.4%	50,000	750,000	1.4%
60,000,000	50,000	700,000	1.2%	100,000	1,400,000	2.3%	50,000	800,000	1.3%
65,000,000	50,000	750,000	1.2%	100,000	1,500,000	2.3%	50,000	850,000	1.3%
70,000,000	50,000	800,000	1.1%	100,000	1,600,000	2.3%	50,000	900,000	1.3%
75,000,000	50,000	850,000	1.1%	100,000	1,700,000	2.3%	50,000	950,000	1.3%
80,000,000	50,000	900,000	1.1%	100,000	1,800,000	2.3%	50,000	1,000,000	1.3%
85,000,000	50,000	950,000	1.1%	100,000	1,900,000	2.2%	50,000	1,050,000	1.2%
90,000,000	50,000	1,000,000	1.1%	100,000	2,000,000	2.2%	50,000	1,100,000	1.2%
95,000,000	50,000	1,050,000	1.1%	100,000	2,100,000	2.2%	50,000	1,150,000	1.2%
100,000,000	50,000	1,100,000	1.1%	100,000	2,200,000	2.2%	50,000	1,200,000	1.2%
200,000,000	**1,000,000**	**2,100,000**	**1.1%**	**2,000,000**	**4,200,000**	**2.1%**	**1,000,000**	**2,200,000**	**1.1%**
300,000,000	**1,000,000**	**3,100,000**	**1.0%**	**2,000,000**	**6,200,000**	**2.1%**	**1,000,000**	**3,200,000**	**1.1%**
400,000,000	**1,000,000**	**4,100,000**	**1.0%**	**2,000,000**	**8,200,000**	**2.1%**	**1,000,000**	**4,200,000**	**1.1%**
500,000,000	**1,000,000**	**5,100,000**	**1.0%**	**2,000,000**	**10,200,000**	**2.0%**	**1,000,000**	**5,200,000**	**1.0%**
600,000,000	**1,000,000**	**6,100,000**	**1.0%**	**2,000,000**	**12,200,000**	**2.0%**	**1,000,000**	**6,200,000**	**1.0%**
700,000,000	**1,000,000**	**7,100,000**	**1.0%**	**2,000,000**	**14,200,000**	**2.0%**	**1,000,000**	**7,200,000**	**1.0%**
800,000,000	**1,000,000**	**8,100,000**	**1.0%**	**2,000,000**	**16,200,000**	**2.0%**	**1,000,000**	**8,200,000**	**1.0%**
900,000,000	**1,000,000**	**9,100,000**	**1.0%**	**2,000,000**	**18,200,000**	**2.0%**	**1,000,000**	**9,200,000**	**1.0%**
1,000,000,000	**1,000,000**	**10,100,000**	**1.0%**	**2,000,000**	**20,200,000**	**2.0%**	**1,000,000**	**10,200,000**	**1.0%**
1,500,000,000	**5,000,000**	**15,100,000**	**1.0%**	**10,000,000**	**30,200,000**	**2.0%**	**5,000,000**	**15,200,000**	**1.0%**

DEAL SIZE	INCREMENTAL LEHMAN VARIATION FORMULA FEES	TOTAL FEES	% OF DEAL	INCREMENTAL FEE % BASED PORTION	MINIMUM PLUS % TOTAL FEES	% OF DEAL	INCREMENTAL FEE % BASED PORTION	MINIMUM PLUS % TOTAL FEES	% OF DEAL
1,000,000	50,000	50,000	5.0%	30,000	480,000	48.0%	**40,000**	**190,000**	**19.0%**
2,000,000	50,000	100,000	5.0%	30,000	510,000	25.5%	**40,000**	**230,000**	**11.5%**
3,000,000	50,000	150,000	5.0%	30,000	540,000	18.0%	**40,000**	**270,000**	**9.0%**
4,000,000	50,000	200,000	5.0%	30,000	570,000	14.3%	**40,000**	**310,000**	**7.8%**
5,000,000	50,000	250,000	5.0%	30,000	600,000	12.0%	**40,000**	**350,000**	**7.0%**
6,000,000	30,000	280,000	4.7%	10,000	610,000	10.2%	**20,000**	**370,000**	**6.2%**
7,000,000	30,000	310,000	4.4%	10,000	620,000	8.9%	**20,000**	**390,000**	**5.6%**
8,000,000	30,000	340,000	4.3%	10,000	630,000	7.9%	**20,000**	**410,000**	**5.1%**
9,000,000	30,000	370,000	4.1%	10,000	640,000	7.1%	**20,000**	**430,000**	**4.8%**
10,000,000	30,000	400,000	4.0%	10,000	650,000	6.5%	**20,000**	**450,000**	**4.5%**
15,000,000	50,000	450,000	3.0%	50,000	700,000	4.7%	**37,500**	**487,500**	**3.3%**
20,000,000	50,000	500,000	2.5%	50,000	750,000	3.8%	**37,500**	**525,000**	**2.6%**
25,000,000	50,000	550,000	2.2%	50,000	800,000	3.2%	**37,500**	**562,500**	**2.3%**
30,000,000	50,000	600,000	2.0%	50,000	850,000	2.8%	**37,500**	**600,000**	**2.0%**
35,000,000	50,000	650,000	1.9%	50,000	900,000	2.6%	**37,500**	**637,500**	**1.8%**
40,000,000	50,000	700,000	1.8%	50,000	950,000	2.4%	**37,500**	**675,000**	**1.7%**
45,000,000	50,000	750,000	1.7%	50,000	1,000,000	2.2%	**37,500**	**712,500**	**1.6%**
50,000,000	50,000	800,000	1.6%	**50,000**	**1,050,000**	**2.1%**	**37,500**	**750,000**	**1.5%**
55,000,000	50,000	850,000	1.5%	**50,000**	**1,100,000**	**2.0%**	37,500	787,500	1.4%
60,000,000	50,000	900,000	1.5%	**50,000**	**1,150,000**	**1.9%**	37,500	825,000	1.4%
65,000,000	50,000	950,000	1.5%	**50,000**	**1,200,000**	**1.8%**	37,500	862,500	1.3%
70,000,000	50,000	1,000,000	1.4%	**50,000**	**1,250,000**	**1.8%**	37,500	900,000	1.3%
75,000,000	50,000	1,050,000	1.4%	**50,000**	**1,300,000**	**1.7%**	37,500	937,500	1.3%
80,000,000	50,000	1,100,000	1.4%	**50,000**	**1,350,000**	**1.7%**	37,500	975,000	1.2%
85,000,000	50,000	1,150,000	1.4%	**50,000**	**1,400,000**	**1.6%**	37,500	1,012,500	1.2%
90,000,000	50,000	1,200,000	1.3%	**50,000**	**1,450,000**	**1.6%**	37,500	1,050,000	1.2%
95,000,000	50,000	1,250,000	1.3%	**50,000**	**1,500,000**	**1.6%**	37,500	1,087,500	1.1%
100,000,000	50,000	1,300,000	1.3%	**50,000**	**1,550,000**	**1.6%**	37,500	1,125,000	1.1%
200,000,000	**1,000,000**	**2,300,000**	**1.2%**	1,000,000	2,550,000	1.3%	750,000	1,875,000	0.9%
300,000,000	**1,000,000**	**3,300,000**	**1.1%**	1,000,000	3,550,000	1.2%	750,000	2,625,000	0.9%
400,000,000	**1,000,000**	**4,300,000**	**1.1%**	1,000,000	4,550,000	1.1%	750,000	3,375,000	0.8%
500,000,000	**1,000,000**	**5,300,000**	**1.1%**	1,000,000	5,550,000	1.1%	750,000	4,125,000	0.8%
600,000,000	**1,000,000**	**6,300,000**	**1.1%**	1,000,000	6,550,000	1.1%	750,000	4,875,000	0.8%
700,000,000	**1,000,000**	**7,300,000**	**1.0%**	1,000,000	7,550,000	1.1%	750,000	5,625,000	0.8%
800,000,000	**1,000,000**	**8,300,000**	**1.0%**	1,000,000	8,550,000	1.1%	750,000	6,375,000	0.8%
900,000,000	**1,000,000**	**9,300,000**	**1.0%**	1,000,000	9,550,000	1.1%	750,000	7,125,000	0.8%
1,000,000,000	**1,000,000**	**10,300,000**	**1.0%**	1,000,000	10,550,000	1.1%	750,000	7,875,000	0.8%
1,500,000,000	**5,000,000**	**15,300,000**	**1.0%**						

APPENDIX 6.1 Deal Fee Engine

The following Appendices, as well as those presented earlier, are available for viewing or download on the Web site for this book at: www.wiley.com/go/emott. Please see the About the Web Site page at the back of this book for login information.

APPENDIX 6.2 Banker/Seller Engagement Letter

APPENDIX 6.3 Buy-Side Finder Fee Engine

APPENDIX 6.4 Buy-Side Reverse Fee Structure Chart: (a) Broker Fee Goes Up as Purchase Price Goes Down and (b) Broker Fee Percentage Goes Up as Purchase Price Goes Down

TOPIC 7

Financial and Strategic Buyers

Topic 7 provides an overview of the characteristics and intentions of financial buyers and strategic buyers. Their interests and intentions are quite different.

FINANCIAL BUYERS

- Financial buyers acquire businesses with the goal of eventually selling them (alone or as part of a group of acquired entities—e.g., a roll-up) to realize financial returns on the investors equity invested.
- The financial buyers' objective is to turn over the equity capital invested in a deal in approximately a three- to seven-year period from the date of acquisition and realize a target internal rate of return on equity capital invested in the deal generally in excess of 20% to 25% (see Topic 43).
  - The largest portion of the financial buyer's eventual return on the equity investment arises from possibly an interim recapitalization event plus the final exit event: initial public offering (IPO) or sale.
  - The financial buyer has great expertise in timing the exit to coincide with the most opportune industry and credit market cycles where the value of the exit option chosen is maximized.
- Financial buyers generally purchase sound, profitable operating businesses with prospects for value growth attributable to sound management and execution in strong industry sectors and reasonable prospects for exit potential.
- Financial buyers generally do not possess particular industry knowledge or skills to exercise the benefits of integration or operating synergy. More recently financial buyers are retaining or hiring such industry knowledge and skills to strengthen their investment activities and improve operating results.
- Financial buyers generally cannot pay the premium levels equivalent to those of strategic buyers (who can identify and leverage operating synergies and competence overlaps).
- Financial buyers attempt to add value through management selection, cost reduction, and management incentives to perform, including equity incentives and application of strong accountability and governance.

- Financial buyers occasionally acquire a platform entity then roll up more than one subsequently acquired business (thereby realizing operating synergies) into the exit entity.
- Financial buyers employ heavily leveraged capital structures in their deals.
- Financial buyers generally devote free cash flow to retirement of acquisition debt as opposed to dividend flow.
- Financial buyers, in the end, must depend on their ability to develop exit strategies to entice second-round buyer(s) or create IPO interest, based on the target's story of the future, to realize the exit price required when the financial buyer is ready to exit.
- Financial buyers may be more inclined to keep the place (people) intact as this is integral to what they eventually have to sell.

STRATEGIC BUYERS

- The strategic buyer's objective is to build value through the exercise of competency and knowledge overlaps or complements with the target by realizing the economic benefits of integration synergies.
- Strategic buyers are usually operators engaged in the same or an adjacent industry to the target and usually have well-engineered integration capabilities. Strategic buyers are well aware of the industry segment and opportunities served by the target, and they exercise that knowledge to create value.
- Strategic buyers will aggressively execute integration plans to realize synergy benefits. The seller's business (people, facilities) will experience significant change.
- Strategic buyers do not have a target holding period—their horizon is as long term as the duration of the buyer.
- Strategic buyers are in a position to pay the highest premium for a target.
- Strategic buyers realize returns through long-term synergy and integration benefit realization, resulting in growth in target enterprise value and cash flow take-out.
- Cash flow take-out is second in priority to reinvestment in the business to grow value.
- Strategic buyers also will employ leveraged capital structures in completing deals.

TOPIC 8

How Long Will It Take to Complete the Deal?

Deals take time to complete, often longer than you think or plan for. The issue is issues! Topic 8 explores what to expect and the timelines to expect.

DEAL ISSUES TAKE TIME

- Deals will take as long as it is necessary to discover and resolve the issues pertinent to the deal.
- All deals have issues, and issues take time.
- Plan on 60 to 90, possibly 120, days from receipt of prospectus (or equivalent) to cycle through preliminary due diligence and valuations to a finally agreed value on negotiated deals. Auctions are generally much shorter. (See Topic 12.)
- Plan on 60 to 90, possibly 120, days from agreement on value to closing on a typical negotiated deal. Auctions are generally much shorter.
- As an acquirer, do not be rushed.
- Sellers or auction bosses will push to tighten up the timelines.
- Buyers must run all the traps to ensure adequate risk identification.
- Rush but do not be rushed.
- Tell auction bosses or sellers you are in a rush to do it right but will not be rushed to do it.
- Required preclosing filings with governmental agencies to assure compliance with anticompetitive regulations can take considerable time and push out closings. Filings are required in the United States under the Hart-Scott-Rodino Antitrust Improvements Act of 1976, depending on various considerations. As of February 2011, for transactions that close after that date, filings are required if:
  - Buyer's or target's sales and or assets exceed $131.9 million and the other party's sales or assets exceed $13.2 million.
  - The transaction value exceeds $66.0 million.
  - The transaction value exceeds $263.8 million regardless of the size of the buyer or target.

Similar filing requirements exist in many countries. Check with your attorney, as this is a very complex area.

TOPIC 9

Confidentiality Agreements

The exchange of information between parties considering entering into an acquisition transaction must be governed by confidentiality agreements that set forth the terms of what information is to be exchanged, what is and is not confidential, and the terms of nondisclosure of information exchanged. Information exchanged between competing parties requires special attention well beyond the exchange of confidentiality agreements.

ENTER INTO CONFIDENTIALITY AGREEMENTS EARLY

- Enter into a binding nondisclosure or confidentiality agreement, as illustrated in Appendix 9.1, *prior to entering into meaningful conversations* with a prospective target about any aspect of M&A. Whenever sellers (and the buyer) will be disclosing confidential (excluding anticompetitive) information to facilitate the discussions in the search for complementary strategic interests that lead to a deal, they should have a binding confidentiality agreement in place. Seller's attorneys typically serve up the agreement for consideration by buyer.

DISCUSSION BETWEEN COMPETITORS REQUIRES GREAT CARE

- Where discussions regarding M&A possibilities are taking place between competitors in the same served market segments, great care must be exercised between the parties over what may and may not be discussed pursuant to government regulations (e.g., in the United States, Department of Justice or Federal Trade Commission regulations).
- Generally, the negotiating parties *may not discuss* any matters or exchange any information pertaining to each party's own:
  - Strategic plans and directions
  - Operating capacity
  - Product's pricing or plans
  - Product's unit cost
  - Customers or customer plans
  - Competitive issues in territories or sub markets
  - Market, customer, unit cost, or product synergies expected to result postacquisition

- Generally, negotiating parties *may discuss* certain matters and exchange certain information having to do with the combined postmerger or acquisition entity:
  - Vision and mission of the combined entity
  - Broad strategic goals of the combined entity
  - Broad strategic initiatives the combined entity should engage in postacquisition
  - High-level drivers and trends in the marketplace as a rationale for a merged entity
  - Possible areas of synergy expected to be realized as a result of the acquisition and high-level cost savings estimates (other than as may draw on restricted information, without exchange of any detailed cost or financial information or stand-alone cost avoidance benefits). Such areas of synergy may include:
    - Selling general and administration cost avoidance or duplication
    - Headquarters cost avoidance or duplication
    - Facilities cost avoidance or duplication
- The parties may exchange high-level financial statements (including high-level product family profitability but excluding individual product information) to enable valuation exercises.
- It is essential that an experienced antitrust law firm maintain oversight and distribution of all information exchanged and attend all discussions between negotiating parties.

USE A FIREWALL

- For purposes of performing valuation and detail synergy estimation, restricted information on unit cost, facility capacity and efficiency, pricing, markets, customers, and so on is often provided (through attorneys) by each party to a firewall (a specialist firm working as a intermediary to protect confidential information).
- Specialist firms can include accounting practices and business consulting firms. The cost of a firewall in a merger transaction is generally split between the parties; otherwise the buyer pays the fee.
- The firewall performs the detail valuation or integration option and synergy potential exercises and presents the results of such work to attorneys for each party in the case of a merger or the buyer's attorney in the case of a buyout. The attorneys summarize the work into formats that may be disclosed to each party, often as ranges, without disclosure of the plant closure or redundancy options associated with the ranges or any competitive or other restricted information that would enable that material to be traced.
- The work performed at this stage in a deal is to ensure the parties that adequate ranges of financial synergy exist. The detail work product available to each party after the deal closes can form the basis of much of the detail integration plan.
- In all cases, experienced deal or antitrust attorneys must be employed in the drafting of all confidentiality related agreements and act as the conduit for the exchange of all information between the parties.

CONFIDENTIALITY AGREEMENT

[ ] 200x
Mr. [ ]
[ ]
[ ] Company
Dear Mr. ________

In connection with your possible interest in acquiring the assets of the XXXXX Division of YYYYYYYY (the "Company"), we will furnish you with certain oral and written information, documents, and material which is nonpublic, confidential, or proprietary in nature. Such information, documents, and material furnished to you and the Company's willingness to consider such a transaction, as well as all analyses, compilations, forecasts, studies, or other documents prepared by you, your agents, representatives, or employees, which contain or otherwise reflect such information, documents, or material, or your review of, or interest in, the Company, is hereinafter referred to as the "Information." In consideration of our furnishing you with Information, you agree for the benefit of the Company that:

1. The Information will be kept confidential by you and shall not, without our prior written consent, be disclosed by you, or by your agents, representatives, or employees, in any manner whatsoever, in whole or in part, and shall not be used by you, your agents, representatives, or employees, other than in connection with evaluation or pursuit of the transaction described above. Moreover, you agree to reveal the Information only to your agents, representatives, and employees who need to know the Information for the purpose of evaluating the transaction described above, who are informed by you of the confidential nature of the Information, and who shall agree (in writing, if so requested) to act in accordance with the terms and conditions of this letter agreement (this "Agreement").
2. You shall keep the Information in a manner no less secure than you keep your own confidential and proprietary information, and you shall segregate and keep the Information separate from your other records, documents, or similar materials.
3. Without the Company's prior written consent, except as required by law, such requirement to be confirmed by a written legal opinion delivered to the Company, you and your agents, representatives, and employees will not disclose to any person the fact that the Information has been made available, that discussions or negotiations are taking place or have taken place concerning a possible transaction involving you and the Company, or any of the terms, conditions, or other facts with respect to any such possible transaction, including the status thereof.
4. Without the Company's prior consent, you will not contact, directly or indirectly, any of the Company's director's, officers, employees, or shareholders

(*Continued*)

APPENDIX 9.1 Confidentiality Agreement

regarding the Information or your interest in the Company or any possible transaction involving the Company. For a period of one year from the date hereof, you will not, directly or indirectly, solicit for employment or hire any employee or independent contractor of the Company or otherwise encourage any such person to terminate employment with the Company; provided that nothing contained herein shall prevent you from employing any person who responds to a general media advertisement or nondirected search inquiry, or who makes an unsolicited contact for employment.

5. You understand that the Company has endeavored to include in the Information those materials which the Company believes to be reliable and relevant for the purpose of your evaluation, but you acknowledge that neither the Company nor any of its respective agents, representatives, or employees makes any representation or warranty, either express or implied, as to the accuracy or completeness of the Information.
6. The term "Information" shall not include such portions of the Information which (i) are or become generally available to the public other than as a result of a disclosure by you, by your agents, representatives, or employees, or (ii) become available to you on a nonconfidential basis from a source other than the Company or its agents which is not prohibited from disclosing such information to you by a legal, contractual, or fiduciary obligation to the Company.
7. All copies of the Information, including documents or other materials prepared by you, your agents, representatives, or employees that include portions of or are derived from the Information, will be kept confidential and subject to the terms of this Agreement, and returned by you to us upon request within ten (10) business days of such request.
8. In the event you or anyone to whom you transmit the Information pursuant to this Agreement becomes legally compelled to disclose any of the Information, you will provide the Company with prompt notice so that the Company many seek a protective order or other appropriate remedy and/or waive compliance with the provisions of this Agreement. You will furnish only that portion of the Information which you are advised by written opinion of counsel, which you will deliver to the Company, is legally required and will exercise your best efforts to obtain reliable assurance that confidential treatment will be accorded the Information.
9. Unless and until a definitive agreement between the Company and you with respect to the transaction described above has been executed and delivered, neither the Company nor you will be under any legal obligation of any kind whatsoever with respect to such a transaction by virtue of this Agreement or otherwise.
10. You acknowledge and agree that the Company has not granted you any license, copyright, or similar right with respect to any of the Information, and the Company is and shall remain the exclusive owner of the Information.
11. You shall not assign any of your rights or obligations hereunder without the prior written consent of the Company.

APPENDIX 9.1 (*Continued*)

12. This Agreement contains the entire agreement between you and us with respect to the subject matter hereof. This Agreement may be amended only by a written instrument signed by you and us.
13. This Agreement shall be governed by and construed in accordance with the substantive and procedural laws of the state of ZZZZZZZZZ.
14. You agree that no failure or delay by the Company in exercising any right, power, or privilege hereunder shall operate as a waiver thereof, nor shall any single or partial exercise thereof preclude any other or further exercise of any right, power, or privilege hereunder.
15. This Agreement may be executed by the parties in separate counterparts, each of which when so executed and delivered shall be an original, but all such counterparts shall together constitute one and the same instrument. Signatures may be exchanged by facsimile. Each of the parties agrees that it will be bound by its own facsimile signature and that it accepts the facsimile signature of the other party.
16. The invalidity or unenforceability of any provision of this Agreement shall not affect the validity or enforceability of the remaining provisions of this Agreement.
17. This Agreement shall inure to the benefit of the Company, its security holders, and any person which acquires the assets or stock of the Company and shall be enforceable by any such person.
18. You represent and warrant that you are duly authorized to enter into this agreement on behalf of XYZ Acquisition Company. This Agreement shall be binding on your successors and permitted assigns.

Sincerely,

ACCEPTED AND AGREED
As of the Date First Written Above

XYZ Acquisition Company

By: ______________________________

Mr. Bucks

APPENDIX 9.1 (*Continued*)

TOPIC 10

"Concern Capture" Due Diligence

This topic presents the essentials of the critical due diligence process that buyers must undertake with each deal. The due diligence process must focus on concern capture at every turn—some concerns you have from the start, some you find along the way. Due diligence is about finding out what you do not know about the target, confirming what you may know, and synthesizing the knowledge acquired in terms of the significance of the information, what you should do about it, and how it affects the process of doing (or not doing) a deal.

Due diligence provides the background knowledge critical to completion of the acquisition criteria evaluation presented in Topic 4. This topic provides complete due diligence worksheets focused on typical concern issues for each business function to enable readers to jump start the due diligence activity.

The reader is encouraged to take the time to read the text in conjunction with the referenced Appendices to gain the appropriate level of understanding of the subject matter discussed in the narrative. Appendices are either presented at the end of this Topic or are available for review and download on the companion Web site noted at the end of this Topic.

DESCRIPTION OF THE DUE DILIGENCE PROCESS

- The due diligence process is an intense, focused effort of discovery about the target company.
- The truth is in the details so take the time to find it.
- Read, interview, discuss, listen, and read some more.
- Ask why, why, why about all issues of concern that demand answers.
- The normal due diligence process should take 120 to 180 days elapsed time before the closing (see Topic 8).
- Unusual problem discovery and evaluation can extend the process. Such problems may include:
  - Environmental issues
  - Inventory valuation issues
  - Customer/product warranty liability or recall issues
  - Proprietary technology ownership and licensing issues
  - Pension plan transfer and valuation issues

- The *first goal* of due diligence is to bring to light what we need to know about the target company's:
  - Business strengths and weaknesses
  - Customer assessment of target products and services
  - Business qualities and opportunities
  - Business vulnerabilities and weaknesses
  - Business risks and threats
  - Basis of sustainable competitive advantage
  - Basis for realizing opportunities for synergy
  - Ability to satisfy the acquisition criteria of the buyer
- *The second goal* is to bring to light what we need to know about risks and concern issues:
  - The potential financial impact of discovered risks, issues, and concerns should be negotiated away or positioned in the offering conditions and closing documents so that the buyer assumes only an acceptable level of risk.
  - Knowledge acquired is used to assist the buyer to determine whether to proceed with a deal, how far the risk-adjusted offer should go as reflected in the bid price, and other issues requiring attention in contract negotiation.
  - The acquisition criteria should also be used to focus the key diligence issues, topics, and questions that should be addressed during the process.
  - The knowledge acquired from due diligence provides the background for the due diligence team to complete the acquisition criteria evaluation (see Topic 4).
- Appendix 10.1 presents an overview of the due diligence concern capture process and the interrelationship among the data collected, acquisition criteria, implication of the results, and indicated resolution of concern issues surfaced.
- The due diligence work plans and collection formats must gather what is needed about each material point of intersection between the subject matter as presented in Appendix 10.1.
- *Due diligence usually occurs in two phases.*

PHASE ONE: PRELIMINARY DILIGENCE

- Preliminary diligence enables the buyer to evaluate the target business to a point where a conditional offer (conditional based on further diligence, etc.) can be made and presented in a nonbinding letter of intent or term sheet (see Topics 68 and 88).
- Preliminary due diligence should also clarify further issues to be explored in Phase Two.
- *Appendix 10.2 presents a preliminary due diligence information request list* typically provided by the buyer to the seller. This list is drawn from the concern capture work plan formats presented in Appendix 10.3.

- *Appendix 10.3 presents a concern capture work plan format* designed to focus the Phase One (and Phase Two) work effort on the identified concerns that matter most to the buyer and the information sources to get answers, provide a paper trail work product, summarize the knowledge gained about each concern issue, and enable the diligence team to provide a *learned assessment* about the target covering:
  - A strategic (and scored) assessment of each concern issue's strength, weakness, opportunity, and threat (SWOT) impact. It also should allow for the completion of the Business Driver Assessment Engine in Appendix 10.4, the Valuation Driver Assessment Engine in Appendix 10.5, the target Acquisition Criteria Rating Engine in Appendix 4.1, and the target's capabilities versus the market and competitive requirements (Appendices 1.5 and 1.6).
  - An assessment of the target's road map required for technology, new product, capacity, and others.
  - An assessment of each concern issue's integration and synergy creation impact, if material.
  - An assessment of each concern issue's risk potential and indicated risk disposition that rises to a material level (higher price, negotiate away, indemnity, escrow, insurance).
  - An assessment of each concern issue's overall closing risk impact that rises to a material level, taking into consideration the risk disposition methods.

PHASE TWO: DETAIL DUE DILIGENCE

- Detail due diligence generally follows offer acceptance and captures the balance of the pertinent due diligence concern areas and follow-up items from Phase One.
- While detailed checklists of general due diligence issues, topics, and questions are available from attorneys, accounting firms, investment banks, and other sources, it is advisable for the due diligence team first to ask and list their general and specific concerns in each focus area—*what do we need to know and learn about each concern*—and then develop the required information list that will hopefully provide the answers, as demonstrated in Appendix 10.3.
- Phase Two follows the concern capture work plan format. The value added is to capture enough knowledge about each concern to assess accurately what the findings from any functional department or process assessment mean to the goal of due diligence: how it affects value, risk, negotiations, and business and deal attractiveness.
- The concern capture work plan format presented in Appendix 10.3 is used to focus the Phase Two effort on functional or process assessment areas; to some degree, however, learning may lead to further due diligence beyond the targeted concern areas as a result of "following your nose" as something of relevance presents itself during the work. These additional concern issues are then added to the formats.

IDENTIFY NON-NORMATIVE TRENDS AND BEHAVIOR

- In most all due diligence areas, exceptions and changes to normative and appropriate trends, behaviors, transactions, accounting entries, and risk exposures should be identified by comparison of target results, practices, and answers to historical practices, prior periods, industry norms, competitors, and best practices. If exceptions are detected, their relevance must be determined. (Is this a singular exception, not to be repeated, or is it indicative of a control breakdown or a negative trend likely to continue, etc.?)
- The buyer should assemble a due diligence team composed of representatives from sales and marketing, operations, finance and tax, contracts, purchasing, environmental, human resources, risk management, and legal functions.
- The buyer due diligence team assigned to each due diligence functional area should assemble the work plan based on the concern list for the assigned focus areas and complete the work.
- The knowledge capture and accumulation process requires diligent linear thinking and effort to gather the facts: follow the trail, run all the traps, ask why, why, why.
- The learning distillation and assessment process is often intuitive and dynamic: What do the facts mean, how important are they, and what are the implications and related effects and issues?

BUSINESS DRIVER ASSESSMENT ENGINE—DETERMINE STRENGTH OF INCOME DRIVERS

- Appendix 10.4 presents the Business Driver Assessment Engine designed to capture the affinity between (a) the strength of the target's business process drivers (right side) and (b) the target's acquisition criteria fit (left side) and the joint impact on (c) the target's income (and cash flow) investment drivers (center).
    - The goal of the affinity matrix in Appendix 10.4 is to develop a composite rating of the strength and quality of the target's acquisition criteria fit and business process driver impact on income drivers. Is the fit strong and is the impact high or not?
- *The impact of the target's business process drivers on income* is assessed and scored by interviews and inspection resulting from the due diligence knowledge capture process.
    - The goal is to determine the state of development of the target's business processes versus world-class levels and rate the impact on income of the target's business processes on a scale of 1 (weak-low impact) to 5 (strong-high impact).
- *The target's degree of fit to the acquisition criteria*, (attractiveness of the target's markets, its business, and of its quantitative criteria) is also assessed by interviews and inspection resulting from the due diligence knowledge capture process.

  - The goal is to assess the attractiveness of the target's market and business versus world- class levels and rate the attractiveness accordingly from 1 (very unattractive) to 5 (very attractive).
- The strength of each driver's affinity on the income and investment drivers is a preestablished weighting: 2 (weak affinity) to 5 (strong affinity), as set by the due diligence team.
- The composite strength of fit is the sum of the score times the affinity weight for each criterion or business driver divided by the maximum cumulative weighted score possible if all scores were the highest, 5. In the example, the fit is 74% versus a maximum fit of 100%.
- The higher the composite strength of fit, the greater the confidence in the income and cash flow drivers.

VALUATION DRIVER ASSESSMENT ENGINE-DETERMINE STRENGTH OF VALUATION DRIVERS

- Appendix 10.5 presents the Valuation Driver Assessment Engine designed to capture the affinity between (a) the composite income (and cash flow) investment driver rating as determined from Appendix 10.4; (right side) and (b) the state of development and impact of financial policy drivers (if the target will remain a stand-alone entity; left side) and the joint impact on (c) business valuation drivers (center) .
  - The goal of this affinity matrix is to capture a composite rating of the strength and quality of income and financial policy drivers on valuation drivers.
- The state of development and impact of financial policy drivers is assessed by interviews and inspection resulting from the due diligence knowledge capture process.
  - The goal is to assess the attractiveness of the target's financial policy drivers on valuation drivers and rate that attractiveness from 1 (very unattractive) to 5 (very attractive).
- The strength of each driver's affinity on the valuation drivers is a preestablished weighting: 2 (weak affinity) to 5 (strong affinity).
- The composite strength of fit is the sum of the score times the affinity weight for each criterion or business driver divided by the maximum cumulative weighted score possible if all scores were 5. In the example, the fit is 79% versus a maximum fit of 100%.
- The higher the composite strength of fit, the greater the confidence in the valuation and drivers.

CONCLUSION

- If possible, do the diligence work with in-house personnel.
- The acquirer's team will have to sweat the details after a deal is closed to make it work. For that reason, the acquirer better knows the issues and has the conclusions before the deal closes.

- External experienced due diligence teams can be hired from the major accounting firms as well as from specialists.
- Due diligence source data often are provided in data rooms located at the seller's investment bank or attorney. More recently, they are available in electronic data room formats accessible by remote computer access.
- In the end, the due diligence effort must provide management with a risk-based assessment designed to allow management to make a recommendation to proceed with the deal or not.
- It is often useful to force rank the most critical due diligence issues by employing a list of affirmative threshold questions that the due diligence team must answer positively if the deal is to proceed. (See Appendix 10.6 for an illustration.)
  - Such an approach compels the due diligence team to deeply assess the risk associated with critical make-or-break issues.
- Special issues associated with the due diligence of operating working capital elements are presented in Appendix 10.7.

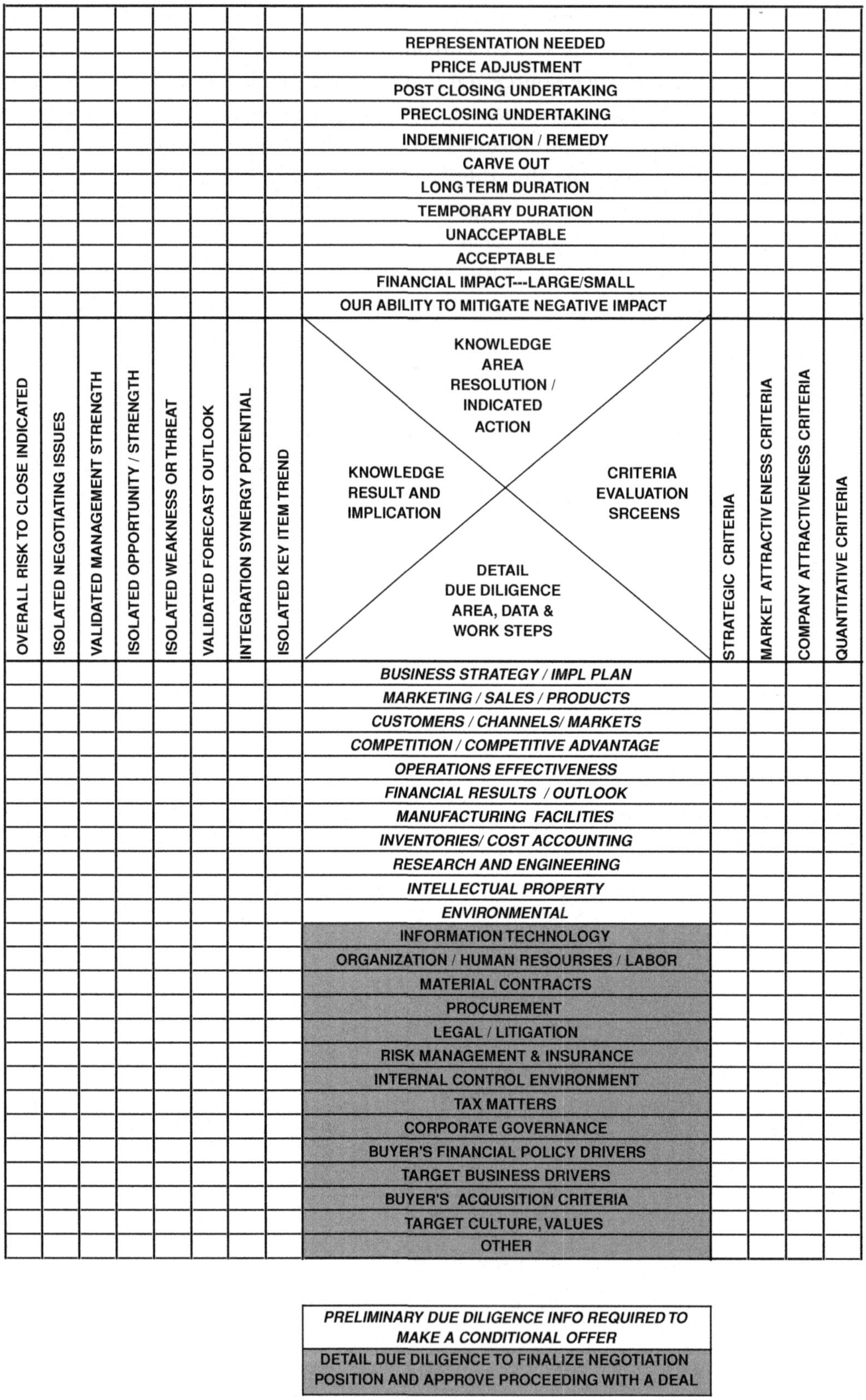

OVERALL RISK TO CLOSE INDICATED	ISOLATED NEGOTIATING ISSUES	VALIDATED MANAGEMENT STRENGTH	ISOLATED OPPORTUNITY / STRENGTH	ISOLATED WEAKNESS OR THREAT	VALIDATED FORECAST OUTLOOK	INTEGRATION SYNERGY POTENTIAL	ISOLATED KEY ITEM TREND	KNOWLEDGE AREA RESOLUTION / INDICATED ACTION KNOWLEDGE RESULT AND IMPLICATION CRITERIA EVALUATION SRCEENS DETAIL DUE DILIGENCE AREA, DATA & WORK STEPS	STRATEGIC CRITERIA	MARKET ATTRACTIVENESS CRITERIA	COMPANY ATTRACTIVENESS CRITERIA	QUANTITATIVE CRITERIA
								REPRESENTATION NEEDED				
								PRICE ADJUSTMENT				
								POST CLOSING UNDERTAKING				
								PRECLOSING UNDERTAKING				
								INDEMNIFICATION / REMEDY				
								CARVE OUT				
								LONG TERM DURATION				
								TEMPORARY DURATION				
								UNACCEPTABLE				
								ACCEPTABLE				
								FINANCIAL IMPACT---LARGE/SMALL				
								OUR ABILITY TO MITIGATE NEGATIVE IMPACT				
								BUSINESS STRATEGY / IMPL PLAN				
								MARKETING / SALES / PRODUCTS				
								CUSTOMERS / CHANNELS/ MARKETS				
								COMPETITION / COMPETITIVE ADVANTAGE				
								OPERATIONS EFFECTIVENESS				
								FINANCIAL RESULTS / OUTLOOK				
								MANUFACTURING FACILITIES				
								INVENTORIES/ COST ACCOUNTING				
								RESEARCH AND ENGINEERING				
								INTELLECTUAL PROPERTY				
								ENVIRONMENTAL				
								INFORMATION TECHNOLOGY				
								ORGANIZATION / HUMAN RESOURSES / LABOR				
								MATERIAL CONTRACTS				
								PROCUREMENT				
								LEGAL / LITIGATION				
								RISK MANAGEMENT & INSURANCE				
								INTERNAL CONTROL ENVIRONMENT				
								TAX MATTERS				
								CORPORATE GOVERNANCE				
								BUYER'S FINANCIAL POLICY DRIVERS				
								TARGET BUSINESS DRIVERS				
								BUYER'S ACQUISITION CRITERIA				
								TARGET CULTURE, VALUES				
								OTHER				

Legend
PRELIMINARY DUE DILIGENCE INFO REQUIRED TO MAKE A CONDITIONAL OFFER
DETAIL DUE DILIGENCE TO FINALIZE NEGOTIATION POSITION AND APPROVE PROCEEDING WITH A DEAL

APPENDIX 10.1 Due Diligence Overview

The following Appendices, as well as those presented earlier, are available for viewing or download on the Web site for this book at: www.wiley.com/go/emott. Please see the About the Web Site page at the back of this book for login information.

APPENDIX 10.2 Preliminary Due Diligence Information Request List

APPENDIX 10.3 Due Diligence Work Plan Formats

APPENDIX 10.3 A p1-3 Due Diligence Work Plan Formats, Business Drivers Rating

APPENDIX 10.3 B p1-2 Due Diligence Work Plan Formats, Acquisition Criteria Rating

APPENDIX 10.3 C Due Diligence Work Plan Formats, Financial Policy Driver Rating

APPENDIX 10.3 D Due Diligence Work Plan Formats, Culture, Values

APPENDIX 10.3 E Due Diligence Work Plan Formats, Business Strategy

APPENDIX 10.3 F p1-2 Due Diligence Work Plan Formats, Marketing/Sales/Products

APPENDIX 10.3 G Due Diligence Work Plan Formats, Customers, Channels, Markets

APPENDIX 10.3 H Due Diligence Work Plan Formats, Competition, Competitive Advantage

APPENDIX 10.3 I Due Diligence Work Plan Formats, Operations Effectiveness

APPENDIX 10.3 J Due Diligence Work Plan Formats, Manufacturing Facilities and Property

APPENDIX 10.3 K p1-3 Due Diligence Work Plan Formats, Accounting, Financial Results & Forecast

APPENDIX 10.3 L Due Diligence Work Plan Formats, Inventory, Cost Accounting

APPENDIX 10.3 M Due Diligence Work Plan Formats, Research and Development

APPENDIX 10.3 N Due Diligence Work Plan Formats, Intellectual Property

APPENDIX 10.3 O Due Diligence Work Plan Formats, Environmental

APPENDIX 10.3 P Due Diligence Work Plan Formats, Information Technology

APPENDIX 10.3 Q Due Diligence Work Plan Formats, Organization, Human Resourses and Labor

APPENDIX 10.3 R Due Diligence Work Plan Formats, Material Contracts

APPENDIX 10.3 S Due Diligence Work Plan Formats, Procurment

APPENDIX 10.3 T Due Diligence Work Plan Formats, Legal, Litigation

APPENDIX 10.3 U Due Diligence Work Plan Formats, Risk Management and Insurance

APPENDIX 10.3 V Due Diligence Work Plan Formats, Internal Control Environment

APPENDIX 10.3 W Due Diligence Work Plan Formats, Tax Matters

APPENDIX 10.3 X Due Diligence Work Plan Formats, Corporate Governance

APPENDIX 10.4 Business Driver Assessment Engine

APPENDIX 10.5 Valuation Driver Assessment Engine

APPENDIX 10.6 Due Diligence Threshold Issues

APPENDIX 10.7 Due Diligence Working Capital Issues

TOPIC 11

Keep Deal Conversations Quiet

Deal discussions are not anyone's business other than those with a need to know. However, the longer discussions go on, more people get in the loop and leaks often occur. As a buyer or seller, be prepared to deal with the inevitable question: Are you for sale? Are you buying so-and-so?

WHAT TO DO WHEN IT LEAKS OUT

- It is to the advantage of both buyers and sellers to keep their conversations to themselves and unknown to competitors, vendors, customers, and public investors until disclosure is agreed or required (by applicable regulation).
- When the fact that discussions are taking place leaks out—which it often does as time passes and the number of people in the loop increases—and buyer or seller receives inquiries from customers, employees, vendors, or others, each party should be prepared with a response designed to close off further inquiry and protect the confidentiality surrounding the transaction. Suggested responses might be:
  - "We look at opportunities from time to time. We may or may not be doing so now. I can only answer you by saying that either way, such knowledge is of no business to anyone other than those with a need to know."
  - "If we were talking to anyone, we would be bound by confidentiality agreements to protect and inform only those with a need to know. If we were not talking, and you had a need to know, you would know we are not talking. In either case, if you had a need to know, you'd know. Therefore, you would have no need to ask, but since you are asking, you don't have a need to know—so, with all respect for you and me, don't ask!"
  - "It's none of your business!"

TOPIC 12
Auctions

Auctions are a generally successful way for a seller to sell out fairly quickly and often realize a higher value than if the business were sold in a privately negotiated sale with a single buyer. Those auctions that succeed do so due to the fear factor driving potential buyers. Topic 12 discusses the auction process and what to expect, when, and suggests a buyer's approach to bidding in an auction.

The reader is encouraged to take the time to read the text in conjunction with the referenced Appendices to gain the appropriate level of understanding of the subject matter discussed in the narrative. Appendices are either presented at the end of this Topic or are available for review and download on the companion Web site noted at the end of this Topic.

FEAR IS A COMPELLING DRIVER TO AUCTION SUCCESS

- Auction deals are managed by investment bankers (or others) with the intention of obtaining the highest price possible resulting from the tension derived from a competitive buyer qualification and bidding process designed to drive to a closing in the least amount of time.
- *Fear is a compelling factor* in gaining bidder participation in the auction process, particularly in auctions of targets with strategic capabilities applicable to a group of potential strategic buyers:
  - Fear that a needed strategic capability found in the target will not be gained and a synergistic competitive advantage will be lost.
  - Fear that the target's capability will go to someone else who can gain competitive advantage.
  - Fear that by not taking part and eventually winning the auction, future growth will be limited.
  - Fear that by not taking part, one loses face in the eyes of owners or managing boards.
- Auction bosses hope that the subtle influence on bidders of the fear factor and having to beat competing bids will result in offers that have been stretched to the seller's advantage.
- By design, buyers are denied the time to gather extensive due diligence knowledge with which to negotiate directly with the seller and gain any negotiating advantage or identify deep seller issues.

- The auction process and timeline is highly compressed and is theoretically to the seller's advantage. See the example of a timeline in Appendix 12.1.
- Bidders must exercise control over their bid process and not overreach.
- Auctions can have more than two or three bid rounds in an attempt to stretch the offers.
- Winning bidders should consider assuring that they were not bidding against themselves in rebid contests by requiring nonconfidential evidence of the losing rebids if they win a bid and the deal closes.

AUCTION PROCESS—BID SOLICITATION

- The auction process generally unfolds as follows:
- Prospective buyers are solicited for interest by direct cold call letters or phone calls. Auction bosses and sellers assemble and vet the list of potential buyers.
- See Appendix 12.2 for an example of a bid solicitation letter.

AUCTION PROCESS—INVITATION TO BID

- Interested prospective buyers enter into confidentiality agreements with the buyer, banker, and seller prior to obtaining the seller's prospectus information (see Topic 9).
- Seller information is summarized in an offering prospectus prepared by the banker and is provided to prospective buyers upon receipt of the confidentiality agreement (see Topic 13).
- Nonbinding letters of interest and preliminary valuation ranges are requested for delivery 15 to 30 days following prospectus receipt.
- See Appendix 12.3 for an example of an invitation to bid instruction letter.
- Seller's investment bank provides draft purchase and purchase and sale agreements along with the invitation to bid letters to prospective buyers (see Topic 90).
- Bidders are given three to four weeks to deliver preliminary offers and purchase and sales agreements with buyer-proposed changes.

AUCTION PROCESS—FIRST ROUND CONDITIONAL OFFER

- Bidders' first-round offers made at this stage are generally highly qualified.
- Offering valuations are usually stated as a range.
- Offers are conditional on satisfactory due diligence covering a number of areas, including environmental, customer, technology, manufacturing, value chain, vendors, and so on.
- See Appendix 12.4 for an example of a first-round auction conditional offer letter.

AUCTION PROCESS—MANAGEMENT PRESENTATION, DUE DILIGENCE, MORE BID ROUNDS

- The bidder list is reduced to three to four second-round bidders in five to ten days based on responses received by the investment bank.
- The remaining prospective buyers are scheduled to hear the seller's management presentation and perhaps to review preliminary information made available in a data room located at the seller's, banker, or attorney offices or perhaps at the target company. Data rooms are often Internet-accessible Web sites (virtual data rooms).
- Facility tours are provided if visits to the target company are arranged.
- Private sellers are often very concerned with informing employees, customers, vendors, and others that the company is for sale until a deal is felt by the seller to be imminent, in which case facility tours and customer and employee interviews are final steps in the due diligence process.
- On very large deals, the seller's bankers also provide highly detailed "vendor due diligence" reports prepared by outside experts retained by the seller for the purpose of limiting or eliminating subsequent on-site due diligence work by the selected buyer groups.
- Vendor due diligence reports include detail data and information on essentially all areas defined in Topic 10. Such data may require vetting by attorneys before release to certain bidders if there are potential antitrust issues between seller and bidder (see Topic 9).
- There may be more than two rounds of diligence, bidding, and offer letters in the process of narrowing the bid field to a single winning bid.

AUCTION PROCESS—SELECT A WINNER

- Bidders' offers are ranked by the investment banker on several award criteria, including:
  - Offer price (most important)
  - Conditions contained in the offer letter concerning further due diligence requirements, board approval, financing contingencies, time to closing, and so forth
  - The extent of changes to the draft purchase and sale agreement
  - The ability of the buyer to finance the transaction and the form of consideration (cash, stock, a take-back note payable obligation, or a combination thereof)
  - Likelihood of closing
- The seller and the investment bank select one bidder with which to negotiate the purchase and sale agreement.
- The second-ranked bidder is usually notified that if the first bidder does not proceed, the second bidder will be brought in.
- The successful bidder usually demands an exclusive negotiation period.
- The winning bidder must prepare integration plans in a very short time frame with limited knowledge.

PREEMPTIVE OFFERS

- Occasionally, a bidder makes a preemptive, close-out offer at the very beginning or during the bidding process with the intent of closing out the bid process and obtaining an exclusive period to negotiate the deal. See Appendix 12.5 for an illustration of a preemptive offer and request for exclusivity letter.
- Such bidders either fear the auction process or feel they have an ace in the hole in the form of synergies or integration benefits that compel them to offer a preemptive premium early.
- Typically, the auction bosses stretch preemptive bid offers by demanding that the bid must be very compelling to take the target off the market and grant an exclusive to the bidder.
- Preemptive bidders are also provided a copy of the purchase and sale agreement, which must be returned very quickly to the auction boss with all requested changes. The major deal points in the agreement must be negotiated to the seller's satisfaction before the exclusive right is provided to the bidder.

AUCTION PROCESS—GRANT EXCLUSIVITY

- The exclusive arrangement is provided to the winning bidder via an exclusive letter agreement dictating the terms of the exclusive including duration, due diligence access, and so on.
- Exclusivity agreements are nonbinding on either party. If the seller violates the buyer's no-shop provisions (contained in the exclusivity agreement) during the period of exclusivity, buyers often require sellers to reimburse their costs and expenses.
- See Appendix 12.6 for an example of an exclusivity letter.
- If an exclusive deal fails and comes apart during due diligence, the auction generally can be restarted with the second-place bidder, but the seller will find it difficult to regain the initial auction tension and momentum.
- Contracts are intended to be signed within a few weeks of receipt of final offers and are expected to authorize deal closing following completion in two to four weeks of outstanding preclosing due diligence activities, which may include:
  - Customer visitation
  - Employee introduction and interviews
  - Vendor visitation
  - Environmental and intellectual property evaluation
- It is often difficult for buyers to break or slow an auction and interact with the target's management alone to assess its quality and strength until a bidder is selected.
- When a bidder is selected, the negotiating leverage shifts a bit. The bidder's demand to meet with management alone in a setting of its choice is often successful.

- Auctions are often difficult to manage and conclude in contrast to private, relationship-based transactions, which often take much longer to nurture and develop but can be negotiated more easily in time frames suited to the parties, as each side recognizes the mutual benefits of the evolving transaction.

FAILED AUCTIONS

- Failed auctions (the deal is pulled from the market at some point in the process) are not necessarily fatal to a subsequent sale process.
- The biggest risk to pulling a deal from the market is, in spite of confidentiality agreements, the target's information, financial, and a certain level of proprietary information, is "out there."
- Deals can be pulled for a variety of reasons:
  - General lack of bidder interest and participation
  - Price expectations not met by offers
  - Unforeseen economic dislocation events
  - Health
  - Target business issues that materialize during the process (intellectual property, environmental, and so forth)
- Business issues that materialized during the auction process would certainly require correction prior to a subsequent sales process. Generally, the same circle of potential bidders will be approached in a subsequent sale process and they will look for issue resolution.

AN AUCTION BIDDING STRATEGY

- *On first-round bids*, determine the most likely range of high and low enterprise values based on the limited information provided and gathered knowledge of the market; less preferable, create a range by increasing and decreasing a single-point valuation by 15% to 20%.
  - The underlying reason for presenting a range offer is the uncertainty (pending confirmation with more disclosure or during due diligence) of the relevant business drivers and the impact on enterprise value.
  - Include the range offer in a conditional offer letter (see Appendix 12.4).
- *On second-round bids* tighten up the high/low assumptions and narrow the range to ±5% to 10%.
  - Request more specific information on the business drivers in question prior to making second and subsequent round bids: "The better the information, the sharper our pencil."
- *On final bids*, determine the highest price and the best terms and level of risk assumption you can live with based on the knowledge profile you were able to assemble in the time available to make the deal work, then reduce the value by 5% to 10% when you make the "final" offer; do not overreach just to win, and do not offer your final position.

- You will be asked to improve your "final" bid probably twice so leave some dry powder to increase your offer.
- If you lose, you lost on your best effort.
- If you win, you win knowing some of the key risks and most of the resources needed to manage them to make the deal work.

BEWARE OF THE CRAZIES

- *To bid well beyond your knowledge limits is a bad place to be.* The best play for bidders is to bid based on what they know and have learned about the business and their analysis of the deal.
- Beware of "the crazies." Auctions often stir bidders into a case of the crazies, where bidders lose the goal of doing a smart deal in the fever of winning the deal; winning becomes the end game, not an event along the way, and often leads to the winner's curse: the perception that because everyone else bid less, you must have bid too much![1]
- Final offer letters must allow room (offer conditions) to undertake enough detail due diligence either to validate the seller's value proposition and the buyer's offer assumptions or to invalidate them and provide the ability to back away.

[1] Robert F. Bruner, *Applied Mergers and Acquisitions* (Hoboken, NJ: John Wiley & Sons, 2004), p. 801.

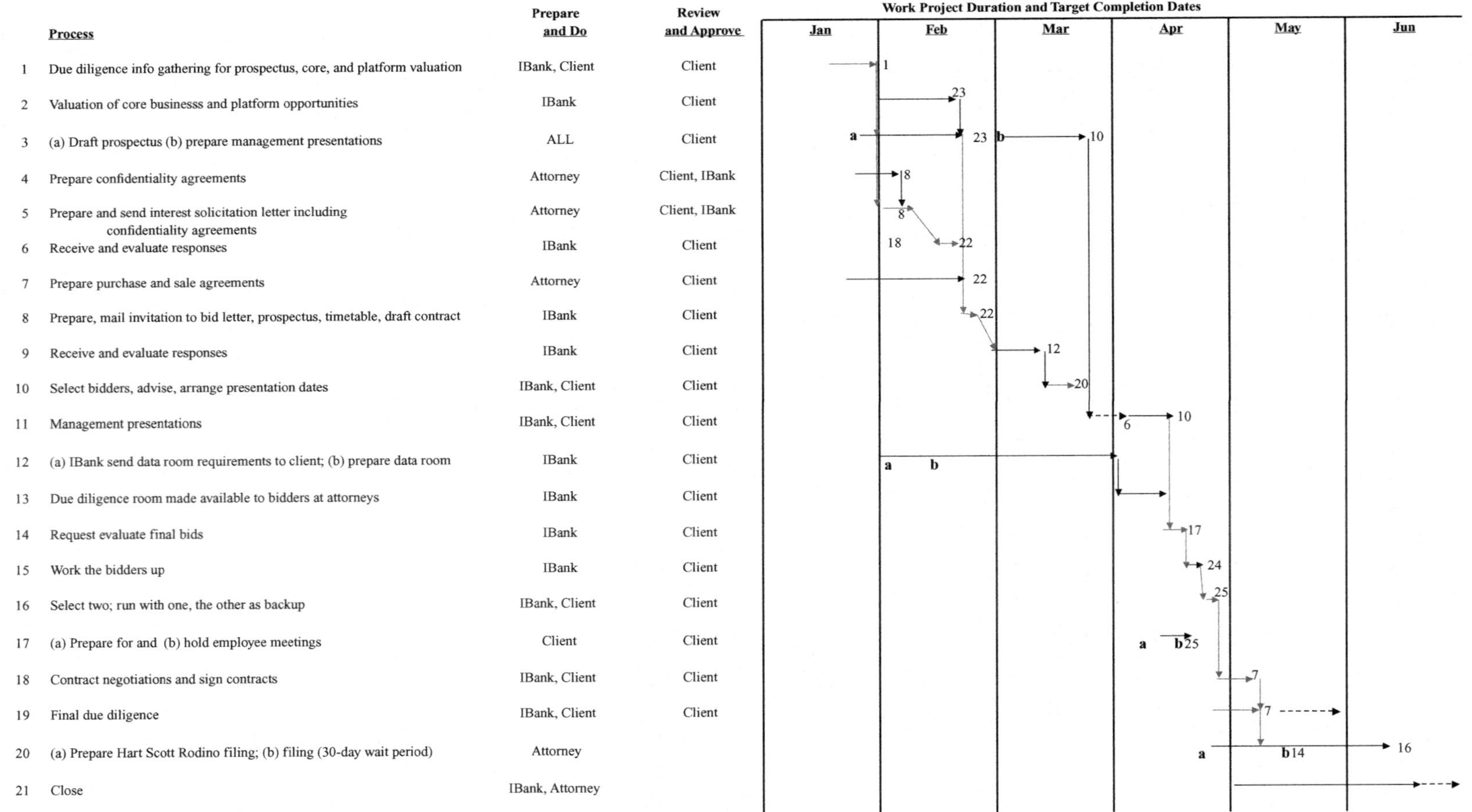

	Process	Prepare and Do	Review and Approve
1	Due diligence info gathering for prospectus, core, and platform valuation	IBank, Client	Client
2	Valuation of core businesss and platform opportunities	IBank	Client
3	(a) Draft prospectus (b) prepare management presentations	ALL	Client
4	Prepare confidentiality agreements	Attorney	Client, IBank
5	Prepare and send interest solicitation letter including confidentiality agreements	Attorney	Client, IBank
6	Receive and evaluate responses	IBank	Client
7	Prepare purchase and sale agreements	Attorney	Client
8	Prepare, mail invitation to bid letter, prospectus, timetable, draft contract	IBank	Client
9	Receive and evaluate responses	IBank	Client
10	Select bidders, advise, arrange presentation dates	IBank, Client	Client
11	Management presentations	IBank, Client	Client
12	(a) IBank send data room requirements to client; (b) prepare data room	IBank	Client
13	Due diligence room made available to bidders at attorneys	IBank	Client
14	Request evaluate final bids	IBank	Client
15	Work the bidders up	IBank	Client
16	Select two; run with one, the other as backup	IBank, Client	Client
17	(a) Prepare for and (b) hold employee meetings	Client	Client
18	Contract negotiations and sign contracts	IBank, Client	Client
19	Final due diligence	IBank, Client	Client
20	(a) Prepare Hart Scott Rodino filing; (b) filing (30-day wait period)	Attorney	
21	Close	IBank, Attorney	

APPENDIX 12.1 Auction Timeline Example

The following Appendices, as well as those presented earlier, are available for viewing or download on the Web site for this book at: www.wiley.com/go/emott. Please see the About the Web Site page at the back of this book for login information.

APPENDIX 12.2 Bid Solicitation Letter

APPENDIX 12.3 Invitation to Bid Instruction Letter

APPENDIX 12.4 Conditional Offer Letter

APPENDIX 12.5 Preemptive Offer and Request for Exclusivity Letter

APPENDIX 12.6 Exclusivity Letter

TOPIC 13

Seller's Prospectus

A prospectus, or selling document, is required as part of the process of engaging in an auction. Sellers and their bankers collaborate in the preparation of this document. Bankers provide the format and outline, and sellers provide the description of the business, market, customers, competition, operations, and so forth, and the technical background. Bankers provide the financial and transaction information, value proposition, and position the business opportunity and write the document.

CONTENTS OF THE SELLING DOCUMENT

- The seller's prospectus is a selling document prepared by the seller and/or the seller's banker. The primary function of the prospectus is to present the compelling story and attributes of the target's business model.
- The compelling story should start at the end user level and run through the target's internal fulfillment chain. Readers must find credible, testable resonance with the rationale presented in support of the financial outlook provided in the document, such as:
  - End user market drivers that support unit volume demand growth (evidenced by regulatory requirements, demographics, technology replacement trends, supply imbalances, and so forth)
  - Served market share drivers (evidenced by price leadership, low-cost leadership, innovative/unique solutions, competitive advantage, customer surveys, performance, and so forth)
  - Competitive advantage (deriving from proprietary technology and know-how; relative quality, delivery, and solution performance, and so forth)
  - Barriers to entry or intrusion (deriving from proprietary technology and know-how, performance legacy, high switching risk and cost, and so forth)
  - Channel access advantages
  - Stable, low cost, repeatable, agile fulfillment/manufacturing/delivery process (deriving from an evolving or in place customer requirements driven, lean enterprise environment and so forth)
- The banker provides the prospectus to parties interested in bidding on a target business following receipt of a confidentiality agreement. The prospectus

provides a bidder enough information to allow the preparation of a conditional offer for the target.

- Development of a prospectus can take up to two months due to the nature of the information required and the need for collaboration between seller and banker.
- The prospectus should be started well in advance of the bid solicitation letters, as interested parties should receive a prospectus shortly after the seller receives letters of bidder interest.
- The prospectus usually presents target information in a format similar to the following outline:

Executive Summary

Company, Industry Served, and Strategic Intent

Markets Served and Growth Drivers

Technical Innovations and Recent Developments

Company Operations and Facilities

Company Strengths, Capabilities, and Competencies

Financial Results Highlights, 2003 to 2008

Financial Position Highlights, 2003 to 2008

Projected Financial Results Highlights, 2009 to 2013

Projected Financial Position Highlights, 2009 to 2013

Description of the Core Opportunity for an Acquirer

Description of the Platform Opportunities and Platform Value for an Acquirer

Investment Opportunity Detail

Company History and Ownership

Company Products, Integrated Technologies, and Services Offered

Engineering, Technology Achievements, and Research and Development

Key Market Growth Drivers Now and in the Future

Product Segments and End Use Markets Served

Competitor Profiles and Barriers to Entry Relative Competitive Advantage

Facilities and Organization

Sales, Marketing, and Software Development

Customer Technical Services and Training

Manufacturing Operations, Capacity, Process, and Value-Added Activities

Key Vendors and Relationships

Computer Systems

Intellectual Property

Human Resources, Organization, and Benefit Programs

Insurance

Transaction

Preferred Deal Structure and Consideration

Preferred Acquirer Profile

Financial Results, 2003 to 2008

Financial Position, 2003 to 2008

Projected Financial Results, 2009 to 2013

Projected Financial Position, 2009 to 2013

TOPIC 14

Pay for Inherent Capabilities Only

Topic 14 discusses the necessity for buyers to focus their offers on the level of business capabilities existing in the business at the time of the acquisition and on the financial results related thereto. Projected seller financial results may be based on a much-expanded capability base that does not exist at the closing of the acquisition. Do not overpay.

THE BASKET OF CAPABILTIES ACQUIRED HAS A FINITE LIFE AND VALUE

- The business and capabilities acquired *at closing* (hopefully) possess the potential to capture the benefits of a *given level of "franchise" differentiation* or competitive advantage resulting from the know-how, technology, and process advantage resident in the business at closing.
- Presumably, the business acquired has a given franchise time frame (T) during which continued earnings, growth, superior returns, and value creation resulting from the acquired capabilities can occur. At the conclusion of that period, the franchise capability base will be somewhat diminished and returns would be no better than those of other competitors.[1]
- *Acquired franchise-creating capabilities existing at closing* with duration longer than four to seven years would be exceptional; three to five years is more likely for most acquired franchise capabilities before the marketplace closes the gap and new generations of capability are required to maintain franchise level returns.
- This is not to say a target has a three- to five-year life. It is to say that superior franchise level returns from the *as-is basket of capabilities acquired* have a limited duration, after which the returns eventually will settle to a continuum level into the future, barring the introduction of new franchise capabilities.

[1] G. Bennett Stewart III, *The Quest for Value* (New York: HarperBusiness, 1991), pp. 289, 290.

SELLER PROJECTIONS OFTEN COMINGLE CURRENT AND FUTURE CAPABILITIES

- *Buyers' beware.* Sellers' projections of revenue, earnings, and value potential derived from "existing" franchise capabilities often are confused and intermingled with *future franchise capabilities* and potential future *opportunities* available to the buyer that *do not exist in the business at the closing.* Often the projected costs of future development expense and investment in capacity and intellectual property required to create new capabilities have not been included in such forecasts.
- Value-creating potential and superior returns beyond the acquired franchise horizon T from successfully executing initiatives leading to new franchise capabilities and realizing the benefits of future scenarios *will be determined and implemented at the risk and cost of the purchaser* after the closing (if the purchaser chooses to do so).
- *Future "franchise generations"* will evolve and expand the entities' lifetime value creation potential, which is different from acquired franchise capabilities.
- Buyers will prepare strategic plans for the acquired target as a testament to the value proposition they expect to achieve longer term. The financial projections related thereto will capture the buyers' future cash flow requirements for new capabilities and capacities required to realize their strategic rationale for the acquisition. This value proposition plan and forecast will and should be very different from that used to value the business for the purpose of an acquisition.

PAY ONLY FOR EXISTING VALUE POTENTIAL

- Buyers should strive to *pay only for the acquired franchise value creation potential resident in the target at the closing plus some recognition of the underlying capability platform* that may enable buyers to exploit new opportunities and evolve new future franchise capabilities (see Topic 15).
- Buyers should not pay for the *forecasted potential value of nonexistent future capability.* (No one knows exactly what future capability will look like, will cost to develop, or will return.) See illustration in Appendix 14.1.
- Buyers should do their homework here, and recognize there is a potential to overpay.
- To avoid the potential of overpayment, buyers should consider structuring offers in this way:
  - Offer up-front payments for the acquired as is franchise capability value, plus platform value.
  - If such offers are not successful, offer contingent performance based earn-outs for the difference in value between the buyers and sellers franchise value forecasts.
- See also Topic 15 (Platform Value) and Topic 76 (Earn-Outs).

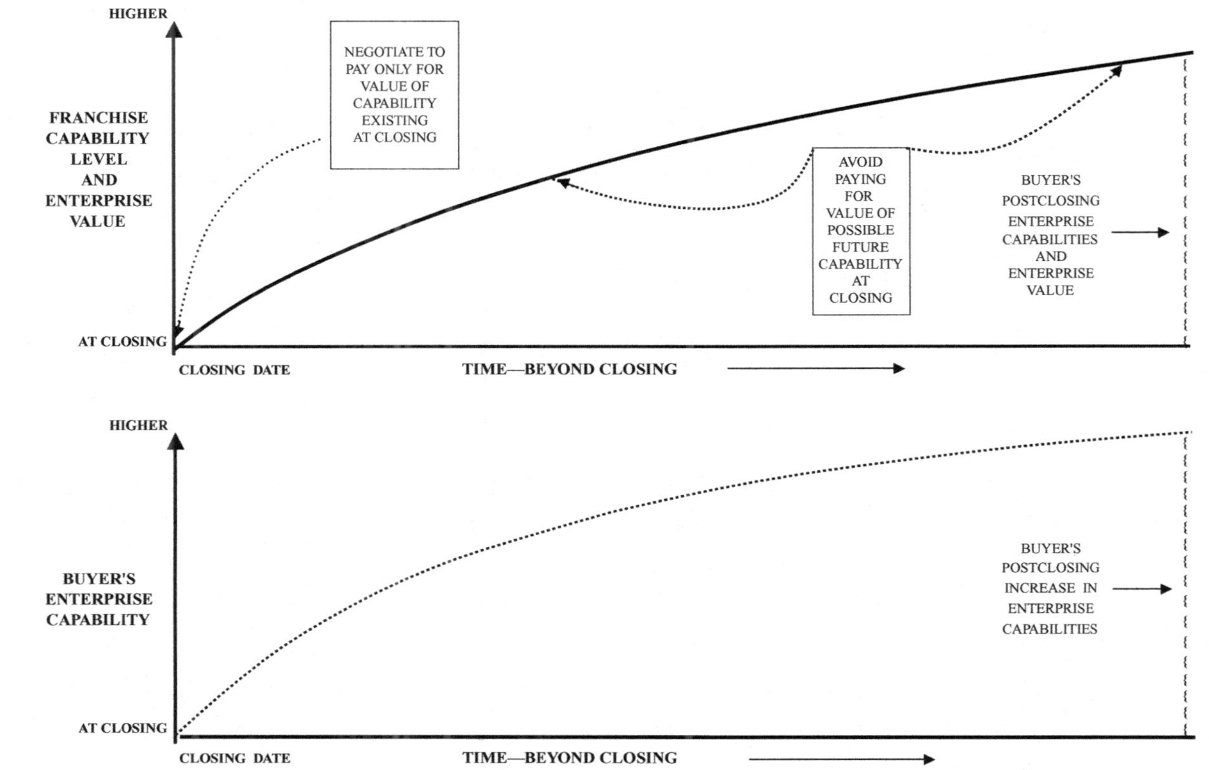

APPENDIX 14.1 Franchise Capability Evolution Postclosing

TOPIC 15
Platform Value

Sellers expect to realize a portion of the platform value of their firm by extracting a premium in the purchase price. Platform value is an enabler that allows the buyer to invest in the acquired business and thereby realize the benefits of new opportunities. Without the platform (the acquired business), the benefits of new opportunities could not be achieved. Topic 15 explores this value dimension and proposes a practical approach to valuing platform value.

WHAT IS IT, HOW MUCH IS IT WORTH

- *To sellers, platform value* is the maximum amount they could expect to extract from a buyer arising from the value sellers think will accrue to the buyer from the cumulative value of future franchise capability benefits.
- *To buyers, platform value* is the value of future franchise capability benefits that arise from investment in new technology, markets, products, or services the benefits of which *can be derived only* from new buyer investments in the as-is platform acquired. Without the acquired platform capabilities, buyers would be unable to realize (or would encounter significant difficulty in realizing) the advantages of future franchise positions arising from exploiting new opportunities. (See Topics 16 and 17.)
- A very realistic approach for buyers to determine platform value is to answer this question: *How much would a buyer be willing to pay to determine with reasonable certainty* the future incremental franchise value that can be created from investment in new opportunities (research and development [R&D], technology, markets, product, etc.) that are available only from owning this target?
- A reasonable answer to this question lies in structuring the issues associated with these opportunities as a "real option" or series of real options: What and how large are the incremental opportunities (new returns arising from new products, new markets)? What is the likely size of the variation (or risk) in these returns? How long will it take for the returns to come to fruition? What is the size of the required future investment in the platform, and when must it be made to realize the returns?

THE REAL OPTION APPROACH TO PLATFORM VALUATION

- *The real option approach provides an answer to the value of (how much should you pay for) the right to wait and see how good is good before making an investment in a new platform direction.*
- The deeper value found from engaging in real options analysis is found in how management strategically manages scarce resources and the events encountered in a world filled with uncertainty and answer the following questions before making the investment decision: Will the technology work or the R&D pay off? When will it be ready? Will customers realize value from it? What will the products cost? What will competition do? How volatile will the returns be? and so on.
- Sellers attempt intuitively to estimate the value of benefits accruing to buyers and to extract an such amount as a premium in price demands, or they simply assume that such value is included in the pricing multiples demanded.
- Platform value premiums may be identified by the seller as additional purchase price expectations over and above the value of the core business or platform value may simply be included in the seller's offer demand as a premium designed to stretch the buyer's offer.
- Buyers, not sellers, will be taking the business and financial risk of exploitation of any future value emanating from the platform purchased.
- *How much should a buyer expect to pay for platform value?* Buyers must focus their offers and negotiation strategies on paying no more than the fundamental value of the core business acquired as it is *plus not more than the real option value of new* opportunities arising from platform ownership (net of the value lost, if any, from replacement of acquired capabilities resulting from implementing the new opportunities; e.g., Product B replaces the free cash flow stream of Product A after B is fully accepted). (See Topic 14.)
- See Topics 45, 46, and 85 for explanation and illustrations of valuing real options.

TOPIC 16

Buyer and Seller Value Perspectives

In the end, the total consideration paid for a business equals the purchase price plus liabilities and the economic impact of risk assumed. Theoretically, the purchase price paid should not exceed the actual opportunity and risk-adjusted value of the target business, including platform value and synergies, or value may not be created. Topic 16 explores the issues and thought processes considered by sellers and buyers as they compose offer and counteroffer scenarios.

WHAT IS THE OTHER SIDE THINKING THE VALUE OF THE BUSINESS IS?

- Before negotiations begin, be familiar with the thought process engaged in by the other side when positioning your side. Appendix 16.1 presents the issues relevant to buyers and sellers in determining value positions.
- *Sellers must determine* their own composite valuation ranges for the target and estimate the potential ranges buyers may likely offer and why.
- *Buyers must determine* their own composite valuation ranges for the target and estimate the potential ranges sellers may likely expect and why.
- Each party should have a very clear idea of:
  - *The target core business value* "as it is."
  - *The upside and downside potential* adjustments to the as-is value and the probability of realization.
  - *The value of integration and combinative synergies* if the buyer owned and ran the target (see Topics 51 and 52).
  - *The value of deal-structuring advantages* (taxes, debt, net operating loss carry forwards, etc.) (see Topics 42, 84, and 85).
  - *The platform value* of the future opportunities potentially available to the buyer arising from the target's capabilities in the business that the buyer must attempt to realize (see Topics 15, 45, and 46).
  - The quantification of these items and ranges of value.
  - The assets expected to be received and the liabilities and risks to be assumed.

- *Buyers must assess their ceiling offer value*—where they have to walk away—and stick to it.
- The more you know about the deal, the future potentials and risks, and your ability to manage them, the farther you can stretch your offer and the clearer the ceiling offer becomes (see Topics 26, 27, and 28).
- Buyers must have a realistic perception of the seller's lowest acceptable offer value and have a good feel for:
  - How the seller will assess your offer
  - Whether your offer range overlaps with your estimate of the seller's range
  - Where the seller will walk away
- Buyers must have a realistic perception of the seller's after-tax cash take-out position and goal:
  - What is the seller's cash take-out before and after taxes, debt repayment, and fees depending on the deal structure, asset or stock sale?
  - How much is the estimated seller's equity investment tax basis and what he or she should fairly expect as a return on this investment?
  - How do your offer ranges compare to seller expectations? Be prepared to address the differences.
  - What are the risks assumed or transferred between buyer and seller?
  - The target's value will emerge from a quantitative exercise—read on!
- The buyer's target offer level is that price (and risk assumption) that will provide the desired targeted returns to the investors.
- The buyer's initial offer in negotiated deals should be 15% to 20% or so below the target offer level but must be close to the seller's lowest acceptable offer level, based on the buyer's judgment of what will be acceptable to the seller (see Topic 67).
- Offers are often presented as a range, depending on the level of business knowledge made available to the buyer. An increase in this knowledge will enable the buyer to sharpen the range and eventually make a single-value offer.
- Buyers must leave room in their offers or ranges for upward movement during negotiations.
- In the end, the real value will be realized from what buyers do with the business to add value to customers and stakeholders.
- The amount paid should be an affirmation of an effective negotiation process where both parties are equally dissatisfied with the result but can live with it and justify it to themselves and others (see Topic 67).

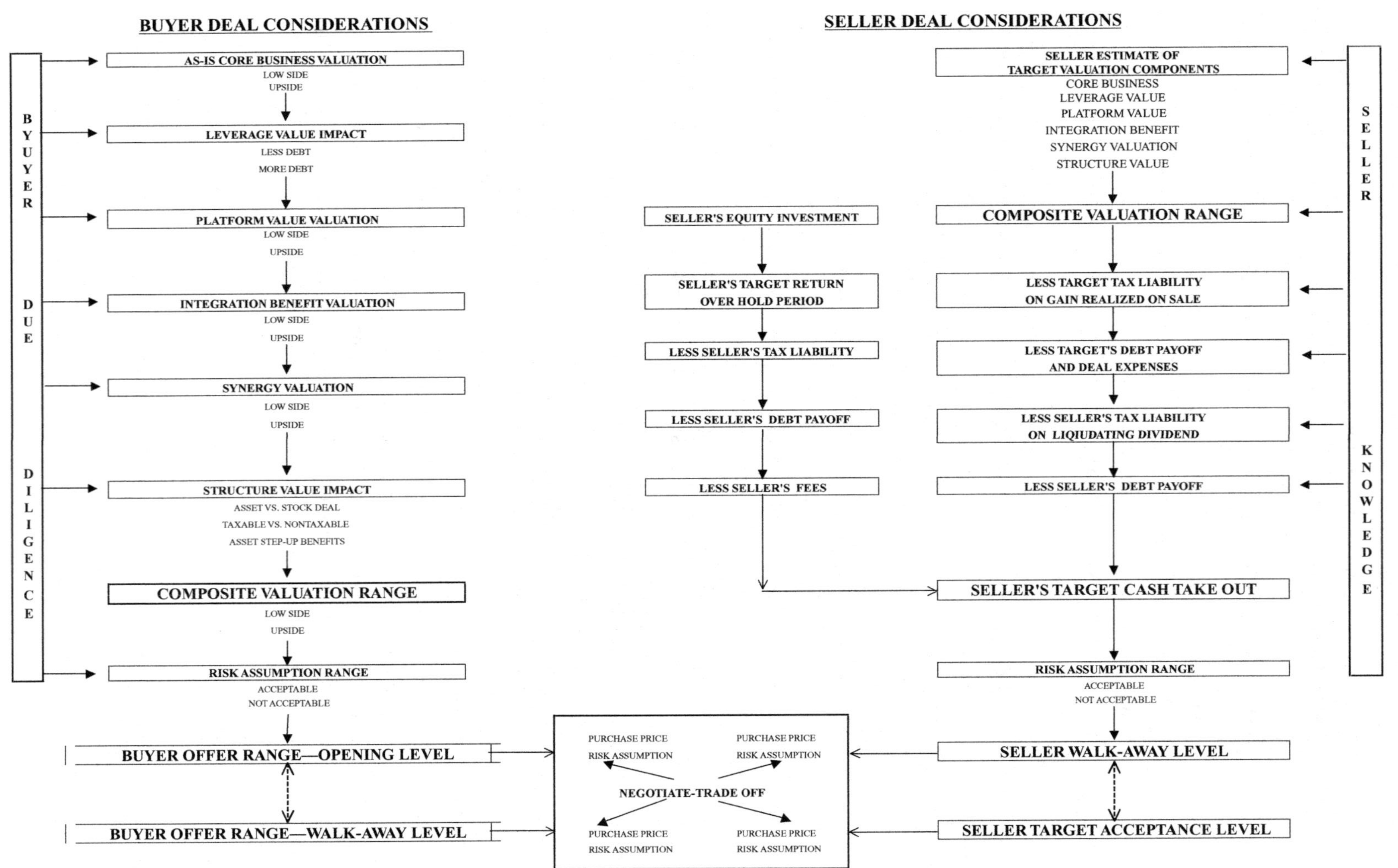

APPENDIX 16.1 Offer Determination and Deal Negotiation Process

TOPIC 17

Integration Initiatives Will Determine Deal Value

Without the ability to see and implement integration initiatives leading to improved operational results, buyers likely will have to settle for painful returns on their investment. Deals are fully priced, and if buyers do not have the ability to drive value improvements, their returns will suffer.

KNOW WHAT YOU ARE GOING TO DO TO CREATE ADDED VALUE IN YOUR DEAL

- Deals will be fully priced in willing buyer and seller negotiations conducted on even negotiating terms.
- Given the dynamics of the negotiation process, buyers' offers will be stretched to get the deal done.
- Nominal pure-play buyer returns on as-is deals will be driven to painful levels if buyers close deals without the ability to add value to them postclosing.
- Buyers must see (and justify the deal based on) how they can create added value beyond the as-is value to bring the all-in returns to acceptable levels.
- Added value is created by doing things differently after the deal closes.
- Strategic buyers must take advantage of capability overlaps with the target and complementary gap-closing capabilities acquired and leverage both leading to:
  - Improved operating cycle time
  - Improved delivery lead time to customers
  - Improved order fill rates
  - Improved quality
  - Improved customer satisfaction
  - Facility/capacity consolidation and cost reduction
  - Staff/function redundancy and consolidation and cost reduction
  - Expanded volumes through market penetration, new customers, new products/services
  - Technology improvements leading to new product development and launch
  - Faster inventory turnover

  - Reduced waste through lean value chain processes (i.e., in order processing and selling, manufacturing, distribution, vendor management and procurement, etc.) (see Topics 18 and 19).
  - Reduced manufacturing, overhead, and operating costs leading to improved gross margins
  - Improved distribution channel access
  - Distribution, marketing, selling and administrative consolidation, cost reduction, or productivity improvements
  - Reduced raw materials cost from procurement efficiencies
  - Lower effective tax rates
  - Identification and realization of future options available to the firm
- If buyers cannot see ways to implement postclosing integration initiatives, they will have to settle for pure-play financial returns.
- Alternatively, if buyers cannot see ways to implement postclosing integration initiatives, they should consider looking elsewhere.
- Buyers must, in the end, earn what they pay (see Topics 18 and 19).

TOPIC 18

Unlock Hidden Value: The Lean Enterprise

Postclosing initiatives must include a thrust to reduce waste, improve throughput and productivity, reduce working capital employed, and increase cash flow. Lean enterprise thinking is the answer, if you know how to do it. Evaluate lean opportunities during due diligence, and you will enhance your ability to make your deal successful and will have an advantage in the negotiation process.

EVALUATE LEAN OPPORTUNITIES DURING DUE DILIGENCE

- Virtually every business process has waste in it (perhaps 25% to 50%).
- "Look under the rocks" of the target as you do your due diligence to find waste. Value the impact of eliminating it, and you will learn how far you can stretch your offer or improve your returns and you will be a step ahead in making your deal really work.
- During due diligence, evaluate the most significant business processes of the target, which usually include sales and customer order processing, order fulfillment and material conversion, materials procurement and payables, returns, distribution, billing, receivables and cash collection, capital equipment procurement, and so on.
- These business processes generally are identified by discussions and observations of the seller's principal activities and capabilities during the due diligence process (see Topics 1 and 10).
- The order fulfillment and material conversion process in manufacturing (and other) companies is usually a key place to start evaluating lean opportunities.
- The lean opportunities evaluation work should be done by savvy operations types who live and breathe lean process improvement as a way of life.

STAPLE YOURSELF TO AN ORDER

- Start by "stapling yourself to an order": Walk through the flow of the ordering, order fulfillment, and material conversion process on the shop floor, then procurement and payables, then billing and collection, and so forth.

- Consider these questions as you do your walk-through:
  - *How is stuff (material, supplies, parts, etc.) ordered from vendors?* Are large orders placed, to get volume discounts? Are prices driven by an efficient, well-controlled, and centralized material requirements planning or enterprise resource planning system?
  - *What is the vendor relationship?* Are there many vendors utilized, thus allowing the company to play one off against the other to gain the lowest price and best purchase quantity terms?
  - *How is stuff delivered and received?* Does the company order large quantities (to assure lowest unit cost) shipped to efficient, secure, central warehouses with automated storage, identification retrieval, and locator systems?
  - *How is stuff put into play to convert it from a raw material to an in-process subassembly?* Are efficient, large-batch runs used based on a centralized, well-controlled automated scheduling system so machine utilization is high and unit output cost per batch or run is low?
  - Look for efficiently stacked and moved in-process parts or staged raw materials.
  - Watch the large operating machines and machine centers.
  - *How are the machines loaded with demand to churn out parts?* Is this machinery efficiently scheduled from an automated central nerve center to run large batches and absorb overhead?
  - Are these machines set up and changed over infrequently to ensure high machine utilization rates and output levels?
  - Are the in-process parts efficiently staged and moved to caged-in process storage areas before sub- and final assembly areas call for parts?
  - How are the in-process parts moved, how frequently, how far? Are the in-process parts moved by dedicated available movers?
  - Are the caged storage areas secure and attended?
  - Is final assembly well supplied with in-process parts inventory availability?
  - *How are sub- and final assembly loaded with demand?* Is an efficient central scheduling system used that provides build-to inventory schedules to ensure low unit cost based on high batch runs to optimize repetitive labor and machine utilization?
  - *Where does the finished product go?* Does it go to an efficient, secure distribution warehouse? Why is the warehouse efficient?
  - Are there adequate central storage facilities and people on hand to keep the raw material organized, retrieve it, and deliver it to the floor based on the scheduling system?
  - Are the raw material storage areas secure and separated from in-process areas?
  - Are there adequate people available to move the in-process inventory efficiently and timely to the next stage?
  - Are there adequate people to move the assembled goods to the warehouse or for delivery to the distribution center?
  - Are there adequate people and systems available to store and efficiently track the finished goods inventory and load outgoing distribution as orders are picked, staged, and fulfilled?

- Are purchase orders generated by a centralized material requirements planning purchasing system based on scheduled production requirements?
- Are raw materials received matched to purchase orders to ensure that quantity delivered equals orders? Are there adequate staff and controls in place to deal with exceptions? Do copies of the matched receivers and purchase orders go to accounts payable for matching and reconciliation with purchase orders and vendor invoices received prior to payment?

CONCLUSION

- If you recorded yes to some or most of these questions, thank everyone for the tour and keep the answers to yourself. You can conclude that:
  - The target is doing all the wrong things.
  - The operation is very efficient at doing very inefficient things. Cost and investment saving opportunities await the trained eye and hand.
  - Hidden value unknown to the seller is yours for the taking and deal return making.
- See Topic 19.

TOPIC 19

The Real Deal: Lean

Lean enterprise thinking is a field of knowledge directed at continuous process improvements and elimination of all non-value-added activities in the enterprise, resulting in increasing customer satisfaction, reduced waste, improved throughput and productivity, reduced working capital employed, increased cash flow, and improved returns on capital employed. This topic explores some of the principles and essentials of lean thinking and illustrates the need for implementation of this critical mind-set in any acquisition target.

LEAN ENTERPRISE OVERVIEW: IDENTIFY THE NON-VALUE-ADDED ACTIVITIES

- The ultimate goal of today's lean enterprise model is to eliminate time, distance, and space from every stage of order fulfillment, material conversion, and all other business support processes.
- For the acquirer, the goal is to identify during due diligence the gaps and differences between the as-is and the "ideal lean enterprise" operating environment in order to isolate value-creating lean initiatives that can be undertaken post-closing.
- During a walk-through, the goal is to size up the gaps and identify and quantify the opportunities to create value by eliminating most of the so-called efficient activities observed in Topic 18.
- Generally speaking, in a lean enterprise, any non-value-added activities such as storage, moving, queuing, pushing, packing, stacking, receiving, recording, waiting, staging, overseeing, and inspecting are eliminated from any conversion process, including product design and development, selling, order taking, manufacturing, distribution, billing, collection, accounts payable, and field service.
- A value-added activity can be defined as one that an end customer would pay for and that improves stakeholder satisfaction.
- A value-added activity can be defined as one that productively touches and transforms the product being produced into the final state desired by a customer in the least amount of time.

- A non-value-added activity is one that the customer would not pay for and that does not productively touch and transform the product toward final completion.
- Ideally, material conversion flow should be pulled from the downstream stage based on customer order demand rates, not pushed by an automated material requirements planning system.

ONE-PIECE FLOW IS THE GOAL

- *Make stuff at the same rate stuff is sold*, and you will eliminate inventory and reduce indirect costs.
- *Employ kanbans* to trigger needed upstream production activity.
- Kanbans are essentially visual triggers (an empty space or rack) that, when empty, cause a producer action to fill the space or rack with production to a prescribed level available for the downstream producer.
- Raw materials should be delivered by vendors directly to the shop floor only when and where they are required for use by producers based on kanban or other pull signals. (Eliminate the warehouses, stock picking, and moving activities.)
- *Purchase orders, invoices, and receivers from certain vendors are potentially eliminated*: Pay vendors based on shipments of finished goods for the vendors' material component content, if possible (plus counted scrap and waste).
- *Form and level load work cells.* The in-process cycle time of any work center or work center combination (e.g., one minute to make a component) should equal the rate at which the downstream component is pulled (e.g., one item per minute).
- *If appropriate, eliminate production lines and consider contiguous work cells* containing a number of in-process steps under the control of multidisciplined, cross-trained producers.
- *Empower producers* to operate their work cells independently, verify quality, and shut the cell down if a problem arises.
- *Eliminate quality checkers;* empower producers to own the quality of their output.
- Correct quality issues where and when they occur, not later.
- Limit supervision; empower producers to own their process.
- Limit inspection; empower producers to own inspection.
- *Cross-train producers* to perform a number of activities.
- *Employ standard work*, do not work to a standard.
- *Run small batches* of only what is needed at the next stage to fill the kanban requirement.
- *Reduce setup and changeover time* to as near to zero as possible. That way, changeover to meet demand and specification changes will be painless.
- The only inventory in the place should be the item being worked on at each stage in production.

- "Efficient" moving, picking, cuing, and delivery systems are not required; get rid of them.
- *Build, assemble, and deliver to customer orders*, not to an inventory replenishment plan.

CONCLUSION

- A wealth of information is available on the subject of lean enterprise management; access it, learn it.[1]
- The lessons learned from leaning out order fulfillment, manufacturing, and other material conversion or fulfillment process are applicable to most other white-collar business processes: credit, billing and collection; procurement and accounts payable; capital asset procurement, returns; and the like.
- Lean implementation provides the key to unlocking hidden value: lowered unit cost, improved delivery lead times, less inventory (higher inventory turns); improved on-time delivery, quality, and customer satisfaction; higher-than-anticipated free cash flow; improved economic value added (EVA); higher rates of return and value creation potential.
- Modify the financial reporting systems to support the actual value stream process costs, not the traditional standard cost, manufacturing variances, and over- and underabsorbed overheads cost accounting model.
- Provide a balanced scorecard to measure progress on key shop floor and financial metrics as lean is implemented in the organization. The Lean Value Pyramid in Appendix 19.1 illustrates the goal and the flow of the value creation results from lean.
- Figure out how to evaluate the impact of lean opportunities during the due diligence process and how to implement lean in your acquired companies. It is the key to unlocking internally generated wealth creation in your deals.

[1] An excellent source for material on lean is Productivity Inc; email: info@productivityinc.com; telephone: 212-686-5900, or read James P. Womack, Daniel T. Jones, and Daniel Roos, *The Machine that Changed The World: The Story of Lean Production* (New York: Free Press, 2007); James P. Womack and Daniel T. Jones, *Lean Solutions: How Companies and Customers Can Create Value and Wealth Together* (New York: Free Press, 2005); Mark R. Hamel, *Kaizen Event Fieldbook* (Dearborn, MI: Society of Manufacturing Engineers, 2010); *Jerrold M. Solomon, Who's Counting, a Lean Accounting Business Novel* (Fort Wayne, IN: WCM Associates, 2003).

Strategic Performance — Semiannual Metrics

Monthly Metrics

Monthly Metrics

Tactical Performance — Monthly Metrics

Operational Performance — Weekly Metrics Shop Floor

Operational Performance — Daily Metrics Shop Floor

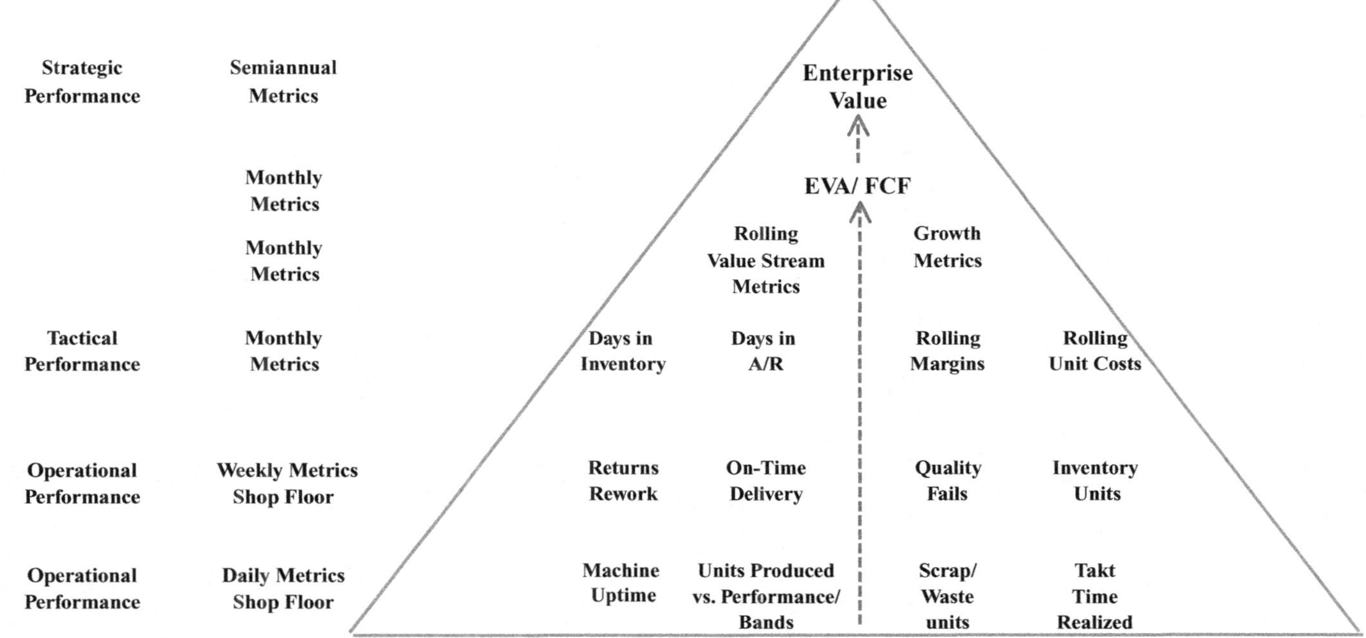

Need Lean Scorecard for management and board meetings
Need a definition glossary of each Metric and why it is critical to follow
Management and board needs to know where Lean is going, why, and what they should measure to gauge progress

APPENDIX 19.1 Lean Value Pyramid

TOPIC 20

Valuation: An Introduction

Topic 20 presents an overview of the essential approaches used in the process of valuation determination. To simplify it, any valuation exercise is an attempt using the method selected to convert the economic profile of the enterprise being valued to a cash-equivalent value at the date of the valuation.

VALUATION CONSIDERATIONS AND METHODS OVERVIEW

- Valuation exercises can range from the simple to the complex.
- The goal of the valuation exercise is multifaceted, as indicated by the following issues (see also Topics 16 and 17):

Value Considerations of the Buyer

- As-is value scenarios, risk adjusted.
- Synergy value scenarios, risk adjusted.
- Future "real option" values that may exist for the target business.
- Structuring impact on value.
- Leverage impact on value.
- Other asset and liability valuation issues (carry-forward losses, pension plans, investments).

Value Considerations of the Seller

- As-is fair market value (comparables, determinative methods) (see Topics 47 and 48).
- Platform value sharing, how much (see Topic 15)?
- Synergy value sharing, how much?
- Seller cash take-away scenarios (after debt repayment, fees, taxes).
- Structuring impact on seller take-away value (taxable versus nontaxable structures) (see Topics 84 and 85).

Offer-Level Considerations

- Initial offers.
- Counteroffers and cross-counteroffer scenarios.
- Buyer final total consideration walk-away offer level.
- Seller final walk-away offer level.

- Valuation exercises and the methods employed in M&A transactions are both *determinative* of value and *corroborative* of the value derived from other methods.
- The most widely employed methods are:
- *Comparable methods*, so-called market approach[1] (see Topics 57, 58, and 59).
- *Capitalization of benefits methods and discounted cash flow (DCF) methods*, so-called income approaches[2] (see Topic 39).
- *Cost replication methods* attempt to estimate value by determining the cost today of replicating the target's capability from ground up, including:
  - Facilities, property
  - Machinery and equipment
  - Intellectual property and patent estates
  - Working capital

The cost replication method is not widely used in M&A transactions.

COMPARABLE METHODS: MARKET APPROACH OVERVIEW

- *Comparable methods* determine values by multiplying the target's current financial results (e.g., sales, income, etc.) by *multiples of various financial measures* (e.g., sales, income, etc.) of "comparable" companies and businesses as *valued in the public markets* or in *purchase and sale transactions* of public or private companies (or securities).
- The *multiples* are determined by dividing the enterprise value or transaction sales price value of the comparable company by a reported financial result (sales, *earnings before interest, depreciation, and amortization* [*EBIDA*], earnings before interest and tax [EBIT], net income, cash flow, etc.) (see Topic 58).
- The shortcoming of the market approach as a determinative M&A valuation method is the degree of meaningful comparability of the company or companies selected with the target (size, business, operating characteristics, and financial performance, etc.). See Topics 57 to 59.
- In addition, mechanical adjustments are often made to the comparable company multiples as they are to make them more closely fit the target company's operating characteristics and size.
- For this reason, comparable valuations often are used as corroborative measures of value as determined by economic modeling income approaches.
- Comparable method multiples are, however, generally faster to develop and less data intense than economic modeling income methods.
- Comparable multiple methods are discussed further in Topics 57, 58, and 59.

---

[1] See also Shannon P. Pratt, *Valuing a Business: The Analysis and Appraisal of Closely Held Companies*, 2nd ed. (New York: McGraw-Hill, 1989), pp. 52–56, for a full discussion.
[2] Ibid.

- Comparable multiple methods include:

Multiple Employed	Value Determined	See Topics
Net Income (P/E) multiple method	Equity value	57–60
Cash Flow multiple method	Enterprise value	57–60
EBITDA multiple method	Enterprise value	57–60
EBIT multiple method	Enterprise value	57–60
Sales multiple method	Enterprise value	57–60

CAPITALIZATION OF BENEFITS METHOD OVERVIEW

- *Capitalization of benefit method* determines value (V) by dividing a sustainable economic return benefit (R_1) by a capitalization rate (cap rate) of return (r) *expected* over the (perpetual) life of the benefit stream as follows.[3]

$$V = \frac{R_1}{r}$$

where R_1 = the value of the return (R) at the end of year 1, the first year

- From the buyer's perspective, *value (V) is the maximum amount* the buyer would logically be *willing to pay* for a business with expected returns (R) to result in a target return on investment (r).
- The shortcoming of applying the capitalization of benefits method to M&A valuation lies in the difficulty of determination of the appropriate sustainable value R_1, the proposition that such a sum is continuous and that growth if any, is accurate and constant. It is less problematic to determine an applicable capitalization rate.
- The attractiveness of the capitalization approach lies in its simplicity, in the fact that value is determined quickly, and in that the method is less data intense than economic modeling methods.
- *The effect of estimated future (constant) annual growth* (g) in an economic benefit (R) is captured by reducing the discount rate (r) by g (except when g is equal to or greater than r). This is called the Gordon growth model.

$$V = \frac{R_1}{r - g}$$

- Growth (g) in the economic return (R) from a business is driven by the collective impact of served market growth, market share growth, and continuous improvements in profitability and capital employed efficiency, which are discussed in the topics that follow. See also Topic 10 and Appendices 10.4 and 10.5 for an illustration of value growth drivers.
- The following illustrations walk through illustrations of the capitalization of benefits approach.

[3] See ibid., pp. 94–101, for a full discussion.

ILLUSTRATION 1: CAPITALIZATION ILLUSTRATION: VALUATION OF A PERPETUITY

What is the value (V) today of a constant future annual after-tax cash income stream (a perpetuity) (R) of $1,000 received at the very end of year 1 and at the end of each year thereafter with a posttax target return (r) of 20%? Value is defined as follows (where R_1 = the value of the return (R) at the end of year 1, the first year of the perpetuity period):

$$V = \frac{R_1}{r} = \frac{\$1{,}000}{.2} = \$5{,}000$$

That is, a $1,000 annual cash stream received at the end of each year from today into perpetuity at a target return of 20% has a value today of $5,000.

Or, a $5,000 investment made today that yields a $1,000 annual free cash flow forever payable at the end of each year from today into the future results in an annualized compound rate of return on the investment of 20% (so-called internal rate of return).

The concept behind an *internal* rate of return is that as each $1,000 is received, it is immediately reinvested at the stated internal rate of return.

ILLUSTRATION 2: CAPITALIZATION ILLUSTRATION: VALUATION OF A GROWING PERPETUITY

What is the value today of a periodic cash flow (R_0) of $1,000 received at the end of each year from today if it grows each year in the future at a constant annual growth rate (g) of 5%? Value is defined as follows (where $R_1 = R_0 (1+g)$, or R_1 = the value of R after one year of growth, and r is equal to 20%):

$$V = \frac{R_1}{r-g} = \frac{1000(1.05)}{.20-.05} = \frac{\$1{,}050}{.15} = \$7{,}000$$

That is, a $7,000 investment today that yields $1,050 at the very end of the first year of compounding and grows 5% each year thereafter provides a compound annual rate of return on the investment of 20%.

Note that this method (the Gordon growth model) is workable only when r is greater than g.

DISCOUNTED CASH FLOW METHOD

- *DCF methods* determine values by discounting the projected future economic benefits of economic modeling scenarios (see Topics 21, 39, and 44).

TOPIC 21

Discounted Cash Flow: An Introduction

Topic 21 presents the mechanics of the discounted cash flow (DCF) valuation process and how it is done. The DCF process is more data intensive than the valuation methods discussed in Topic 20. The flexibility of modeling and valuing the possible economic profiles of a business forecast generally outweigh the data intensity and time required to prepare meaningful DCF valuations.

The reader is encouraged to take the time to read the text in conjunction with the referenced Appendices to gain the appropriate level of understanding of the subject matter discussed in the narrative. Appendices are either presented at the end of this Topic or are available for review and download on the companion Web site noted at the end of this Topic.

DCF—INTRODUCTION, ADVANTAGE, DISADVANTAGE

- *The discounted cash flow valuation process* yields identical results to the capitalization or perpetuity value methods illustrated in Topic 20, where the returns (R) and growth (g) are constant and the life is perpetual.
- The advantage of DCF versus capitalization is that value can be derived from *uneven future periodic flows* and uneven growth rates for any number of future periods (n).
- The disadvantage is that it is more computationally intensive.
- *The discounting process is the exact opposite of the compounding process.*[1]

COMPOUNDING

- In compounding, a future value is determined by multiplying an amount times 1 plus a constant compounding factor, then multiplying that result times

[1] Robert F. Bruner, *Applied Mergers and Acquisitions* (Hoboken, NJ: John Wiley & Sons, 2004), p. 260.

1 plus the constant compounding factor, and so forth, for as many periods as the compounding is required.

- For example, \$1,000 today (time 0, or the beginning of year 1) compounded at 20% for three years from today results in a future value of \$1,728 (see Illustration 21.1).

ILLUSTRATION 21.1 COMPOUNDING TO A FUTURE VALUE

Compound Value of $1,000 at the end of:			
R	R_1	R_2	R_3
Today	Year 1	Year 2	Year 3
1,000 × 1.20 ↳			
	= 1,200 × 1.20 ↳		
		= 1,440 × 1.20 ↳	
			= 1,728

- This is also computationally equal to:

$= \$1,000 \times 1.20^3 (1.20^3$ is 1.20 compounded for three periods $(1.20 \times 1.20 \times 1.20)$, or 1.728))

$= \$1,000 \times 1.728$

$= \$1,728$ at the end of year 3

DISCOUNTING

- In discounting, the question is: What is the present value today of a future amount (or a series of future amounts)?
- The present value is equivalent to dividing the future amount to be discounted by 1 plus the compounding factor, then dividing that result by 1 plus the compounding factor, and so on, for as many periods (n) as necessary to arrive at the present value today (the reverse of the compounding process).
- For example, the present value today of \$1,728 received three years (n = 3) from now (at the end of the third year) at a 20% *discount rate* is \$1,000 (see Illustration 21.2).

ILLUSTRATION 21.2 DISCOUNTING TO A PRESENT VALUE

	Value at end of:		
Today	Year 1	Year 2	Year 3
			$\frac{1,728}{1.20}$
		1,440 = $\frac{}{1.20}$ ↵	
	1,200 = $\frac{}{1.20}$ ↵		
1,000 = ↵			

- This is also computationally equal to

$= \$1,728 \div 1.20^3$

$= \$1,728 \div 1.728$

$= \$1,000$ present value today at the beginning of year 1 (time 0)

The same result is obtained by multiplying the future value to be discounted by the reciprocal of 1 plus the discount rate raised to the nth period (with the nth period being the number of periods the future value is from today):

$= 1728 \times 1/[1.20^3]$

$= 1728 \times 1/1.728$

$= 1728 \times .5787$

$= \$1,000$ present value today at the beginning of year 1 (time 0).

DISCOUNTED CASH FLOW

- DCF valuations of business forecasts calculate the present value today of a number of future cash flows to be received at the end of each of a successive number of future years (n) and cumulate each of the year's respective present values to arrive at a present value of the flows of all the years.
- The next expression presents this methodology:

$$V = \sum_{n=1}^{\infty} \frac{FCFn}{(1+r)^n}$$

where V = value today of all future flows
FCF = free cash flow amount (see Topic 22) received at the end of each future year n
n = year 1 to ∞ (practically, say 200 years)
r = discount rate

In cases where the DCF valuation is for a period less than perpetuity, n equals the last period.

- Appendix 21.1 presents the discounted cash flow valuation of the data presented in Illustration 2 of Topic 20, the valuation of a growing perpetuity value of $1,000 today, and is also equal to $7,000. DCF valuations *into perpetuity* calculate and sum the value today of *each future flow amount* in a series of expected future flows expressed as:
  - In Appendix 21.1, the free cash flow amount for each future year is equal to the base year FCF value of $1,000 ($FCF_0$) times the nth period compound growth factor, and the DCF expression is equal to:

$$V = \sum_{n=1}^{\infty} \frac{FCF_0(1+g)^n}{(1+r)^\wedge n}$$

  - The discount factors for each future year in Appendix 21.1 equal the reciprocal of the compound growth factor for that year as follows:

$$\text{Year 1}: 1/(1+.20)^1 = .8333$$

$$\text{Year 2}: 1/(1+.20)^2 = .6944$$

$$\text{Year 3}: 1/(1+.20)^3 = .5787$$

- The disadvantage of discounting is that more computational complexity is required. That is why there are spreadsheet models, personal computers, and smart people to run them!

The following Appendix is available for viewing or download on the Web site for this book at: www.wiley.com/go/emott. Please see the About the Web Site page at the back of this book for login information.

APPENDIX 21.1 Discounted Cash Flow Valuation

TOPIC 22

Free Cash Flow

Topic 22 explores free cash flow (FCF) and how to calculate and use it in the DCF valuation process. FCF is the cash that is available from business operations after tax after meeting all *operating* needs of the business (excluding financing) and is available to pay posttax interest expense on debt, meet debt principal payment requirements or other nonoperating obligations, or be returned to stockholders in the form of dividends or stock repurchases.[1] FCF is the economic value R (introduced in Topic 20) that provides the basis for doing discounted cash flow (DCF) valuations.

FCF DEFINED

- FCF from ongoing operating results is what matters in valuing a business—not net income plus depreciation or cash flow as determined on a generally accepted accounting principles (GAAP) accounting financial statement presentation format.
- FCF is the amount of cash available from the business from ongoing operations:

  After payment of:
  - All cash operating expenses
  - Cash income tax payments reflecting the effect of deducting tax-deductible cash and noncash charges (excluding interest expense on third-party debt) and

  After reinvestment for:
  - New plant and equipment or other operating asset requirements (for new capacity or to maintain capacity)
  - Operating working capital requirements (for growth), but

  Before payment for or receipt from:
  - Interest expense or income or other nonoperating income items
  - Dividends
  - Debt reduction payments or proceeds
  - Equity redemptions or proceeds

[1] G. Bennett Stewart III, *The Quest for Value* (New York: HarperBusiness, 1991), pp. 307–310.

FCF DETERMINATION

- FCF can be determined in a straightforward manner on an earnings before interest, tax, depreciation, and amortization (EBITDA) basis or an earnings before interest and tax (EBIT) basis (see Illustration 22.1 below).
- Either method results in the same FCF value.
- All recurring operating charges and income related to the core business are included in EBITDA and EBIT. All nonoperating charges and income are excluded.
- Inventory and cost of sales are stated on a first-in, first-out (FIFO) inventory basis.
- The cash flow effect of last-in, first-out (LIFO) basis inventory accounting (usually lower tax expense) is captured in the cash tax payment and is discussed in illustration 22.1 below.
- Illustration 22.1 presents the key elements associated with each method.

ILLUSTRATION 22.1 FCF CALCULATION: EBITDA OR EBIT METHOD

EBITDA Method	EBIT Method
EBITDA is earnings on a FIFO inventory basis *before* interest (expense or income), income taxes, nonoperating charges (income), and book basis depreciation and amortization expense.	EBIT is earnings on a FIFO inventory basis *before* interest (expense or income), income taxes and nonoperating charges (income) *after* book basis depreciation and amortization expense.
FCF equals: **EBITDA**	FCF equals: **EBIT**
Less: Effective cash taxes payable on (projected) EBITDA. (Cash taxes are taxes payable at [projected] marginal tax rates after the effect of the [projected] tax basis depreciation and amortization deduction; **less** the [projected] change in deferred tax arising from: LIFO inventory accounting book-tax difference; other book-tax timing differences such as payments versus accruals for pension benefits, and so on.) (Cash taxes exclude the [projected] effect of net operating loss carry-forward or carry-back impacts, which are valued separately, and nonoperating charges [income].)	Less: Effective cash taxes payable on (projected) EBIT. (Result is equivalent to NOPAT: net operating profit after tax.) (Cash taxes are taxes payable at [projected] marginal tax rates; **less** the [projected] change in deferred tax arising from: tax basis depreciation and amortization shield; LIFO inventory accounting book-tax difference; other book-tax timing differences such as payments versus accruals for pension benefits, and so on.) (Cash taxes exclude the [projected] effect of net operating loss carry-forward or carry-back impacts, which are valued separately, and nonoperating charges [income].)

(*Continued*)

EBITDA Method	EBIT Method
Less: Cash required (available) for operating working capital requirements (operating working capital excludes short-term investments and excess cash).	Plus: Book depreciation and amortization included in EBIT
Less: Cash required for new plant, equipment, and other operating asset requirements including intellectual property.	Less: Cash required (available) for operating working capital requirements (operating working capital excludes short term investments and excess cash).
	Less: Cash required for new plant, equipment, and other operating asset requirements including intellectual property.
Equals: FCF	Equals: FCF

- The cash effect of (material) net operating loss carry-forwards or carry-backs (NOL) utilization is excluded from the projected cash tax expense. If material NOLs are acquired, NOLs should be separately valued in the negotiation process pursuant to the NOL utilization regulations and court precedent governing the issues giving rise to the NOLs. The risk of creation of the taxable income required to utilize the NOLs available must also be considered in the NOL valuation process.

WHILE THE ELEMENTS OF FCF ARE SOMETIMES RESTATED TO MEASURE ROI, THERE IS NO EFFECT ON FCF

- EBITDA, EBIT, and the elements of operating capital employed (operating working capital and fixed assets including intangibles and other operating assets) may be stated after adjustments for other capitalized expenses (net capitalized research and development [R&D], net capitalized operating leases, etc.).
  - In the measurement of return on investment (ROI) and in valuation exercises, EBITDA, EBIT, and capital employed are often restated to reflect the capitalization of certain continuing expenses to better state the normalized economic profit, capital, and return of the enterprise.[2]
  - The restatement is made for expenses that are material in the income statement and are deemed to generate profit over a term longer than the period of expenditure and include R&D, certain new product development and marketing, operating leases, LIFO reserve changes to restate cost of sales to a FIFO basis, bad debt and other reserves, and so forth.[3]

[2] Aswath Damodaran, *The Dark Side of Valuation: Valuing Old Tech, New Tech, and New Economy Companies*, Upper Saddle River, NJ: Prentice-Hall, 2001, pp. 109–119.

[3] G. Bennett Stewart III, *The Quest for Value* (New York: HarperBusiness, 1991), pp. 112–117.

- For example, in the case of R&D and new product development and marketing, the restatements to capital employed require the determination of the capitalized *value* of the spending pattern of R&D to determine the capitalized gross R&D asset value at an expected normal rate (a life of say, five years, e.g., to bring a new product to market) *net* of amortization at each balance sheet date.[3]
- The current unadjusted expense charged to the income statement is reversed and included in the capitalized value at the current balance sheet date and is replaced with the amortization amount.[4]
- The *net* value determined is "added" to operating capital and the equity equivalent sides of the balance sheet in an attempt to properly measure the economic value of capital employed.
- The period-to-period change in the restated net operating capital value (reversed expense net of amortization) is charged to the income statement for the measurement period as income or expense.[5]
- Because the restatements (change in the net operating capital value) increase or decrease income and operating capital in the same amount, there is no effect on the determination of FCF if such restated values are used to determine FCF. Appendix 22.1 presents restatements of certain expenses to illustrate that FCF is the same whether determined before or after such restatements.

CONCLUSION

- The essential goal in assessing FCF is to determine how much cash is available to or required of the investors (debt and equity holders) after meeting the operating (not financing) needs of the business.
- Limited or negative FCF is not a bad thing if it is accompanied by growing operating earnings and revenues and reflects the related and appropriate working capital and fixed capital cash requirements to fund and support the growth.
- Growing, profitable companies may have negative free cash flow as working capital and new capacity investments are incurred, consuming FCF.
- The good news is that if the growth leads to larger and larger EBITDA and EBIT, eventually FCF will catch up and become positive as the growth acceleration path levels out. Remember that the franchise capability acquired (which is what should be valued) has a certain time period T during which superior returns and growth will take place (see Topic 14).
- See Topics 39, 43, 76, and 85 for illustrations of FCF-based valuation applications.

[4] Ibid.

[5] See G. Bennett Stewart III, *The Quest for Value* (New York: HarperBusiness, 1991), pp. 112–117 and Aswath Damodaran, *The Dark Side of Valuation: Valuing Old Tech, New Tech, and New Economy Companies* (Upper Saddle River, NJ: Prentice-Hall, 2001), pp. 109–119, for a discussion of the restatement approaches.

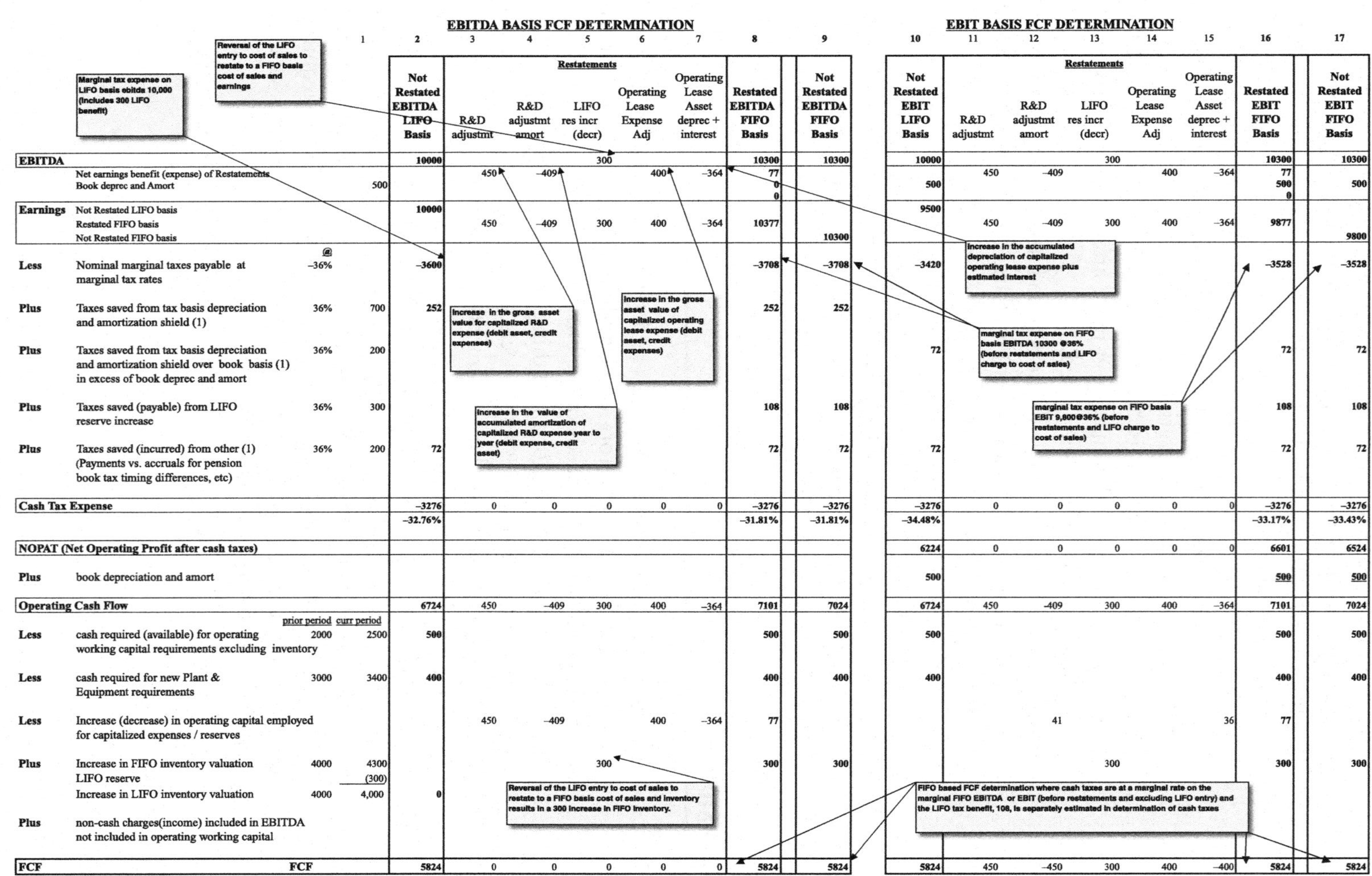

EBITDA BASIS FCF DETERMINATION

			1	2	3	4	5	6	7	8	9
					Restatements						
				Not Restated EBITDA LIFO Basis	R&D adjustmt	R&D adjustmt amort	LIFO res incr (decr)	Operating Lease Expense Adj	Operating Lease Asset deprec + interest	Restated EBITDA FIFO Basis	Not Restated EBITDA FIFO Basis
EBITDA				**10000**			300			**10300**	**10300**
	Net earnings benefit (expense) of Restatements				450	–409		400	–364	**77**	
	Book deprec and Amort		500							**0**	
										0	
Earnings	Not Restated LIFO basis			**10000**							
	Restated FIFO basis				450	–409	300	400	–364	**10377**	
	Not Restated FIFO basis										**10300**
Less	Nominal marginal taxes payable at marginal tax rates	@ –36%		**–3600**						**–3708**	**–3708**
Plus	Taxes saved from tax basis depreciation and amortization shield (1)	36%	700	**252**						**252**	**252**
Plus	Taxes saved from tax basis depreciation and amortization shield over book basis (1) in excess of book deprec and amort	36%	200								
Plus	Taxes saved (payable) from LIFO reserve increase	36%	300							**108**	**108**
Plus	Taxes saved (incurred) from other (1) (Payments vs. accruals for pension book tax timing differences, etc)	36%	200	**72**						**72**	**72**
Cash Tax Expense				**–3276**	0	0	0	0	0	**–3276**	**–3276**
				–32.76%						**–31.81%**	**–31.81%**
NOPAT (Net Operating Profit after cash taxes)											
Plus	book depreciation and amort										
Operating Cash Flow				**6724**	450	–409	300	400	–364	**7101**	**7024**
		prior period	curr period								
Less	cash required (available) for operating working capital requirements excluding inventory	2000	2500	**500**						**500**	**500**
Less	cash required for new Plant & Equipment requirements	3000	3400	**400**						**400**	**400**
Less	Increase (decrease) in operating capital employed for capitalized expenses / reserves				450	–409		400	–364	**77**	
Plus	Increase in FIFO inventory valuation	4000	4300				300			**300**	**300**
	LIFO reserve		(300)								
	Increase in LIFO inventory valuation	4000	4,000	**0**							
Plus	non-cash charges(income) included in EBITDA not included in operating working capital										
FCF	FCF			**5824**	0	0	0	0	0	**5824**	**5824**

EBIT BASIS FCF DETERMINATION

		10	11	12	13	14	15	16	17
			Restatements						
		Not Restated EBIT LIFO Basis	R&D adjustmt	R&D adjustmt amort	LIFO res incr (decr)	Operating Lease Expense Adj	Operating Lease Asset deprec + interest	Restated EBIT FIFO Basis	Not Restated EBIT FIFO Basis
EBITDA		**10000**			300			**10300**	**10300**
	Net earnings benefit (expense) of Restatements		450	–409		400	–364	**77**	
	Book deprec and Amort	**500**						**500**	**500**
								0	
Earnings	Not Restated LIFO basis	**9500**							
	Restated FIFO basis		450	–409	300	400	–364	**9877**	
	Not Restated FIFO basis								**9800**
Less	Nominal marginal taxes payable at marginal tax rates	**–3420**						**–3528**	**–3528**
Plus	Taxes saved from tax basis depreciation and amortization shield (1)								
Plus	Taxes saved from tax basis depreciation and amortization shield over book basis (1) in excess of book deprec and amort	**72**						**72**	**72**
Plus	Taxes saved (payable) from LIFO reserve increase							**108**	**108**
Plus	Taxes saved (incurred) from other (1) (Payments vs. accruals for pension book tax timing differences, etc)	**72**						**72**	**72**
Cash Tax Expense		**–3276**	0	0	0	0	0	**–3276**	**–3276**
		–34.48%						**–33.17%**	**–33.43%**
NOPAT (Net Operating Profit after cash taxes)		**6224**	0	0	0	0	0	**6601**	**6524**
Plus	book depreciation and amort	**500**						**500**	**500**
Operating Cash Flow		**6724**	450	–409	300	400	–364	**7101**	**7024**
Less	cash required (available) for operating working capital requirements excluding inventory	**500**						**500**	**500**
Less	cash required for new Plant & Equipment requirements	**400**						**400**	**400**
Less	Increase (decrease) in operating capital employed for capitalized expenses / reserves			41			36	**77**	
Plus	Increase in FIFO inventory valuation				300			**300**	**300**
	LIFO reserve								
	Increase in LIFO inventory valuation								
Plus	non-cash charges(income) included in EBITDA not included in operating working capital								
FCF	FCF	**5824**	450	–450	300	400	–400	**5824**	**5824**

1. deferred tax change element

APPENDIX 22.1 FCF Determination on a FIFO and LIFO Basis with and without Restatements Example

TOPIC 23

Fair Return on a Deal

Topic 23 addresses what a fair return to reasonably expect on a deal is and provides insight into and methodology to determine a fair return. The proper determination of a fair return provides the basis for the discount rate used in discounted cash flow (DCF) and other valuation.

The reader is encouraged to take the time to read the text in conjunction with the referenced Appendices to gain the appropriate level of understanding of the subject matter discussed in the narrative. Appendices are either presented at the end of this Topic or are available for review and download on the companion Web site noted at the end of this Topic.

FAIR RETURN

- What is a fair return to expect on a given deal? It depends: the long-term return on Treasury bills, mutual funds, stocks, the Standard & Poor's index, what your venture capital fund or hedge fund manager friend tells you is possible, and so forth.
  - All of them are fair answers.
  - What separates them is *risk*.
- Realistically, a fair return to expect on a deal is what you should expect to earn on an investment with equivalent risk and opportunity as the deal target—*your opportunity return.*[1]
- For business acquirers, the most frequently used, and somewhat controversial, target return used to determine the investor's required return on equity in valuing deals is that resulting from the capital asset pricing model (CAPM).

CAPITAL ASSET PRICING MODEL

- *CAPM is an opportunity-based return—what you can expect to get elsewhere for comparable risk.*[2]

[1] G. Bennett Stewart, *The Quest for Value* (New York: HarperBusiness, 1991), pp. 431, 432.
[2] Ibbotson Associates, *2010 Valuation Yearbook, Market Results for Stocks, Bonds, Bills and Inflation 1926–2009* (222 W. Washington, Chicago, Illinois: Morningstar, Inc., 2010), pp. 21, 22.

- CAPM was developed by Harry M. Markowitz, James S. Tobin, and William F. Sharpe, recipients of the Nobel Prize in Economic Science for their efforts.[3]
- CAPM derives a target return an equity investor should expect to earn on a security investment over a long time period by estimating a risk premium in excess of a riskless investment return. The size of the risk premium is in linear proportion to the amount of systematic risk assumed.[4]
- CAPM is not without its detractors, but it is time tested and is widely used in practice.
- CAPM is a bottoms-up construction of the *cost of equity capital (excluding the effect of debt)* composed of:[5]
  - *A risk-free return,* R_f (see Topic 24).
  - Plus a factor for general equity risk: so-called *equity risk premium* (ERP) (see Topic 25).
  - Plus an adjustment to ERP for *systematic equity risk*, called *beta*, which tends to be inversely related to the size (risk) of the market cap of the securities from which beta is calculated (see Topics 29 to 35).
  - Plus as promulgated by Ibbotson (not captured in the original CAPM model) a risk premium for size appropriate to the size of the target resulting in an *adjusted* CAPM model. (See the following comments and Illustration 23.1.)
- The essential problems with CAPM-derived returns (without the size premia) are:
  - The correlation of CAPM-predicted returns with actual returns (in capital securities markets) does not result in a high degree of relationship, as measured by r^2.[6] (r^2, the coefficient of determination or the regression analysis correlation coefficient squared, is a measure of the proportion of the variability in a dependent variable that is explained by another independent variable [s])).
  - The application of beta (see Topics 29 to 35) does not adequately capture return volatility, particularly as it relates to the valuation of closely held and small-company stocks.[7]
  - The predicted returns (cost of capital) resulting from CAPM are not as high as actual returns for small-company investments. As a result, they tend to overstate small-company valuations: Beta does not capture all the risk premia associated with small companies.[8]
- The Ibbotson Associates size premia studies attempt to isolate the amount by which the cost of equity is underestimated by CAPM for each size decile of the capital markets studied and provides such data as a size premium in its annual publication *Stocks, Bonds Bills and Inflation Yearbook* (see Topic 36).

---

[3] Ibid. p. 43.
[4] Ibid.,
[5] Ibid., pp. 44, 45.
[6] Robert F. Bruner, *Applied Mergers and Acquisitions* (Hoboken, NJ: John Wiley & Sons, 2004), p. 267.
[7] Ibbotson Associates, *2010 Valuation Yearbook*, p. 90.
[8] Ibid., pp. 89, 90, and 91.

- The relationships between the elements of CAPM and adjusted CAPM, including the Ibbotson size premia, are portrayed on the Security Market Line in Appendix 23.1.[9]

SECURITY MARKET LINE

- CAPM-predicted returns, including the beta adjustment for systematic risk, are presented on the Security Market Line (the solid line noted as CAPM expected returns) in Appendix 23.1.
- Actual returns by size decile as measured over time exceed the CAPM expected returns as beta increases—market cap decreases (the dotted line rising from the solid line), suggesting the need for a size premium adjustment for each decile in the construction of CAPM (see Topic 29).
- *The adjusted CAPM return is a risk-adjusted target return on equity* that can be used in the determination of a weighted average cost of capital (see Topic 37) that is employed in either capitalization or DCF valuation methods.

COSTS OF CAPITAL DEFINED AND USES: C_U, C_L, I, AND C*

There are four costs of capital discussed here, noted herein as C_U, C_L, i (cost of debt capital), and C* (weighted average cost of capital).[10]

- C_U is the cost of equity capital determined by CAPM, *without the effect of debt* (as debt affects beta), *also referred to as* the unlevered cost of equity. The cost of equity may also be expressed as a target return on equity *including the effect of debt* (as debt affects beta), in the acquired company's capital structure, C_L, the levered cost of equity, also determined by CAPM.
- The levered cost of equity capital, C_L, may be combined with the after-tax cost of debt capital (interest cost, i, times (1 – tax rate t)), on a weighted basis of debt to equity in the capital structure, resulting in a weighted average cost of capital, C* (see Topic 37).
- C* may also be derived directly from CU (see Topic 37).
- C_L is comparable to a calculated total shareholder return (TSR) on investment for the equity holder (see Topic 86). The book accounting return measure, return on equity (ROE), defined as net income divided by book equity is sometimes used as a rough proxy comparable to C_L.
- C* is the basis for determining the periodic discount rates used in many discounted cash flow (DCF) valuations (other than in those DCF valuations when the value of free cash flow (FCF) is separately determined from the value of debt (see Topics 43 and 44)).

---

[9] Ibid., p. 91.

[10] As characterized by Stewart, *The Quest for Value*, p. 432.

- C^* is comparable to the internal rate of return (the rate that equates the expected free cash flow from the business plus terminal value to the *market* enterprise value of net operating capital employed [working capital plus net plant and equipment plus other operating assets and goodwill]) as measured at any time in the business life of the enterprise. The book accounting return measure, return on net assets (RONA), defined as net operating profit after tax to operating capital employed is sometimes used as a rough proxy comparable to C^*.
- C_U provides the basis for determining the periodic discount rates used in DCF valuations when the value of FCF is separately determined from the value of debt such as the valuation of leveraged buyouts (see Topics 43 and 44).
- C^* is also integral to determining corroborating *comparable multiples* (see Topics 57 to 59).

VALUATION RISKS

- Not all valuation risks are captured in the construction of CAPM target returns.
- While *systematic risks* (captured by beta: the volatility of a security versus the stock market volatility as a whole) are captured in CAPM, *unsystematic risks* (business asset risks) are *not* captured in CAPM. In terms of portfolio theory, while unsystematic business volatility risk can be diversified away in a broadly distributed portfolio,[11] such risks remain in the valuation of a given acquired business entity. (See Topics 29 and 30.)
- As relates to specific target valuations, the business asset risk can be captured somewhat by modeling the expected variation in FCF returns resulting from such risk.

OTHER METHODS OF RETURN ON EQUITY ESTIMATION

- Other methods of target return on equity derivation include the build-up method, the Fama and French three-factor model and the arbitrage pricing theory (APT) model.
  - The *build-up method* is the sum of the risk-free rate, the equity risk premium (beta is not applied; it is implicitly assumed to be 1.0), a size premium without an adjustment for beta, and possibly an industry premium (or reduction).[12]
  - The essential shortcoming of this method is that it does not capture the *relative riskiness* (beta) of a particular security investment versus the market as a whole.

[11] Stephen A. Ross, Randolph W. Westerfield, and Jeffery Jaffe, *Corporate Finance*, 4th ed. (New York: McGraw-Hill, 1996), pp. 293–298.

[12] Ibbotson Associates, *2010 Valuation Yearbook, Market Results for Stocks, Bonds, Bills and Inflation 1926–2009* (222 W. Washington, Chicago, Illinois: Morningstar, Inc., 2010), pp. 27–41.

- The *Fama and French three-factor model* was developed by professors Eugene Fama and Kenneth French.[13]
- The model develops expected market returns based on their findings that returns on stocks are better explained as a function of a company's *size* (market capitalization), *financial risk* (determined by book value to market value ratio), and *covariance* with the market.
- As Ibbotson points out, it is not conclusive whether the returns from the Fama and French model are better or worse than CAPM. The Fama and French model produces similar expected return results for large cap companies but generally higher returns for small cap companies.[14]
- The *arbitrage pricing theory model (APT)* was developed by Stephen A. Ross and elaborated by Richard Roll.[15]
- APT develops expected market returns for a security as the sum of the risk-free rate plus the sum of the product of various systematic risk factors times the securities factor loading for that risk factor (regression coefficient).[16]
- Although the risk factors might include, for example, changes in gross national product, inflation, production, and others, there is generally no agreement on a correct or complete set of factors.[17]

CAPM CALCULATION

- The elements of the CAPM return and how they are combined are shown in Illustration 23.1.

ILLUSTRATION 23.1 CAPM

CAPM Determination of C_L (used for determination of C* and resulting levered enterprise value) (a)

Risk-free Rate		7.000%	R_F	(See Topic 24)
Equity risk premium (large cap)	7.600%		ERP	(See Topic 25)
× comparable levered equity beta [(b)]	1.1546		B_L	
= beta-adjusted equity risk premium	8.775%			(See Topic 32)
+ **beta-adjusted equity risk premium**		8.775%		
= **CAPM-derived return** on equity target for large cap companies with Leverage (C_L)		15.775%	C_L	

(Continued)

[13] Ibid., pp. 61 and 109–114.
[14] Ibid., p. 111.
[15] Ibid., pp. 46.
[16] Ibid.
[17] Ross, Westerfield, and Jaffe, *Corporate Finance*, p. 306.

+ Small-cap size premium (if valuing other than a large-cap company) (c)	2.600%	See Topic 36
= **CAPM return on equity target for target "smaller-cap"** companies with leverage C_{LS}	18.375%	C_{LS}

[a]All values indicated are for illustration clarity only. The values are not static and should reflect the most current data available at the time of CAPM construction.

[b]From an analysis of look-alike comparable companies adjusted to reflect the long-term expected debt to capital structure of the target (see Topics 29 and 32).

[c]Size premiums vary in amount (see Topic 36).

Ibbotson Associates, Chicago, Illinois, a subsidiary of Morningstar, Inc., is a frequently used source for risk-free rates, beta, and size premium data. It provides and updates this data annually, has exceptionally well-documented literature, and has a Web site source (www.ibbotson.com).

TREATMENT OF INHERENT VOLATILITY FROM UNSYSTEMATIC RISK IN VALUATIONS

- *The goal of the capital asset pricing model is to derive a target opportunity rate of return on equity that the investor should expect to earn on an equity investment in a comparable business of comparable size, equivalent risk, and opportunity, and leverage appropriate to the target company being acquired—the opportunity return.*
- The target return should reflect the appropriate beta and size risk premium comparable to the target company and industry, not the acquirer of the target.
- While other risk adjustments (for unsystematic business risks), such as currency risk, key man dependency risk, customer, product or market concentration risk, and so forth *may* be included in the derivation of C_L, *it is not preferable to do so* if information is available to model the effect of these factors on cash flow directly.
  - The valuation impact of these other unsystematic risks is best assessed by sensitizing the projected FCF returns directly for the potential impact and leave the base CAPM discount rate intact (see Topic 61).
- *The construction and application of systematic risk-adjusted discount rates for purposes of valuation does not address the impact of inherent volatility (standard deviation) of economic returns associated with the business assets in its markets on a given deal, see Topic 31.*
- The value of a business to a buyer (or subsequent buyers) is the present value as measured at a point in time, of the *perceived potential* of the business to produce inherently volatile economic returns over the long term. The inherent volatility of the returns (up or down) arising from unsystematic risk factors is part and parcel of the acquired business and cannot be eliminated regardless of what was paid for the business.

- The function of the discount rate (and the valuation process) is to set a floor under the expected rate of return acceptable to the buyer. The valuation mechanics establish a value of the expected economic returns that inherently include certain volatility. Certain aspects of the volatility in the economic returns will be controllable as they present themselves; others will not.
- Attempting to price a deal by valuing the expected economic returns at an arbitrarily high discount rate, C*, designed to mitigate or eliminate the impact of the potential *downside volatility* of returns at the best provides indications of value sensitivity for use in negotiation preparation.
  - More than likely overstated discount rates will lead to valuation ranges that do not result in completed deals (buyer undervaluations).
  - In addition, the credibility acquired from negotiating from a totally sound conceptual framework is lost.
  - It is far better to disagree during negotiations over expected FCF forecasts than poorly constructed discount rates.
- Valuing arbitrarily reduced (severely haircut) *expected* economic returns at a rationally determined C* discount rate to mitigate the impact of potential downside volatility of returns may provide useful indications of value sensitivity to employ in negotiation preparations but likely results in deals that do not happen rather than enviably high returns on completed deals.
- The process of evaluation and due diligence, and eventually negotiation, should be used to establish the range (most likely, least likely) of expected economic returns to be valued. The volatility associated with each range is unchanged. Disagreement on the seller's versus buyer's perception of the expected economic return levels therefore value, should be addressed by obtaining greater clarity and agreement on fundamental business FCF drivers or if a large valuation gap cannot be bridged, settled through deal structuring (earn-outs for example, see Topic 76) not in discount rate construction.

INTERNATIONAL COST OF EQUITY CAPITAL—OVERVIEW

- Investments should be evaluated utilizing cost of capital, C_L, reflecting the risks indigenous to the country of investment. As Ibbotson points out, the data required for the construction of CAPM in the United States are not available outside the United States as many foreign markets either are not integrated, do not have a long track record of meaningful historical data on companies and industries, or are much smaller and as a result less diversified and tend to be concentrated.[18]
- International cost of capital calculations are therefore often done on a "country-specific basis" employing a number of methods summarized below.

[18] Ibid., p. 115.

- CAPM can be converted to a country specific basis by utilizing the equity risk premium (ERP), beta and risk free rate for the country of investment.[19]
  - The ERP is first calculated on a worldwide basis by dividing the ERP in the United States by the beta of the U.S. market to the world market. Ibbotson indicates that the U.S. beta for the period 1970 to 2009 is .9190. With a large cap ERP in the United States of 6.67%, the ERP for the world would be 7.26% (6.67% /.9091).[20]
  - Beta is calculated for the returns of the country of investment as a whole versus the world market returns. The resulting beta is then applied to the worldwide ERP, resulting in a beta adjusted ERP for the country of investment.
  - C_L would equal the risk free for the country plus the country-specific ERP. Ibbotson points out that the betas thus calculated show significantly less statistical significance for developing markets.[21]
- The country risk rating model overcomes some of the data limitations of the country specific CAPM. The country risk rating model regresses country returns (dependent variable) against the natural log of the country credit rating for the prior period. The resulting regression equation provides the basis to estimate equity returns for any country with a credit rating.[22]
- The country-spread model calls for the determination of the spread between the yield on dollar denominated foreign bonds and the yield on U.S. Treasury bond (presumably of the same duration) as a measure of the risk of a foreign investment. The spread is then added to the CAPM cost of equity of 11.3%, as at the end of 2009 (risk free rate of 4.6% plus ERP of 6.7%).
- Other methods include the globally nested CAPM and the relative standard deviation method.[23]
- FCF forecasts for foreign country investments should be prepared on a nominal basis, including inflation in the local currency of the country of investment. Foreign currency risk and political risk are theoretically captured in the adjustments to CAPM data utilized in the estimation of country specific CAPM or in the other cost of equity capital estimation methodologies.

[19] Ibid., p. 116.
[20] Ibid., p. 117.
[21] Ibid.
[22] Ibid., p. 119.
[23] Ibid., pp. 118–119.

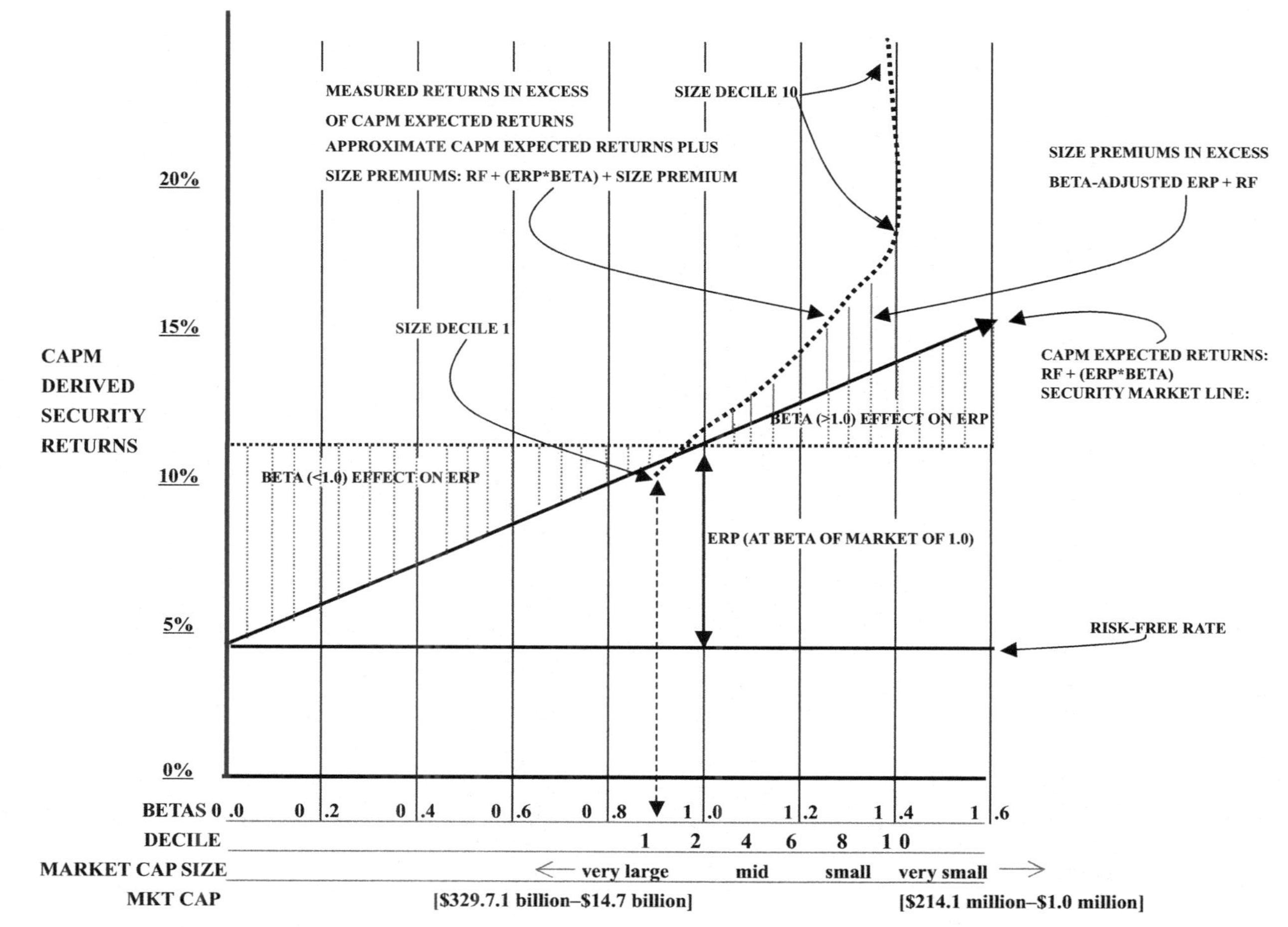

APPENDIX 23.1 Security Market Line

Source: Adapted from Ibbotson Associates, *2010 Valuation Yearbook, Market Results for Stocks, Bonds, Bills and Inflation 1926–2009* (222 W. Washington, Chicago, Illinois: Morningstar, Inc., 2010), p. 93.

TOPIC 24

Risk-Free Rates

This topic explores the notion of risk-free rates as a component of the capital asset pricing model (CAPM) as introduced in Topic 23.

RISK-FREE RATE DEFINED

- The risk-free rate is what an investor would expect to earn on investments in long-term government-issued securities held to maturity.[1]
- The "risk-free" part is the notion that the central government will not default on the interest or repayment obligation of the security.[2]
- Risk is what separates equity investments from investments in risk-free government securities.
  - With equity investments, you might get back less, get it later, or get nothing.
- Expect more return if you buy a business! Welcome to equity risk!
- The term of the quoted underlying risk-free rate used in a discounted cash flow valuation generally should reflect the expected life of the investment asset, not the expected life of the investor's holding.[2]
- Usually the longest-term government Treasury rate is utilized.
- Ibbotson utilizes the 20-year U.S. Treasury Bond Yield as the risk-free rate. At year end 2009, this rate was 4.6%.[3]
- A frequently used source for risk-free data is from Ibbotson Associates, Chicago, Illinois, a subsidiary of Morningstar, Inc., which provides and updates this data annually, provides exceptionally well-documented literature, and has a Web site source (www.ibbotson.com).

[1] Ibbotson Associates, *2010 Valuation Yearbook, Market Results for Stocks, Bonds, Bills and Inflation 1926–2009* (222 W. Washington, Chicago, Illinois:Morningstar, Inc., 2010), p. 44.
[2] Ibid.
[3] Ibid.

TOPIC 25
Equity Risk Premiums

Topic 25 explores the background to the determination of the equity risk premium and how it is used in the capital asset pricing model (CAPM) as introduced in Topic 23.

EQUITY RISK PREMIUM DEFINED

- As reported by Ibbotson Associates, the overall equity return for large-company equity securities as a whole on the U.S. equity markets in excess of risk-free rates over the last 84 years for the period ending December 31, 2009, is 6.7%.[1]
- The large-company equity risk premium equals the actual arithmetic average of the long-term total return of the stock market as included in the Standard & Poor's (S&P 500) return index, less the arithmetic average government bond income return, the risk-free rate.[2]
- Ibbotson Associates currently uses the income return of a series of Treasury bonds with approximately 20 years to maturity as the risk-free rate in determination of the equity risk premium.[3] Although the 30-year Treasury bond is preferable for this purpose, that bond was introduced only in 1977 (and subsequently has been withdrawn and reintroduced).[4]
- Equity risk premiums are opportunity based—you should expect to realize this premium on equity investments versus risk-free investments, so you should expect to get at least such a premium from an acquisition.
- A frequently used source for equity risk premium data is from Ibbotson Associates, a subsidiary of Morningstar, Inc., which provides and updates this data annually, provides exceptionally well-documented literature, and provides a Web site source (www.ibbotson.com).

[1] Ibbotson Associates, *2010 Valuation Yearbook, Market Results for Stocks, Bonds, Bills and Inflation 1926–2009* (222 W. Washington, Chicago, Illinois: Morningstar, Inc., 2010), p. 59.
[2] Ibid, pp. 54, 55.
[3] Ibid., p. 55.
[4] Ibid.

TOPIC 26

What Is Business Risk?

Risk often is defined as variability measures, such as standard deviation, which are easily measurable. While business risk, particularly in terms of doing M&A, includes variability, it may be more appropriately defined in terms that the operating manager or responsible acquirer can relate to more readily. Topic 26 explores the notion of business risk in mergers and acquisitions (M&A).

BUSINESS RISK IN M&A DEFINED

- *Business risk can be defined as the composite effect of the tendency for actual results to vary (negatively) from expectations, the timing of the occurrence and duration of the resulting impact, and the degree of control possessed to mitigate the (negative) variation.*
- *Control is the ability to prevent or limit* the effect of the convergence and consequence of events that may, singly or jointly, result in minor, severe, or disastrous negative variation from expectations.
- Control is what separates managing risk from simply gambling.
- *Negative variation and impact* is, of course, the concern and, more often than not, the result in deals (see also Topics 17 and 27).
  - *Variation* is expressed as the magnitude of return variation and time variation.
  - *Return variation* is the extent to which actual returns are less than expected (negative impact).
  - *Time variation* is the extent to which returns are realized later than expected and continue longer than expected.
- *The level of necessary control* is expressed relative to the amount of potential variation and its likelihood.
  - Little control is needed if the potential negative deviation from expected returns (impact), the duration resulting from an event or series of events, and the likelihood of an occurrence are very small.
  - Some control is needed if the potential negative deviation from expected returns (impact) and the duration resulting from an event or series of events are small, but the likelihood of an occurrence or series of occurrences is large.

- Great control will be needed to prevent or mitigate the impact if the potential negative deviation from expectations of returns (impact) and the duration resulting from an event or series of events are large and the likelihood of occurrence is either small or large.
- If the control possessed by management is not what is required to prevent or mitigate potential negative variation (impact and duration), *unmanageable risk is evident.* If appropriate, the risk must be financed away through insurance devices or not undertaken.
- If the control possessed is appropriate to that required to prevent or mitigate potential negative variation (impact, and duration), *manageable risk* is evident
- If the potential impact of negative variation in returns, even if unlikely, is most likely acute and disastrously extreme (go out of business or suffer significant permanent impairment) as opposed to chronic and of moderate impact, aspects of more or less control may make little difference; the risk must be financed away through insurance or other hedging devices if available and acceptable, or the risk should not be undertaken.

CONTROL AND RISK MANAGEMENT EMANATES FROM KNOWLEDGE OVERLAPS

- Control emanates from knowledge, know-how, capability, and activity overlaps of the acquirer with the business demands of the target (see Topic 17).
- The more you know about the business characteristics of the acquired entity, the greater the control, resulting in, it is hoped, manageable deal risk.
- If you want to assess your risk by your ability to control variation and the resulting impact, do your homework (due diligence) and stay close to what you know and are very good at when acquiring.
- As you assess each deal, ask yourself: How well can I or someone I retain or hire prevent or control the possible negative impact of events that can result in negative variation of returns associated with each aspect of the target business in its markets?
- Do a risk assessment of customers, delivery channels, operations, vendors, technology, operations, and so forth.
- An example of the risk frontier apparent in any deal is presented in Appendix 26.1. As each element of risk moves farther away from the point of convergence (increasing impact, increased duration, less control), composite business risk increases.
- The area of the frontier is the composite risk.
- The smaller the area, the smaller the risk.
- Get a handle on the risk frontier you face with your deal or any risk situation by drilling into these questions:
  - What can go wrong? What events can take place that can result in a negative effect?
  - What could be the negative return or time variation of the event?

    - How material could the negative impact be? Disastrous?
    - Can you really control it (prevent it) or manage it when things start to go bad?
    - Is the level of control you possess sufficient to mitigate the potential impact quickly?
    - Can you finance or hedge it away? At a reasonable cost?
- If you can neither control identified risk effectively nor finance it away acceptably, you are effectively gambling—not a good place for deal making!
- Be a risk manager, not a gambler, when you assess your deals.

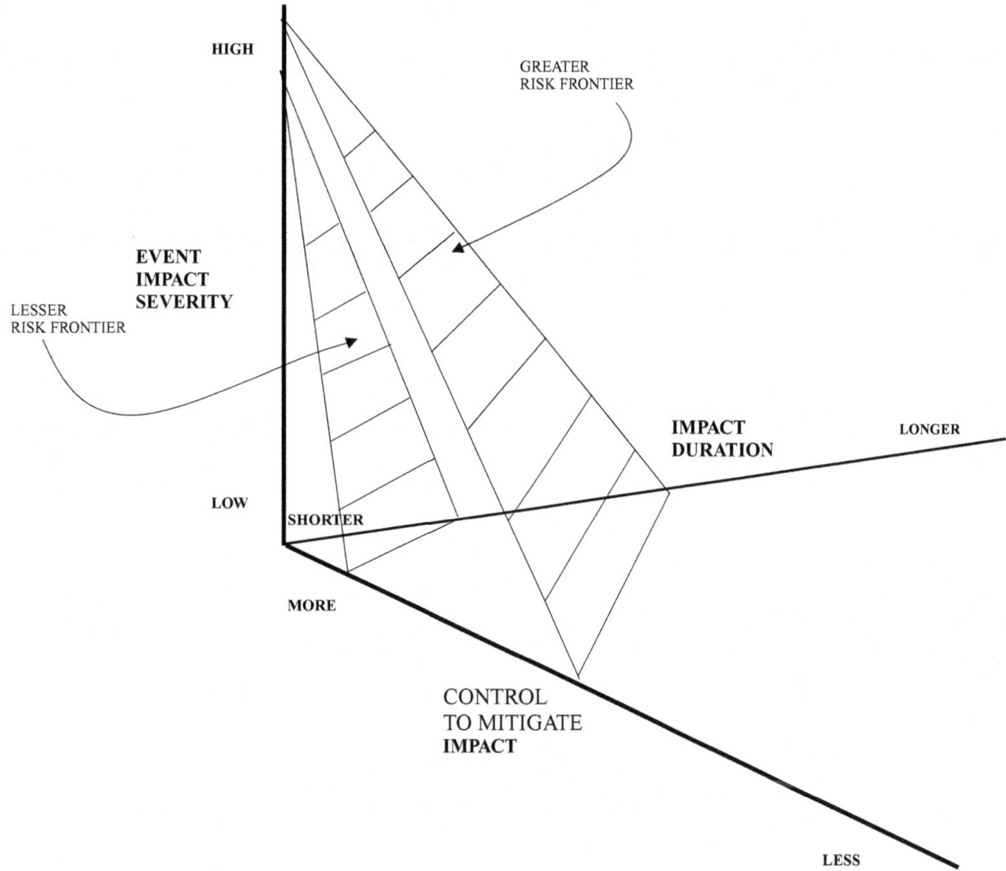

APPENDIX 26.1 Deal Risk Frontier Example

TOPIC 27

Entropy: Tendency toward Negative Variation

Topic 27 explores the notion of entropy in M&A deals: things tend to go wrong, and negative variation from expected returns often occur. Entropy may be one of the reasons why there is a tendency toward negative variation.

ENTROPY DEFINED

- The *Second Law of Thermodynamics* is an expression of the universal principle of decay observable in nature. It is measured and expressed in terms of a property called *entropy*.
- Entropy is "the tendency for all matter and energy in the universe to evolve toward a state of inert uniformity." Entropy is the "inevitable and steady deterioration of a system or society."[1]
- Entropy is also defined "as a measure of unusable energy within a closed or isolated system (e.g., the universe). As usable energy decreases and unusable energy increases, entropy increases. Entropy is also a gauge of randomness or chaos within a closed system. As usable energy is irretrievably lost, disorganization, randomness, and chaos increase."[2]
- Generalizing, left to itself without outside assistance, an isolated system tends toward a state of energy loss described as entropy.

ENTROPY IN M&A DEALS

- Perhaps, then, there is an irreversible loss of effectiveness when all the elements of a business (particularly after a deal) are brought together in an ongoing fashion and left alone without continuing outside assistance in the form of leadership, management, accountability, and correction processes.
- This tendency toward disorder, entropy, rather than toward higher order, anti-entropy, perhaps explains the tendency of actual deal returns to vary

[1] The Free Dictionary, www.thefreedictionary.com/entropy.

[2] All About Science.org, www.allaboutscience.org/second-law-of-thermodynamics.htm.

negatively from deal expectations (therefore requiring continuous outside influence to somewhat mitigate the negative variations).

- Perhaps this is the basis for Murphy's Law: If it can go wrong, it will.
- If you leave your deal to itself after the closing, beware of the inevitable effect of entropy.
- Be sure you have the ability to bring control to the inevitable disorder that is sure to take place.
  - Be sure to have capability overlap in your deals to minimize the impact of entropy (see Topic 3).
  - Be sure to have a well-thought-out integration plan and execution process (see Topics 51 and 52).

TOPIC 28
Equity Investor Risk

Topic 28 adds to the concepts of the equity risk premium demanded in M&A deals by focusing on the priorities generally governing access to free cash flow. The equity holder usually is the last in line—yet another reason to demand the equity risk premium.

OVERVIEW

- In liquidations (and in going concerns), equity investors usually are the last in line to realize the economic benefit of available free cash flows. The general order is:
  - Taxes due get paid first.
  - Then secured senior creditors or debt holders.
  - Then subordinated debt holders.
  - Then preferred stockholders.
  - Then general creditors and unsecured creditors.
  - Then common equity holders.
- Equity holders have, therefore, demanded an equity risk premium in recognition of being last in line (both when things are going well or when things go wrong and last for a long time and cannot be well controlled).
- Equity owners' risk in an acquired equity stake can be mitigated if management can exercise control over those factors affecting the target's business (so-called unsystematic risks, see Topic 31).

TOPIC 29
Beta

Beta is a measure that captures the systematic risk of a security in the construction of the cost of equity capital determined with the capital asset pricing model (CAPM), as introduced in Topic 23.

BETA IS AND IS NOT

- In portfolio theory, because investors can hold large diversified portfolios of securities, unsystematic risk (general business risk) can be diversified away across the portfolio. (Factors that drive values up in some securities will drive values down in other securities.)[1]
- The specific unsystematic risk of a security can therefore be ignored when considering adding it to a large investment portfolio.[2]
- The impact of unsystematic business risks on the valuation of an acquisition target are best dealt with by modeling the potential economic impact of those events that can create variation in returns.
- Other risks of equity ownership not controllable by management that cannot be diversified away—so-called systematic risk—must also be evaluated in valuing an equity investment.
- Beta, central to the CAPM (see Topic 23), is employed to do this.
- Beta measures the systematic risk (volatility) exhibited by a security as it moves sympathetically with the securities markets as a whole.[3]
- Beta is a computationally derived measure of how much a securities market value increases or decreases (its volatility) versus the increase or decrease in the securities market as a whole.
- The Standard & Poor's (S&P) 500 stock market index has a beta of 1.0.[4]
- A beta of 1.10 for a security means the security is more volatile than the S&P 500 as a whole and will move 10% more than the movement of the market, up or down.

[1] Stephen Ross, Randolph W. Westerfield, and Jeffery Jaffe, *Corporate Finance*, 4th ed. (New York: McGraw-Hill, 1996), pp. 239–240 and 302–305.
[2] Ibid.
[3] Ibid.
[4] Ibid.

- A beta of 1.0 for a security means the security is as volatile as the market as a whole.[5]
- A beta of .9 for a security means the security is less volatile than the market as a whole and will move up or down more slowly than the market as a whole.
- When calculating the cost of equity capital using the CAPM, beta (for a security comparable to the target) is used to adjust the equity risk premium (ERP) of the market as a whole in determining the expected return for *a* security.
- ERP is about 6.7% for large-cap securities versus risk-free investments[6] (see Topic 23).
- The well-determined beta increases or decreases the market ERP to an adjusted ERP inclusive of the appropriate systematic risk.
- Betas are inversely related to the size of the security's market cap. The larger the market cap, the smaller the beta; the smaller the market cap, the larger the beta. See Appendix 23.1 for a presentation of the security market line, which displays the inverse relationship of beta to market cap.
- Betas are determined by a statistical process measuring the covariation of a security versus the market as a whole divided by the variance of the market[7] or by regressing the excess returns of a security across time against the excess returns of the market across time.[8]

DEBATE OVER BETA

- Significant debate remains whether beta, determined from a historical analysis of a security's variability to the stock market, adequately captures meaningful volatility risk for purposes of a business valuation, particularly for small businesses, because the relationship between average returns, for monthly time periods tested over the last 20 to 40 years, is not positively related to its beta, the basic element of CAPM[9] (see Topic 23).
- Returns on small-company stocks exceed that implied by their betas.[10]
- In recognition of this, Ibbotson has developed and refined the use of small cap size premium data for use with CAPM (see Topic 36).
- A frequently used source for beta, size premium data, and risk-free rates is Ibbotson Associates, Chicago, Illinois, a subsidiary of Morningstar, Inc., which provides and updates these data annually, provides exceptionally well-documented literature, and provides a Web site source (www.ibbotson.com).

---

[5] Ibid.

[6] Ibbotson Associates, *2010 Valuation Yearbook, Market Results for Stocks, Bonds, Bills and Inflation 1926–2009* (222 W. Washington, Chicago, Illinois: Morningstar, Inc., 2010), p. 59.

[7] Stephen Ross, Randolph W. Westerfield, and Jeffery Jaffe, *Corporate Finance*, 4th ed. (New York: McGraw-Hill, 1996), pp. 317–319.

[8] Ibbotson Associates, *2010 Valuation Yearbook, Market Results for Stocks, Bonds, Bills and Inflation 1926–2009* (222 W. Washington, Chicago, Illinois: Morningstar, Inc., 2010), p. 70.

[9] Stephen Ross, Randolph W. Westerfield, and Jeffery Jaffe, *Corporate Finance*, 4th ed. (New York: McGraw-Hill, 1996), p. 290.

[10] Ibbotson Associates, *2010 Valuation Yearbook, Market Results for Stocks, Bonds, Bills and Inflation 1926–2009* (222 W. Washington, Chicago, Illinois: Morningstar, Inc., 2010), p. 90.

- Other sources for beta data may be found at:
  - http://finance.yahoo.com (get stock quote then go to key statistics)
  - http://www3.valueline.com/vlquotes/quote.aspx (enter stock quote)
  - http://moneycentral.msn.com/home.asp (enter stock quote)
- An informative Web site for beta sources and explanations is found at: http://www.bu.edu/library/management/tutorials/beta/index.html.

TOPIC 30

Systematic Risk

Topic 30 explores the factors giving rise to systematic risk. Systematic risk is captured in the beta of a security, which measures the volatility of a security arising from systematic risk to the market as a whole.

SYSTEMATIC RISK DEFINED

- Systematic risk, as measured by beta, is a composite measurement of the volatility of a securities return associated with the sensitivity of the security with significant factors that affect the return on all securities.[1] Such risk factors cause return variation throughout the financial markets and result from broad economic, political, or social change.[2] Such factors may include:
  - Relative political stability
  - International events and perceived instability
  - Government tax policy effects
  - Inflation
  - Government monetary policy and actions
  - Interest rates
  - Economic health domestically and internationally
  - Investor confidence
- The stock market will move up and down over time as these drivers exert their impact on all companies, their markets, and buyers and sellers in the market.
- A security will systematically resonate with the market's response to these conditions either more or less than the market as a whole as measured by the beta of the security.

[1] Shannon P. Pratt, *Valuing a Business: The Analysis and Appraisal of Closely Held Companies*, 2nd ed. (Burr Ridge, Illinois; New York, New York: Irwin, 1989), p. 47.

[2] D. Gasiorek, *Merger and Acquisition: Valuation and Structuring* (Norcross, Ga., Corporate Development Institute, 1997), p. 63.

- In determining the appropriate discount rate for valuing a target, buyers must consider the appropriate beta in the capital asset pricing model (CAPM) to determine an appropriate cost of equity capital to compensate for the level of systematic risk (an opportunity cost element) exhibited by that investment.
- Generally, measures of beta are inversely related to the size of the firm.
- See Topics 23 and 29.

TOPIC 31
Unsystematic Risk

Topic 31 explores the factors giving rise to unsystematic risk. Unsystematic risk has its foundation in the operating risk of conducting business in its markets and is not captured in beta. Theoretically, unsystematic risk can be mitigated by holding broadly diversified portfolios of many securities. For any one security, unsystematic risk remains evident.

UNSYSTEMATIC RISK DEFINED

- Unsystematic risk is a composite driver of the return on a security due to operating conditions associated with and indigenous to the target business in its markets and industry.[1] It may include factors such as:
  - Sustainable competitive advantage or disadvantage resulting from technology changes
  - Predatory competitors
  - Relative product quality and functionality (relative to competition)
  - Relative manufacturing efficiency
  - Labor unrest and labor management
  - Vulnerability to technological replacement (products or services)
  - Management strength and depth
  - Research and development competence
  - Financing reach and viability
  - Customer base and depth
- Although the market's perception of the company's control over the impact of such risks is reflected in a securities market valuation, beta does not capture these effects in equity risk premium (ERP) determination.
- Although the impact of an entity's unsystematic risk should be considered in the valuation of the target by modeling the effect on free cash flow, practitioners often make subjective adjustments to the discount rate for such risk (see the discussion of this issue in Topics 23 and 61).

[1] Shannon P. Pratt, *Valuing a Business: The Analysis and Appraisal of Closely Held Companies*, 2nd ed. (Burr Ridge, Illinois; New York, New York: Irwin, 1989), pp. 47 and 76.

TOPIC 32

Beta with or without Debt

Measures of beta can be stated with or without the effect of debt in the firm capital structure. Betas generally are stated to include the impact of debt in the capital structure unless otherwise noted.

OVERVIEW

- Gathering beta data that includes or excludes the impact of debt depends on how the beta is going to be used in the valuation process.
- Beta initially is measured and generally is reported reflecting the underlying debt and equity in the capital structure of the company being evaluated (also called a levered beta).
- Companies with debt have financial risk in addition to systematic risk, both of which are captured in the measurement of a levered beta.
- The more debt, the greater the risk of financial distress in an economic downturn, and the greater the financial risk.
- The financial risk component of the levered beta can be estimated and removed to isolate an asset beta without the risk of debt.
- Stating beta on an unlevered basis, without the impact of debt, is necessary if an unlevered beta is to be used in the construction of a C_U, the cost of equity capital without the effect of debt on beta using the capital asset pricing model (CAPM) (see Topics 23 and 33).

TOPIC 33

Beta: Levered or Unlevered

Topic 33 surveys the method of selecting betas and the process of deleveraging levered betas and releveraging unlevered betas.

The reader is encouraged to take the time to read the text in conjunction with the referenced Appendices to gain the appropriate level of understanding of the subject matter discussed in the narrative. Appendices are either presented at the end of this Topic or are available for review and download on the companion Web site noted at the end of this Topic.

GATHERING APPLICABLE AND COMPARABLE BETAS

- Select public companies comparable to the target based on factors of comparability such as:
  - Size and profitability
  - Industry, product segment
  - Key business processes
  - Markets served
  - Customers served
  - Competitors serving the same markets
- Levered betas for public securities are readily available from Ibbotson Associates, Chicago, Illinois, a subsidiary of Morningstar, Inc., which provides and updates this data annually, provides exceptionally well-documented literature, and provides a Web site source (www.ibbotson.com).
- Ibbotson reports both levered and unlevered betas for many large and small public companies; all are available online.
- Other sources for beta data may be found at:
  - http://finance.yahoo.com (get stock quote then go to key statistics)
  - http://www3.valueline.com/vlquotes/quote.aspx (enter stock quote)
  - http://moneycentral.msn.com/home.asp (enter stock quote)
- An informative Web site for beta sources and explanations is found at: http://www.bu.edu/library/management/tutorials/beta/index.html.
- Obtain (or calculate) the reported levered betas for the selected comparable securities.

DELEVERAGING LEVERED BETAS AND DEVELOPING A COMPARABLE UNLEVERED BETA FOR THE TARGET

- If levered comparable betas have been gathered, they may be delevered to yield *unlevered* asset betas (beta without debt risk) for each comparable company security as shown below.

To Delever a Levered Equity Beta

$$B_U = \frac{B_{LC}}{1 + \left[(1 - t)\frac{D}{E}\right]}$$

where B_U = unlevered asset beta of comparable company
B_{LC} = levered beta for the comparable company
t = marginal tax rate for comparable company
D = market value of comparable company's actual debt employed
E = market value of comparable company's equity capital (public market quoted total equity value)

This process removes the impact of debt embedded in the levered asset beta resulting in an unlevered beta. The unlevered beta then may be relevered at a tax rate and debt-to-equity ratio appropriate for the target.

- Next, determine by inspection or computation (mean, median, etc.) the *unlevered asset beta for the comparable group*. The group unlevered beta is then employed to construct C_U for the target.

TO RELEVER AN UNLEVERED ASSET BETA

- If a weighted average cost of capital, C*, is to be used in the target valuation exercise, relever the comparable group's unlevered asset beta to determine a *levered beta for the target company* as shown below.

To Relever an Unlevered Asset Beta to Derive a Levered Beta for the Target Company

$$B_{LT} = B_U\,[1 + [(1 - t)D/E_F]]$$

where B_{LT} = Levered beta for the target company
B_U = Comparable company (or group average) unlevered asset beta
D/E_F = Financeable debt-to-equity ratio for target company
t = Tax rate for target company

The financeable debt-to-equity ratio for the target company (D/E_F) should be the *expected ratio* of the potential amount of debt the company *could* borrow from lenders in the debt market to the expected market value of the equity capital. The financeable debt-to-equity ratio is used to determine the levered beta regardless of the debt level expected to be utilized by the target; the point being that D/E_F could be obtained by an acquirer; therefore, the levered beta, C* (and enterprise value resulting from the valuation), should reflect the potential leverage impact that could be obtained in the market, not the actual capital structure expected of the target.

- A comparable group unlevered asset beta for the target company may or may not need to be relevered, depending on the valuation exercise.
- If the valuation of the target company is to be done on an unlevered basis, the asset beta does not require releveraging (see Topic 34 regarding the application of betas in valuations of leveraged and in highly leveraged buyout transactions).
- Appendix 33.1 presents an example of the process of deleveraging a levered beta of 1.2, resulting in a unlevered beta of .9, and releveraging at a different debt-to-equity ratio, resulting in a relevered beta of 1.15 using the computational methods presented.

The following Appendix is available for viewing or download on the Web site for this book at: www.wiley.com/go/emott. Please see the About the Web Site page at the back of this book for login information.

APPENDIX 33.1 Beta Deleveraging and Releveraging Example

TOPIC 34

Beta Application in Determination of C_U

Topic 34 explores the application of beta in the determination of C_U, the unlevered cost of equity capital, which is the appropriate discount rate for the valuation of free cash flow in leveraged buyouts and highly leveraged transactions.

- If the acquisition of the target is to be valued as a leveraged buyout transaction where the *unlevered free cash flows* are valued separately from the *value of debt employed*, the unlevered beta is used without releveraging in the determination of the target's C_U using the capital asset pricing model (CAPM), as shown in Illustration 34.1.

ILLUSTRATION 34.1 CAPM DETERMINATION OF C_U (FOR VALUATION OF UNLEVERED ENTERPRISE VALUE[a])

Risk-free Rate		7.000%	R_F	(See Topic 24)
Equity Risk Premium (large cap)	7.6%		ERP	(See Topic 25)
× comparable **unlevered** asset beta[b]	.9		B_U	(See Topic 32)
= Risk-adjusted equity risk premium	6.84%			
+ beta-adjusted equity risk premium		6.840%		
= CAPM-derived return on equity target for large-cap target companies *without* leverage (C_U)		13.840%	C_U	
+ Small-cap-size premium (if valuing other than a large-cap company)[c]		2.600%		(See Topic 36)
= CAPM return on equity target for small cap companies excluding leverage (C_{US})		16.440%	C_{US}	

[a]All percentage values indicated are for illustration clarity only. The amounts used are not static and should reflect the most current data available at the time of CAPM construction.
[b]From an analysis of comparable companies, see Topics 29, 32, and 33.
[c]Size premiums vary in amount (see Topics 23 and 36).

- A frequently used source for risk-free rates, beta, and size premium data is from Ibbotson Associates, Chicago, Illinois, a subsidiary of Morningstar, Inc., which provides and updates these data annually, provides exceptionally well-documented literature, and provides a Web site source (www.ibbotson.com).
- See Topics 43 and 44 for an illustration of how C_U is used in a leveraged buyout valuation.
- Although other risk factors may be added to the unlevered cost of equity, it is preferable to sensitize the free cash flow (see Topic 23).

TOPIC 35

Levered Beta Moves as Debt to Equity Moves

Topic 35 explores the impact the capital structure has on the levered beta.

LEVERED BETA IN A WORLD WITHOUT TAXES

- By definition, levered betas (B_L) are higher than unlevered betas (B_U) due to the impact of the risk of debt.
- For a given security in a world without taxes, the levered beta will be greater than the unlevered asset beta, in direct proportion to the increase in the debt-to-equity (D/E) ratio: the market value of debt (D_M) divided by the market value of equity (E_M) in the capital structure, as shown in Illustration 35.1.

ILLUSTRATION 35.1 PERCENTAGE INCREASE IN B_L OVER B_U IN A WORLD WITHOUT TAXES

B_U	×	$(1 + D_M/E_M)$	=	B_L	% Increase in B_L $(B_L \div B_U) - 1.0$	$\$D_M$	$\$E_M$	D_M/E_M Ratio	Cumulative Change D/E Ratio
1.0	×	(1 + 0)	=	1.0	–	0	100	0%	
1.0	×	(1 + .10)	=	1.10	**+ 10%**	10	100	10%	**+ 10%**
1.0	×	(1 + .30)	=	1.30	**+ 30%**	30	100	30%	**+ 30%**

LEVERED BETA IN A WORLD WITH TAXES

- In a world with taxes, levered betas increase over unlevered asset betas in direct proportion to the market value of debt less the effect of the tax shield provided by debt: the value of taxes not paid equal to tD_M divided by the market value of equity in the capital structure.
- That is, levered betas in a world with taxes (t) increase more slowly versus the levered beta in a world without taxes, as debt is increased in the capital structures. See Illustration 35.2.

ILLUSTRATION 35.2 PERCENTAGE INCREASE IN B_L OVER B_U IN A WORLD WITH TAXES (T = 34%)

B_U	×	$(1 + (D_M - tD_M)/E_M)$	=	B_L	% Increase in B_L $(B_L \div B_U) - 1.0$	D_M	tD_M	D_{Mt} $(D_M - tD_M)$	E_M	D_M/E_M Ratio	Cumulative Change D/E Ratio
1.0	×	(1 + (0 – 0)/100)	=	1.0	–	0	0	0	100	0%	–
1.0	×	(1 + (10. – 3.4)/100	=	1.066	+6.6%	10	3.4	6.6	100	6.6%	+6.6%
1.0	×	(1 + (30 – 10.1)/100	=	1.198	+19.8%	30	10.2	19.8	100	19.8%	+19.8%

TOPIC 36

Size Premium

Topic 36 explores the size premium deciles as developed and reported by Ibbotson Associates. Actual returns by size decile of the New York Stock Exchange (NYSE), American Stock Exchange (AMEX), and Nasdaq as measured over time exceed the returns expected by capital asset pricing model (CAPM) as the market cap of the size deciles decreases. This suggests the need for a size premium adjustment in the construction of CAPM returns, particularly for smaller target companies (see Topic 29).

SIZE PREMIUMS ARE INVERSELY RELATED TO FIRM SIZE

- As reported by Ibbotson, the overall equity return for large-company equity securities as a whole on the U.S. equity markets in excess of risk-free rates over the last 84 years for the period ending December 31, 2009, is 6.7%.[1]
- The size premium (return in excess or under the return expected from the CAPM) for the largest-cap companies in the first decile (over $14.7 billion market cap) of the NYSE, AMEX, Nasdaq as reported by Ibbotson is −.37%.
- The size premium (return in excess or under the return expected from the CAPM) for the small-cap companies in the tenth decile (up to $214 million market cap) of the NYSE, AMEX, Nasdaq as reported by Ibbotson is 6.28%.
- The deciles reported by Ibbotson are from securities data from the NYSE, AMEX, and Nasdaq exchanges.
- Mid-cap, low-cap, and micro-cap companies have exhibited higher returns than large-cap companies (and in excess of the return expected from the CAPM) over long time periods to compensate investors for the size risk as well as the size-related systematic risk of the security (see Topics 23 and 29).
- Smaller companies are more vulnerable and bear higher risk than large-cap companies due to:
  - Inability to withstand downturns in the economic cycle over larger companies.
  - Less ability to attract capital at as favorable rates and terms as larger companies.

[1] Ibbotson Associates, *2010 Valuation Yearbook, Market Results for Stocks, Bonds, Bills and Inflation 1926–2009* (222 W. Washington, Chicago, Illinois: Morningstar, Inc., 2010), p. 198.

  - Less ability to attract and retain management talent than larger companies.
  - Less ability to compete due to lack of depth in management, research and development, technology deployment, and so on.
- Adjusted derivations of the cost of unlevered equity, C_U, and the cost of levered equity, C_L, for small-cap companies therefore bear an additional premium for size over the beta-adjusted equity risk premium. The size premium generally is inversely related to the market cap of the securities in each decile.[2]
- Illustration 36.1 presents the range of size premiums for mid- to micro-cap companies based on MVE ranges.

ILLUSTRATION 36.1 SIZE PREMIUM RANGES

Cap-Decile	MVE	Beta-Adjusted Size Premium
Large Cap 1	>$14.7 Bil	−0.37%
Large Cap 2	>$5.9 Bil <$14.7 Bil	0.74%
Mid Cap 3-5	>$1.6 Bill <$5.9 Bil	1.08%
Low Cap 6-8	>$431.3 Mil <$1.6 Bil	1.85%
Micro Cap 9-10	>$1.0Mil <$431.3 Mil	3.99%

Source: Ibbotson Associates, *2010 Valuation Yearbook, Market Results for Stocks, Bonds, Bills and Inflation 1926–2009* (222 W. Washington, Chicago, Illinois: Morningstar, Inc., 2010), pp. 92 and 198.

- Ibbotson reports[3] that:
  - Beta-adjusted size premiums are most appropriate for the CAPM valuation method.
  - The *beta-adjusted size premium* excludes the excess returns over large-cap returns *due to the higher betas of the smaller-cap companies and are therefore* more appropriate *size premiums* than non–beta-adjusted size premiums.
  - That is, they reflect the size premium impact of excess returns vs. CAPM only, without the effect of higher betas for the systematic risk associated with smaller companies.
  - Using *non–beta-adjusted size premiums* (including the effect of higher small-company betas in the measurement of the excess returns) *in addition to the application of a small-cap beta* derived from comparable small-cap companies in the construction of CAPM tends to duplicate the effect of the beta adjustment in the CAPM-determined cost of capital for smaller-cap companies.

---

[2] Ibid.

[3] Ibid., p. 45.

- The *2010 Valuation Yearbook* indicates that the size premiums in the micro-cap tenth decile have wide variations, as shown in Illustration 36.2.

ILLUSTRATION 36.2 MICRO-CAP SIZE PREMIUMS IN THE TENTH DECILE

Cap-Decile	MVE	Beta-Adjusted Size Premium
Micro-Cap 10th a	>$123.5 Mil <$214.1 Mil	4.45%
Micro-Cap 10th b	>$1.0 Mil <$123.5 Mil	10.01%

Source: Ibbotson Associates, *2010 Valuation Yearbook, Market Results for Stocks, Bonds, Bills and Inflation 1926–2009* (222 W. Washington, Chicago, Illinois: Morningstar, Inc., 2010), p. 198.

- The *2010 Valuation Yearbook* also indicates that the size premiums in the micro-cap 10b decile are further separated into even smaller segments, y and z, as shown in Illustration 36.2.

ILLUSTRATION 36.2 MICRO-CAP SIZE PREMIUMS IN THE TENTH B DECILE

Cap-Decile	MVE	Beta-Adjusted Size Premium
Micro-Cap 10b y	>$76.1 Mil <$123.5 Mil	9.05%
Micro-Cap 10b z	>$1.0 Mil <$76.1 Mil	12.06%

Source: Ibbotson Associates, *2010 Valuation Yearbook, Market Results for Stocks, Bonds, Bills and Inflation 1926–2009* (222 W. Washington, Chicago, Illinois: Morningstar, Inc., 2010), p. 198.

TOPIC 37

Weighted Average Cost of Capital

Topic 37 explores the methods of determination of C*, the weighted average cost of capital (WACC). The WACC is the weighted average of the levered cost of equity, C_L, and the after-tax cost of debt, $i(1 - t)$, included in the capital structure.

INTRODUCTION TO WEIGHTED AVERAGE COST OF CAPITAL

- Given C_U, the unlevered cost of equity from the capital asset pricing model (CAPM), if some level of debt is employed in the capital structure financing mix, a WACC for the debt and equity in the capital structure can be derived that is the basis for the discount rate used in discounted cash flow (DCF) valuations. (The weighted average cost of capital is noted as WACC or k in many works or as C* by Stewart.[1])
- The level of debt (expressed as the debt-to-capital ratio, D/C) assumed in the financing mix used to determine C* should reflect a level consistent with:
  - The target company's industry characteristics.
  - The debt-carrying capacity of the target, not the investor. How much debt is practically financeable in the market?
  - Note that the actual anticipated D/C structure of the target is not used for the purpose of determining C* unless such structure equals the target's debt-carrying capacity.
- The reason for this is that the enterprise value of the target should reflect and be based on the amount of debt *the market (lenders and other bidders) would allow to be placed on the target.*
  - Debt in a capital structure increases enterprise value.
  - The seller will expect full value.
  - See Topics 40, 41, and 42.

[1] G. Bennett Stewart III, *The Quest for Value* (New York: HarperBusiness, 1991), p. 282.

- Unless there is no debt in the capital structure, C* will always be less than C_U, and C_L, because the posttax cost of debt is (generally always) less than C_L.
  - C_U is determined using an unlevered beta reflecting no debt in the financing mix (see Topic 33).
  - C_L is determined using a levered beta at the assumed level of debt in the financing mix (see Topic 33).
  - C* is the weighted blend of C_L and the posttax cost of debt.
  - See Illustration 37.1.
- C* may be used as the target return in the DCF valuation process.
- C_U also may be used in the DCF valuation process where the enterprise value impact of the debt employed is determined separately from the value of unlevered free cash flow (FCF) (see Topics 40 to 44 on leveraged buyout valuation).

WEIGHTED AVERAGE METHOD OF C* DETERMINATION

- C* usually is determined by weighting the cost of debt (after tax) by the target D/C and adding this to the weighted cost of equity, (C_L) times the equity to capital ratio (1 – D/C)[2] (where D/C = the *market value* of debt to *market value* of capital ratio, not a book value–based D/C ratio). See Illustration 37.1.
- Each time a new target D/C mix is assumed, the weighted average approach requires that C_L be recalculated with a *relevered* beta (B_L) in the determination of C* (see Topic 33).
  - Note that C_L is different from C_U due only to the difference in the levered beta applied to the equity risk premium (ERP) as the target D/C level changes (see Topic 34).
  - Remember that $B_L = B_U\left[1+\left[(1-t)\frac{D}{E}\right]\right]$ (see Topic 33).
  - C_L is determined by applying B_L to ERP (see Topic 23).
  - C_U is determined by applying B_U to ERP (see Topic 34).
- With an unlevered beta, B_U, of 0.9, a D/C of 30%, a risk-free rate (RF) of 7.00%, ERP of 7.6%, the levered beta, B_L, is 1.1546 (see Topic 33), C_L is 15.775% (see Topic 34), and C* is determined to be 12.428% using the weighted average approach, assuming a pretax cost of debt, i, of 7.0% and a tax rate of 34%. See Illustration 37.1.

[2] Ibid., p. 284.

ILLUSTRATION 37.1 C*: WEIGHTED AVERAGE METHOD WITH D/C OF 30%

	Cost	Weight	Weighted Cost
Debt	4.620%	30%	1.386%
Equity (C_L)	15.775%	70%	11.042%
(C*) WACC		100%	12.428%

$$B_L = 1.1546 = .9\left[1 + \left[(1 - .34)\frac{.30}{.70}\right]\right]$$

$$C_L = RF + (ERP)(B_L)$$

$$C_L = .15775 = .07 + ((.076)(1.1546)) \quad \text{(See Topic 23)}$$

- With a 34% tax rate, the after-tax cost of debt is 4.62% – ((7.0%) (1 – .34)).

- *If the debt to capital ratio is raised to 35%,* C* may be determined only if C_L is recalculated based on a new relevered beta at the higher debt-to-capital ratio. C_L is would equal 16.271%, as shown in Illustration 37.2.

ILLUSTRATION 37.2 C*: WEIGHTED AVERAGE METHOD WITH D/C OF 35%

	Cost	Weight	Weighted Cost
Debt	4.620%	35%	1.617%
Equity (C_L)	16.271%	65%	10.576%
(C*) WACC		100%	12.193%

- C_L will rise along with B_L as debt is added to the target capital structure as B_L is recalculated based on the revised D/C ratio (see Topic 35).

$$B_L = 1.2199 = .9\left[1 + \left[(1 - .34)\frac{.35}{.65}\right]\right]$$

$$C_L = RF + (ERP)(B_L)$$

$$C_L = .16271 = .07 + ((.076)(1.2199))$$

DIRECT METHOD OF C* DETERMINATION

- G. Bennett Stewart demonstrates that C* can be determined directly from C_U as shown with the same assumptions as in Illustration 37.1:[3]

$$C^* = [C_U(1 - ((D/C(t))]$$

where C* = WACC

C_U = cost of equity without the effect of debt and *without small-cap size or other risk premium* = (13.84%) = (RF + (ERP)(B_u)) = 7.0% + ((7.6%) (.9))

D/C% = target % of the market value of debt to the market value of debt plus equity capital = 30%

t = marginal cash tax rate (34%)

C* = [.1384(1 − ((.30)(.34)))]

C* = .12428 = 12.428% (which value is equal to C* in Illustration 37.1) above determined using the weighted average method)

- If D/C is changed to 35%, C* is found to be 12.193% by inserting the new D/C % of 35%:

$$C^* = [.1384(1 - ((.35)(.34)))]$$

$$C^* = .12193 = 12.193\%(\text{equal to } C^*\text{Illustration } 37.2)$$

- The advantage of this direct approach is that C* may be recalculated directly from C_U by altering the target D/C% avoiding the step of recalculating B_L and C_L for the change in leverage.
- This direct approach yields the same result as the weighted average approach when the *risk-free rate* employed in the determination of C_U is *equal to the pretax cost of debt* employed in the determination of C*.

ADJUSTED DIRECT METHOD OF C* DETERMINATION

- When the *risk-free rate* employed in the determination of C_U *is different* from the target's *pretax cost* of debt employed in the determination of C*, the expression to determine C* directly from C_U requires an adjustment (italics in the equation below) for the difference in the target's borrowing rate and the risk-free as shown:

$$C^* = [(C_U)(1 - ((D/C)(t)))] + [((i - RF)(1 - t))(D/C)]$$

- If RF = i, the value in italics is zero and therefore effectively drops out of the adjusted direct expression.
- C_U must exclude the effect of debt and small cap size or other risk premium.

---

[3] Ibid.

- The direct approach is therefore adjusted to include the small-cap effect on C* with the adjustment shown in italics in the next equation.

$$C^* = [(C_U(1 - ((D/C)(t)))] + [((i - RF)(1 - t))(D/C)] + \mathit{sc}(1 - D/C)$$

where C^* = WACC

C_U = cost of equity without debt and *without small-cap premium* = (13.84%) = RF + (ERP) (Bu) = 7.0% + (7.6%)(.9) = 13.84%

D/C% = target % of the market value of debt to the market value of debt and equity capital = 30%

t = marginal cash tax rate = 34%

i = target company interest rate on new borrowing = 8.0%

RF = risk-free rate in target companies cost of capital = 7.0%

sc = small-cap premium = 2%

- With B_U of 0.9, a D/C of 30%, RF of 7.00%, ERP of 7.6%, sc of 2%, B_L is 1.1546, C_L is 17.775%, and C* is determined to be 14.026% *using the weighted average approach* as shown in Illustration 37.3, assuming a pretax cost of debt of 8.0 % and a tax rate of 34%.

ILLUSTRATION 37.3 C*: WEIGHTED AVERAGE METHOD

	Cost	Weight	Weighted Cost
Debt	5.28%	30%	1.584%
Equity (C_L)	17.775%	70%	12.443%
WACC (C*)		100%	14.026%

$$B_L = 1.1546 = .9\left[1 + \left[(1 - .34)\frac{.30}{.70}\right]\right]$$

$$C_L = .17775 = .07 + ((.076)(1.1546)) + .02$$

- With a 34% tax rate, the after-tax cost of debt is 5.28% (8.0% × (1 – .34)).

- *Per the adjusted direct approach* (including the adjustment for the difference in the borrowing rate and the risk-free rate and the small-cap premium), C* is also determined to be 14.026%:

$$C^* = [(C_U)(1 - ((D/C)(t)))] + [((i - RF)(1 - t))(D/C)] + sc(1 - D/C)$$

$$C^* = [(.1384)(1 - ((.30)(.34)))] + [((.08 - .07)(1 - .34))(.30)] + .02(1 - .30)$$

$$C^* = .12428 + .00198 + .0140$$

$$C^* = .14026 = 14.026\%$$

- *If D/C is changed to 35%,* C* is found to be 13.724% by inserting the new D/C percentage of 35% into the adjusted direct approach, including an adjustment for the difference in the borrowing rate and the risk-free rate as follows:

$$C^* = [(C_U)(1 - ((D/C)(t)))] + [((i - RF)(1 - t))(D/C)] + sc(1 - D/C)$$

$$C^* = [(.1384)(1 - ((.35)(.34)))] + [((.08 - .07)(1 - .34))(.35)] + .02(1 - .35)$$

$$C^* = .12193 + .00231 + .013$$

$$C^* = .13724 = 13.724\%$$

- *C* is also found to be 13.724% using the weighted average approach. This figure is consistent with the direct approach,* including the adjustment for the difference in the borrowing rate and the risk-free rate, as shown in Illustration 37.4. See also Appendix 37.1.

ILLUSTRATION 37.4 C*: WEIGHTED AVERAGE METHOD

	Cost	Weight	Weighted Cost
Debt	5.28%	35%	1.848%
Equity (C_L)	18.271%	65%	11.876%
WACC (C*)		100%	13.724%

$$B_L = 1.2199 = .9\left[1 + \left[(1 - .34)\frac{.35}{.65}\right]\right]$$

$$C_L = .18271 = .07 + ((.076)(1.2199)) + .02$$

- Note that C_U in Appendix 37.1 of 13.840% may also be derived directly from C* of 13.724% by rearranging the adjusted direct approach (see Topic 34):

$$C_U = \left[\frac{C^* - [((i - RF)(1 - t))(D/C) + sc(1 - D/C)]}{1 - ((D/C)t)}\right]$$

$$C_U = .1384 = \left[\frac{.13724 - [((.08 - .07)(1 - .34))(.35) + .02(1 - .35)]}{1 - ((.35).34)}\right] = 13.84\%$$

HISTORICAL CAPITAL STRUCTURE (5-YR AVG)

	to relever:	to delever: input levered beta:
a CO L T MARGINAL DEBT COST	8.00%	
b CO MARGINAL TAX RATE "T"	34.00%	34.00%
c 1 - CO MARGINAL TAX RATE	66.00%	
d POSTTAX COST OF DEBT	5.28%	

	to relever:	to delever: input levered beta:
DEBT AS % OF TOTAL MARKET VALUE OF CAPITAL	35.000%	35.00%
MARKET VALUE OF EQUITY AS % OF TOTAL MKT VALUE OF CAP	65.000%	65.00%
DEBT TO MARKET VALUE OF EQUITY %	53.846%	53.85%

DERIVATION OF C & C*

					to relever:		to delever:
	SPECIFIC RISK PREMIUM				0.00%		
	COUNTRY RISK PREMIUM (30 yr local-30 yr US Treas.)				0.00%		
	S TOTAL SPECIFIC + COUNTRY RISK PREM				0.00%		
a	**EQUITY RISK PREMIUM SMALL-CAP INCREMNT**			Ibbotson	2.00%		
b	**LONG-TERM RISK-FREE BORROWING RATE**				7.00%		
c	EQUITY RISK PREMIUM LARGE CAP			Ibbotson	7.60%		
	EQUITY RISK PREMIUM				0.00%		delevered input beta
d	**EQUITY RISK PREMIUM LARGE CAP**			Ibbotson	7.60%		
e	**BUSINESS RISK BETA**			Ibbotson	0.900	<<<	0.9000
f	FINANCIAL RISK BETA				0.3198		
g	TOTAL LEVERED RISK BETA		e+f		1.2198		1.2199
	UNLEVERED EQUITY COST	C_U	a+b+c+(dxe)		15.840%		input levered beta
	LEVERED EQUITY COST	C_L	a+b+c+(dxg)		18.271%		

WEIGHTEDAVERAGE COST OF CAPITAL C* (FINANCING APPROACH)

	POSTTAX COST	*	WEIGHT		POSTTAX WEIGHTED AVERAGE C*	DERIVED COST OF CAPITAL C, INCL. BIZ, INDUSTRY, AND COUNTRY RISK WITHOUT DEBT
DEBT	5.280%	*	35.00%	=	1.848%	
EQUITY C_L	18.271%	*	65.00%	=	11.876%	
TOTAL WACC – C* USING FINANCING APPROACH					13.724%	15.840%

DERIVED AVERAGE COST OF CAPITAL AND EQUITY COST OF CAPITAL GIVEN CUNLEVERED BUSINESS COST OF CAPITAL

UNLEVERED EQUITY COST C_u	= X (1- (T X	0 5% HIST D/C))	HIST D/E)	INTEREST RATE	RISK FREE RATE	SPECIFIC +COUNTRY RISK PREMIUM	SMALL-CAP RISK PREMIUM	COST OF CAPITAL C*	DERIVED LEVERED EQUITY COST CI	DERIVED UNLEVERED EQUITY COST C	TOTAL BETA	DERIVED BUS RISK BETA	FINCL RISK BETA
15.840%	34.0%	35.00%	53.85%	8.00%	7.00%	0.00%	2.00%	13.724%	18.271%	15.840%	1.220	0.900	0.320
15.840%	34.0%	40.00%	66.67%	8.00%	7.00%	0.00%	2.00%	13.422%	18.850%	16.267%	1.296	0.900	0.396
15.840%	34.0%	45.00%	81.82%	8.00%	7.00%	0.00%	2.00%	13.119%	19.534%	16.772%	1.386	0.900	0.486
15.840%	34.0%	50.00%	100.00%	8.00%	7.00%	0.00%	2.00%	12.817%	20.354%	17.377%	1.494	0.900	0.594
15.840%	34.0%	55.00%	122.22%	8.00%	7.00%	0.00%	2.00%	12.515%	21.358%	18.117%	1.626	0.900	0.726
15.840%	34.0%	60.00%	150.00%	8.00%	7.00%	0.00%	2.00%	12.213%	22.612%	19.043%	1.791	0.900	0.891

DELEVERAGE OF TARGET OR COMPARABLE ENTITY INPUT EQUITY BETA USING ENTITIES FINANCING PARAMETERS

derived delevered asset beta from given levered equity beta	=	levered equity beta	/ 1+[	(1 -	tax rate)	x	(debt to market equity cap ratio) (d to cap% /equity to cap %)	]
bu = 0.9000	=	1.2199	/ 1+[	(1 -	34.0%)	x (	35.0% / 65.0%	)]

RELEVERAGE OF TARGET OR COMPARABLE ENTITY INPUT EQUITY BETA USING ENTITIES FINANCING PARAMETERS

derived levered equity beta from derived delevered asset beta	=	delevered equity beta (asset beta)	x 1+[	(1 -	tax rate)		x	(debt to market equity cap ratio) (d to cap% /equity to cap %)	]
bl = 1.2199	=	0.900	x 1+[	(1 -	34.0%)	x	x (	35.0% / 65.0%	)]

DELEVERAGE OF TARGET OR COMPARABLE ENTITY INPUT EQUITY BETA USING ENTITIES FINANCING PARAMETERS

derived delevered asset beta from given levered equity beta	=	levered equity beta	/ 1+[	(1 -	tax rate)	x	(debt to market equity cap ratio) (d to cap% /equity to cap %)	]
bu = 0.900	=	1.220	/ 1+[	(1 -	34.0%)	x (	35.0% / 65.0%	)]

derived levered equity beta from derived delevered asset beta	=	delevered asset beta	x 1+[	(1 -	tax rate)		x	(debt to market equity cap ratio) (d to cap% /equity to cap %)	]
bl = 1.2198	=	0.900	x 1+[	(1 -	34.0%)	x	x (	35.0% / 65.0%	)]

APPENDIX 37.1 Cost of Capital Engine

TOPIC 38

Terminal Values, Terminal Value Multiples, and Terminal Value DCFs

Terminal values typically represent the largest portion of the enterprise value in discounted cash flow (DCF) valuations. Topic 38 explores the definition of terminal values and presents methods of determination.

The reader is encouraged to take the time to read the text in conjunction with the referenced Appendices to gain the appropriate level of understanding of the subject matter discussed in the narrative. Appendices are either presented at the end of this Topic or are available for review and download on the companion Web site noted at the end of this Topic.

TERMINAL VALUE DEFINITION

- Terminal values represent that portion of the enterprise value of the entity existing beyond period T (the period in which the acquired capabilities existing at the closing should achieve above-average returns). The terminal value amount is conceptually equivalent to the present value as at the end of period T of the residual free cash flow into perpetuity following period T.

OVERSTATING TERMINAL VALUES IS A DEAL VALUATION RISK

- Terminal values and therefore deal values run the risk of overstatement when the terminal value at the end of period T is based on an exit multiple of *earnings before interest, tax, depreciation, and amortization (EBITDA), earnings before interest and tax (EBIT), or free cash flow (FCF) that is equal to comparable full deal value transaction or trading multiples.*
  - Terminal value multiple equivalents should reflect the discounted weighted impact of *only* the *residual free cash flow and market growth remaining* from the date of the last forecasted franchise growth period (T) into the future for the capabilities acquired.

  - Terminal value exit multiples should be lower than full deal value comparable multiples because the dominant period of franchise-level *growth* and above-average returns that the entity is capable of achieving based on the capabilities acquired will be realized only over time period T (see Topic 14).
  - Thereafter, as differentiation wanes and the *acquired franchise capability fades in the face of competition,* growth from the *franchise capability acquired* will be lower than during the franchise period; so therefore should residual value multiples.
  - Comparable full deal value transaction or trading multiples used in the determination of terminal values reflect the impact of *all the franchise growth* during T plus the *declining growth impact* of the capability acquired. Therefore, they lead to an overvaluation of the terminal value.
  - If the firm prospers under an acquirer who takes the risk and makes the required investment, a new capability base will have evolved at the end of period T. *Why pay the seller for the value of this new capability base in the form of inflated terminal values when it does not exist at the time of the acquisition?* (See Topics 14 and 15.)
- *Notwithstanding the foregoing, in many valuations, terminal value exit multiples often are close to enterprise value comparables multiples. The reasons probably are:*
  - Buyers think they will find another buyer in the future that will pay such a multiple, so they are protected from overpaying.
  - That is what it takes to close a deal.
  - Financial buyers doing leveraged buyouts or management buyouts plan to spin off the acquired entity in three to seven years. They expect to find a buyer willing to pay a full deal value terminal-value multiple or realize the equivalent in an initial public offering.
  - Sellers would continue the capability development if the business was not sold, so they should expect terminal values reflecting full deal value multiples.
  - Sellers also attempt to extract a share of the platform value of the entity at the time of the sale (see Topic 15), in part in the form of inflated terminal value multiples.
  - In order to argue successfully against excessive terminal value multiples estimates, buyers must understand and model the franchise capability growth over its useful life and reasons for its decline beyond T (see Topic 15).

TERMINAL VALUE DETERMINATION METHODS

- *Terminal values of going concerns generally are determined (or cross-corroborated to other methods) using:*
  - Discounted cash flow methods reflecting the perpetuity period growth
  - Multiples of EBITDA

    - Terminal value EBITDA multiples generally could approximate (plus or minus) 4 to 5 times lagging EBITDA (EBITDA in the last T period) depending on the post-T period business/market outlook and growth, which usually is lower following period T.
- Multiples of EBIT
    - Terminal value EBIT multiples generally could approximate (plus or minus) 4 to 5 times lagging EBIT (EBIT in the last T period), depending on the past-T period business/market outlook and growth.
- Multiples of free cash flow (FCF)
    - Terminal value FCF multiples generally could approximate (plus or minus) 8 to 9 lagging FCF (in the last T period), depending on the post-T period business/market outlook and growth.
- *FCF perpetuity growth capitalization models* where the capitalized FCF is equal to the:
    - FCF in the last forecast year of period T, or
    - An average of the FCF during the forecast period, or
    - An adjusted normalized continuation FCF value (i.e., in the T+1 period)
    - The capitalization rate is C* (or C_u) adjusted for growth during the perpetuity period.
- Estimated liquidation value

PERPETUITY GROWTH CAPITALIZATION METHOD

- *Where a single-period normalized continuation FCF value beyond T is to be used for purposes of capitalization, the T+1 period FCF normalized continuation value to be discounted or capitalized should reflect:*[1]
    - *Capital spending* (beyond the T forecast period) to maintain the free cash flow level during the perpetuity (lower-growth) period.
        - Growth is slower beyond the T forecast period so less capital is required to support the FCF level.
        - If the perpetuity period growth rate is 25% of the T period compound average growth rate, it is not unreasonable to reduce the average normalized level of ongoing capital expenditure requirements in period T by a similar amount.
    - *Working capital requirements* reflective of the T+1 perpetuity period growth rate, usually expressed as the percent of sales realized in the T time period.
    - *A cash tax rate* reflecting book-tax depreciation timing differences (deferred tax changes), if any, carrying forward from the franchise growth period and created during the perpetuity period based on the capital spending level in the perpetuity period.
    - An example of the *adjusted FCF perpetuity growth model* is presented in Appendix 38.1.

[1] See also Alan D. Gasiorek, *Merger and Acquisition: Valuation and Structuring* (Norcross, Ga: Corporate Development Institute, 1997), Chapter 6, for an excellent discussion.

DISCOUNTED FREE CASH FLOW INTO PERPETUITY METHOD

- *The most conceptually understandable terminal value is derived from a discounted cash flow into perpetuity reflecting the long-term growth rates and relationships of the FCF elements.*
- Discounted cash flow or FCF perpetuity growth capitalization terminal value models should reflect modest free cash flow growth factors not greater than the long-term market real growth plus any *net* impact of expected long-term inflation on FCF for the served market segment.
  - The most complex areas requiring great care are capital expenditure, depreciation, and working capital investments required during the perpetuity period to maintain the firm under the more modest post-T growth assumptions.
  - As the level of capital expenditures in the post-T period will be lower than during T as earnings expansion slows, so also will the resulting book and tax depreciation expense and therefore tax shield.
  - The level of additional working capital required per additional dollar of sales during period T is a reasonable measure to employ during the perpetuity period.
  - All other elements of FCF—sales, cost of sales, period expenses and, therefore, EBITDA—will expand at the perpetuity period growth rate(s).
  - *Book depreciation expense* during the perpetuity period requires modeling based on an assumed composite average book life of the capital expenditures mix (machinery, office equipment, auto, etc.) expected during the perpetuity period plus the residual book depreciation in perpetuity arising from the book depreciation asset balance available at the end of the T period prior to the perpetuity period.
  - *Tax depreciation expense* requires modeling based on the assumed composite average tax life and accelerated depreciation method of the mix of the capital expenditure level expected during the perpetuity period plus the residual tax depreciation into perpetuity arising from the tax depreciation asset balance available at the end of the T period prior to the perpetuity period.
  - Lapsing schedules are required to determine the roll-out of the book tax timing difference and the resulting tax effect on cash flow. See the illustration in Appendix 38.2.
  - Appendices 38.3 and 38.4 present examples of the *DCF into perpetuity terminal value valuation model.*

DISCOUNTING THE TERMINAL VALUE AMOUNT AT THE END OF YEAR T

- Terminal values resulting from discounted cash flow or other methods are stated as at the end of period T. Such amount is then discounted to time 0, the beginning of Year 1, the valuation as of date, using the end-of-year basis discount factor for year T equal to:

$$\frac{1}{(1 + C^*)^T} \quad \text{(See Topic 54.)}$$

where T = the number of years of expected franchise growth in period T.

C_U should be used in place of C^* in a leveraged buyout terminal value valuations (see Topic 43).

LIQUIDATION OF ASSETS TERMINAL VALUE METHOD

- *The liquidation of assets* method of estimating terminal values generally is not used in going-concern valuations. Such methods require making an estimate of the appropriate realization percentages for each asset class, such as:
  - 80% of receivables (or other %)
  - 50% of inventory (or other %)
  - 10 to 30% of net property, plant, and equipment (or other %)

The following Appendices are available for viewing or download on the Web site for this book at: www.wiley.com/go/emott. Please see the About the Web Site page at the back of this book for login information.

APPENDIX 38.1 Adjusted Free Cash Flow Perpetuity Method to Derive Terminal Value Example

APPENDIX 38.2 Lapsing Schedule of Projected Book Tax Depreciation Difference

APPENDIX 38.3 Adjusted Free Cash Flow Perpetuity Method to Derive Terminal Value Example

APPENDIX 38.4 Terminal Value at C* at End of Year T for DCF Valuation

TOPIC 39

Discounted Cash Flow Valuation Illustrated

This topic provides an overview of performing a discounted cash flow (DCF) valuation utilizing the principles and methodologies presented in the previous topics. It then explores the steps after the valuation to determine the buyer's offer.

The reader is encouraged to take the time to read the text in conjunction with the referenced Appendices to gain the appropriate level of understanding of the subject matter discussed in the narrative. Appendices are either presented at the end of this Topic or are available for review and download on the companion Web site noted at the end of this Topic.

DCF VALUATION PROCESS

The key components of the DCF value determination process based on the use of a levered C* discount rate are described and numbered below and in Appendix 39.1. The reader is encouraged to follow the text along with the flow on Appendix 39.1 and the other Appendices referenced.

1. *Identify* expected risk-adjusted *as-is unlevered* free cash flow (FCF) for the target resulting from deal value drivers and earnings before interest, tax, depreciation, and amortization (EBITDA) or net operating profit after tax (NOPAT) during the T period.
   See also Appendix 44.2(h)–(j) for the deal value drivers (profit and loss, capital employed, and cash flow statements) and FCF components.
2. *Construct* levered cost of equity, C_L, for this business (see Appendix 39.2).
3. *Determine the target debt to capital ratio, interest rate on debt* employed and calculate C*, the weighted average cost of capital (see Appendix 39.2).
4. Perform a DCF analysis and value the unlevered FCF using C* as the discount rate (see Appendix 39.3 for the DCF illustration). Appendix 39.3 presents the FCF determination and valuation using the earnings before interest and tax (EBIT, NOPAT) approach and the EBITDA approach as discussed in Topic 22. The calculation of the terminal value amount in the DCF valuation in Appendix 39.3 is presented on Appendices 38.3 and 38.4.

5. Determine the amount of excess cash or securities to come with the deal.
6. Determine the levered "as is" enterprise value (see Appendix 39.3).
7. Value the buyer risk-adjusted operating synergies resulting from operating or strategic initiatives grounded in the buyer integration plan.
8. Value the buyer risk-adjusted benefits resulting from tax structure benefits such as asset step-ups or noncompete payments.
9. Determine the adjusted levered enterprise value by totaling: the as-is levered enterprise value (6), synergy value (7), and deal tax and structure value benefits (8).
10. Determine the value of other nonoperating assets or liabilities to be assumed, such as net operating loss carry-forwards, net pension plan liability net of assets, net postretirement health retirement plan, site environmental liabiltiies, and so forth (other than seller debt).
11. Determine the total amount of seller debt to be assumed in the transaction and/or new debt employed at closing consistent with the target debt-to-capital ratio in the weighted average cost of capital determination.
12. Determine the buyer's total levered enterprise value and ranges by adding the net value of other nonoperating assets and liabilities assumed (10) plus cash or short-term investments (5) to the adjusted levered enterprise value (9).

OFFER DETERMINATION PROCESS

13. The buyer enterprise value offer determination and evaluation process starts with and is impacted by the deal valuation process results (6). The buyer must consider the value ranges for the business opposite what the buyer feels may be acceptable to the seller.
14. As part of the offer negotiation determination process, estimate the platform value and sharing expectation of the buyer, if any (see Topics 15 and 45).
15. Preliminary offers, equals the levered as is enterprise value (6 and 13) plus the values resulting from the platform valuation and sharing determination process (14) less an amount that leaves adequate room for negotiation.
    - See Topics 16 and 67 for the discussion of determining the enterprise value offer to the seller.
    - The value of synergies and deal structuring potentially accruing to a buyer resulting from the as-is platform acquired is not lost on the seller.
    - Sellers will expect to share in some portion of the platform value benefit accruing to the buyer (see Topic 15).
    - The degree of sharing will depend on the business, the difficulty of achieving the benefit resulting from owning the platform, the negotiation process, and so forth.
16. Determine the amount of debt assumed by the seller at the closing, if any.
17. The levered enterprise offer value to a seller equals the preliminary enterprise value *offer* amount (15) plus other nonoperating assets acquired less seller's

other liabilities assumed (10) plus cash and/or securities acquired (5) less an amount that leaves adequate room for negotiation.

18. Sellers will have expectations for the takeaway value of the business.
19. Buyers and sellers will enter into a negotiation of the finally acceptable enterprise (or equity value) value to be paid for the business. The difference and tension created between the buyer's levered enterprise value offer (17), the buyer's levered enterprise value (12), and the seller's takeaway expectation (18) define the negotiation space in the transaction.

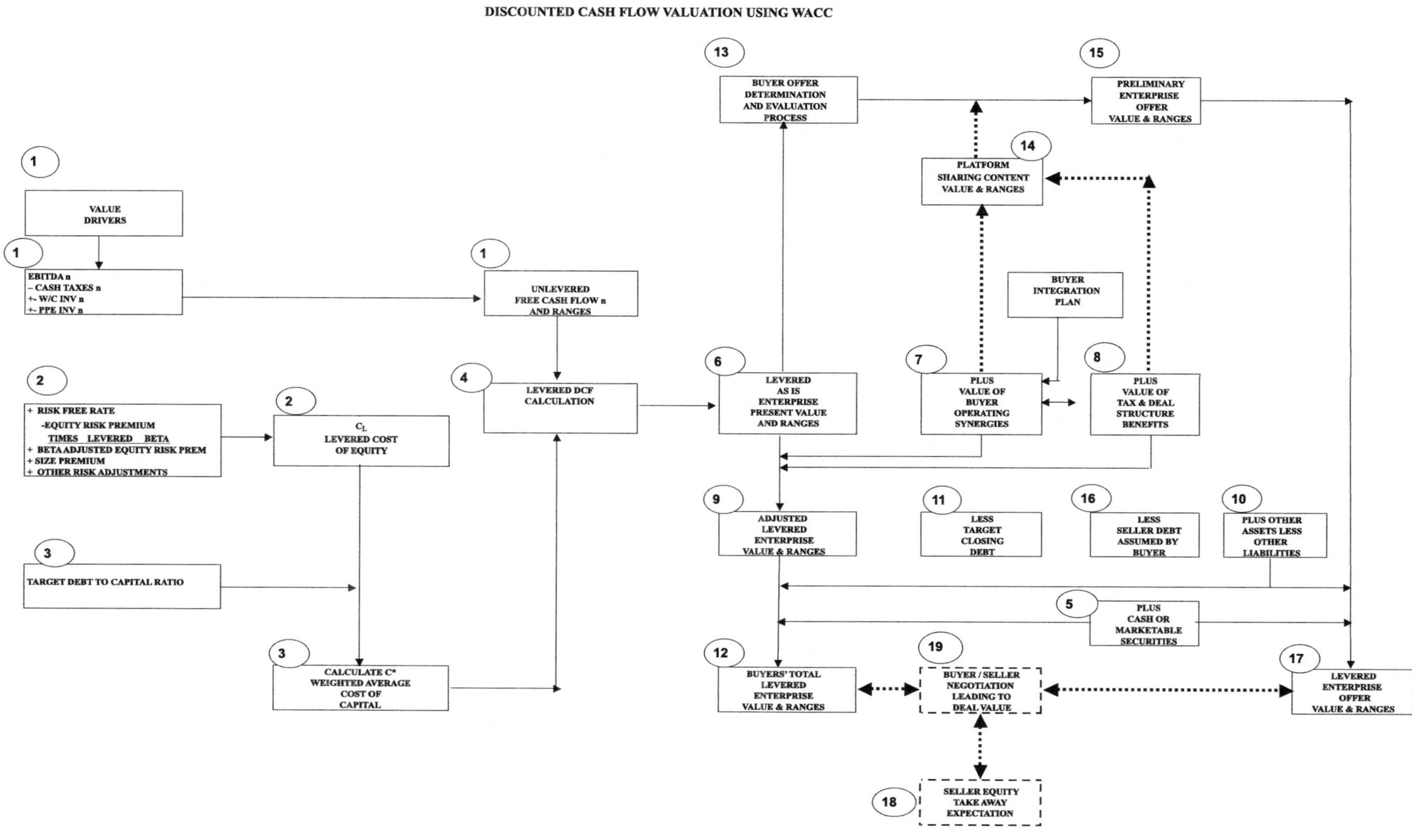

APPENDIX 39.1 Discounted Cash Flow Valuation and Offer Determination Engine

The following Appendices, as well as those presented earlier, are available for viewing or download on the Web site for this book at: www.wiley.com/go/emott. Please see the About the Web Site page at the back of this book for login information.

APPENDIX 39.2 Cost of Capital Calculation Example

APPENDIX 39.3 Discounted Cash Flow Valuation Example

TOPIC 40

Leverage: The Real Deal

Using a reasonable amount of debt to finance an acquisition will enable the buyer to increase the offer value to the seller and realize the buyer's target return on equity, C_L.

LEVERAGE INCREASES DEAL VALUATIONS

- Debt (leverage or gearing, as it is sometimes called outside the United States) is a good thing in doing acquisitions.
- Debt enables buyers to offer higher prices to sellers due to the fact that less costly debt is used in place of more costly equity capital in financing the deal.
- *Here's the real deal and the theoretical basis for the use of debt:* The government acts as a third partner in financing the deal (equity partner, lender partner, government [tax] partner).
  - The government allows a corporate tax deduction for the interest payment to the debt holders (versus no deduction on dividend payments to equity holders).
  - *With debt in the capital structure, less cash taxes are paid on the same level of operating profit (profit before interest and taxes) versus no debt, because of tax- deductible interest.* Therefore, total cash flow available to all investors (debt and equity holders) in the form of dividends and interest is higher by the amount of the income taxes not paid arising from the use of leverage.
  - Annual *free cash flow before interest expense increases* in an amount equal to the *taxes not paid*—cash taxes are lower, resulting from the interest shield.
  - The enterprise value (V) of the target company is higher with the use of debt in an amount equal to the present value of the taxes not paid due to the use of debt (Dt)

    where D = amount of debt employed in the capital structure
    t = target's marginal tax rate on earnings
    (See Topic 42.)

  - *Equity value is higher as well by the same amount* because the *increase* in cash flow, equal to the taxes not paid resulting from deductible interest, is available to the equity holders over time (as dividends), not to the debt holders.

- Although dividend payments (at the same payout ratio) are generally lower with debt in the financing mix (net income is lower), the equity investor normally has *proportionally less cash invested* than the proportional reduction in the net income (debt was invested in place of equity).

CONCLUSION

- *The use of debt is one of the primary reasons that buyers in highly leveraged transactions (leverage buyouts, etc.)* pay premiums for targets (in an amount equal to the present value of the taxes not paid due to the interest shield).
- *The new equity holder is repaid over time*, in the form of less taxes paid, for the premium paid to the seller resulting from the use of debt.
- See Topics 41, 42, and 43.

TOPIC 41

Debt Limits

The use of debt in financing a transaction has practical and proscribed limits. Topic 41 explores the general level of constraints placed on borrowers by lenders.

THE PRACTICAL LENDING LIMIT IS UP TO LENDERS

- Theoretically, debt financing that creates interest expense that approaches the level of earnings before interest and tax (EBIT) would surely maximize returns on the equity holder's investment, keeping in mind that operating profit is not affected by leverage and that free cash flow is higher by the amount of taxes not paid due to the interest shield (see Topic 40).
- Practically, however, lenders will lend only up to limits they are comfortable with. The aim of these limits is to avoid the costs of financial distress resulting from economic cyclicality or mismanagement.[1]
- Lenders' comfort limits are negotiated by lenders and equity investors as levered deals are put together.
- Typical deal lending limits reflect the following constraints, depending on the business cycle and the resulting business and lending climate. In the early to mid-2000s, lending limits were considerably higher than in the late 2000s. In the earlier period lending limits approached:
  - Up to 3.0 to 4.5 times leading (next year's) earnings before interest, tax, depreciation, and amortization (EBITDA) for senior lenders.
  - Up to 1.0 to 2.0 times leading EBITDA for typical subordinated or mezzanine lenders.
  - Interest expense coverage was 1 to 1.25 times leading EBITDA.
- In today' lending climate (2010), lending limits are more likely:
  - Up to 2.0 to 2.5 times leading (next year's) EBITDA for senior lenders.
  - Up to 1.0 times leading EBITDA for typical subordinated or mezzanine lenders.
  - Interest expense coverage may be a bit higher than in the past.

[1] Stephen Ross, Randolph W. Westerfield, and Jeffery Jaffe, *Corporate Finance*, 4th ed. (New York: McGraw-Hill, 1996), p. 426.

- Depending on the type of indebtedness incurred (senior, subordinated, mezzanine), covenants may be included in the loan documents whose aim also is avoiding the costs of distress.[2]
  - *Negative covenants* prohibiting what the company may do include dividend restrictions and limitations regarding asset pledges to others, acquisition sale or lease of assets over certain amounts, lease obligations, and technology disposition.
  - *Positive covenants* specifying what the company will do include interest coverage, EBITDA to debt coverage, minimum working capital, maximum capital spending, and related periodic or continuous maintenance tests of the covenant limits and reporting of results.
- The theoretically optimal amount of debt is where the incremental present value of the cost of distress from additional debt equals the increase in the present value of the tax shield. Beyond this point, additional debt reduces the value of the firm[3] (see Topic 43).
- In reality, such an amount is not actually measured or practically measurable—the debt limitations just outlined must suffice in determining the optimal level.[4]

[2] Ibid., pp. 424, 425.
[3] Ibid., p. 426.
[4] Ibid.

TOPIC 42

Debt Adds Value: The Derivation of Dt

Topic 42 explores the mechanics of deriving and fully understanding the benefit of debt and provides the background for applying the methodology in doing levered merger and acquisition transactions.

The reader is encouraged to take the time to read the text in conjunction with the referenced Appendices to gain the appropriate level of understanding of the subject matter discussed in the narrative. Appendices are either presented at the end of this Topic or are available for review and download on the companion Web site noted at the end of this Topic.

DERIVATION OF Dt AND TAX ADVANTAGE OF A FIXED LEVEL OF DEBT

- The present value (PV) of the taxes saved by assuming a level amount of debt is equal to Dt and is derived as:
  - The *PV of the stream of interest* payments paid out in perpetuity on a fixed amount of debt plus the eventual debt repayment will *equal the fixed amount of debt* if discounted at the pretax nominal interest rate on the debt.
  - The reason is that the *ultimate* debt repayment that is presumed to occur at the end of the interest stream takes place so far into the future—the end of perpetuity (whether by terms or as multiple refinancings)—that its PV is effectively zero. *Therefore, the only outflow entering into the PV of the cost of a permanent debt level is the interest stream.*
  - *Illustration 42.1 presents the derivation of this conclusion.*

ILLUSTRATION 42.1 DERIVATION OF Dt

The PV of the total cash stream (TCS_{PV}) of interest payments (i_ND) and debt repayment due in 200 years (effectively at the end of a perpetuity) (D_{200}),

(*Continued*)

where interest (i) = 10%, Debt (D) = $100, and N = from 1 to 200 years is:

$$TCS = i_1D + i_2D + i_3D + i_4D + i_5D \cdots + D_{200}$$

$$TCS = \$10_1 + \$10_2 + \$10_3 + \$10_4 + \$10_5 \cdots + \$100_{200}$$

$$TCS_{PV} = \frac{i_1D}{(1+i)} + \frac{i_2D}{(1+i)^2} + \frac{i_3D}{(1+i)^3} \cdots \frac{D}{(1+i)^{200}}$$

$$TCS_{PV} = \frac{\$10}{1.10} + \frac{\$10}{1.21} + \frac{\$10}{1.31} \cdots + \frac{\$100}{189{,}905{,}276.00}$$

$$TCS_{PV} = \$9.1 + \$8.3 + \$7.5 \cdots + \text{NIL}$$

$$TCS_{PV} = \$100$$

See Appendix 42.1 for the full discounted cash flow calculations.

- The derivation of the conclusion presented in Appendix 42.1 can also be expressed as a PV amount using the perpetuity method as:

$$i_N D_{PV} = TCS_{PV} = \frac{iD}{i} = \frac{\$10}{.10} = \$100$$

- If iD, the interest payment ($10), always is deducted currently, taxes saved (TS) (not paid) on the operating profit that enables the current deduction are equal to iD times the tax rate t (40%):

$$TS = iDt$$

$$TS = .10 \times \$100 \times .4$$

$$TS = \$4 \text{ tax not paid in each year the interest is fully deducted}$$

- *The present value* of the taxes not paid T_{SPV} over the life of the interest *stream using the perpetuity method* equals:

$$TS_{PV}\frac{iDt}{i} = \frac{.10 \times \$100 \times .4}{.10} = \frac{\$4}{.10} = \$40$$

- Or finally, the derivation of Dt:

$$\frac{iDt}{i} = \frac{\not{i}Dt}{\not{i}} = Dt$$

$$Dt = \$100 \times .40 = \$40$$

- See Appendix 42.2 for the discounted cash flow equivalent.

TAX ADVANTAGE OF DEBT WITH A VARYING LEVEL OF DEBT

- Note that Dt will equal the value of tax savings assuming a *level amount of debt.*
- *The value of the tax savings resulting from a varying debt level and therefore a varying interest expense level* always is determined using the discounting process. The discounting process is equal to the *PV* of the taxes saved (taxes not paid) over the life of the interest stream discounted at the pretax nominal interest rate on the debt resulting in TS_{PV} as presented in the next equation.

$$TS_{PV} = \sum_{N=1}^{200} \frac{iDt_N}{(1+i)^N}$$

- TS_{PV} is found by inserting t into the discounting process presented in Illustration 42.1 to derive TCS_{PV}, = D, as follows:
  - *The PV of the taxes saved (TS_{PV})* of interest payments (i_ND) and debt repayment due in 200 years (effectively at the end of perpetuity) (D_{200}) where the tax rate (t) = 40%, interest rate (i) = 10%, Debt (D) = \$100, and N = from 1 to 200 years is:

$$TS = i_1Dt + i_2Dt + i_3Dt + i_4Dt + i_5Dt \cdots + Dt_{200}$$

$$TS = \$4_1 + \$4_2 + \$4_3 + \$4_4 + \$4_5 \ldots + \$40_{200}$$

$$TS_{PV} = \frac{i_1Dt}{(1+i)} + \frac{i_2Dt}{(1+i)^2} + \frac{i_3Dt}{(1+i)^3} \cdots + \frac{Dt}{(1+i)^{200}}$$

$$TS_{PV} = \frac{\$4}{1.10} + \frac{\$4}{1.21} + \frac{\$4}{1.31} \cdots + \frac{\$40}{189{,}905{,}276.00}$$

$$TS_{PV} = \$3.6 + \$3.3 + \$3.0 \cdots + \text{NIL}$$

$$TS_{PV} = \$40$$

DEBT ADVANTAGE IN M&A TRANSACTIONS

- With the use of a fixed or varying level of debt:
  - The up-front offer price can be increased by the *PV of the benefit of debt,* \$40, from the illustration above (not the amount of the debt) arising from the debt incurred to finance the deal, \$100.
  - The buyer gets the \$40 back over time in the form of lower tax payments (versus no debt), which repays the price premium paid.
  - To make this work, the interest must continue to be deducted currently.
  - The debt amount valued, \$100 in this example, must remain in place; *early repayment will unwind the advantage.*

- When debt is used, levered company values always will exceed unlevered values:

$$\frac{R}{C^*} > \frac{R}{C_U}$$

- The difference in the value of a target's free cash flow R discounted first at C_U and then at C* (including the effect of debt in the capital structure; see Topic 37) will equal the PV of the taxes saved. (This difference will equal Dt when a level amount of debt is employed.)

$$\frac{R}{C_U} - \frac{R}{C^*} = \text{Dt (with level amount of debt)}$$

- Also true, therefore, is that:

$$\frac{R}{C^*} = \frac{R}{C_U} + Dt$$

- When a fixed amount of debt is used, and when a varying amount of debt is used:

$$\frac{R}{C^*} = \frac{R}{C_U} + TS_{PV}$$

- That is, levered values determined using C*, will equal values determined using a component approach of first determining an unlevered business value (V_U) using the unlevered discount rate C_U, then adding the value of debt (TS_{PV}). This will be true if C* is an average C* reflecting a varying capital structure over the life of the cash flows.
- When a varying amount of debt is employed in the capital structure, C*, is slightly different for each period of the discounted cash flow forecast as the debt to market value ratio changes. C* would have to be recalculated for each period and separately applied to the free cash flow (FCF) for that period when using the C* discounting approach to result in a value equal to the component approach (a very cumbersome process).
- We are now ready to proceed to pricing the leveraged buyout (see Topic 43).

The following Appendices are available for viewing or download on the Web site for this book at: www.wiley.com/go/emott. Please see the About the Web Site page at the back of this book for login information.

APPENDIX 42.1 Discounted Cash Flow Derivation of TCS_{PV}

APPENDIX 42.2 Discounted Cash Flow Derivation of TCS_{PV} and Dt

TOPIC 43

The Leveraged Buyout; Definition and Valuation

Topic 43 defines the characteristics of a highly leveraged transaction and the methodology employed to price a leveraged buyout (LBO).

LBO DEFINED

- A leveraged transaction or LBO is a buyout transaction financed with a significant amount of debt in the capital structure.
- Debt allows the acquirer to increase the price paid for the target based on specific valuation of the leverage benefit (see Topic 42).
- The amount and type of debt and the characteristics of debt employed in financing such transactions is a function of the lender's perceived risk-adjusted cash flows of the target as well as the *state of the lending markets* at the time the transaction is structured (see Topic 44).
  - Generally speaking, senior debt lenders today generally lend up to 2.0 to 2.5 times leading (next year's) earnings before interest, tax, depreciation, and amortization (EBITDA), sometimes higher (depending on the industry, business, and economic conditions prevailing at the time and other covenants).
  - Mezzanine subordinated lenders generally lend up to 1.0 times leading EBITDA (again depending on the industry, business, and economic conditions prevailing at the time and other covenants).
  - All in, LBO debt today could approximate 2.0 to 3.5 times leading EBITDA (sometimes higher), depending on the lender relationship, lending climate, target fundamentals, outlook, and value proposition.

LBO VALUATION OVERVIEW

- The leveraged transaction enterprise value, EV_{LBO}, is the sum of two components: V_U and TS_{PV}. (The reader is also referred to Topic 44 indicating that the LBO enterprise value is also equal to the amount of debt (D) that can be placed on the deal plus the amount of equity (E) invested.)

1. The *unlevered enterprise value* (V_U) of the target is determined by discounting the unlevered free cash flow (FCF) using the unlevered cost of equity capital (C_U) as the discount rate.
2. The *present value* of the *taxes saved* on the debt employed to finance the deal, TS_{PV}, is separately determined (see Topic 42).

- The as-is LBO enterprise value is equal to $V_U + TS_{PV}$ per the next equation. (It is also known as the adjusted present value [APV] approach.)

$$EV_{LBO} = V_U + TS_{PV}$$

  - The value of the taxes saved is determined using the discounted cash flow method as the debt employed in an LBO is a function of the type of debt employed, the debt retirement ability of the target's FCF, and the requirements of the lenders. Therefore, it is not a constant value over the life of the LBO deal.
  - Therefore, Dt is usually not the appropriate method of determining the value of debt (see Topic 42).

DEBT LEVELS EMPLOYED

- LBO debt usually starts out as a significant proportion of the target's capital structure at the closing (depending on EBITDA levels and prevailing lending conditions) and declines as FCF is utilized to retire the debt.
- Debt usually is targeted to decline over a three- to five-year period to a "normalized" level in the capital structure consistent with the industry and prospects for the firm.
  - Senior-based debt lenders will require repayment before mezzanine or subordinated lenders receive payment.
  - Dividend payments will be restricted throughout the debt repayment period.
  - The value of the taxes saved from the interest stream is therefore determined based on the modeled retirement of the debt layers pursuant to the lending documents and the FCF stream.

RECAPITALIZATIONS AND EQUITY INVESTORS' END GAME

- *LBOs often are recapitalized* with new senior debt after a number of years of successfully demonstrated debt retirement capability.
  - The proceeds are used to reduce the equity investors' equity position.
  - The proceeds are taken out in the most tax-efficient manner for the investors, such as share redemptions, dividends, or repayment of equity investors' subordinated loans.
- *The end game for the LBO* investor is typically an initial public offering (IPO) or a sale of the business to a strategic or financial buyer after realizing a

sufficient increase in equity market value to provide a satisfactory return on the equity investment.

- The LBO equity investors' measure of success is total shareholder return (TSR) (see Topic 86).
- TSR is expressed as the internal rate of return at which the present value (PV) of the posttax cash flow benefits from the investment (pretax to the investor) equals the investor's *equity investment:*
  - The level of *equity capital invested* (I) versus the *PV* of dividend flows posttax (d), plus recapitalization proceeds (R), plus net proceeds from liquidity events posttax (L) (IPO or strategic sale) determines TSR (see Topic 86).
- LBO deal pricing usually is determined at a level that provides a target return on equity (TSR) for the equity investors, generally 20% to 25+%.
- The levels of debt and equity in the deal and the offering price is iterated in a circular fashion until the TSR requirement of the equity investors and the requirements of the lender and, it is hoped, the seller are in balance (see Topic 44).
- TSR is generally in excess of C_L as equity investors realize the largest portion of TSR through timing of the exit event, when the exit values can be realized at a premium. Equity investors generally wait for the opportune time in the economic cycle to ensure this.

LEVERAGED BUYOUT CAPITAL STRUCTURE AND COMPANY CHARACTERISTICS

- A typical LBO capital structure and general company characteristics are shown in Illustration 43.1.

ILLUSTRATION 43.1 TYPICAL LBO CAPITAL STRUCTURE AND LBO COMPANY CHARACTERISTICS

Nominal Structure	Typical Terms and Issues
Senior Debt	Represents 30% to 50% of capital structure. Revolving credit working capital facility or term loans. Generally banks or bank syndicates as lenders. Senior security on all assets and payments. Spreads of 1% to 3% over cost of funds (London Interbank Offered Rate [LIBOR]). 5 to 8 years maturity, amortizing, plus balloon. Typical Covenants: Leading EBITDA to cash interest should exceed 2.5 to 3.5 times. Leading EBIT to cash interest should exceed 1.5 to 1.75 times interest coverage.

(Continued)

Nominal Structure	Typical Terms and Issues
	Asset coverage 25% to 75%. Dividend, debt to capital, and net worth tests. Limitation on new debt. Restriction on change of business ownership or asset sales. Limitation on dividends. Preference as to repayments versus mezzanine or subordinated lenders. Lender amount placed is function of financeable secured assets available, EBITDA, and cash flow. In recent years, so-called cov-lite senior debt was being employed in large M&A deals. Typical covenants were reduced in the senior financing. (See Topic 44.)
Mezzanine or Subordinated Debt	Represents 10% to 30% of capital structure. Fixed interest rate spread: 4% to 7% over Treasuries. Interest spreads can decline based on improving results below covenant hurdles. Payment in kind (PIK) often employed (such as added equity securities or principal in place of interest). Subordinated to senior debt security and payment preferences. Second-lien position possible. 5 to 12 years maturity. Often no amortization until senior debt is satisfied. Limited covenants compared to senior debt lenders. Limits on new debt. Redemption rights on change of control. Dividend and distribution limitations. 15% to 20% all in return requirements—interest plus equity kicker. Equity kicker at maturity or liquidation event (IPO or sale): Warrants or equity options often used, which dilute equity holders. 3% to 8% one-time up-front fees to place and structure financing. Lenders are banks, investment banks, insurance companies, specialists. Subject to intercreditor agreements with senior leaders. Stand-still rights (180 days). Default provision is limited. Lender looks to cash flow and earnings prospects and IPO or sale for all-in return.
Equity Investors	Represent 20% to 40% of capital structures (90% to 95% of equity). 20% to 25+% return requirements realized through dividends, recapitalizations, and end-game cash out (IPO, sale). No dividend paid until senior and mezzanine paid out or down. Equity investors hold 90% to 95% of equity. 3- to 7-year realization horizon. Looks to earnings and value creation prospects (IPO or sale) for the return.

Nominal Structure	Typical Terms and Issues
Management Investors	Represent 1% to 4% of capital structures (5 to 10% of equity).
	Consist of top management team, select others.
	Managers required to buy initial equity position in target (sweat equity).
	Buy-in price equal to LBO equity value (less a discount).
	Management often receives *incentive options or warrants* based on performance targets realized at time of IPO or sale. These options dilute equity investors and other warrant or option holders.
	Options exercise upon liquidity event (IPO or strategic sale).
	Number of option shares or warrants exercisable per share of equity owned is based on target internal measures achieved:
	Return on investment level thresholds achieved.
	Economic value added level thresholds achieved.
	Equity options do not require buy-in.
	Tax consequences need attention.
LBO Company Characteristics	Proven operating management in place.
	Products/markets not subject to rapid technological change.
	Proprietary products with stable market share.
	Low-cost producer.
	Stable (slow) growth markets.
	Limited advertising and promotion requirements.
	Cash flow predictability high, not subject to wide or prolonged cyclical swings.
	Balance sheet has high level of leverageable current and fixed assets.
	Can maintain margins consistently.

TOPIC 44

Valuing the Leveraged Buyout

Topic 44 explores the steps to value the leveraged buyout (LBO) employing the methodologies presented in the previous topics and discusses how large leveraged deals are priced in auction transactions.

The reader is encouraged to take the time to read the text in conjunction with the referenced Appendices to gain the appropriate level of understanding of the subject matter discussed in the narrative. Appendices are either presented at the end of this Topic or are available for review and download on the companion Web site noted at the end of this Topic.

STEPS TO VALUE THE LBO

- The steps to value a (LBO) transaction are presented in Appendix 44.1.
  1. Identify expected risk-adjusted as-is unlevered free cash flow (FCF) for the target resulting from deal value drivers and resulting earnings before interest, tax, depreciation, and amortization (EBITDA; Appendix 44.2(h) and 44.2(j), line 44). See also Appendix 39.3, which presents the FCF determination using the earnings before interest and tax (EBIT; net operating profit after tax [NOPAT]) approach and the EBITDA approach as discussed in Topic 22.
  2. Construct unlevered cost of equity, C_U, for this business (Appendix 44.2(f), line 15) (see Topics 23 and 37).
  3. Value the unlevered FCF during the T period (Appendix 44.2(c), lines 8–14) and the terminal value perpetuity (Appendix 44.2(c), lines 3–5).
  4. Identify excess cash or equivalents to come with the deal (Appendix 44.2(c), line 34).
  5. Determine the unlevered as-is enterprise value (EV) using the unlevered cost of equity, C_U (Appendix 44.2(c), line 15). It includes the unlevered value of the terminal value (Appendix 44.2(c), line 5) plus the unlevered FCF during the T period (Appendix 44.2(c), line 14).
  6. Value buyer risk-adjusted synergies resulting from operating or strategic initiatives grounded in the buyer integration plan (operating and consolidation benefits) (Appendix 44.2(c), line 16) (see Topic 85).
  7. Value buyer risk-adjusted benefits resulting from tax and deal structure benefits and the buyer's integration plan (Appendix 44.2(c), line 16) (asset step-ups, noncompete payments, etc.) (see Topic 85).

8. Identify the value of other target assets and other liabilities (other than seller debt) to be acquired by buyer (Appendix 44.2(c), line 34).
   - This may include net operating loss carry-forwards, net pension plan liability net of assets, net postretirement health retirement plan, site environmental, and so forth.
9. Determine unlevered adjusted enterprise value by adding synergy value (6), platform value (20) (see Topic 15) and deal structure value (7) (see Topic 85) to unlevered as-is EV (5) (Appendix 44.2(c), lines 15–17).
10. Identify and model potential closing debt and capital structure options, terms, covenants, and requirements (Appendix 44.2(i), line 31).
    - This may include seller debt assumed by the buyer at closing in addition to new buyer debt incurred (Appendix 44.2(b), line 23).
    - The amount of total debt today will be limited to a maximum amount equal to approximately two to three and a half times leading EBITDA (Appendix 44.2(b), line 14) (see Topic 43).
11. Determine the leveraged cash flow available from the deal to retire debt per the negotiated debt retirement schedule (Appendix 44.2(j), line 16).
12. Determine the expected debt balance after scheduled debt retirement and resulting capital structure during the holding period of the deal (Appendix 44.2(i), line 31).
13. Determine the debt-to-capital ratio during the perpetuity period. This ratio may be different from that at the end of the holding period (Appendix 44.2(f), line 13).
    - This perpetuity debt-to-capital ratio is usually the normalized debt level appropriate for the business over the long term.

    Determine the interest rate applicable during the perpetuity period (Appendix 44.2(f), line 5). This rate may be different from that at the end of the holding period as the debt in place at the end of the holding period may well be refinanced, reflecting a longer-term capital structure.
14. Determine the levered cost of capital, C*, after the holding period into perpetuity (Appendix 44.2(f), line 28).
15. Determine the annual amount of interest paid over the deal holding period (Appendix 44.2(c), line 20, Appendix 44.2(d), line 4).
16. Determine the amount of taxes not paid resulting from the interest deduction (from 15) during the deal holding period arising on assumed seller debt or new debt (Appendix 44.2(d), line 6).
17. Determine the value of the debt (the present value [PV] of the taxes not paid) during the expected deal holding period using the discounted cash flow method (Appendix 44.2(d), lines 7–9 and Appendix 44.2(c), line 20) (see Topic 42).
    - Note that the taxes not paid resulting from the interest deduction (Appendix 44.2(d), line 6) may be discounted at the pretax interest rate on the mix of debt, i, or by C_U, the unlevered cost of equity, (which was used in the illustration) example (Appendix 44.2(d), line 7).
    - Generally, if all the FCF are dedicated by loan covenants to reduce debt, then C_U is the more appropriate discount rate, as the amount of debt outstanding and the interest shield are as risky as the operating FCF.

- If the debt payments are scheduled and do not consume all or most of the FCF, then the pretax cost of debt is generally the more appropriate discount rate.
- If the LBO is of a smaller firm by a large private or public firm and the debt levels assumed are that which would be obtained from a third party in a sponsored LBO but is in fact from the acquirer's internal resources and therefore without covenant restriction, then the pretax cost of debt is the more appropriate discount rate.

18. Determine the value of the debt after the holding period (the PV of the taxes not paid) resulting from interest payments after the holding period (e.g., into perpetuity) (Appendix 44.2(d), lines 11–15).
    - The value of the debt after the holding period is the difference between a terminal value (TV*) of the business determined using the value of C* (from 14) determined as at the end of the holding period (Appendix 44.2(e, p1), line 43) and Appendix 44.2(d), line 12) and a terminal value (TV_U) determined using C_U (Appendix 44.2(e, p2), line 43, and Appendix 44.2(d), line 11).
    - TV* is a terminal value reflecting a weighted average cost of capital, C*, calculated using the debt-to-capital ratio expected into the future during the perpetuity period (from 14) (Appendix 44.2(f), line 28).
    - TV_U will be lower in value than TV* as TV_U has been determined using the unlevered discount rate C_U (Appendix 44.2(f), line 15) (see step 2).
    - The difference between TV* and TV_U can be due only to the effect of debt in the financing mix assumed during the perpetuity period and, therefore, is equal to the value of the taxes not paid into perpetuity arising from the interest expense assumed at the long-term debt-to-capital ratio after the holding period (Appendix 44.2(d), lines 11–13).
    - The value of $TV_U - TV^*$ determined at the end of the holding period must be discounted to the present, time 0, at either i or C_U (which was used in the illustration), using the end-of-year discount rate convention, where N equals the number of the last year of the holding period (Appendix 44.2(d), line 15, and Appendix 44.2(c), line 27).
19. Determine the adjusted levered enterprise value (19) by adding the value of the debt (taxes not paid during (17) and after (18) the holding period) to the unlevered adjusted enterprise value (9) (Appendix 44.2(c), lines 17–31).

STEPS TO DETERMINE LBO OFFER

20. As part of the offer negotiation determination process, estimate the platform value-sharing expectation of the buyer, if any (see Topic 15).
    - Sellers will expect to share in some portion of the platform value benefit accruing to the buyer (see Topic 15).
    - The degree of sharing will depend on the business, the difficulty of achieving the benefit resulting from owning the platform, the negotiation process, and so forth.

21. The buyer's offer determination and evaluation process starts with and is impacted by the deal valuation process results (8). The buyer must consider the value ranges for the business opposite what the buyer feels may be acceptable to the seller.
22. The preliminary enterprise value offer reflects the output from the buyer's offer determination process (21) and the buyer's consideration of platform value and sharing (20).
    - See Topics 12 and 67 for the other elements associated with determining the enterprise value offer to the seller.
    - In addition, the value of synergies (6) and deal structuring (7) potentially accruing to a buyer resulting from the as-is platform acquired are not lost on the seller.
23. The amount of the seller's debt to be assumed by the buyer must be determined, if any, and included in the total debt valuation process (15–18).
24. The buyer's total levered enterprise value is the sum of the buyer's adjusted levered enterprise value (19) plus the value of other assets to be acquired (8) less the value of other liabilities to be assumed (8) plus the value of cash and marketable securities to be acquired (4) (Appendix 44.2(c), line 31–35).
25. The buyer's levered enterprise value offer to the seller will be the sum of the buyer's preliminary enterprise value offer (22) plus other assets to be acquired (8) less other nonoperating liabilities assumed (8) plus cash and/or securities acquired (4).
    - The buyer's initial levered enterprise offer value (25) will reflect a reduction from the preliminary levered enterprise value (24) for a portion of buyer synergy benefits (6), structuring benefits (7), and platform value (20) to allow negotiation space.
26. Sellers will have equity takeaway expectations from the sale of the business. Buyers must consider the range of these expectations in determining offer ranges and negotiation strategies.
27. Buyers and sellers will enter into a negotiation of the finally acceptable enterprise (or equity value) value to be paid for the business. The difference and tension created between the buyer's levered enterprise value offer (25), the buyer's total levered enterprise value (24), and the seller's takeaway expectation (26) defines the negotiation space in the transaction.

BENEFIT OF USING DEBT VERSUS NO DEBT ON ENTERPRISE VALUE AND OFFERS

- Appendix 44.3 presents a summary of the benefits of debt by sensitizing the valuation illustration presented in Appendix 44.2 with various amounts of leverage.
    - Leverage can represent a 15% to 25% increase in enterprise value versus no leverage. The benefit in the example in Appendix 44.2 is a 15% increase.
    - The internal rate of return (IRR) on shareholder equity doubles in the example as leverage is added from 23% (no debt) to 46% (with 4.3 times beginning debt to leading EBITDA).

LBO OFFERS EQUAL THE EQUITY INVESTED PLUS THE DEBT

- Offers made in LBO transactions (LBO_O) are in the end equal to the amount of debt (D) that can be placed on the deal plus the amount of equity (E) invested. This amount is also equal to the value of the LBO (EV_{LBO}) equal to the sum of the value of the unlevered FCF (V_U) plus the value of the debt (TS_{PV}) as discussed in Topic 43 and as discussed above:

$$LBO_O = EV_{LBO}$$

$$D + E = V_U + TS_{PV}$$

- The basic tax implications and limitations on the amount of leverage employed and the target IRR return on the equity invested remain the same regardless how the offer value is expressed. The calculus of the theoretically correct valuation (EV_{LBO}) is implicit in the total of the debt plus equity.
- The LBO offer determination process unfolds generally as follows in large auction LBO transactions.
  - The seller's investment bank often makes available to sponsors (investors) a complete and fully committed debt financing package, consisting of senior and subordinated debt, a so-called staple financing. The staple sets a financing package bar for the sponsors either to improve on with other lenders or to avail themselves of.
  - The only usual exit from the commitment provided by a seller's investment bank in a staple may be a final review of the sponsor's business plan to assure consistency with the assumptions in place when the staple was provided.
  - In the deal, the amount of debt employed in the staple (or in a sponsor's financing package) is a function of the sponsor's ability to syndicate lenders or to underwrite the debt obligation itself.
  - The lending amounts will be driven by the state of liquidity and cost of debt in the lending markets and the perceived cash flow–generating capability of the target to meet the lender's desired debt repayment schedule and covenants.
    - In the mid- to late 2000 period, *cov-lite deals* were being done. Senior debt is arranged with fewer covenants or with covenants similar to bond deals. Maintenance covenant tests often are replaced with period-end tests or occurrence tests on new debt. In many deals, often maximum total debt to EBITDA is one of the few surviving covenants. Cov-lite deals reflected a period of excessive liquidity available, very competitive lenders, and low interest rates. Such deals were a cyclical market event.
    - The economic advantages of cov-lite debt include greater flexibility for management and equity owners to work through economic slowdowns or business issues without needing outside lenders who do not know the business as well.
    - The macroeconomic disadvantages of cov-lite debt include greater flexibility for management and equity owners to work through economic slowdowns without the impact of outside lenders. The theory of separation of authority, responsibility, obligation, and accountability between

lender and borrower in the pursuit and measurement of performance is well tested and proven over time. Eliminating the friction in this embrace in a lending structure can lead to a lopsided risk assumption environment with a wide division regarding when course corrections are needed.

- A prevailing multiple of EBITDA at the time of the syndication often is employed to characterize (not necessarily determine) the amount of the lending obligation (e.g., four times leading EBITDA).
- Once the debt availability is known, the buyer will assess the amount of equity to be placed at risk. (The seller is making the same calculation as the buyer, which calibrates the parties' negotiation space.)
- The sum of the debt financing package plus the equity placed at risk determines the initial and subsequent offers to the seller during the auction process.
- The amount of the equity to be placed in the deal is a function of the buyer's perceived exit value in a given time frame and the buyer's resulting total shareholder return (TSR) target.
- Targeted TSR generally will be 20-25% plus, depending on the business, stability, size, market position, and so forth.
- The auction tension is designed to cause a buyer to place more equity at risk at a lower TSR or result in altering the business case or exit assumptions as to timing and value to maintain TSR targets. The other option is to pursue more debt.
- The matrix in Appendix 44.4 presents the type of sensitivity analysis employed by buyers in assessing their equity placement, assuming a five- or seven-year hold.
  - With a maximum debt package of $13,128, equity investors could place up to $6,850 in the deal at a expected return of not less than 26% over a five- to seven-year hold, for a total enterprise value offer of $19,978. If the required price is higher and the debt package cannot be changed, the return to the equity investor decline as more equity is required to close the deal.
- Buyers will evaluate the target's ability to repay the debt package according to its terms over the expected holding period and thereby increase the market value of the equity.
- The increase in the market value of the equity at exit can result only from a reduction in the LBO debt or an increase in the EV.
- The increase in EV will be driven by growing EBITDA at expected nominal multiples, buyer-induced EBITDA enhancements, and/or a cyclical step change increase in EV multiples at the time of exit due to general market or business sector attractiveness factors.
- A very significant factor in determining actual sponsor TSR is the acuity of sponsors to time the exit at the point of greatest market acceptance.

FINAL NOTE ON THE VALUE PAID IN LEVERAGED BUYOUTS

- While the enterprise value of the leveraged buyout (EV_{LBO}) equals the unlevered value plus the value of the debt employed, in reality, the levered EV paid in auction and sometimes in privately negotiated deals often equals the unlevered value plus the value of the debt employed plus *mu* (*u*), where *u* equals a buyer-desire-premium over EV_{LBO} resulting from the dynamics of the negotiation process and the status of the credit markets at the time.

- When debt finance is readily available at attractive pricing and buyer desire runs high, the normally expected negotiating range of EV_{LBO} can be significantly exceeded by the almost indeterminable value, *u*.
- The financing of the *u* requirement is met by a combination of pressing lenders to provide more debt and/or more sponsor equity.
- Whether *u* is justified as it should be by hard integration, deal structuring synergies, and realistic cash flow and exit multiple expectations—and not from deal fever—often remains to be seen.
- See Topic 60.

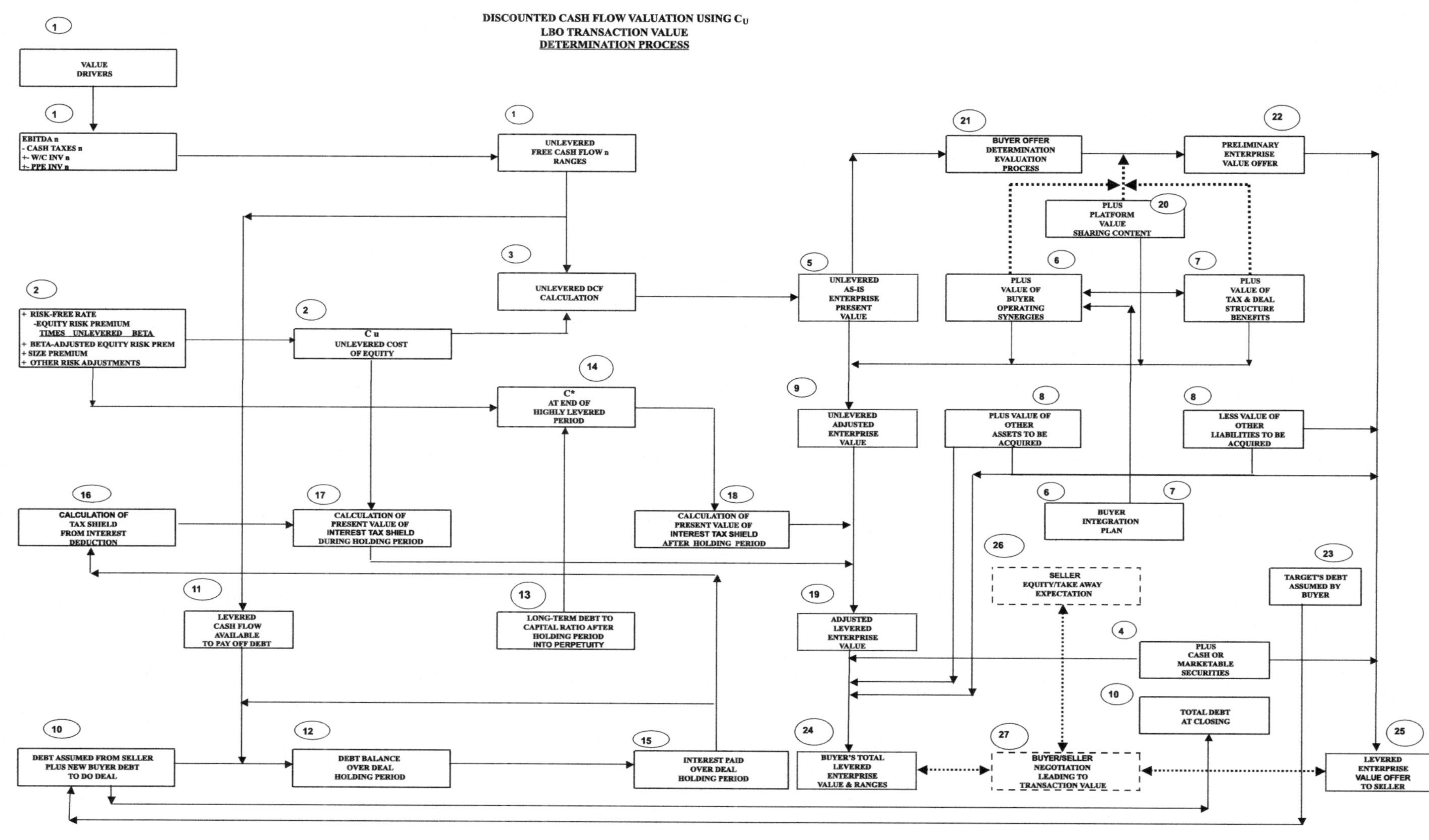

APPENDIX 44.1 LBO Valuation Engine

The following Appendices, as well as those presented above, are available for viewing or download on the Web site for this book at: www.wiley.com/go/emott. Please see the About the Web Site page at the back of this book for login information.

APPENDIX 44.2 Leveraged Buyout Example, A to K

APPENDIX 44.3 Benefit of Using Debt versus No Debt on Enterprise Value and Offers

APPENDIX 44.4 Sponsor Entry/Exit Equity Sensitivity Example

TOPIC 45

Real Option Valuation: An Introduction

The valuation of real options is a methodology applicable to the process of evaluating M&A opportunities. Topic 45 explores the definition of real options, the applications of real option analysis to M&As, the interpretation of the real option result and what it really means, and the methodology of how to perform real option valuation in an M&A setting.

DEFINITION AND DEEPER VALUE OF REAL OPTIONS

- "Real options" are potential investments in income-producing hard assets—hence "real"—at some time in the future (as opposed to an option to invest in a financial instrument at some future date).
- A real option is the right to make, sell, or delay an investment at some future time.[1]
- The value of a real option is the value today of the flexibility of having the right to make (or sell or delay) the future investment, just before the real investment opportunity is no longer available or determined to be viable.
- Real options have value under conditions where an investment, if made, is irreversible (e.g., pouring concrete and erecting steel for a new plant, entering into a long-term contract, acquiring technology). They are made in a world where potential returns and their timing are uncertain and very volatile.
- The greater the volatility (standard deviation) of the potential returns from the investment (make a lot or lose a lot) net of the cash investment required (the "exercise price"), the greater is the "option value": the value of the flexibility, the right to wait and see before making the final investment decision at the exercise date.
- The greater the length of time required between today and the future exercise date, the greater is the option value resulting from having more time to evaluate the opportunity.
- The deeper value found from engaging in the process of real options valuation in a business context is in how management strategically manages the dynamic

[1] Tom Copeland and Vladimir Antikarov, *Real Options: A Practitioner's Guide* (New York: Norton, 2001), p. 5.

events encountered in reaching a decision to make significant bets in a world filled with uncertainty: will the technology work, when will it be ready, will the customers realize value from it, what will the products cost, what will competition do, how volatile will the returns be, and so forth.[2]

REAL OPTIONS VALUATION AND DISCOUNTED CASH FLOW VALUATION

- Real option valuation is not a replacement for traditional discounted cash flow (DCF) valuation methods, which view risky investments in a digital, linear fashion: Evaluate the decision to invest now by contrasting the investment required with the risk-adjusted returns from a number of scenarios and invest if the return criteria are met or do not if they are not.
- In fact, real option valuation utilizes DCF methods in determining the future returns resulting from paying the exercise price at the exercise date.
- For example, a timing real call option valuation asks management to consider paying now for the right—the option—to wait as long as possible until there is greater clarity that the investment should or will be successful based on DCF analysis, then invest.

UNDERSTANDING THE RESULT FROM A REAL OPTION VALUATION

- The result from a real option valuation is fairly simple to understand.
- The calculated value of a real option is the expected *income value*, the present value (PV) of all the *upside* DCF valuation possibilities each (calculated at the weighted average cost of capital, C* discount rates), resulting from the future investment (those that exceed the central, most likely future DCF valuation case), less the PV of the future real investment to be made (for plant and equipment, etc.) to realize the results.
- The expected value of all the potential downside possibilities is ignored in determining the option value because investing in the option allows management to wait and see if the downside uncertainty associated with the investment is going be resolved and the upside is to be realized before making the investment.
- The PV of the upside DCF valuation possibilities and of the real investment is determined at a risk-free rate. There is no uncertainty associated with the underlying asset, as the investment will not be made unless the upside is going to be realized.[3] The term of the risk-free rate is for the same time period as the option.
- The expected income value is effectively the probability of each upside DCF outcome times the PV of that outcome.

---

[2] Martha Amram and Nalin Kulatilaka, *Real Options: Managing Strategic Investment in an Uncertain World* (New York: Oxford University Press, 1999), pp. 4–7.

[3] Ibid., p. 33.

- The upside DCF valuations result from the upside volatility surrounding the opportunity.
- The downside volatility possibilities do not matter in call option valuation.
- The cost of structuring various arrangements to allow the dynamic uncertainties to resolve themselves before making the final investment decision is the cost of the option, or the *option price*. This is the cost for the flexibility of waiting before making the investment.
- Structuring arrangements could include leasing payments for facility and staff to conduct research to prove technical viability, fees for toll manufacturing arrangements to prove a product cost and determine manufacturing viability, and retainage fees for test marketing facilities and staff to prove market acceptance and competitive advantage.
- The cumulative cost of these strategic structures—the option price payments—should not exceed the value of the real option during the time period in which such values are measured (see Topic 46).
- As the exercise date moves closer and the option value is recalculated, the option value will either increase or decrease in value as the uncertainty surrounding the dynamic risks is resolved or not.
- If the volatility of the expected option returns (or the expected returns themselves) increases as the risks resolve themselves during the term of the option price payments, the option value will increase, and continued spending on structuring costs will remain justified.
- If the volatility of the expected option returns decreases as the risks resolve themselves as option payments are made, the option value will decrease. At some point it may be less than the cumulative option cost payments made. At that time, further spending will no longer be justified, and the option to make the final investment is abandoned.
- The advantage to management of waiting before making the irreversible investment is the ability to manage scarce cash resources of the business in light of the uncertainties surrounding return possibilities over time and thereby to optimize shareholder return.

FORMS OF REAL OPTIONS AND VALUATION DETERMINATION METHODS

- Real option forms include *entry or growth options* (a call option—right to buy an asset or right to invest in research and development), *exit or abandonment options* (a put option—right to sell or exit a business or contract), *timing options* (the right to defer or delay investment in a plant, project, or business), and *switching options* (the right to switch operating method). They include a number of varieties including simple options, compound options (options on options), and expiring or deferred options.[4]

[4] Robert F. Bruner, *Applied Mergers and Acquisitions* (Hoboken, NJ: John Wiley & Sons, 2004), pp. 426–430.

- Option valuation methods include the use of the Black-Scholes method (a partial differential calculus application first published in 1973 for the purpose of valuing European financial options), lattice solution methods, decision tree analysis, simulation analysis (Monte Carlo simulation), and others that are explained in the pertinent references.[5]
- The mathematics involved in a thorough exercise of the various approaches to option valuation can be daunting. Often an experienced resource is needed to get it right.
- Real options analysis may be an appropriate strategic approach when these criteria are present:
  - There is an identifiable underlying asset.
  - An exclusive right exists for the option holder.
  - There is an identifiable uncertainty or contingency to the asset and its value.
  - The right is costly.
  - The option has a finite life.[6]

REAL OPTION APPLICATIONS IN M&A

- Real option analysis in M&A may be appropriate in these applications:
  - Determination of the platform value associated with an acquisition (see Topics 14 and 15)
  - Taking a minority position before a full acquisition
  - Evaluating expansion opportunities
  - Establishing a market sector position with a roll-up platform acquisition approach
  - Evaluating the advantage of being a second versus first mover
  - Obtaining rights to obtain or exploit uncertain resources such as research and development projects or patent rights
  - Evaluating undervalued acquisition targets
  - Evaluating rights to exploit synergy opportunities[7]
- Topic 46 presents a simple illustration of the mechanics of a timing call option valuation with two likely outcomes. It demonstrates the key valuation issues and why volatility and increased time increases the option value and why strategic management is enhanced. The topic contrasts the results with the application of a Black-Scholes valuation approach.

---

[5] Ibid., p. 438.
[6] Ibid., p. 434.
[7] Ibid., p. 432.

TOPIC 46

Real Option Valuation: Application and Illustration

Topic 46 presents an example of the mechanics of doing real option valuation. The discounted cash flow example is contrasted with the real option approach to value a timing call option.

The reader is encouraged to take the time to read the text in conjunction with the referenced Appendices to gain the appropriate level of understanding of the subject matter discussed in the narrative. Appendices are either presented at the end of this and each remaining Topic or are available for review and download on this book's companion Web site (see the About the Web Site page for login information).

OVERVIEW

- Any investment opportunity has a range of potential results and volatility:
  - The investment can overrun or underrun cost estimates.
  - The returns have the potential to be very good or very bad.
  - The returns can occur sooner or later than expected.
- The volatility range and time to exercise are what make option valuation a risk management tool and yields the flexibility advantage of waiting before investing. Waiting has value. Real option valuation determines the value of the right to wait before investing, hence the value of the option.

REAL OPTION VALUATION: AN EXAMPLE

- For purposes of illustrating how a real option value is determined, consider the simple timing call option scenario in Appendix 46.1 valued which contrasts:
  - The net present value approach
  - A simplified illustration presenting the elements of the real option approach
  - A real option solution using the modified Black-Scholes method.
- An initiative requiring an investment of $35 million today for manufacturing plant capacity, working capital, and creating the market acceptance of a patented new product/technology can result in an expected free cash flow (FCF) of $7 million per year starting one year after initial investment.

NPV APPROACH

- *Using the net present value (NPV) approach* of valuing a high-low best-case, worst-case scenario, with each possibility having a 50% probability, FCF with a high of $14 million per year growing at 3% per year or a loss of $7 million per year (see Appendix 46.1 item (1A) in the DCF valuation section), the expected NPV of this range of values at a cost of capital of 15% (determined using the capitalization method) is a break-even proposition (see Appendix 46.1 item (2) in the DCF valuation section), meaning that the project should be rejected. (The weighted expected present value of the upside and downside results in a value of $35 million versus the investment of $35 million.)

ILLUSTRATION OF ELEMENTS OF REAL OPTION APPROACH

- *Now consider the real option illustration in the lower real option valuation section of Appendix 46.1.* If the decision to invest the $35 million were deferrable for two years, resulting in a present value (PV) of $33.7 million today at a 4% risk-free rate (the exercise price) and management could invest $10 million in year 1 and $5 million in year 2 in tolling and other temporary facility and personnel arrangements for the purposes of proving the case (effectively an option at a PV of $14 million, the option price), would this be a smart decision for the shareholders?
- Assume that the volatility of three standard deviations (around the estimate of $7 million) at a 62% standard deviation (a variance of 38%, standard deviation squared) with the value of each standard deviation equal to $4.3 million, results in a high FCF of $20 million per year growing at 3% per year with a 50% probability; or a low FCF of $(3.7) million per year with a 50% probability. (See item 1) in Appendix 46.1.
- The real option approach results in an *option value* of this initiative of $24.2 million as presented in the real option valuation section of Appendix 46.1 at (item 3), assuming *the distribution of all possible upside expectations* is best represented by the single-point high value of $15 million FCF per year (estimated at 75% of the 3 sigma value of $20 for illustration purposes).
- The option value of $24.2 million equals the expected value of the PV of the upside DCF valuation two years hence due to the delay equal to $57.8 million less the PV of the exercise price of $33.7 million as follows:
  - $57.8 million is equal to $125.1 million upside DCF value in two years (item 7) on Appendix 46.1 times the risk-free discount rate of 4% for two years ($(1 + .04)^2$) which equals $115.7 million ($125.1 times .9246).
  - The expected value of the $115.7 million at a 50% probability equals $57.8 million.
  - $57.8 million less $33.7 million equals $24.2 million) (item 3).
- As the cumulative option cost of $14.2 million (PV of the first and second year's option price of $10 million in year 1 plus $5 million in year 2) (item 4)

is less than the option value of $24.2 million, resulting in an initial *option premium value* of $10 million (item 5), it makes sense to proceed with the first year's spending for the option price of $10 million (tolling, temporary facilities, etc.). The second year's $5 million tolling fee can be reevaluated at the end of year 1.

- The option payoff for this option would approach $57.8 million, as presented in the option payoff section of Appendix 46.1, (item 6). This is equal to the PV of the upside return equal to $115.7 less the exercise price of $33.7 (investment in plant, working capital, etc.) less the cost of the option, $24.2 million (assuming the tolling fee payments to prove the case were equal to the option value). If the option cost was limited to the expected option price for tolling expenses of $14.2 million (versus the calculated option cost of 24.2 million), the option payoff would be $67.8 million ($115.7 less $33.7 less $14.2).

INTERPRETATION OF THE REAL OPTION RESULT

- The reason the option value of $24.2 million exceeds the expected value break-even position under the DCF valuation method is that option valuation ignores the expected value of the distribution of all the potential downside expectations in determining the option value. Investing in the option allows management to wait and see if the downside uncertainty associated with the investment is going be resolved and eliminated and the upside to be realized before investing the irreversible amount of $35.0 million. Hence, the flexibility of waiting yields the ability to eliminate downside from determination of the option value.
- *The conceptual way to interpret entering into this real option structure example is this*: If all the upside option assumptions made two years prior to the investment date are accurate and the investment is going to succeed, one should pay (or should have paid in retrospect) $14.2 million (as much as $24.2 million) now for the option to wait two years before investing the $35 million. It will become clear by waiting that just before the investment is to be made, the actual annual upside FCF of $20 million (the 3 sigma upside distribution of all possible upside expectations) is going to be realized as a result of management's decision to prove the case by tolling and other temporary facility and personnel arrangements. The PV of the returns is going to be $67.8 million. Not bad for a $47.9 million investment ($14.2 + $33.7 (PV of $35.0)).
- *The corollary to this view* is that if the assumptions made two years prior to the investment date are not validated during the first year, and the tolling arrangements do not prove the case, the firm is out $10 million in tolling and other expenses but did not spend $35 million and excessive management time, making it a better use of scarce resources.
- Only the upside volatility portion of the distribution of possibilities is considered in the mathematics of option valuation.

- If the volatility were even greater, the option value would have even greater value than illustrated: Only the upside matters.
- Real option valuation allows management the ability to contrast the tolling expense to prove the case against the option value of the opportunity.

USING THE MODIFIED BLACK-SCHOLES REAL OPTION MODEL

- Using the modified Black-Scholes model to value this scenario (Appendix 46.2, pp. 1–3), if the PV of the average free cash flow of the scenario at the 4% risk-free rate was $54 million ($7 million/12% (1/(1.04^2))), the exercise price was $33.7 million (PV of $35 million at 4% risk-free rate), the time of competitive advantage is the life of the potential patent of 17 years, the dividend yield lost is 6% (1/17 years), the standard deviation in the average cash flows was 62%, and the risk-free rate for two years was 4%, the option value is $15.9 million. This is versus $24.2 million in the illustration in Appendix 46.1. The cumulative option premium value is $1.7 million ($15.9 – $14.2 option cost).
  - Page 1 of Appendix 46.2 presents a summary of the inputs to the modified Black-Scholes model as summarized above and an overview of how the elements of input are combined in the array of a probability distribution.
  - Page 2 of Appendix 46.2 presents the detail computation of the option value utilizing the differential calculus of the modified Black-Scholes approach.
  - Page 3 of Appendix 46.2 presents the interpretation of the output results from the modified Black-Scholes approach.
- The decision to proceed at the option price for the first year is the same as in the real option illustration in Appendix 46.1.

REVIEW THE TOLLING ARRANGEMENT AND OPTION VALUE AT THE END OF THE FIRST YEAR: IF LOWER VOLATILITY IS EXPECTED

- In Appendix 46.3, at the conclusion of the first year, the second year's option price (tolling expenses) of $5 million and the option value are reevaluated by capturing the results of the first years' learning from the tolling arrangements.
- If the distribution of potential payoffs after waiting and proving the case for one year as presented in Appendix 46.3 is not as favorable as presented in Appendix 46.1 (less volatility—the standard deviation goes to 25%), while the option value is a positive $8.4 million item (item 8) in Appendix 46.3, the option premium value is $(6.4) million (item 9) (after payment of the first year's option price of $10 million plus the remaining second-year option price of $5 million).
- Therefore, using real option valuation, the investment opportunity indicates abandonment in year 2.

- Recognition of the volatility range of returns is a key element to making option valuation work for management and yields the flexibility advantage of waiting before investing.
- *Using the modified Black-Scholes model* to value this scenario at the end of year 1 (Appendix 46.4, pp. 1–3), the option value is $11.1 million (versus $8.4 million in the illustration in Appendix 46.3) and the option premium value is $(3.7) million, also indicating abandonment of the second year spending ($11.1 option value less $14.8 option cost of tolling fees for two years from Appendix 46.3 equals $(3.7)). The $(3.7) option premium per Black-Scholes is versus an option premium of $(6.4) million in the illustration in Appendix 46.3.
- Using the NPV approach, the expected NPV of these alternatives at a cost of capital of 15% is $(11.6) million (see Appendix 46.3 in the DCF valuation section), also indicating that the project should be abandoned.

REVIEW THE TOLLING ARRANGEMENT AND OPTION VALUE AT THE END OF THE FIRST YEAR: IF HIGHER VOLATILITY IS EXPECTED

- The effect of the volatility range is demonstrated in Appendix 46.5, where the distribution of returns is more volatile than in Appendix 46.1. With a 70% standard deviation, the option value is $40.9 million (item 8) in Appendix 46.5 and the option premium is $26.1 million (item 10) after the payment of the first and remaining second year's option price. This indicates that the option should continue in place, the second year's option price (tolling expense) should be paid, more learning should take place in the second year, and management should continue to wait and see before committing to or abandoning the investment initiative.
- *Using the modified Black-Scholes model* to value this scenario (Appendix 46.6, pp. 1–3), the option value is $18.5 million versus $40.9 million in the illustration in Appendix 46.5, and the option premium value is $3.7 million ($18.5 less the $14.8 option cost), also indicating that the option should continue in place.
- Using the NPV approach in Appendix 46.5, the expected NPV of these alternatives at a cost of capital of 15% is $(9.2) million (see Appendix 46.3 in the DCF valuation section), indicating that the option should be abandoned.

CONCLUDING REMARKS ON REAL OPTION VALUATION

- See Topic 85 for application of the option valuation framework to a product development possibility as part of an integration planning exercise.
- As with any tool, management diligence and credibility is required in the determination of the option model drivers and assumptions. Remember the axiom: garbage in, garbage out.

The following Appendices are available for viewing or download on the Web site for this book at: www.wiley.com/go/emott. Please see the About the Web Site page at the back of this book for login information.

APPENDIX 46.1 Real Option Valuation Illustration No. 1: Timing Call Option

APPENDIX 46.2 Call Option Engine No. 1: Modified Black-Scholes Pages 1, 2, and 3

APPENDIX 46.3 Real Option Valuation Illustration No. 2: Timing Call Option

APPENDIX 46.4 Call Option Engine No. 2: Modified Black-Scholes pages 1, 2, and 3

APPENDIX 46.5 Real Option Valuation Illustration No. 3: Timing Call Option

APPENDIX 46.6 Call Option Engine No. 3: Modified Black-Scholes pages 1, 2, and 3

TOPIC 47

M&A Values Are Not All the Same

Topic 47 explores the definition and applicability of the various values that are encountered in evaluating M&A opportunities.

INVESTMENT VALUE

- *Investment value* is the enterprise or equity control value of a business to a particular buyer. Therefore, it includes all of the integration, structure, and tax synergies expected to be realized by that buyer.[1]
  - Acquisition premiums paid in deals generally result in total consideration amounts approaching buyer's investment value and generally include the effect of control premiums.
  - The negotiation process will determine how much of the expected integration, tax, platform, and synergy values of a particular buyer are shared with the seller.

CONTROL VALUE

- *Control value* is the enterprise or equity value of a business to any number of buyers. It includes a notional control premium reflecting an owner's sole power and capability of realizing and accessing all the economic cash flow benefits possible arising from the exercise of control over the policy and operations of the target, including management appointment and compensation, company policy and direction, acquiring assets, making acquisitions, dividends, changing articles of incorporation or by-laws, going public, and so forth.[2]
  - The control premium reflected in a control value is not necessarily equal to an acquisition premium.
  - Such value may or may not be expressed after discounts for lack of marketability (see Topic 48).

[1] Shannon P. Pratt, *Business Valuation Body of Knowledge: Exam Review and Professional Reference*, 2nd ed. (New York: John Wiley & Sons, 1998), p. 29.
[2] Ibid., p. 157.

FAIR MARKET VALUE

- *Fair market value* is the (enterprise or equity) value at which a business would change hands between a hypothetical willing buyer and seller, both being fully informed and neither being compelled to buy or sell, and both having the means and willingness to do so and knowledge of the relevant facts.[3]
  - Fair market value can be determined at a control or minority valuation level, depending on the valuation purpose: control enterprise or equity value, minority enterprise or equity value.

ENTERPRISE VALUE

- Enterprise value can be viewed and defined in a number of ways.
  - *In an acquisition transaction, enterprise value* is the total leveraged market value of the target business operations and operating capabilities at the date of a transaction (including the valuation benefit of employing a financeable level of debt in the acquisition capital structure) (see Topic 42).
    - Depending on the intended use and/or transaction contemplated, *enterprise value* in an acquisition transaction may also be expanded to include excess cash and marketable securities, platform value, integration synergies, and other nonoperating assets acquired, if any, net of any nonoperating liabilities assumed, if any (excluding debt) (see Topic 42).
  - *From an operating asset point of view, enterprise value* is equivalent to the total market value of all of the net assets of the business: total assets including goodwill (at market value) less current liabilities.
  - *From a financing point of view, enterprise value* is equivalent to the total of the market value of the equity plus the market value of the funded debt held by all such security holders.
  - *Enterprise value for publicly traded companies* is equivalent to the market value of all of the equity securities (common, preferred) at any trading date held by all such security holders (which includes the value of cash and marketable securities net of other long-term liabilities excluding debt) plus the market value of all funded debt securities (senior, subordinated, mezzanine, etc.) held by all such security holders.
- Enterprise value may be stated on an investment, control, or minority basis.

EQUITY VALUE

- *Equity value* in a valuation exercise is the enterprise value less the market value of funded debt actually employed in the capital structure.
  - Depending on the intended use and/or transaction contemplated, such value may also be expanded to include excess cash and marketable securities, platform value, integration synergies, and other nonoperating assets acquired,

[3] Ibid., p. 28.

if any, net of any nonoperating liabilities assumed, if any (excluding debt) (see Topic 42).

- Equity value for publicly traded companies may also be defined as the market value of the enterprise (which includes cash and marketable securities net of other long-term liabilities excluding debt) less the market value of funded debt.
- Equity value may be stated on an investment, control, or minority basis.

MINORITY VALUE

- *Minority value* is the value of a minority interest in the total enterprise or equity value that does not have the ability to exercise control over the target and thereby access all the potential economic benefits.
  - A minor shareholding of less than 50% of the outstanding equity is usually but not necessarily a minority interest.
  - Minority value depends on the control the minority interest shareholder can exercise over the business, such as blocking or supermajority rights.
  - A minority interest value reflects a discount from the control value, the extent of which depends on the control rights (ability to affect policy and access value) held by the minority shareholder.[4]
  - A minority interest with no rights is subject to a full minority discount (see Topic 48).
  - A minority interest with some rights, such as supermajority or blocking rights, is subject to less than a full discount.
  - A minority interest value may or may not also be discounted for lack of marketability.
  - Public company shares with very broad public holding (float) traded day to day on public markets are valued at a minority value, without suffering any discount for marketability (also referred to as a fully distributed minority value).
  - Privately held company minority interests without ready access to many knowledgeable buyers usually will be valued after a minority discount and a marketability discount.
  - Put rights to the issuing company to demand purchase of such minority share interests would mitigate the level of a marketability discount.

OFFER VALUE

- *Offer value* is the purchase price offered by a buyer to a seller, generally stated as an enterprise value, and reflects the buyer's estimate of what the buyer feels is a reasonable offer that a seller should fairly expect to receive (see Topic 67).
  - A buyer will not generally ever offer a buyer's total investment value to a seller.

---

[4] Shannon P. Pratt, *Valuing a Business: The Analysis and Appraisal of Closely Held Companies*, 2nd ed. (New York: McGraw-Hill, 1989), p. 397.

TRANSACTION VALUE

- *Transaction value* is the actual price or consideration paid in a particular transaction after any closing or post closing adjustments.
  - Transaction value may reflect investment value (unlikely), control value, fair market value, minority value, and so forth, and may or may not reflect discounts for lack of marketability (liquidity), depending on the deal.

NET REALIZED SELLER VALUE

- *Net realized seller value* is the transaction value less taxes payable by the seller on the gain resulting from the sale or transfer of the business, the amount of any debt to be paid off after the closing by the seller (if not already deducted from the transaction value at the closing) and fees (legal, investment banking, accounting, etc.) associated with the sale of the business.
- A visual depiction of the relationships between values and their determinants is presented in Appendix 48.1. (See Topic 48.)
- In addition to the most often encountered M&A values as just described, business entity enterprise or equity value will also reflect the different goals of business owners giving rise to the valuation exercise: estate valuation versus business sale, stock buy-backs versus stock flotation, insurance valuation versus liquidation, and so forth.

TOPIC 48

Discounts and Premiums

Topic 48 explores the nature and application of discounts and premiums in the determination of values encountered in the M&A process. The basis used to determine discounts or premiums must be clearly understood to ensure proper application in the determination of values. Also, the base value to which the discount or premium is applied must be consistent with the basis used to determine the discounts or premiums.

ACQUISITION PREMIUMS

- Acquisition premium is the additional value (paid) over the total value of the fully distributed minority value of an enterprise that emanates from the ability and right of the controlling acquirer to exercise control over the management and affairs of the enterprise. This control provides the beneficiary with the ability to ultimately maximize value and have full access to the free cash flow (FCF) of the business. This value generally includes the value to the buyer of expected synergies and platform value potentials.[1]
- Acquisition premiums, including control and probably synergy effects, paid in acquisition transactions of public companies *have been about 30% to 45%* higher than the fully distributed minority values prior to the transactions.[2]
  - It is not clear whether such acquisition values fall at the lower, middle, or upper end of the range of the buyer's target control or investment value level, as the levels are known only to the buyer in the deal.
  - No doubt the buyer feels that something below the upper-level control value was paid to the seller.
  - No doubt the seller feels that something above the lower-level control value approaching the upper level value was received. A zero-sum game?

CONTROL PREMIUMS

- Control premiums, employed in the determination of control value, are the additional value over the total value of the fully distributed minority value

[1] Robert F. Bruner, *Applied Mergers and Acquisitions* (Hoboken, NJ: John Wiley & Sons, 2004), p. 466.

[2] Shannon P. Pratt, *Valuing a Business: The Analysis and Appraisal of Closely Held Companies*, 2nd ed. (New York: McGraw-Hill, 1989), pp. 398, 399.

of an enterprise. Control premiums emanate from the ability and right of the controlling acquirer to exercise control over the management and affairs of the enterprise and ultimately maximize value and have full access to the FCF of the business.[3]

- Strictly speaking, control premiums exclude premiums associated with synergy effects in a particular transaction. However, the two are difficult to unbundle in the determination of either alone.[4]
- The conceptual basis for the existence and size of control premiums emanates from control premium studies of acquisition transactions of public companies where the acquisition price per share was at a premium to the minority price per share as traded prior to the acquisition.[5]
- The appropriate application of control premiums to the fully distributed minority value of the enterprise to determine control value depends greatly on the basis used to determine the fully distributed (before marketability or liquidity discounts) minority value of the enterprise being valued.[6]
- *The derivation of a comparable earnings multiple resulting from an analysis of guideline public company trading multiples* (where the underlying earnings data and enterprise value data do not reflect the prerogatives of control) will result in a multiple that, when applied to the noncontrol earnings of the enterprise being valued, generally will result in a fully distributed minority value to which an appropriate control premium may be applied.
  - Care must be exercised to apply such comparable earnings multiple to a comparable (noncontrol basis) earnings level for the enterprise being valued.
  - The earnings basis and market value of the guideline public companies should also reflect elements of debt-to-capital ratio, size, beta, and so forth comparable to the enterprise being valued.
  - If the foregoing is taken into account in determining the fully distributed minority value, application of a control premium is appropriate in the determination of a control value of such enterprise.
- *The derivation of a capitalization of earnings rate from guideline public company data* (where the earnings data does not reflect the prerogatives of control) will, when applied to the noncontrol earnings base of the enterprise being valued, generally result in a fully distributed minority value.
  - The earnings and market value of the guideline public companies must also reflect elements of the debt-to-capital ratio, size, and beta comparable to the enterprise being valued.
  - If the foregoing is taken into account in determining the fully distributed minority value, application of a control premium is appropriate in the determination of a control value of such enterprise.

[3] Shannon P Pratt, *Business Valuation Body of Knowledge: Exam Review and Professional Reference*, 2nd ed. (New York: John Wiley & Sons, 1998), p. 57.
[4] Bruner, *Applied Mergers and Acquisitions.*
[5] Pratt, *Valuing a Business*, pp. 397, 398.
[6] Ibid.

- *The derivation of a comparable earnings multiple developed from guideline public company acquisition transaction multiples of noncontrol earnings* generally will result in a fully distributed control, perhaps investment, value multiple. When applied to the earnings of the enterprise being valued (where the earnings data do not reflect the prerogatives of control), it will result in a fully distributed control/investment value.
  - In this case, the application of such a transaction multiple to target noncontrol earnings will reflect the effect of the acquisition premiums paid (including the effect of control) in the acquisitions sampled. The application of a further control premium is neither appropriate nor applicable.
- *A discounted cash flow (DCF) valuation of the as-is enterprise free cash flows generally results in a fully distributed minority value* unless the underlying financial data and free cash flows have been restated to reflect the prerogatives of control. In that case, DCF valuation will reflect the benefits of control, and further application of a control premium is not applicable.
  - In the former case, the application of a control premium to the fully distributed minority value is appropriate, as the base is a fully distributed minority value without the benefits of control.
- Acquisition transactions of 100% of the controlling equity of privately held companies take place at valuations including some level of control premium.
- Such valuations probably also reflect some level of purchaser synergies and possibly liquidity discounts if there are very few seller liquidity options.
- Control premiums are included in the acquisition premiums in takeover transactions of public and private companies where the acquirer secures the full power of control.

MINORITY DISCOUNTS

- *Minority discounts,* employed in the determination of the value of a minority position, are the reduction in value from the *control value* of the enterprise with full liquidity. Minority discounts are applicable where a minority owner lacks the ability to exercise control over management and affairs of the enterprise and ultimately to maximize value and have full access to the business's FCF.[7]
- *Full minority discounts are usually in the range of 25% to 30%* and are deducted from the proportionate (minority) share of the total fully distributed entity acquisition/control value.[8] (The proportionate (minority) share results from multiplying the minority share ownership percentage times the fully distributed entity control value).
  - Public company fully distributed shares are effectively valued after a full minority discount as the minority owners are not able to exercise control (see Topic 47).

[7] Ibid., pp. 397–399.
[8] Ibid., pp. 398, 399.

- The conceptual basis for the existence and size of minority discounts emanates from control premium studies of acquisition transactions of public companies, where the acquisition price per share was at a premium to the minority price per share as traded prior to the acquisition.[9] The minority discount is the corollary to the control premium.[10] (Twenty-three percent of control value (minority discount) is equivalent to 30% of minority value (control premium)).
- The appropriate application of minority discounts to determine a minority value depends on whether the value of the enterprise being valued is a control value or not.
- *A comparable multiple approach using guideline public company trading multiples* (where the underlying earnings data does not reflect the prerogatives of control) generally will result in *a fully distributed minority value multiple,* which, when applied to the earnings of the enterprise being valued (where the earnings data does not reflect the prerogatives of control), results in a fully distributed minority value, *In this case, application of a minority interest discount is not warranted.*
  - Care must be exercised to apply such guideline earnings multiple to a comparable (noncontrol basis) earnings level for the enterprise being valued.
- *A capitalization of earnings approach using guideline public company data to derive capitalization rates* (where the earnings data does not reflect the prerogatives of control) will, when applied to the earnings base of enterprise being valued, generally result in a fully distributed minority value. In this case, application of a minority interest discount is not warranted.
- *A comparable earnings multiple approach using guideline public company acquisition transaction multiples* generally will result in a fully distributed acquisition multiple, which, when applied to the earnings (where the earnings data do not reflect the prerogatives of control) of the enterprise being valued, will result in a fully distributed control value.
  - In such case, a minority discount is applicable in the determination of a minority interest.
  - The impact of the synergy effects included in the acquisition multiples is very difficult to unbundle from the pure control value portion of the acquisition multiple. An attempt to unbundle the impact should be considered prior to application of the acquisition multiple to the non–control earnings of the enterprise being valued.
- *A discounted cash flow valuation* of the as-is enterprise being valued generally results in a fully distributed minority value. In this case, the application of a minority discount is not appropriate.
  - If the underlying financial data of the enterprise being valued have been restated to reflect the prerogatives of control, the DCF valuation will reflect the benefits of control, and the application of a minority discount is applicable in the determination of a fully distributed minority value.

[9] Ibid.
[10] Ibid.

MARKETABILITY (OR LIQUIDITY) DISCOUNTS

- *Marketability (right to sell) or liquidity (rapid salability) discounts* are the reduction in the valuation of privately held (nonpublic) equity interests where there is a lack of marketability (restrictions on the holder's ability to readily convert a holding to cash) or readily available liquidity (no organized market of potential willing and informed buyers to enable the seller to convert a holding to cash).[11]
- The conceptual basis for such discounts arise from:
  - Marketability discount studies of discounts realized on sales of lettered (restricted from public sale for a period of time) shares of publicly traded companies compared to the prices of unrestricted shares traded on the public markets (25% to 45% discounts).[12]
  - Discounts realized on sales of privately held companies shares compared to prices realized upon and after going public (40% to 70+% discounts).[13]
  - The costs incurred in a public share offering (registration, disclosure, sale).
  - In the 1974 Securities and Exchange Commission study, the average cost of compensation and expenses was approximately 12%.[14]
- Such discounts are applied to the fully marketable minority value *of the security being valued.*
- *Marketability or liquidity discounts reflect the economic disadvantage of:*
  - *Not having a broad active market of willing, able buyers knowledgeable regarding the risk of the business assets underlying the equity value.*
  - *Having to find a buyer from a limited pool of hard-to-identify potential buyers and the consequence of a seller's potentially poor negotiating position.*
- Marketability/liquidity discounts generally are not applicable to the valuation of the common equity of broadly held public companies (with the exception of lettered or restricted shares).
- Valuations of *minority interests* in *privately held* companies usually reflect marketability/liquidity discounts. The level of the discounts depends on the rights of the minority owner such as put rights of the shares back to the issuing company, other permitted restrictions on sale of the company without consent or other supermajority blocking rights. A marketability discount rate of 35% to 50% for closely held companies appears to be supported by the evidence.[15]
  - Restrictions on sales of a minority holding to outsiders without an ability to put the shares back to the company, for example, would call for a steep liquidity discount in valuing a minority interest.
  - The only apparent exit in such case would be if the company agrees to respond to a minority seller's offer to sell shares back to the company, likely at a discount, or if the company lifts the restrictions.

---

[11] Bruner, *Applied Mergers and Acquisitions*, p. 462.

[12] Pratt, *Valuing a Business*, pp. 240–248.

[13] Ibid., pp. 249–255.

[14] Ibid., p. 257.

[15] Ibid., p. 59.

- Marketability/liquidity discounts generally are *not applicable to valuations of negotiated buyouts of 100% of the equity of privately held companies* unless the property can be of interest only to a particular sole buyer and that buyer has no ability subsequently to dispose of the acquired entity alone or as part of the acquirer's business.
  - Generally, liquidity is not an issue in private company 100% buyout transactions, auctions, and privately negotiated deals *as the buyer* presumably is selected from *a few or many possible buyers.*
- *In the determination of the fully distributed total entity equity value of a privately held company for a purpose other than a buyout,* composed of the fully distributed equity value of operating entities plus a very material amount of nonoperating cash or cash equivalents, the liquidity discount should be deducted only from fully distributed equity value of the operating entities, not to the cash portion of the entities total value.
  - *The fully distributed equity value of the operating entities would be subject to the liquidity discount* in determination of the expected cash value a seller should expect to realize if these holdings were converted to cash. The fully distributed value of the operating entities do not enjoy having access to an organized market of potential willing and informed buyers to enable the seller to convert this holding to cash.
  - The material amount of nonoperating cash or cash equivalents would be added to the discounted equity value of the operating entities to determine the discounted total entity equity value of the privately held company.
  - *Material amounts of excess cash or cash equivalents do not suffer the underlying business risks associated with operating entities* and therefore the economic disadvantages of a lack of a market of knowledgeable buyers.
  - On the contrary, cash, even if it represents the material value of a privately held security, enhances and at the very least does not restrict the marketability of such a security to a broad market of ready buyers and the conversion of the security to cash.
    1. There is no threshold of knowledge of the business risk applicable to cash that would preclude identifying a market of potential buyers. On the contrary, the marketing of a security composed of cash (readily accessible to the security holder) opens the security to a universe of potential buyers (knowledgeable regarding the underlying asset risk). As the first or any subsequent security holder is not encumbered in converting the security to cash dollar for dollar, the applicability of a liquidity or marketability discount is inappropriate.
    2. As the marketing of a security composed of readily accessible cash creates a universe of potential buyers without a threshold of knowledge of the business risk to overcome, the seller cannot be in a poor negotiating position that would lead to the applicability of a liquidity or marketability discount.
    3. As material excess cash is easily disgorged from the total entity dollar for dollar by the seller at the moment of valuation, a shareholder must be indifferent to whether excess cash is held in the company and represented

in the per share value or held in hand if paid in the form of a dividend to the shareholder moments before the share valuation. In the latter case, the operating entities held in the company are subject to the liquidity discount; the cash is not, as it has been disgorged. At the moment of valuation, the shareholder holds the same total value in hand regardless of where the excess cash is resident.

- The same understanding must extend itself to the material amount of excess cash included in the value of a fully distributed equity value distinct from the treatment of the risk of the business assets of operating entities. *Material* amounts of excess cash or equivalents should have the same value to the total entity valuation before or after a liquidity discount.

KEY MAN DISCOUNTS

- Key man discounts represent the reduction in the control value of the enterprise, an entity-level discount, associated with the risk of dependence on an individual or small group of individuals.[16]
- Inconclusive studies (public company values before and immediately after announcement of the departure of a known key management member and others) seem to indicate that discounts approximating 5% to 9% of enterprise value may be appropriate for situations where management is very thin or dependent on a key man. The smaller the company and the smaller the management team, the greater the discount.[17]
- It is preferable to sensitize cash flows for the potential impact of losing a key man (customer loss, product/technology decline) rather than adjust the discount rate or apply a valuation discount in determining a key man valuation adjustment.[18]
- The control basis valuation of a small- or micro-cap company that is heavily dependent on the continuance of a key individual or small group of individuals, should reflect a key man discount from the control value, offset possibly by life insurance proceeds, to reflect this risk.[19]
- If small-company valuations result in a fully distributed minority basis valuation, the key man discount will be applied to the minority basis valuation.

CONGLOMERATE DISCOUNTS

- Valuation of enterprises that are composed of diversified unrelated business entities are often subject to conglomerate discounts (so-called entity-level discounts) at the entity level approximating 10% to 25% of the aggregate fully

[16] Shannon P. Pratt, *Business Valuation Discounts and Premiums* (Hoboken, NJ: John Wiley & Sons, 2001), p. 225, from a study by Steven Bolton and Yan Wang.
[17] Ibid.
[18] Ibid., p. 227.
[19] Ibid.

distributed control value of the diversified entity, depending on the size, complexity, and diversity of the conglomerate company.[20]

- Analysts' estimates of the difference in breakup value of a public conglomerate company versus the conglomerate's trading value provide insight into the factors driving such discounts.[21] The estimated composite breakup values generally exceed the conglomerate trading value.
- The conglomerate discount reflects the equity market's perception of the cumulative value lost through retaining ownership of a portfolio of diverse entities that may be more difficult to manage than a stand-alone company and of the time, costs, and risk associated with a sell-off of a business unit versus the aggregate value of stand-alone component valuations.[22]
- If the company valuation results in a fully distributed minority basis valuation, a conglomerate discount will be applied to the minority basis valuation.

FUZZY LOGIC BETWEEN DISCOUNTS AND VALUATION LEVELS EXAMPLE

- Appendix 48.1 presents a schematic showing the fuzzy logic between the various discounts and valuation levels for baseline valuation methods employed. The highlighted boxed-in values result from the valuation method noted at the top of each column. For example a discounted valuation of a large public company would result in a fully distributed minority value, $100 in the first column. Applicable premiums increase this amount to the indicated increased value levels, and applicable discounts decrease it reflecting the nature of the discount to decreased value levels.

[20] Ibid., pp. 260–268.
[21] Ibid., pp. 263, 264.
[22] Ibid., p. 260.

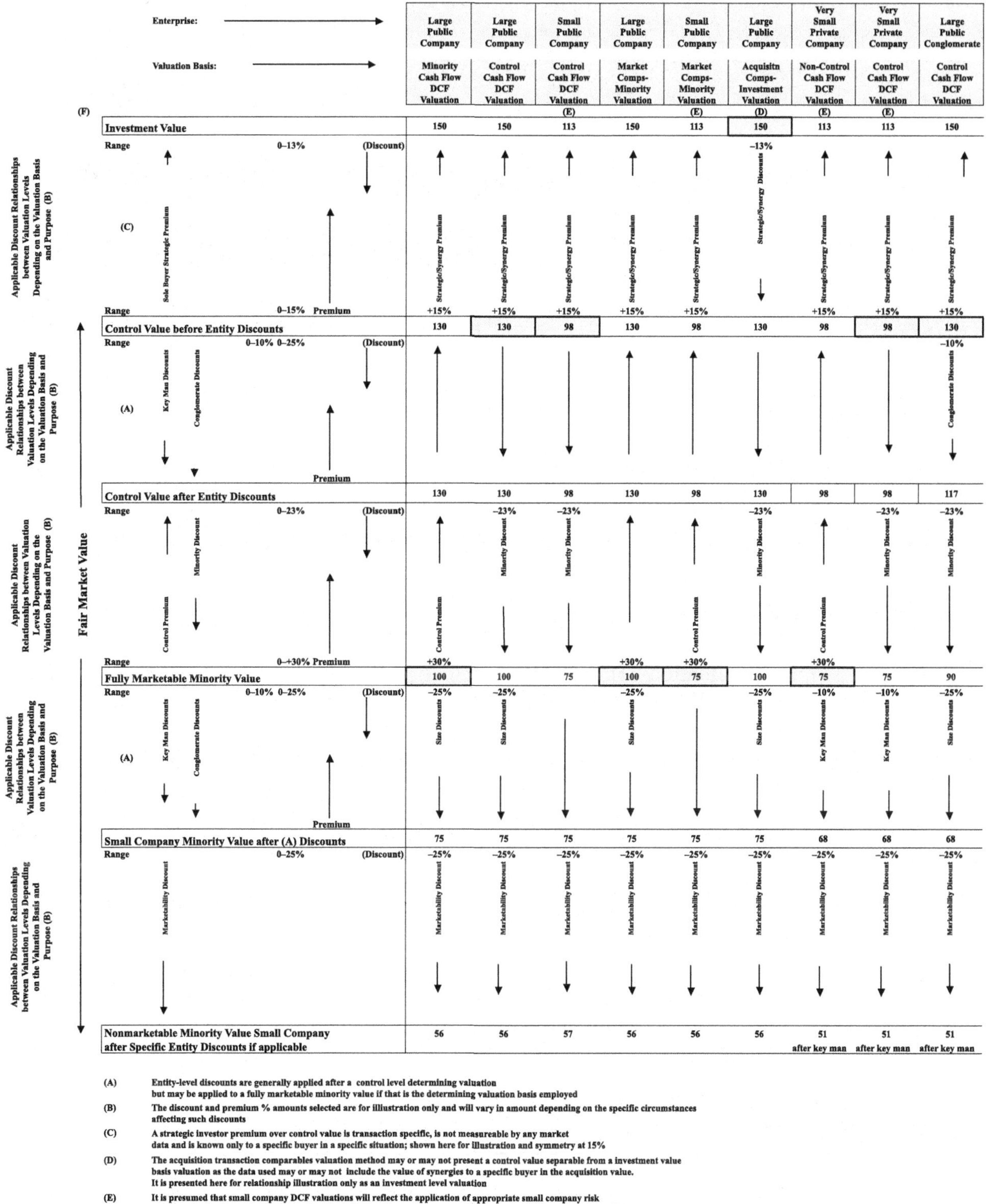

Enterprise:
Large Public Company | Large Public Company | Small Public Company | Large Public Company | Small Public Company | Large Public Company | Very Small Private Company | Very Small Private Company | Large Public Conglomerate
Valuation Basis:
Minority Cash Flow DCF Valuation | Control Cash Flow DCF Valuation | Control Cash Flow DCF Valuation (E) | Market Comps-Minority Valuation | Market Comps-Minority Valuation (E) | Acquisitn Comps-Investment Valuation (D) | Non-Control Cash Flow DCF Valuation (E) | Control Cash Flow DCF Valuation (E) | Control Cash Flow DCF Valuation
(F)
Investment Value: 150 | 150 | 113 | 150 | 113 | 150 | 113 | 113 | 150
Range 0–13% (Discount) | –13%
(C) Sole Buyer Strategic Premium | Strategic/Synergy Premium | Strategic/Synergy Discounts
Range 0–15% Premium: +15% | +15% | +15% | +15% | +15% | | +15% | +15% | +15%
Control Value before Entity Discounts: 130 | 130 | 98 | 130 | 98 | 130 | 98 | 98 | 130
Range 0–10% 0–25% (Discount) | –10%
(A) Key Man Discounts | Conglomerate Discounts | Premium
Control Value after Entity Discounts: 130 | 130 | 98 | 130 | 98 | 130 | 98 | 98 | 117
Range 0–23% (Discount): | –23% | –23% | | | –23% | | –23% | –23%
Control Premium | Minority Discount
Range 0–+30% Premium: +30% | | | +30% | +30% | | +30%
Fully Marketable Minority Value: 100 | 100 | 75 | 100 | 75 | 100 | 75 | 75 | 90
Range 0–10% 0–25% (Discount): –25% | –25% | | –25% | | –25% | –10% | –10% | –25%
(A) Key Man Discounts | Conglomerate Discounts | Size Discounts | Premium
Small Company Minority Value after (A) Discounts: 75 | 75 | 75 | 75 | 75 | 75 | 68 | 68 | 68
Range 0–25% (Discount): –25% | –25% | –25% | –25% | –25% | –25% | –25% | –25% | –25%
Marketability Discount
Nonmarketable Minority Value Small Company after Specific Entity Discounts if applicable: 56 | 56 | 57 | 56 | 56 | 56 | 51 after key man | 51 after key man | 51 after key man
Fair Market Value
Applicable Discount Relationships between Valuation Levels Depending on the Valuation Basis and Purpose (B)
(A) Entity-level discounts are generally applied after a control level determining valuation but may be applied to a fully marketable minority value if that is the determining valuation basis employed
(B) The discount and premium % amounts selected are for illustration only and will vary in amount depending on the specific circumstances affecting such discounts
(C) A strategic investor premium over control value is transaction specific, is not measureable by any market data and is known only to a specific buyer in a specific situation; shown here for illustration and symmetry at 15%
(D) The acquisition transaction comparables valuation method may or may not present a control value separable from a investment value basis valuation as the data used may or may not include the value of synergies to a specific buyer in the acquisition value. It is presented here for relationship illustration only as an investment level valuation
(E) It is presumed that small company DCF valuations will reflect the application of appropriate small company risk premiums in the discount rate construction. By definition, the market comparables methods will also reflect the market pricing risk in the small company pricing multiples
(F) Fair market value can present at any of the value levels illustrated as it is a specific transaction value driven concept

APPENDIX 48.1 Fuzzy Logic between Valuation Levels and Discounts Example

TOPIC 49

Discounted Cash Flow Valuations: Minority or Control

Topic 49 explains why discounted cash flow (DCF) valuations usually result in fully distributed minority value but can result in control value.

DCF VALUATIONS

- DCF valuations of publicly traded (or privately held) businesses generally result in a fully distributed minority value (before marketability discounts) but may result in a fully distributed control value.[1]
- If the cash flows discounted are restated to "control" basis cash flows that capture all the economic effects of exercising control, a fully distributed control value, perhaps investment value, results from the DCF valuation. Financial statements are often re-stated during detail due diligence in a takeover or acquisition after the books have been opened up and the benefits of synergy and removal of duplicative or other costs are identified by the control (acquiring) party.
- Great care must be taken to understand the underlying nature and content of the entity estimated cash flows to determine whether a control or minority value is derived from a DCF of a public company.

DCF VALUATIONS OF PRIVATELY HELD COMPANIES IN ACQUISITIONS

- DCF valuations of privately held businesses in negotiated acquisition transactions generally result in control values as the buyer usually adjusts the expected operating free cash flows to reflect the impact of having control:
  - Excess prior owner salaries and bonuses and other benefits paid by the company are removed.

[1] Shannon P. Pratt, *Business Valuation Body of Knowledge: Exam Review and Professional Reference* (New York: John Wiley & Sons, 1998), p. 47.

  - Prior owner favorite project activities and spending are removed; those of the buyer are inserted.
  - Duplicative overheads and program-related expenses are identified and removed.
  - The synergistic cash flow benefits of plant and facility closure and relocation are identified.
  - The synergistic cash flow benefits of product overlaps, distribution channel, customer and marketing programs are identified.
  - Excess assets are removed.
  - Operating and customer leverage arising from deep overlap with buyer competencies are identified.
  - See Topics 47 and 48.
- Knowledgeable sellers carefully disclose and usually restate historical financial results for such "prior owner preferences" to ensure that expected future free cash flow is not understated in the buyer's valuation exercise and to indicate to the buyer the seller's control value expectations.
- The discount rate used in as-is DCF minority valuations or control valuations should not be different.[2]
- The net effect of exercising control and realizing the impact of integration synergies and platform values results in a buyer's "investment value" (see Topic 47).
  - Buyers hope to pay at or near the bottom of the investment value range and realize most of the synergy value for themselves.
  - Sellers hope to receive a payment equal to the lower-level control value plus some of the synergy values.
  - The negotiation process determines where the final split will be.

[2] Ibid., p. 86.

TOPIC 50

Inflation in DCF Valuations

Topic 50 explores the impact and appropriate treatment of inflation in a discounted cash flow (DCF) valuation.

INCLUDE INFLATION IMPACTS IN DCF VALUATION

- Expected price and cost inflation should be reflected in forward cash flow projections when a nominal cost of capital (versus a real cost of capital excluding inflation) is utilized in a DCF valuation process.
  - The reason for this is that the nominal cost of capital, by definition, includes a nominal inflation component.
  - The inflation component implicit in the unlevered cost of capital,C_U, the leveraged cost of capital,C_L, and the weighted average cost of capital, C^* is found in the risk-free rate, RF (long-term U.S. Treasuries), and in i, the interest rate on debt.
  - RF and i are composed of perceived long-term inflation, approximately 2% to 3%, plus a real return of approximately 1% to 2%.
- The inflation component (in the discount rate) is intended to capture the expected devaluation of the purchasing power of a future value amount.
- Therefore, to derive a meaningful present value of a future cash flow stream, the stream should include the net impact of inflation when a nominal cost of capital is utilized.
- If the projected data used in a DCF valuation exercise are on a real, noninflated basis, when constructing the cost of capital, the nominal cost of capital should be adjusted to a real basis excluding inflation by deducting the implicit inflation factor included in both the risk-free rate and the target's interest rate on debt.
- The equity risk premium component of cost of capital is unaffected by and does not contain an inflation impact and requires no adjustment.
- The reason for this, at least conceptually, is that actual long-term returns on equity and risk-free returns—the components used to derive the equity risk premiums—both contain long-term inflation components.
- Real and nominal basis valuations should result in the same present values.

TOPIC 51

Integration, Alignment, and Synergy Benefits: Plan It Out

Topic 51 explores the necessity of a well-done integration plan, selection of the right people to execute and implement plan initiatives, and the needed organizational commitment to complete the integration effort.

THE STEPS TO DEVELOP THE INTEGRATION PLAN

- Although the effort to effect the integration of two large "equals" into one postmerger operating entity with one new face to the market is more complex and may require more effort than the acquisition and assimilation of a target into the acquirer, the work plan steps outlined in Topic 52 are applicable to both transactions to achieve an effective postclosing operating organization.
- Effective integration alignment of the target into or with the acquirer is a key to identifying and achieving desired synergy benefits.
- *Appoint an integration team* consisting of multidisciplined executive managers from the acquirer and the target (or merger partner).
- *Get the team member resources committed* from their functional superiors to do the following:
  - Work through the integration planning, alignment, and synergy evaluation steps presented in Topic 52 and develop comprehensive agreement on values, strategy, strategic initiatives, culture, organization, management, facilities, and all other alignment elements.
  - Develop a fully aligned postclosing integration work plan to accomplish the identified initiatives (what, when, how, who, where). This is accomplished through the work output of the team and or the cooperation, input, and approval of the merged entities' top management where necessary.
  - Establish achievable milestones and dollar-based measurements of achievement for each synergy initiative identified.
  - Cost out the impact of initiatives and alternatives evaluated—expense and capital requirements.

  - Put the team member work commitments in individual performance and incentive plan goals.
  - Tie team bonus incentives to accomplishment of the plan initiatives and synergy levels realized.
- *Appoint an owner of the integration effort—the team leader.*
  - The team is responsible to the team leader for achievement of results.
  - The team leader must be an excellent facilitator and agenda builder.
  - The team leader must be concerned only with finding the best answer as soon as possible and driving the activities of the team to achieve alignment and realization of synergy benefits.
  - The team leader must be respected and be seen as being an open-minded, fair, analytic, and decisive doer not afraid of recommending or making hard calls on people, options, and priorities.
- *Appoint an integration oversight committee that should:*
  - Track the team's progress closely with progress metrics and milestones.
  - Hold frequent (weekly, monthly) checkpoint meetings.
  - Monitor progress and do not hesitate to make corrections in goals and work plans.
- *Defining and achieving the desired culture,* behavior, values, and a new or combined agenda for the postmerger entity requires:
  - Evolution, not revolution.
  - Culture change and behavior through leadership, inclusion, empowerment, and example, generally not edict.
  - The readiness to quickly eliminate the "tree huggers" who cannot change (e.g., my old way is the only way).
  - Speed, speed, speed.
  - Action at the expense of making mistakes.
  - Moving people who get in the way out of the way.
- See Topic 52 for the essentials of integration alignment and synergy identification and evaluation.

TOPIC 52

Integration, Alignment, and Valuing Synergy Benefits

Topic 52 explores the scope of work required to do effective integration planning and synergy evaluation and the breadth of the issues involved. The integration challenge is to achieve postclosing alignment between the different views of two separate preclosing organizations to ensure achievement of the goals of the newly merged entity (Newco).

The reader is encouraged to take the time to read the text in conjunction with the referenced appendices to gain the appropriate level of understanding of the subject matter discussed in the narrative. Appendices are either presented at the end of this and each remaining Topic or are available for review and download on this book's companion Web site (see the About the Web Site page for login information).

INTRODUCTION-INTEGRATION PLANNING, SYNERGY EVALUATION

- *The basic task in effective integration planning and alignment* is to determine what and who stays and what goes (people and facilities), when (milestones and timelines), and why (strategic and economic benefit) and to eliminate uncertainty and answer "why" questions of employees and constituents. Other tasks are to build support, eliminate rumors, communicate facts, as painful as they may be, and build trust in the management and direction of the company.
- *The basic task in synergy evaluation* is to determine the annual free cash flow effect and net present value (NPV) arising from:
  - cost reduction initiatives associated with redundant facility, capacity, or business function organization, programs and activities,
  - the introduction of "lean enterprise" methods,
  - or market-based initiatives associated with product and marketing advantages arising from new sales to existing or new customers of existing or new products or services.

KEY SUBJECT AREAS REQUIRING ATTENTION

- *Key subject areas requiring attention of the integration team to realize effective integration and realization of the synergy benefits of the posttransaction firm usually encompass the following, which are discussed in the following sections:*
  - Strategy alignment, development, and buy-in
  - Organizational design, management, culture, and policy
  - Communication with all constituencies
  - Capacity and research and development (R&D) facility design
  - Other facility design
  - Business and support function design
  - Market, product, branding, channel, and customer service alignment
  - Technology, intellectual property, and R&D alignment
  - Information technology and management information systems design

STRATEGY ALIGNMENT, DEVELOPMENT, AND BUY-IN

- Synergy identification and evaluation emanates from the initiatives developed from a fully aligned strategic plan conceived by the new management of the Newco. Strategic alignment is particularly necessary for mergers or acquisitions of entities in closely related markets and businesses. (Strategic alignment is also essential for acquisitions of entities in totally unrelated markets and businesses to create a sense of connection and understanding of the overall corporate vision and mission and the contribution expected of each business.)
- Take the time to work through an aligned strategy and identify: where to create value, how to create value, key gaps to be closed, and how to close them. (See Topic 1.)
- The integration team should jointly negotiate the elements of a fully aligned postclosing strategic plan between the two merging or combining companies, Company A and Company B, consisting of the following elements.
  - *Vision and values of Newco* to meet key market and customer strategic initiatives in the views of Company A, Company B, and combined (see Appendix 52.1).
    - Agree on the strategic direction of the served market and customer base and the agreed vision of Newco to complement the market's future.
    - Agree on the core values that will enable Newco to fulfill its vision and how the firm and its employees will conduct business and themselves during its existence.
  - *Newco business mission and mission-critical issues* to fulfill the vision of Newco in the views of Company A, Company B, and combined (see Appendices 52.2 and 52.3).
    - Agree on the mission of Newco.
    - Identify the mission critical market, customer and support/fullfillment issues facing Newco.

- *Newco key strengths, capabilities, and gaps* versus market requirements in the views of Company A, Company B, and combined (see Appendices 52.4 to 52.6).
  - Having identified the critical issues facing Newco, agree on the capabilities required of Newco to deal with the issues
  - Agree on the combined gap that exists between the overall capability requirements and the capabilities of Newco as it is. What capabilities need to changed or be added to close the gap?
- *Strategic initiatives of Newco* to close the strategic gaps, fulfill the business mission, and identify and realize the value of synergies expected of Newco in the views of Company A, Company B, and combined (see Appendix 52.7).
  - Having identified the capability gaps, agree on the initiatives that must be undertaken by Newco to close the capability gaps and the synergistic impact of doing so. What must Newco do to enable performance in its chosen market spaces?
- *Key Newco culture gaps. What culture is needed to complete initiatives and fulfill Newco's mission* in the views of Company A, Company B, and combined (see Appendices 52.8 to 52.10)?
  - Having identified the initiatives required, agree on the culture required of Newco to execute the initiatives.
  - Agree on the combined gap that exists between the culture required and the combined culture of Newco as it is.
  - Agree on what needs to change and the initiatives required to close the culture gaps.
- *Key Newco management capabilities required to meet Newco mission and gaps* versus market requirements in the views of Company A, Company B, and combined (see Appendices 52.11 to 52.13).
  - Having identified the initiatives required, agree on the management capabilities required of Newco to execute the initiatives and conduct the business consistent with its strategic plan.
  - Agree on the combined gap that exists between the management capabilities required and the combined capabilities of Newco as it is.
  - Agree on what needs to change and the initiatives required to close the management capability gaps.
- *Key Newco policy initiatives* to ensure alignment and fulfill the mission in the views of Company A, Company B, and combined (see Appendix 52.14).
  - Agree on the principal employee, customer, vendor, and shareholder policy issues that face Newco and the initiatives required to prepare and adopt new policies that will enable Newco to conduct its business consistent with its strategic plan.
- *Information technology (IT) gaps* and initiatives to meet mission-critical and internal initiatives to fulfill the mission in the views of Company A, Company B, and combined (see Appendices 52.15 to 52.17).
  - Having identified the initiatives required, agree on the IT capabilities required of Newco to execute the initiatives and conduct the business consistent with its strategic plan.

  - Agree on the combined gap that exists between the IT capabilities required and the combined capabilities of Newco as it is.
  - Agree on what needs to change and the initiatives required to close the IT capability gaps.
- Only open-minded, knowledgeable management individuals capable of reaching consensus should participate in the process of working through the strategy alignment development and buy-in process.
- The participants representing each of the merging companies or the acquirer and target should individually and as a group consider all the issues associated with each strategy alignment topic presented earlier and complete the planning formats.
- The participants from both sides should then meet as a group and jointly negotiate final positions representing the best combined solutions for Newco.
- The team leader's diplomacy and decision skills will be fully tested.
- The goal is to achieve integration team buy-in and management resource commitment.
- The earlier the strategy alignment process can take place in the M&A process, the better.
- In mergers of competitive firms, legal and competitive issues may be associated with the exchange of sensitive information that may preclude completing an integration plan before a closing. The plan framework may be designed preclosing, however.
- Consult with legal counsel about which integration plan topics may be undertaken, when, and to what depth prior to closing.
- It is possible to complete some of the identified synergy estimation work by using a firewall consulting firm to gather the relevant data and perform reasonable estimates of the synergy potential for various initiative options that may not be discussed jointly prior to the closing (see Topic 9).

ORGANIZATIONAL DESIGN, MANAGEMENT, CULTURE, AND POLICY

- What is the best organization and culture required to achieve the strategic initiatives; where are the management weaknesses; what are the culture issues between the combining companies; what are the policy issues?
- The next steps may be used in the determination of the management organizational design. The chief executive officer (CEO) of the posttransaction merged firm can lead this effort and often retains an organizational design consultant experienced in the process.

  Step 1. Start at the top of the organization and work down one level below direct reports to the CEO.

  Step 2. Develop position description and requirements definitions (experience, education, motivated ability characteristics required, etc).

  Step 3. Develop market-based compensation packages, considering both sides' current plans with a high level of performance-based incentive pay.

Step 4. Post the position requirements and how internal applicants may respond.

Step 5. Conduct interviews for the open positions reporting to the CEO.

Step 6. After management selection and acceptance, the CEO's direct reports should resolve their direct report requirements in a similar fashion.

Step 7. Consider employee retention issues and incentives to stay, see a deal through, and gain employee sign-on.

- Certain acquisitions may require somewhat less effort in this area if the management organization of the acquirer is in place and is going to absorb and operate the target.
- The CEO of the acquirer may want to assess Newco's management in light of all potential candidates available from the target and the acquirer. In this case, assessment may be assisted using the format in Appendix 52.11.
- Merger or joint venture partners may want to assess Newco's management in light of all potential candidates available from the two organizations. In this case, assessment may be assisted using the formats in Appendices 52.11, 52.12, and 52.13, which require the top management of each side to negotiate and determine the best next-level management team for Newco.
- The integration team should assess culture of Newco to determine if there are significant cultural differences in the integrating organizations and to determine the culture gaps that need to be addressed to best meet the needs of the customer and marketplace and execute the identified initiatives. The formats and work steps on Appendices 52.8, 52.9, and 52.10 require the management of each side to identify the cultural gaps and negotiate the desired culture for Newco.
- Management will want to consider employee benefit plan design for the post-transaction firm considering location, market, and competitive design and affordability (see Appendix 52.14).
- Other policy issue initiatives may also be dealt with in Appendix 52.14.

COMMUNICATION

- Develop a deal prospectus and white paper to ensure consistent communication of the key issues. To each constituency group before and after the closing and during integration. Issues include:
  - Description of the target and business
  - Strategic rationale for the deal: why, what for, when
  - Management team design: who is who as the organization evolves
  - Strategic plan for Newco as it evolves
  - Key conditions to the deal closing
- Communicate early and regularly with the vested constituency groups, including:
  - Employees
  - Customers
  - Vendors

  - Local community
  - Governmental and regulatory bodies
- The goals are to eliminate uncertainty, answer "why" questions, build support, eliminate rumors, communicate facts as painful as they may be, and build trust as decisions are made.
- When available, communicate the integration plan, strategic and tactical goals and milestones, and dates to all employees and follow up on status weekly following the closing.

CAPACITY, R&D PROJECT, AND FACILITY SELECTION DESIGN

- Capacity-related synergies are determined by performing a net present value (NPV) analysis of alternative plant, capacity, and facility closure possibilities. (These analyses are often done behind a firewall.)
- These steps may be used to determine of economic synergies in conjunction with the strategic initiative determination activities as presented earlier:

Step 1. Determine total plant capacity and facility support requirements to meet the strategic plan.

Step 2. Compare the strategic plan capacity and support requirements with the current available combined plant-by-plant capacity and with other available support facility posttransaction capacity.

Step 3. Evaluate the impact on customer satisfaction, product mix, unit cost, and so forth of the continuance, discontinuance, or consolidation of technologies and other projects in the production and R&D processes using NPV and real option analysis: which to keep, which to stop.

Step 4. Develop comparative plant production and R&D facility cost profiles and unit cost or throughput metrics to determine the most cost effective as-is facility.

Step 5. Include direct labor rates, union impacts, indirect labor rates, overhead cost structure, taxes, utilities, and so forth.

Step 6. Evaluate vendor sourcing, unit cost, and overhead benefits resulting from larger purchasing requirements.

Step 7. Evaluate the state of progress of lean enterprise management at each facility and areas of improvement.

Step 8. Utilize the cost of production metrics associated with each site, where appropriate, to complete the cost profile for each closure alternative.

Step 9. Consider alternative plant closure and expansion of alternative plants, adding new capacity and costs and capital spending requirements, transferring equipment from the closed plant and reinstallation costs, relocation costs for employees, severance, training, utilities, taxes, overhead cost structures, supervisory and plant management organizational cost structures, benefit design and cost structures, leased facility exit costs, environmental remediation impacts and costs, and so forth.

Step 10. Develop plant consolidation alternatives based on closing alternative plants and moving to the alternate locations (e.g., move A capacity to B and close A) (or maintaining both if appropriate).

Step 11. Develop NPVs of the resulting capital and net expense savings streams for each alternative considered.

- Community impacts may be material as well.
- Environmental impacts of plant closure may be significant and require great attention.
- The alternative with the greatest NPV should present itself.
- See the comparative example analysis in Appendices 52.18 and 52.19, where the NPV benefit of closing plant B and moving to plant A is preferred to the reverse.

OTHER FACILITY SYNERGY DESIGN

- Headquarters, distribution, or service center or other facility design will follow an alternative closure analysis similar to the capacity-related steps just discussed.

BUSINESS AND SUPPORT FUNCTION SYNERGY DESIGN

- Determine combined synergy benefits related to business support functions (accounting, treasury and finance, information technology, human resources, legal, etc.) by performing a side-by-side analysis of the organization required to support the posttransaction firm versus the combined organization prior to consolidation and an NPV analysis of alternative organizational and location possibilities similar to that done for the alternative plant closure process just discussed.
- Use the next steps in the determination of combined synergy benefits in conjunction with the strategy design process discussed earlier:

Step 1. Compare posttransaction support staff, output, and organizational requirements with the combined organization staffing levels.

Step 2. Develop comparative support function cost profiles and metrics to determine the most cost-effective as-is support organization and cost structure. Include hourly and salary rates, union impacts, overhead and benefit-by-benefit cost structures, taxes, utilities, and so forth.

Step 3. Consider the state of progress of lean enterprise management at each support facility.

Step 4. Develop support function consolidation options based on closing support organizational sites and moving to the alternate locations. Identify the capital, expense, and savings streams associated with each alternative.

Step 5. Utilize the cost metrics associated with each alternative site where appropriate to complete the cost profile for each closure alternative.

Step 6. Consider the impact of adding new organizational support costs and capital spending requirements required to support the new organization, moving support or processing equipment from the closed location, relocation costs for employees, severance, training, utilities, taxes, overhead cost structures, residual supervisory and management organizational cost structures, benefit design and cost structures, leased facility exit costs, and so on.

Step 7. Develop NPVs of the resulting capital and net expense savings streams for each alternative considered.

- Community impacts may be material as well.
- The alternative with the greatest NPV should present itself.
- See the comparative example analysis in Appendices 52.20 and 52.21, where the NPV of closing support facility B and moving to facility A is preferred to the reverse.

MARKET, CUSTOMER-BASED SYNERGIES

- *Market-based synergies* associated with branding, market channel access, service and product issues focus on the amount of expected sales or service of existing or new product or services to new or existing markets through new or existing channels arising from the joint customer initiatives identified in Appendix 52.7.
- Joint post acquisition initiatives leading to new sales and services may include:
  - Product differentiation strategies
  - Low-cost provider strategies
  - Technology innovator or follower strategies
  - Trend innovator or follower strategies
  - Style innovator or follower strategies
  - New features
  - New services
  - Acquired product/services through buyer channels
  - Buyer product/services through acquired channels
  - Bundled product and service offerings
  - Pricing strategies
  - Sales financing strategies
- Lost sales may result as initiatives are implemented, which should be considered.
- Identify the related product margin and related variable selling and distribution costs.
- Identify the capital spent and working capital required to support the new sales levels.
- Develop NPVs of the net free cash flow streams arising from the new sales.
- Evaluate the implications of maintaining or consolidating overlapping products and services.

TECHNOLOGY, INTELLECTUAL PROPERTY, AND R&D

- Effort must be made to evaluate and justify the cost and investment of supporting noncomplementary technologies, intellectual property (IP), and related R&D projects under way versus current and evolving market and customer requirements, current and future product offerings, and branding per the joint customer initiatives identified in Appendix 52.7.
- In cases where the both noncomplementary technology and IP investment streams should continue, justify the synergy impact of doing so by market-based synergies.
- In cases where a technology and IP choice can be made to support the joint market and customer initiatives identified in Appendix 52.7, choices should be made.
- Justify the synergy impact by following an alternative closure analysis similar to the capacity-related synergies steps discussed earlier and in Appendices 52.18 and 52.19.

INFORMATION TECHNOLOGY

- The following evaluation guidelines may be considered in the determination of potentially appropriate Information Technology platforms.
- Evaluate the postclosing IT platforms, given the desired organizational and geographic design and strategic implications and goals of the postmerger firm. Consider these approaches.
- *If the acquiring Newco is a holding company of unaffiliated entities* in differentiated businesses with little overlap with other entities:
  - Consider continuation of the existing (or, if needed and justified, new decentralized and often different from the unafilliated entities) mission-critical IT platforms designed for the operational system support requirements of each business, including the acquired target. Generally there is no economic advantage in having mission-critical operational systems the same in differentiated unafilliated businesses.
  - For business unit financial and metric reporting systems, consider (but not critical) a common (with the holding company) and integrated (with the business unit system general ledger) reporting engine for financial reporting to the holding company. Standard financial and performance metric reporting formats can also be a satisfactory solution.
  - The business unit IT director and staff should report to the business unit with a secondary matrix reporting relationship to the holding company IT director for best practices, development, and policy integration matters.
  - This often means staying with the acquired business system if it serves the mission critical operating needs of the business unit well or, if change is needed, implementing a system best matched with the operating requirements of the business unit (not the holding company) and considering the implementation of a common reporting engine only.

- *If the postclosing Newco is a holding company of closely affiliated plants, entities, or divisions in the same or very similar businesses,* with capability overlap, common business processes, and therefore common business system support requirements:
  - Consider decentralized implementation and utilization of the common mission-critical IT platform of the acquirer (software and hardware may be centrally operated and supported), including an integrated metric and financial reporting engine for reporting to the business unit and the holding company.
  - The business unit IT director and staff should report to the business unit with a secondary matrix reporting relationship to the holding company IT director for best practices, development, and policy integration matters.
  - This often means discontinuing the acquired business system at some point in the integration process and implementing the common mission-critical IT platform.
- *If the postclosing Newco is an integrated multiplant/location operating company of closely affiliated decentralized plants, entities, or divisions in the same businesses,* with capability overlap, common business processes, interplant transactions, and therefore common business system support requirements:
  - Consider decentralized implementation and utilization of the common mission-critical IT platform of the acquirer (software and hardware may be centrally operated and supported), including an integrated metric and financial reporting engine.
  - Where needed to support decentralized plants, entities, or divisions, IT director and staff should report to the decentralized plant unit with a secondary matrix reporting relationship to the operating company IT director for best practices, development, and policy integration matters.
  - This often means discontinuing an acquired business system at some point in the integration process and implementing the common mission-critical IT platform.
- Getting the right answer to the postclosing IT issue is critical to the success of the postclosing strategic plan. Getting it wrong often results in very disruptive, costly consequences, or worse. See Topic 98 for the reasons deals succeed or fail.
- The formats of Appendices 52.15, 52.16, and 52.17 may be used to jointly assess the IT capability gaps and initiatives of Newco versus those required to meet the needs of the market and support other Newco initiatives.

The following Appendices are available for viewing or download on the Web site for this book at: www.wiley.com/go/emott. Please see the About the Web Site page at the back of this book for login information.

APPENDIX 52.1 Newco Business Vision and Values: Company A, Company B, and Combined

APPENDIX 52.2 Newco Business Mission: Company A, Company B, and Combined

APPENDIX 52.3 Mission-Critical Issues: Company A, Company B, and Combined

APPENDIX 52.4 Newco Key Strengths, Capabilities, and Gaps: Company A

APPENDIX 52.5 Newco Key Strengths, Capabilities, and Gaps: Company B

APPENDIX 52.6 Newco Key Strengths and Capabilities: Negotiated Combined View

APPENDIX 52.7 Strategic Initiatives of Newco: Company A, Company B, and Combined View

APPENDIX 52.8 Newco Culture Gap: Company A View

APPENDIX 52.9 Newco Culture Gap: Company B View

APPENDIX 52.10 Newco Culture Gap: Combined View

APPENDIX 52.11 Newco Management Capabilities: Company A View

APPENDIX 52.12 Newco Management Capabilities: Company B View

APPENDIX 52.13 Newco Management Capabilities: Combined View

APPENDIX 52.14 Key Newco Policy Initiatives: Company A, Company B, and Combined View

APPENDIX 52.15 Newco IT Capabilities Requirement Gaps: Company A View

APPENDIX 52.16 Newco IT Capabilities Requirement Gaps: Company B View

APPENDIX 52.17 Newco IT Capabilities Requirement Gaps: Combined View

APPENDIX 52.18 Close Plant B

APPENDIX 52.19 Close Plant A

APPENDIX 52.20 Close Facility B

APPENDIX 52.21 Close Facility A

TOPIC 53

Venture Capital Valuation

Topic 53 explores the goals of venture capital (VC) investors and the fundamental approach often used in the valuation of investment opportunities.

VC INVESTOR INTERESTS, RETURN TARGETS: AN EXAMPLE

- VC investors are concerned with these issues:
  - *The amount of cash made available* by the VC investor to finance a deal *in exchange for a percentage of the target's equity* and when the investment is expected to be returned resulting from a sale or initial public offering (IPO) of the business.
  - *The amount of equity placed at risk by the original owner manager* to finance an opportunity (and the amount of debt that a deal can attract).
  - The VC investor's *exit risk,* which is the perceived *level of attractiveness* of the target's marketplace to the public equity or private sale markets.
  - The *strength of the target's management.*
  - The *marketing, product, and operational effectiveness* of the target.
- Depending on risk assessment, VC investors (VCIs) will seek returns on their investments to compensate them for the perceived equity risk undertaken.
- VC returns to equity are often expressed as a range, depending on the stage of financing:[1]
  - *First-stage financing* is higher risk than financing in subsequent stages because it takes place without any commercial record of success for the target and commands a higher target return and a larger share of the equity. Such returns also reflect the fact that a certain number of investments (in a venture capital investor's portfolio) often fail as the start-up business does not succeed.
  - Generally, venture capital investors will provide the seed capital necessary for the venture to demonstrate commercial viability. Venture capital investors generally do not continue to finance continued operating losses in an attempt to reach commercial viability over extended time frames.

[1] For a discussion of the methodology illustrated here and examples of other VC investment valuation approaches, see Mark Cameron White, "Business Valuation Techniques and Negotiation," White & Lee, White Papers, 2002–2003, www.whiteandlee.com/papers_transactions_bvtn.html.

- *Second- and third-stage financing* occurs after commercial viability is demonstrated.
- The eventual exit event can be a sale to a strategic or financial buyer or an IPO.
- See Illustration 53.1 for the ranges of return generally required with the stage of the financing.

ILLUSTRATION 53.1 VENTURE CAPITAL TARGET RETURNS AND STAGE OF FINANCING

	VC Target	
Stage of Investment	Pretax Internal Rate of Return	Investment Return Convention Terms
First	115%	10 times investment in 3 years
	71%	5 times investment in 3 years
	50%	10 times investment in 5 years
Second	48%	7 times investment in 5 years
	38%	5 times investment in 5 years
Third	31%	3 times investment in 4 years
	26%	4 times investment in 6 years

- *The percentage equity share sought by the VCI* at the time of the investment is often determined by dividing the VCI's target exit amounts (original investment sought plus target return) by the expected company equity value at the exit date (see Illustration 53.2), the so-called hockey stick approach.[2]

ILLUSTRATION 53.2 VENTURE CAPITAL INVESTMENT

VCI Goal: 5 times investment in 5 years (a 38% pretax internal rate of return to the VCI)

Capital sought by the enterprise owner at time of VC investment: $5 million

	Year				
	1	2	3	4	5
Target EBITDA Forecast $000	–200	400	800	2,000	4,000

(Continued)

[2] Ibid.

Exit EBITDA multiple at the end of year 5[a]	Low	18
	High	22
Exit Equity Value (EBITDA multiple)	Lo (18 × $4,000) =	$72,000
Exit Equity Value (EBITDA multiple)	Hi (22 × $4,000) =	$88,000
VC Target Return Total Takeout[b]	$000	25,000
VC Equity Share[c]	High	34.7%
VC Equity Share[d]	Low	28.5%

Conclusion: The VCI will seek between 29% and 35% of the equity of the target to invest $5 million today, which will result in returns at exit equal to VCI target return on investment of five times investment in five years, or an internal rate of return of 38%.

[a] The earnings before interest, tax, depreciation, and amortization (EBITDA) multiples for purposes of value determination come from an analysis of comparable public company IPO or sale transactions. The target exit value is calculated by multiplying the exit year EBITDA times the comparable EBITDA multiple as illustrated.

[b] VC Target Return Calculation:	Capital Invested		Target Return		VC Target Takeout
5 times in 5 years	5,000	×	5	=	25,000

OR

VC Target Return Calculation:	Capital Invested				VC Target Takeout
	5,000	×	1.38^5	=	25,025

[c] Return Exit Equity Value $\frac{25{,}000}{72{,}000} = 34.7\%$

[d] Return Exit Equity Value $\frac{25{,}000}{88{,}000} = 28.5\%$

- VC returns targets are expressed on a pretax basis to the principals in the VC fund. Such funds usually are organized as limited partnerships where the returns realized by the fund are passed through to the limited partner investors for tax purposes and are often taxed as long-term capital gains.

TOPIC 54

Discount Rates and Valuing Free Cash Flow

Topic 53 explores the variety of assumptions that can be made regarding when an annual cash flow amount is received during the year (beginning, end, middle) and the computational adjustments required to the nominal discount rate to properly reflect the impact of the timing of the cash flow on the cash flow valuation.

OVERVIEW

- Discount rates can reflect very different assumptions regarding the timing of the receipt of free cash flow (FCF) during an annual period. Discount rates are computationally adjusted to reflect the timing assumption. Valuation results vary significantly depending on the discount rate construction.

YEAR-END DISCOUNT RATES

- Discount rates in many discounted cash flows (DCFs) or perpetuity DCF calculations are often stated as (and generally known as) year-end rates.
- *Year-end discount rates* by convention value the stated annual cash flow amount in the DCF as if it occurs at the *last moment* on the *last day* of each annual period (N) as shown next:

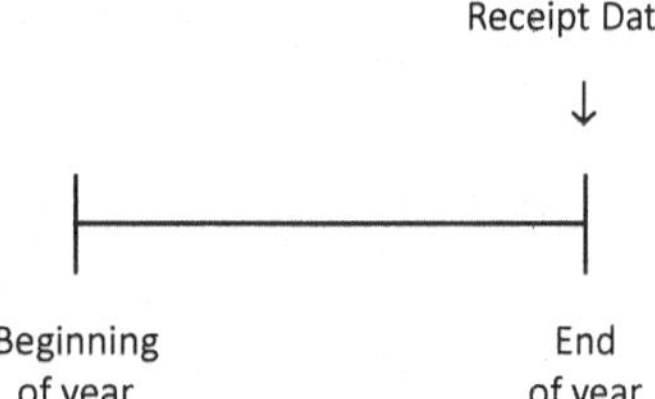

- Year-end discount rates are determined as shown for any year N:

$$\frac{1}{(1+r)^N}$$

where r = annual discount rate
N = year 1, 2, 3 ...

- The end-of-year basis discount rate convention will result in the smallest valuation versus the other conventions as the cash is presumed to be received at the end of each annual period.

- Illustration 54.1 calculates the year-end basis annual discount rate for any year N where r = 10%. The valuation of an annual cash flow of $1,000 for each year indicated is also presented.

ILLUSTRATION 54.1 YEAR-END BASIS DISCOUNT RATE AND THE VALUATION OF $1,000 ANNUAL CASH FLOW (ROUNDED)

	Year 1	Year 2	Year 3	...	Year 20...
	$\frac{1}{(1.1)^1}$	$\frac{1}{(1.1)^2}$	$\frac{1}{(1.1)^3}$	...	$\frac{1}{(1.1)^{20}}$
	.9091	.8264	.7513	...	.1486
FCF	$1,000.00	$1,000.00	$1,000.00		$1,000.00
Value	$909.09	$826.40	$751.30		$148.60

- Alternatively, discount rates for years after year 1 may be determined by dividing each preceding period's discount rate by 1 + r as shown next for years 2, 3, and so on:

$$\text{Year } 2 = .9091/1.10 = .8264$$

$$\text{Year } 3 = .8264/1.10 = .7513$$

- The year 1 valuation may also be interpreted as valuing $1,000 of cash flow received at the end of year 1, plus interest at 10% annual rate of $0 (1,000 $((1 + .10)^0)$) totaling $1,000, by applying a 10% end-of-year discount rate of .9090909 $(1/((1 + .10)^1))$ to the total year 1 annual cash flow amount ($1,000). This is equivalent to $909.09 at the beginning of year 1, the measurement date ($1000 × .90909).
- The year 2 valuation may also be interpreted as valuing $1,000 of cash flow received at the end of year 2, plus zero interest at 10% annual rate of $0 (1,000 $((1 + .10)^0)$) totaling $1,000, by applying a 10% end-of-year discount rate of .8264 (equal to (.9090909/1.1)) to the a total year 2 annual cash flow amount ($1,000). This is equivalent to $826.40 at the beginning of year 1, the measurement date ($1,000 × .8264).

- Operating cash flows usually occur throughout the year.
- Discount rate conventions other than year-end basis discount rates are available to simulate and capture the time value effect of cash flows occurring during the year and are discussed next.

BEGINNING-OF-YEAR DISCOUNT RATES

- *Beginning-of-year discount rates* by convention value the stated annual cash flow amount as if it all occurs at the *first moment* on the *first day* of each annual period and earns interest at the stated nominal rate from the point of receipt to the end of the year, as shown.

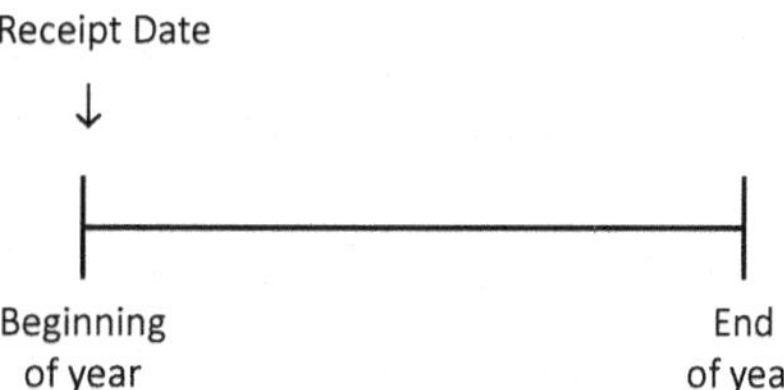

- Beginning-of-year rates are determined as shown for any year N:

$$\frac{1}{(1+r)^{N-1}}$$

where r = annual discount rate
N = year 1, 2, 3 ....

- For year 1, the beginning-of-year discount rate is 1.0 as the Year 1 cash flow is assumed to occur at the present value measurement date, the beginning of year 1.
- The beginning-of-year basis discount rate convention will result in the largest valuation result versus the other conventions as the cash is presumed to be received at the beginning of each annual period.
- Illustration 54.2 is a calculation of beginning-of-year basis annual discount rate for any year N where r = 10%. The valuation of an annual cash flow of $1,000 for each year indicated is also presented.

ILLUSTRATION 54.2 BEGINNING-OF-YEAR BASIS DISCOUNT RATE AND THE VALUATION OF $1,000 ANNUAL CASH FLOW (ROUNDED)

	Year 1	Year 2	Year 3	...	Year 20...
	1.0	$\frac{1}{(1.1)^{2-1}}$	$\frac{1}{(1.1)^{3-1}}$	...	$\frac{1}{(1.1)^{20-1}}$
	1.0	$\frac{1}{(1.1)^{1}}$	$\frac{1}{(1.1)^{2}}$	...	$\frac{1}{(1.1)^{19}}$
	1.0	.9090	.8264	...	.1635
FCF	$1,000.00	$1,000.00	$1,000.00		$1,000.00
Value	$1,000.00	$909.90	$826.40		$163.50

- Alternatively, discount rates for years after year 1 may be determined by dividing each preceding period's discount rate by 1 + r as noted for years 2 and 3:

$$\text{Year 2} = 1.000/1.10 = .9090$$

$$\text{Year 3} = .9090/1.10 = .8264$$

- The year 1 valuation may also be interpreted as valuing \$1,000 of cash flow received at the beginning of year 1 plus a full year's interest of \$100 at 10% annual rate (1000 $((1 + .10)^1)$), totaling \$1,100, by applying a 10% end-of-year discount rate of .9090909 (equal to $1/((1+.10)^1)$) to the total year 1 annual cash flow amount (\$1,100) which is equivalent to \$1,000 at the beginning of year 1, the measurement date (\$1100 × .90909).
- The year 2 valuation may also be interpreted as valuing \$1,000 of cash flow received at the beginning of year 2 plus a full year's interest of \$100 at 10% annual rate (1000 $((1 + .10)^1)$), totaling \$1,100, by applying a 10% end-of-year discount rate as at the end of period 2 of .826446 (equal to 9090909/ (1 + .10) (or $9090909/(1/(1 + .1)^2)$, to the total year 2 annual cash flow amount (\$1,100), which is equivalent to \$909.90 at the beginning of year 1, the measurement date (\$1,100 × .826446).

MIDYEAR DISCOUNT RATES

- *Midyear annual discount rates* by convention value the stated annual cash flow amount as if it all occurs in the *middle of the annual period* and earns interest at the stated nominal rate from the point of receipt to the end of the year, as shown.

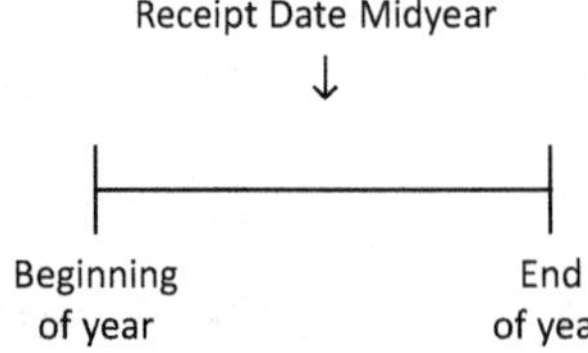

- Midyear rates are determined as shown for any year N:

$$\frac{1}{(1+r)^{N-.5}}$$

where r = annual discount rate
N = year 1, 2, 3 . . .

- The midyear basis discount rate convention will result in a valuation result that is approximately midway between the beginning-of-year and end-of-year conventions, as the cash is presumed to be received midway through each annual period.
- Illustration 54.3 is a calculation of a midyear basis annual discount rate for any year N where r = 10%. The valuation of an annual cash flow of \$1,000 for each year indicated is also presented.

ILLUSTRATION 54.3 MIDYEAR BASIS DISCOUNT RATE AND THE VALUATION OF $1,000 ANNUAL CASH FLOW (ROUNDED)

	Year 1	Year 2	Year 3	...	Year 20
	$=\frac{1}{(1.1)^{1-.5}}$	$\frac{1}{(1.1)^{2-.5}}$	$\frac{1}{(1.1)^{3-.5}}$		$\frac{1}{(1.1)^{20-.5}}$
	$=\frac{1}{(1.1)^{.5}}$	$\frac{1}{(1.1)^{1.5}}$	$\frac{1}{(1.1)^{2.5}}$		$\frac{1}{(1.1)^{19.5}}$
	= .9535	.8668	.7880		.1559
FCF	$1,000.00	$1,000.00	$1,000.00		$1,000.00
Value	$953.50	$866.80	$788.00		$155.90

- Alternatively, discount rates for years after year 1 may be determined by dividing each preceding period discount rate by 1 + r as shown for years 2 and 3:

$$\text{Year } 2 = .9535/1.10 = .8668$$

$$\text{Year } 3 = .8668/1.10 = .7879$$

- The year 1 valuation may also be interpreted as valuing $1,000 of cash flow received midperiod of year 1, plus interest at 10% annual rate from the point of receipt of $48.81 [(1000 ((1 + .10)$^{.5}$)) totaling $1,048.81 at the end of year 1, a composite yield of 4.881%], by applying an end-of-year discount rate of .9090909 (equal to 1/((1+.04881)^2) to the total year 1 annual cash flow amount of $1,048.81, which equals $953.46 at the beginning of year 1, the measurement date ($1,048.81 × .90909). (The composite yield is squared to derive an end-of-year discount rate equivalent as the composite yield was derived based on collection approximately midway during the year.)
- The year 2 valuation may also be interpreted as valuing $1,000 of cash flow received midperiod of year 2, plus interest at 10% annual rate from the point of receipt of $48.81 [(1000 ((1 + .10)$^{.5}$)) totaling $1,048.81 at the end of year 2, a composite yield of 4.881%], by applying an end-of-year discount rate at the end of period 2 of .82644 (equal to .9090909/(1 + .10), or 1/((1 + .04881)^2)^2 to the total year 1 annual cash flow amount of $1,048.81,which equals $866.78 at the beginning of year 1, the measurement date ($1,048.81 × .826446).

QUARTERLY DISCOUNT RATES

- *Quarterly discount rates* by convention value the stated annual cash flow assuming it occurs in four equal amounts at the end of each of four equal periods during the year and earns interest at the stated nominal rate from the point of receipt to the end of the year, as shown next.

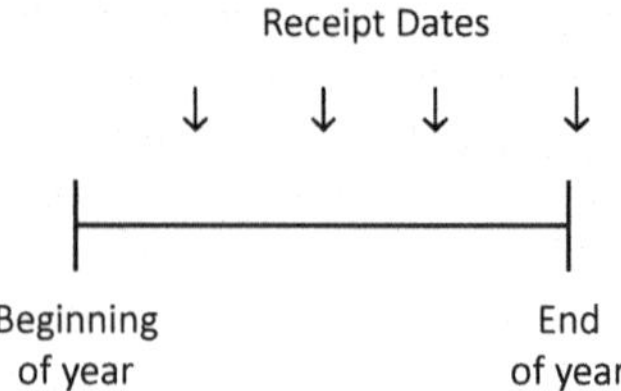

- Quarterly basis annual discount rates may be determined as shown for any year N:

$$\textbf{Year 1 rate} = \frac{1}{1+\left[+\sum_{P=1}^{N-1}\left[1/N\left[(1+r)^{1/N}\right]^{P}\right]\right]}$$

$$\textbf{Subsequent rates for years N} = \left[\frac{\text{Year (N} - 1\text{)Rate}}{(1+r)}\right]$$

where P = number of quarterly compounding periods (1, 2, or 3) associated with each quarter's collection during the year (The fourth-period collection is at the end of the annual period.)
N = number of cash flow collection periods in year 4
r = annual rate of return

- The quarterly basis discount rate convention will result in a valuation result that is approximately midway between the beginning-of-year and end-of-year conventions as the cash is presumed to be received quarterly throughout each annual period.
- Illustration 54.4 is a calculation of a quarterly basis annual discount rate for any year N where r = 10%. The valuation of an annual cash flow of $1,000 for each year indicated is also presented.

ILLUSTRATION 54.4 QUARTERLY BASIS DISCOUNT RATE AND THE VALUATION OF $1,000 ANNUAL CASH FLOW (ROUNDED)

Year 1 rate =			Weight	(1/N) Weighted Average
• First collection period, P = 3	$\left[(1.10)^{1/4}\right]^{3}$	= 1.074099	× .25	= .018525
(end of first quarter, three quarterly compounding periods available until year-end)				

- Second collection period, P = 2 $\left[(1.10)^{1/4}\right]^2$ = 1.048809 × .25 = .012202
  (end of second quarter, two quarterly compounding periods available until year-end)
- Third collection period, P = 1 $\left[(1.10)^{1/4}\right]^1$ = 1.024114 × .25 = .006028
  (end of third quarter, one quarterly compounding period available until year end)

Subtotal .036755

- Plus 1 representing the collection at the end of the last quarter

1.000000

Total 1.036755

Year 1 rate $= \dfrac{1}{1.036755}$

Year 1 rate = .964548

$$\textbf{Subsequent rates for years N} = \left[\frac{\text{Year (N} - 1\text{) Rate}}{(1+r)}\right]$$

where N = year 2, 3, 4, ... etc.
r = annual rate of return

Year 2 rate $= \left[\dfrac{\text{Year }(2-1)\text{ rate}}{(1+r)}\right] = \left[\dfrac{\text{Year 1 Rate}}{(1+r)}\right]$

Year 2 rate $= \dfrac{.964548}{1.10}$

Year 2 rate = .87686

Year 3 rate $= \left[\dfrac{\text{Year }(3-1)\text{ rate}}{(1+r)}\right] = \left[\dfrac{\text{Year 2 Rate}}{(1+r)}\right]$

Year 3 rate $= \dfrac{.87686}{(1.10)}$

Year 3 rate = .79715

Year 1	Year 2	Year 3	...	Year 20
$1,000.00	$1,000.00	$1,000.00	...	$1,000.00

And so on for subsequent years.

Valuation of $1,000 Annual Cash Flow (Rounded)

FCF Value	$964.50	$876.80	$797.10	$157.71

- The year 1 valuation may also be interpreted as valuing $1,000 of cash flow received in four equal amounts of $250 at the end of each of four equal periods during year 1, plus interest at 10% annual rate from the point of receipt of $36.76 (below) totaling $1036.76 at the end of year 1,

(Continued)

a composite yield of 3.6756%, by applying an end-of-year discount rate of .930352 (equal to $1/(1 + .03676)^2$) to the total cash flow of $1,036.76, which equals $964.55 at the beginning of year 1, the measurement date ($1,036.71 × .930352).

- The first $250 received at the beginning of the second of four periods will earn interest of $18.52 ($1000/4(((1 + .10)^{.25})^3)$) totaling $268.52 at the end of year 1.
- The next $250 received at the beginning of the third of four periods will earn interest of $12.20 ($1000/4(((1+.10)^{.25})^2)$) totaling $262.20 at the end of year 1.
- The next $250 received at the beginning of the fourth of four periods will earn interest of $6.03 ($1000/4(((1+.10)^{.25})^1)$) totaling $256.03 at the end of year 1.
- The last $250 is received at the end of the year and earns no interest during the year.
- $18.52 + $12.20 + $6.03 = $36.76 total interest.

- The year 2 valuation may also be interpreted as valuing $1,000 of cash flow received in four equal amounts at the end of each of four equal periods of year 2, plus interest at 10% annual rate from the point of receipt of $36.76 totaling $1,036.76 at the end of year 2, a composite yield of 3.6756%, by applying an end-of-year discount rate of .84578 (equal to .930352/(1+.10)) to the total cash flow of $1,036.76, which equals $876.86 at the beginning of year 1, the measurement date ($1,036.76 × .84578).

MONTHLY DISCOUNT RATES

- *"Monthly basis" discount rates* by convention value the stated annual cash flow amount as if it occurs in *equal amounts* at the end of *each of 12 periods* during the year and earns interest at the stated nominal rate from the point of receipt to the end of the year.

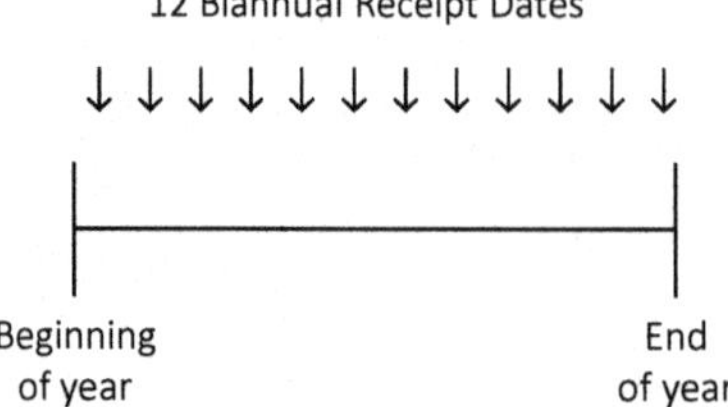

- The first year's monthly basis discount rate is determined using the same method as indicated for first year's quarterly basis discount rates.

where P = collection period (1,2,3,4 . . . 11) during the first year (The 12th period collection is at the end of the annual period.)
N = number of collection periods in the first year, 12

- The monthly basis discount rate convention will result in a valuation result that is approximately midway between the beginning-of-year and end-of-year conventions as the cash is presumed to be received monthly throughout each annual period.
- Subsequent year discount rates are determined using the same method as indicated for quarterly basis discount rates.

DAILY DISCOUNT RATES

- *"Daily basis" discount rates* by convention value the stated annual cash flow amount as if it occurs in equal amounts at the last moment of each of 365 equal periods during the year and earns interest at the stated nominal rate from the point of receipt to the end of the year as shown next.

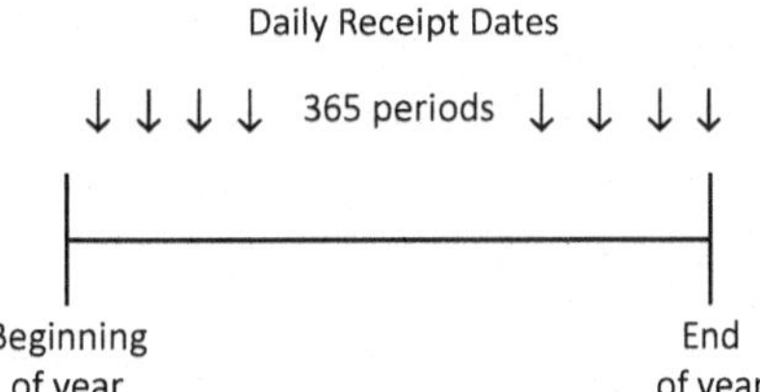

- The first year's daily basis discount rate is determined using the same method as indicated for first year's quarterly basis discount rates.

where P = collection period 1,2,3,4,5 . . . 364 during the first year (The 365th period collection is at the end of the annual period.)
N = number of collection periods in the first year, 365

- Subsequent year discount rates are determined using the same method as indicated for quarterly basis discount rates.
- The daily basis discount rate convention will result in a valuation result that is approximately midway between the beginning-of-year and end-of-year conventions as the cash is presumed to be received at the end of each day through out each annual period.

CONTINUOUS DISCOUNT RATES

- *Continuous basis annual discount rates* value the stated actual cash flow amount as if it occurs in equal amounts at every possible moment during the year as shown next.

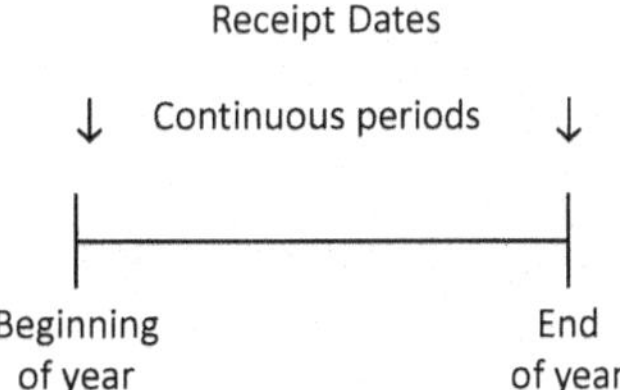

- Continuous rates are determined for any year N as:

$$\frac{1}{(e^r)^{N-.5}}$$

where e = 1.718 (base of a natural log)
r = annual discount rate
N = year 1, 2, 3 . . . N

- Illustration 54.5 shows a calculation of 10% continuous basis annual discount rate for any year N and the valuation of an annual cash flow of $1,000 for each year indicated.

ILLUSTRATION 54.5 CONTINUOUS BASIS DISCOUNT RATE AND THE VALUATION OF $1,000 ANNUAL CASH FLOW (ROUNDED)

	Year 1	Year 2	Year 3		Year 20
=	$\frac{1}{(1.718^{.10})^{1-.5}}$	$\frac{1}{(1.718^{.10})^{2-.5}}$	$\frac{1}{(1.718^{.10})^{3-.5}}$	. . .	$\frac{1}{(1.718^{.10})^{20-.5}}$
=	$\frac{1}{(1.105159)^{.5}}$	$\frac{1}{(1.105159)^{1.5}}$	$\frac{1}{(1.105159)^{2.5}}$	. . .	$\frac{1}{(1.105159)^{19.5}}$
=	$\frac{1}{1.051266}$	$\frac{1}{1.161816}$	$\frac{1}{1.283992}$	. . .	$\frac{1}{7.027267}$
=	.9512	.8607	.7788	. . .	.1423
FCF	1000	1000	1000		1000
Value	$951.23	$864.75	$786.14		$155.53

- The year 1 valuation may also be interpreted as valuing $1,000 of cash flow received continuously throughout period 1, plus interest at 10% annual rate from the point of receipt of $51.27 totaling $1,051.27 at the end of year 1, a composite yield of 5.1271%, by applying a discount rate of .904837 (equal to $1/(1 + .051271)^2$), which equals $951.23 at the beginning of year 1, the measurement date ($1,051.27 × .904837).
- The year 2 valuation may also be interpreted as valuing $1,000 of cash flow received continuously throughout period 2, plus interest at 10% annual rate from the point of receipt of $51.27 totaling $1,051.27 at the end of year 2, a composite yield of 5.1271%, by applying a discount rate of .82258 (equal to .904837/(1 + .10)), which equals $864.75 at the beginning of year 1, the measurement date ($1,051.27 × .82258).

SUMMARY

- The different discount rate conventions used in DCF valuations yield significantly different present value results, as discussed earlier and summarized in the next table.
  - PV results for a $1,000 cash flow into perpetuity at a 10% nominal discount rate are:

Discount Rate Convention Method	Present Value	Cumulative % Decrease in PV
Beginning of Year—Highest PV	11,000	
Quarterly	10,610	–3.55%
Monthly	10,526	–4.31%
Midyear	10,488	–4.66%
Daily	10,485	–4.68%
Continuous	10,464	–4.87%
End of Year—Lowest PV	10,000	–9.09%

- End-of-year rates produce PVs of perpetuity flows that are *9.1% lower* than beginning-of-year rates and *4.7% lower* than midyear rates.
- Midyear rates produce PVs of perpetuity flows that are *4.7%* lower than beginning-of-year rates and *4.9%* higher than end-of-year rates.
- Midyear conventions realistically value the results of operational cash flow activity similar to the monthly pattern of operating cash flows. They are simple to calculate.
- An analysis of the actual (expected actual) annual cash flow patterns of the target should determine the applicability of the annual discount rate convention chosen.
- Keep it simple, however.
- The implications for buyers and sellers in negotiating deal values should be clear.
- Appendix 54.1 presents a table of comparative 10% discount rates for the conventions discussed.

The following Appendix is available for viewing or download on the Web site for this book at: www.wiley.com/go/emott. Please see the About the Web Site page at the back of this book for login information.

APPENDIX 54.1 Discount Rate Engine

TOPIC 55

Growth, C*, and Return: The Engine to Increased Valuations and Deferred Tax Advantage

Topic 55 explores the significance of the interdependency between growth return on operating capital and the weighted average cost of capital, C*. Growth is the engine to increased entity valuation and higher valuation multiples (see Topics 20, 57, and 59).

INTERDEPENDENCIES AMONG GROWTH, RATE OF RETURN, AND COST OF CAPITAL

- The interdependencies among growth during the T period years, (gT), rate of return on operating capital employed (r) (equal to operating profit after tax [NOPAT])/net operating capital) and cost of capital (C*) and the impacts on business results and valuation drivers are presented in Appendix 55.1 and briefly summarized here.
  - The greater the positive spread between r and C*, the greater the firm's valuation and valuation multiples.
  - To the extent gT is equal to r (assuming investment requirements over the long term essentially equal depreciation), *annual growth in valuation* will approximate gT, external financing requirements will be minimized, and cash requirements for growth are met by cash generation.
  - To the extent that gT is less than r, *growth in valuation period to period* will approximate gT, and excess cash will accumulate in the business simply increasing value period to period by the increase in the amount of cash.
  - However, if gT exceeds r, growth in enterprise valuation and gT eventually will settle to a rate to approximate the sustainable growth rate, g_S as the debt capacity reflected in C* is reached. Unless new equity is injected, new debt will not be available to finance growth beyond a pace equal to g_S (see Topic 56).
  - The sweet spot in the interdependency matrix is where $gT \approx r$ and $r >= C^*$.

GROWTH ALSO CREATES A POTENTIAL DEFERRED TAX OPPORTUNITY

- In addition, growth creates the opportunity for equity investors to reinvest cash flow available to fund business growth and realize returns (r) on the reinvested cash flow that would not be possible without growth.
  - Without growth, positive attractive returns, r, create excess cash, which either will accumulate, earning money market rates, or be paid out as dividends to investors.
  - The dividends paid out will attract a personal tax to investors that, once paid, is lost forever.
  - Reinvestment of cash in the business (from the requirements and opportunities of growth when $gT \approx r$ and $r > C^*$) in lieu of a dividend *defers this tax for investors until the dividend eventually is paid.*
  - Earnings on the tax burden *deferred,* through reinvestment of cash in the business created when $gT \approx r$, is continually compounded as the company grows and r returns occur.
- For equity investors, then, *pretax compounding* of earnings on deferred personal taxes remaining in the business and invested at an r potentially ≈ or > C^*, creates incremental value compared to dividend payments, where the effect of compounding earnings on the deferred tax payment is lost forever as the tax (on the dividend received), once paid, is gone.
  - This posttax deferred tax advantage, dta, for any one year's deferred tax amount reinvested in the business is equal to the deferred tax advantage, dta times $1 - t_n$
  - t_n equals the tax rate on dividend payments in year n when the earnings on the deferred taxes are finally paid out as part of a dividend.
  - dta equals [d, the amount of "dividendable" cash reinvested in the business at r return, times t (where t equals the current tax rate on dividends at the time the cash amount (d) is reinvested (in lieu of being paid out as a dividend)) times 1 plus r raised to n (the number of years the deferred tax amount remains in the business), less dt],
  - See the summarized equation following:

$$dta = [(dt((1 + r)^n)) - dt](1 - tn)$$

  - The advantage for all years' tax deferrals is equal to the sum of the yearly advantages.
  - The value-creating effect is optimized where the actual growth remains equal to the sustainable growth rate and where r is greater than C^*.
  - At this point, all excess free cash flow is reinvested at the company's operating r to fund growth.
  - The greater r is, the greater the deferred tax reinvestment advantage for the investor.

The Interdependencies between r, c*, and gT on Value Creation

(Assuming capital expenditure requirements = depreciation over long term, D/C and dividend payout ratios remain at target levels)

Condition: T period Growth Prospect gT	Condition: RONA Prospect r	Condition: Cost of Capital C*	Result: Cash Result	Result: Enterprise Value Result	Result: Ebitda Result	Result: FCF Multiple Result	Result: FCF Result	Result: EVA Result	Shareholder Deferred Tax Benefit Result
gT = 0	r	= 0 < C*	no excess cash creation	possibly equal to liquidation value of capital employed	none	n/a	= depreciation?	very negative, flat into future	none
gT > 0	r	= 0 < C*	unsustainable internally financed growth, cash deficit, new capital required to sustain gT	possibly equal to liquidation value of capital employed, declining in future due to w/c requirement for growth	none	n/a	negative due to w/cap requirement for growth	very negative, negative position growing into future at gT	none
gT = 0	r	> 0 < C*	high excess cash created, no requirement for reinvestment in growth	positive, flat into future	positive, flat into future	=1/C*	positive, flat into future	negative, not growing into future	limited
gT > 0 < <	r gs	> 0 < C*	excess cash, some reinvestment in growth	positive, growing into future @ gT	positive, growing into future @ gT	=1/C*-gd	positive, growing into future @ gT	negative, negative position growing into future at gT	limited
gT => =<	r gs	> 0 < C*	nil to slight excess cash, cash generated mostly reinvested in growth	positive, growing into future @ gT	positive, growing into future @ gT	=1/C*-gd	positive, growing into future @ gT	negative, negative position growing into future at gT	limited
gT > =>	r gs	> 0 < C*	unsustainable internally financed growth if gT > gs, new capital required for growth if gT > gs	positive, growing into future @ gT, eventually gs; gT will settle to gs	positive, growing into future @ gT, eventually gs; gT will settle to gs	=1/C*-gd	positive, growing into future @ gT, eventually gs; gT will settle to gs	negative, negative position growing into future at gT	limited
gT = 0	r	= C*	high excess cash created, no requirement for reinvestment in growth	positive, flat into future	positive, flat into future	=1/C*	positive, flat into future	≈ zero, not growing into future	positive, beneficial, not growing into future
gT > 0 < <	r gs	= C*	excess cash, some reinvestment in growth	positive, growing into future @ gT	positive, growing into future @ gT	=1/C*-gd	positive, growing into future @ gT	≈ zero, not growing into future	positive, very beneficial, growing into future @ gT
gT => =<	r gs	= C*	nil to slight excess cash, cash generated mostly reinvested in growth	positive, growing into future @ gT	positive, growing into future @ gT	=1/C*-gd	positive, growing into future @ gT	≈ zero, not growing into future	positive, very beneficial, growing into future @ gT
gT > =>	r gs	= C*	unsustainable internally financed growth if gT > gs, new capital required for growth if gT > gs	positive, growing into future @ gT, eventually gs; gT will settle to gs	positive, growing into future @ gT, eventually gs; gT will settle to gs	=1/C*-gd	positive, growing into future @ gT, eventually gs; gT will settle to gs	≈ zero, not growing into future	positive, very beneficial growing into future @ gT, eventually gs; gT will settle to gs
gT = 0	r	> C*	high excess cash created, no requirement for reinvestment in growth	very positive, flat into future	very positive, flat into future	=1/C*	very positive, flat into future	very positive, flat into future	positive, very beneficial, not growing into future
gT > 0 < <	r gs	> C*	excess cash, some reinvestment in growth	very positive, growing into future @ gT	very positive growing into future @ gT	=1/C*-gd	very positive growing into future @ gT	very positive growing into future @ gT	positive, very beneficial, growing into future @ gT
gT => =<	r gs	> C*	nil to slight excess cash, cash generated mostly reinvested in growth	very positive, growing into future @ gT	very positive growing into future @ gT	=1/C*-gd	very positive growing into future @ gT	very positive growing into future @ gT	positive, very beneficial, growing into future @ gT
gT > =>	r gs	> C*	unsustainable internally financed growth if gT > gs, new capital required for growth if gT > gs	very positive, growing into future @ gT, eventually gs; gT will settle to gs	very positive, growing into future @ gT, eventually gs; gT will settle to gs	=1/C*-gd	very positive growing into future @ gT, eventually gs; gT will settle to gs	very positive growing into future @ gT, eventually gs; gT will settle to gs	positive, very beneficial growing into future @ gT, eventually gs; gT will settle to gs

APPENDIX 55.1 Interdependencies among r, c*, and g_d on Value Creation

TOPIC 56

How Fast Can the Target Grow?

Topic 56 explores the limitations and drivers of internally generated sustainable growth and presents a method for determining sustainable growth. Testing the growth assumption of target business plans can be very useful during due diligence and negotiations.

- *Barring the introduction of new equity,* internally generated sustainable growth (g_s) in the business (sales, earnings before interest, tax and depreciation and amortization (Ebitda), net operating profit after tax (NOPAT), and free cash flow (FCF)) eventually is limited to approximately a rate equal to the sustainable return on net operating assets, r (equal to NOPAT/Net operating capital) adjusted for dividend payout (d) and leverage (Debt to market value of Capital ratio, D/C) as shown:

$$g_s \approx r\left[\frac{1-d}{1-D/C}\right]$$

- The higher the r, the greater the sustainable growth rate.
- The higher the d, the lower the sustainable growth rate.
- The higher the sustainable D/C, the higher the sustainable growth rate as more capital is available to the firm up to the point that D/C is reached.
- The practical implication of this expression is that if actual growth (gT) exceeds the sustainable rate (g_s), at some point, without an increase in r, the new debt required to fund the growth will climb to a point where D/C is reached. At that point, lenders will curtail the availability of lending or invoke dividend restrictions and other covenants. Growth eventually will be curtailed to a level $\approx g_s$.
- Test the growth assumptions of sellers' business plans by determining their g_s.
  - Sellers cannot sustain growth greater than g_s.
  - Point this out with care, and you will gain credibility.
- Sustainable growth (g_s) is calculated as expansion of business operating earnings but is generally consistent with the associated and interrelated

long-term expansion rates of free cash flow, sales, and invested operating capital.[1]

- If the firm wants to grow organically (and create increasing value opportunities), r must be realized and sustained—r is the gas pedal.
- Illustration 56.1 presents a calculation of g_s.

ILLUSTRATION 56.1 CALCULATION OF g_s

$$g_s \approx r\left[\frac{1-d}{1-D/C}\right]$$

$$g_s \approx .15\left[\frac{1-.2}{1-.33}\right]$$

$$g_s \approx .15\left[\frac{.8}{.667}\right] = .179 = 17.9\%$$

where g_s = internally generated sustainable growth rate
d = target dividend payout rate, 20%
D = target or financeable debt-to-capital ratio, 33%
r = expected (or historical) posttax rate of return on net operating capital employed (NOPAT/Net operating capital), 15%

[1] See also Robert F. Bruner, *Applied Mergers and Acquisitions* (Hoboken, NJ: John Wiley & Sons, 2004), pp. 176, 177, and 263 for a discussion of this the estimation of issue sustainable growth.

TOPIC 57

Cash Flow Multiples, Growth Rates, and Discount Rates

Topic 57 explores the fundamental determinants of free cash flow multiples and introduces the approach of deriving other valuation multiples from free cash flow multiples.

The reader is encouraged to take the time to read the text in conjunction with the referenced Appendices to gain the appropriate level of understanding of the subject matter discussed in the narrative. Appendices are either presented at the end of this and each remaining Topic or are available for review and download on this book's companion Web site (see the About the Web Site page for login information).

LAGGING FREE CASH FLOW MULTIPLES, END-OF-YEAR BASIS, NO GROWTH

- In its simplest form, *free cash flow multiples* (FCF_M) (applied to lagging, most recent actual period free cash flow [FCF] to derive enterprise values), on an end-of-year discount rate basis, where there is no growth expected are equal to the reciprocal of the weighted average cost of capital, C* (see Equation 57.1).

$$FCF_M = \frac{1}{C^*} \tag{57.1}$$

- This concept is easily demonstrated by the fact that the reciprocal of a C* of 12.5% is equal to a multiple of 8.0 on an end-of-year discount rate basis as presented in Illustration 57.1.

ILLUSTRATION 57.1 LAGGING FCF BASIS, END-OF-YEAR RATE BASIS, NO GROWTH

A company with lagging FCF of $1 million with a C* of 12.5% and zero growth expectations would normally have a FCF_M of 8.0 times lagging FCF

(Continued)

on an end-of-year discount rate basis and have an enterprise value (EV) of \$8.0 million, as shown.

$$FCF_M = \frac{1}{C^*} = \frac{1}{.125} = 8.0$$

$$EV = 8.0 \times \$1 \text{ million} = \$8{,}000{,}000$$

- The multiple of 8.0 is also equal to the sum of each year's annual discount rate factors as presented in Appendix 57.1, col 3 (Appendix 57.1 also presents the discount rate adjusted growth rate method, discussed in the section of the same name below, which results in the same free cash flow multiple at the bottom of column 5, as the reciprocal of the discount rate method presented above).

LAGGING FREE CASH FLOW MULTIPLES, MIDYEAR BASIS, NO GROWTH

- The FCF_M and EV on a midyear discount rate basis is shown in Illustration 57.2.

ILLUSTRATION 57.2 LAGGING FCF BASIS, MIDYEAR RATE BASIS, NO GROWTH

$$FCF_M = \frac{1(1 + C^*)^{.5}}{C^*} \qquad (57.2)$$

$$FCF_M = \frac{1(1 + .125)^{.5}}{.125} = 8.485281$$

$$EV = 8.485281 \times \$1 \text{ million} = \$8{,}485{,}281$$

(See also Appendix 57.2 where the discount rate adjusted growth rate method, discussed in the section of the same name below, results in the same free cash flow multiple at the bottom of column 5, as the reciprocal of the discount rate method presented above).

FACTOR TO CONVERT END-OF-YEAR BASIS MULTIPLES TO MIDYEAR'S BASIS

- Alternatively, the factor to convert an end-of-year basis multiple or EV derived from end-of-year multiples (as derived in Illustration 57.1 above) to a midyear basis multiple or EV (as derived in Illustration 57.2 above) is determined as shown.[1]

$$\textbf{End-of-Year to Midyear Basis Conversion Factor} = (1 + C^*)^{.5}$$

$$12.5\%C^* \text{Midyear basis conversion factor} = (1.125)^{.5} = 1.0606602$$

$$\text{EV(midyear)} = \text{EV(end of year)} \times \text{Conversion factor}$$

$$\$8{,}000{,}000(1.0606602) = \$8{,}485{,}300$$

$$FCF_M\text{(midyear)} = FCF_M\text{(end of year)} \times \text{Conversion factor}$$

$$8.0(1.0606602) = 8.485$$

- The same EV results are derived from a perpetuity calculation, as shown next, and from a discounted cash flow (DCF) valuation, as presented in Appendices 57.1 and 57.2.

$$\frac{\$1{,}000{,}000}{.125} = \$8{,}000{,}000 \quad \text{end-of-year basis EV}$$

$$\frac{\$1{,}000{,}000(1 + .12)^5}{.125} = \$8{,}485{,}300 \quad \text{midyear basis EV}$$

LAGGING FREE CASH FLOW MULTIPLES, END-OF-YEAR BASIS, WITH GROWTH

- *With growth*, *lagging* FCF_M are equal to the reciprocal of the discount rate, C^*, less the expected *discount rate and time-weighted compound average growth rate* (g_d) in FCF, expressed in Illustration 57.3.

ILLUSTRATION 57.3 LAGGING FCF BASIS, END-OF-YEAR RATE BASIS, WITH GROWTH

$$FCF_M = \frac{1}{C^* - g_d} \tag{57.3}$$

- A company with *lagging* FCF of \$1 million, a C^* of 12.5%, and nominal FCF expansion prospects of 5% per year would have a FCF_M of 14.0 times *lagging* FCF on an end-of-year discount rate basis and have an enterprise value of \$14.0 million. See Appendix 57.3.
- The FCF_M of 14.0 was derived using the discount rate adjusted growth rate method (discussed in the next section) and the DCF method, both of which result in the same FCF_M.

[1] Enrique R. Arzac, *Valuation for Mergers, Buyouts, and Restructurings* (John Wiley & Sons, 2005), p. 29.

DISCOUNTED RATE ADJUSTED GROWTH RATE METHOD TO DETERMINE FCF_M

- The discount rate weighted long-term growth rate, g_d, as used in Illustration 57.3 and derived in Appendix 57.3, bottom of col 5, is 5.35714%, not the nominal expansion rate of 5%.

$$FCF_M = \frac{1}{12.5 - .0535714} = 13.99999 = 14.0\, \textit{rounded}$$

$$EV = 14.0 \times \$1\text{ million} = \$14{,}000{,}000$$

- If the nominal 5% compound average growth rate, g, was used in Illustration 57.3 in place of g_d, the EV resulting from the *lagging* FCF multiple valuation of $13,333,000 would be 5.0% less than $14 million:

$$FCF_M = \frac{1}{.125 - .05} = 13.333$$

$$EV = 13.333 \times \$1\text{ million} = \$13{,}333{,}333$$

- The use of g_d versus g in the denominator will result in materially different FCF multiples and valuations.
- *The exception to the approach presented in Illustration 57.3 is if a* ***constant*** *annual nominal growth rate (g) is to be used* in the denominator of the *lagging* basis FCF then an adjustment to the numerator is required. The adjustment is made by multiplying the numerator by 1 + g (*essentially converting the lagging FCF to a leading basis*). The resulting expression will also result in an EV of $14,000,000, as in Illustration 57.3, which was on a lagging basis. Equation 57.4 shows the revised equation.

$$FCF_M = \frac{1(1+g)}{C^* - g} \qquad (57.4)$$

$$FCF_M = \frac{1(1.05)}{.125 - .05} = 14.0$$

$$EV = 14.0 \times \$1\text{ million} = \$14{,}000{,}000$$

- This FCF_M expression is an adaption of the Gordon growth model, where the present value (PV) is solved for rather than a FCF multiple, as shown next.

$$PV = \frac{FCF_0(1+g)}{C^* - g}$$

- *If the expected growth in FCF is a two- or three-phase growth pattern* (e.g., x% in T period, y% in the early phase of post T and z% for the remainder into perpetuity), the adjusted FCF_M formula in equation 57.4, inclusive of the adjustment to the numerator, will *not result* in the appropriate FCF_M, as *the nominal compound average growth rate, g, will not capture the time-weighted impact of the discount rate.*
- A *two- or three-phase growth pattern on a lagging or leading basis requires that* (g_d), not (g), be used to determine the appropriate FCF_M and valuation.

DERIVATION OF g_d IN THE DISCOUNTED RATE ADJUSTED GROWTH RATE METHOD

- *The discount rate weighted long-term growth rate g_d, is equal to C* less the reciprocal of the algebraically determined FCF multiple* as presented in Appendix 57.4, described as:
  - Each n year's annual discount rate factor is multiplied by the compound growth rate of the free cash flow from year 1 through year n, resulting in the growth rate adjusted discount factors for each year n. All of the years' adjusted discount factors are summed, resulting in the (discount rate weighted) FCF_M. g_d is equal to C* – 1/FCF_M.
- g_d is used for component by component determination and explanation of FCF multiples as per Illustration 57.3 for either lagging or leading FCF on a midyear and end-of-year discount rate basis.
- *FCF multiples* are equal to the sum of the growth rate adjusted annual discount rate factors extended into perpetuity as presented in the expressions in Appendix 57.5 on both a leading and lagging basis on a year-end and midyear discount rate basis.
- Where a two- or three-phase future growth pattern in FCF is expected and the expression in Illustration 57.3 is to be used to calculate and explain the determination of FCF_M, g_d must be determined *capturing the discount rate weighted growth pattern* according to the method presented in Appendix 57.4.

ILLUSTRATION 57.4 LAGGING FCF BASIS: END-OF-YEAR RATE BASIS (PER EQUATION 57.3)

For example, a company with *lagging FCF* of $1 million, a C* of 12.5%, and annual FCF expansion prospects of 5% per year in period T of five years and 3% per year into perpetuity would have an FCF_M of 11.76343 times FCF (lagging basis) on an *end-of-year discount rate basis* and have an enterprise value of $11.763 million.

$$FCF_M = \frac{1}{.12500 - .0399908} = 11.76343$$

$$EV = 11.76343 \times \$1.0\,\text{million} = \$11{,}763{,}435$$

- See Appendix 57.6 for the derivation of g_d .0399908 in the example above, per the methodology of Appendix 57.4.
- The discount rate weighted long-term growth rate, g_d, in the lagging FCF multiple example in Appendix 57.6 is 3.99908%, not 3.049533%, which is the *nondiscount weighted compound average growth rate*, g, of the growth pattern: 5% per year in period T of five years, and 3% per year into perpetuity, presented in Appendix 57.7.

(Continued)

- If the nondiscount weighted compound average growth rate, g, were used in the lagging FCF_M equation in Illustration 57.4, the EV resulting from the lagging FCF multiple valuation would be 10% less than $11.763 million as follows:

$$FCF_M = \frac{1}{.125 - .03049533} = 10.58148$$

$$EV = 10.58148 \times \$1\text{ million} = \$10{,}581{,}480$$

ILLUSTRATION 57.5 LEADING FCF BASIS: END-OF-YEAR RATE BASIS (PER EQUATION 57.3)

A company with *leading FCF* of $1.05 million (lagging FCF of 1.0 million), a C* of 12.5%, and annual FCF expansion prospects of 5% per year in period T of five years and 3% per year into perpetuity would have an FCF_M of 11.20327 times FCF (leading basis) on an *end-of-year discount rate basis* and have an enterprise value of $11.763 million.

$$FCF_M = \frac{1}{.12500 - .0357404} = 11.20327$$

$$EV = 11.20327 \times \$1.050\text{ million} = \$11{,}763{,}435$$

- See Appendix 57.7 for the derivation of g_d .0357404 in Illustration 57.5, per the methodology of Appendix 57.4 *on a leading end-of-year basis.*
- The same valuation results of $11,763 are derived from a DCF valuation reflecting the growth patterns. See Appendix 57.7.
- The lagging FCF_M on a *midyear discount rate basis* based on the assumptions of Illustration 57.5 is determined as shown in Illustration 57.6.

ILLUSTRATION 57.6 LAGGING FCF BASIS: MIDYEAR RATE BASIS

$$FCF_M = \frac{1}{C^* - g_d}$$

$$FCF_M = \frac{1}{.125 - .0448526} = 12.47701$$

$$EV = 12.47701 \times \$1\text{ million} = \$12{,}477{,}007$$

- Dividing the midyear EV result of $12,477,007 by the midyear to end-of-year adjustment factor of 1.606602 from above, results in the end-of-year basis valuation of $11,763,465 per illustration 57.4 above.

- See Appendix 57.8 for the determination of g_d .0448526 per Illustration 57.6, per the methodology of Appendix 57.4 *on a lagging midyear rate basis*.
- The same valuation results of $12.477 million are derived from a DCF valuation reflecting the growth patterns. See Appendix 57.8.

METHOD FOR DETERMINING AN APPROXIMATION OF g_d AND FCF_M

- An approximation of the value of FCF_M and g_d on an end-of-year or midyear, leading or lagging FCF basis may determined in *lieu of using the FCF_M Engine* per the following method. This method will provide estimated values of FCF_M and g_d comparable to that derived using the FCF_M engine over a reasonable range of large and small cap C* (10 – 15%) and for a reasonable range of gT growth rates (5 – 20%).

$$\text{A years period } FCF_M = [(1/(1+C^*)^{y/2})\,((1+gT)^T((1+g_p)^{(y/2-T)}))]\,y$$

$$\text{B years period } FCF_M = [(1/(1+C^*)^p)\,((1+g_p)^p)]^*p$$

$$FCF_M = \text{A years } FCF_M + \text{B years } FCF_M$$

$$g_d = C^* - 1/FCF_M$$

where C* = weighted average cost of capital
gT = annual growth rate in T period
g_p = annual perpetuity growth rate
y = 20 years
T = years of T period of growth
p = 21 for end-of-year basis lagging FCF_M; p = 15 for midyear basis lagging FCF_M
p = 32 for end-of-year basis leading FCF_M; p = 23 for midyear basis leading FCF_M

- The estimated leading FCF_M and g_d, on an end-of-year basis reflecting the assumptions in illustration 57.5 above following the approximation method above, are 11.0 and 3.42%, versus 11.2 and 3.57% as per the FCF_M Engine calculation in Appendix 57.5, as below.

$$\text{A years period } FCF_M = [(1/(1+.125)^{20/2)}\quad((1+.05)^5(1+.03)^{20/2-5}]20$$

$$= 9.11$$

$$\text{B years periods } FCF_M = [(1/(1+.125)^{32})\quad(^*1.03)^{32}]32$$

$$= 1.90$$

$$FCF_M = \text{A years } FCF_M + \text{B years } FCF_M = 11.01$$

$$g_d = C^* - (1/FCF_M) = 0.125 - (1/11.01)$$

$$g_d = 3.42\%$$

IMPACT OF NOT USING g_d IN FCF_M MULTIPLE CONSTRUCTION

- *If FCF multiples* are to be employed for valuation or corroboration purposes, they should be derived according to Appendix 57.5 using the growth pattern impacted discount rates *equal to the sum of the growth rate adjusted annual discount rate factors extended into perpetuity* (or using the approximation method outlined above) described as:
  - Each n year's annual discount rate factor is multiplied by the compound growth rate of the free cash flow from year 1 through year n, resulting in the growth rate adjusted discount factors for each year n. All of the years' adjusted discount factors are summed, resulting in the FCF_M.
  - It is essential to capture the time-weighted effect of when the growth occurs, sooner or later, weighted by the discount rate appropriate to the target.
  - Growth occurring sooner has more value than growth occurring later and therefore derives a higher FCF_M and enterprise value.
  - A lower C* will result in a higher FCF_M than a higher C* would; g_d must be discount rate weighted (versus only time weighted) to capture the value impact of the discount rate on the derived FCF_M and therefore value.

- For clarity, the calculation of the discount rate and time-weighted compound average growth rate (g_d) derived in Appendix 57.6 by the method presented in Appendix 57.4 and discussed above is demonstrated next for the first three years:

$$1/((1+C^*)^n) \times 1+g_n \times \cdots 1+g_{n-y} = g_{dn}$$

where $y = n - \text{Increments of 1 until } y = 1$

Year 1 $g_d = 1/(1.125^1) \times 1.05_1 = .9333$

Year 2 $g_d = 1/(1.125^2) \times 1.05_2 \times 1{,}05_1 = .8711$

Year 3 $g_d = 1/(1.125^3) \times 1.05_3 \times 1{,}05_2 \times 1.05_1 = .8130$

- The growth rate timing effect on FCF_M and valuation (sooner versus later) can be illustrated by evaluating three different long-term growth rates in FCF, each of which grows to the same FCF amount 200 years hence and therefore has the same *nominal compound annual growth rate* (g_N) over the period but very different *discount rate weighted* compound annual growth rates (g_d), FCF_M, and EV valuations. See Appendices 57.9, 57.10, 57.11, and 57.12.
- While all three growth patterns reach a final-year cash flow of $17,017,084 and therefore have the same lifetime nominal compound annual growth rate % of 3.78974% (Appendix 57.9, line 13), the g_d growth rates on an end-of-year discount rate basis (line 14), and the leading and lagging FCF multiples derived therefrom (line 20 and 36) *differ significantly from the nominal g growth rates (*3.78974%) and the leading and lagging FCF multiples derived

therefrom (lines 19 and 35) due to the growth pattern (lines 10 and 11) applied to a C* of 12.5% *on a end-of-year discount rate basis*. The same significant differences hold on a midyear discount rate basis.

- Therefore, the EVs resulting from application of the FCF multiples derived from growth rates $g_{d,}$(lines 23 and 39) are significantly different from those derived from FCF multiples derived from nominal growth rates (lines 19 and 35).
- Only the EVs resulting from FCF multiples derived from growth pattern impacted discount rates equal those resulting from DCF valuations where a multiple-phase growth pattern is encountered (lines 17 and 33) on either a leading or a lagging basis.

DERIVE FCF_M, C*, OR g_d FROM EITHER OF THE OTHER TWO TERMS

- Given the expression for determining FCF_M, any term in that expression may be derived from the other two.

$$FCF_M = \frac{1}{C^* - g_d}$$

$$C^* = g_d + \frac{1}{FCF_M}$$

$$g_d = C^* - \frac{1}{FCF_M}$$

- The table in Appendix 57.13 presents a range of values for each term as a function of the other two.
- The table in Appendix 57.13 and the method of determining the appropriate growth rate, g_d, described in Appendix 57.4 are useful in validating the growth assumptions of the other side in negotiations or determining the drivers of FCF_M valuation multiples.
- The terms are interrelated. Departures from the results in Appendix 57.13 are easily detected.

SPIDER CHART METHOD FOR VISUAL EXPLANATION OF THE CONSTRUCTION OF C* AND FCF_M

- Appendix 57.14 presents a visual method to present and explain the construction of C* and FCF_M directly using a graphical, spider chart format utilizing the same C* elements and growth drivers as presented in the discounted cash flow valuation presented in Topic 39.
- This visual format may be useful in presenting the basis for the construction of C* and discount rates in valuation presentations, as opposed to strictly numerical CAPM presentations.

- Follow the explanation and numbered items below on the spider chart in Appendix 57.14.
  - The equity risk premium, ERP, of 7%, (starting point 1), on the y axis bottom left quadrant, intersects with the arc of the selected unlevered beta of 1.179 (2) (interpolating between the arc of 1.125 and 1.25), resulting in a beta-adjusted ERP of 8.20% (3) on the x axis bottom left quadrant.
  - Adding a risk-free rate, Rf, of 6% to beta-adjusted ERP of 8.203% by moving along the x axis to the left from the point of intersection results in C_U of 14.203% (4).
  - The intersection of C_U of 14.203% with the arc of the assumed debt to market value of capital ratio, D/C tax rate and borrowing rate leverage drivers (5) results in a C* of 13.536% (before any size premium) on the y axis upper left quadrant (6).
    - The slope arc of the assumed D/C, tax rate, and borrowing rate leverage drivers (5) will vary as these drivers change. Thus, this arc must be reset depending on the D/C, tax rate, and borrowing rate leverage drivers for purposes of a visual explanation.
  - The intersection of C* of 13.536% with the arc of the selected size premium of 9% adjusted for the assumed leverage ((1 – .174) times 9% equals 7.434)) in the upper right quadrant (7) results in a size premium adjusted C* of 20.970% on the x axis of the upper right quadrant (8) (13.536% + 7.434% = 20.970%).
    - The arcs of the small cap premiums assumed, (7) will vary as the D/C driver changes so the slope of these arcs must be reset depending on the D/C ratio assumed for purposes of a visual explanation.
  - Subtracting the discount rate adjusted growth rate, g_d, of 10.87% from the size premium adjusted C* of 20.970% by moving to the left along the x axis by (10.87 points) results in a capitalization rate ($C^*–g_d$) of 10.10% (9).
  - The intersection of the capitalization rate ($C^*–g_d$) of 10.10% with the arc in the lower right quadrant (10) yields a FCF_M of 9.89 on the y axis lower right quadrant (11).
  - For clarity, if the g_d was 7%, the FCF_M would be 7.16 (11A).
- The debt-to-capital ratio component of the cost of capital, C*, assumed in the discounted cash flow illustration in Topic 39 and in the spider chart illustration in Appendix 57.14 was a constant 17.4%.
- The leading basis discount rate adjusted growth rate, g_d, of 10.87% in Appendix 57.14 is the derived lifetime discount rate adjusted growth rate in the free cash flow of the illustration in Topic 39, as presented in Appendix 57.15.

DERIVATION OF PRICE EARNINGS AND OTHER MULTIPLES FROM FCF_M

- It is important to point out that EBITDA and price to earnings multiples (PE) do not directly result from the use of any of the computational methods presented in this topic.

- FCF multiples are the only multiples derived directly from C* and g_d.
- PE and other multiples can be derived from FCF multiples only when sustainable financial measurement relationships are assumed (see Topic 59).
- For example, a PE multiple (a times net income multiple) *is derived* from a FCF_M, as shown (see Topic 59):

$$PE = \left[\frac{FCF_M}{\left[\frac{NI\%}{FCF\%} \right]} \right] \times [1 - DC\%]$$

- And an FCF multiple *is derived* from a PE as follows.

$$FCF_M = \frac{PE}{1 - DC\%} \times \frac{NI\%}{FCF\%}$$

where NI% = sustainable net income as a % of sales
FCF% = sustainable free cash flow as a % of sales
DC% = percentage of debt to market value of capital (debt plus equity)
PE = price to earnings multiple

(See Topic 59 for further development of alternative multiple derivations).

The following Appendices are available for viewing or download on the Web site for this book at: www.wiley.com/go/emott. Please see the About the Web Site page at the back of this book for login information.

APPENDIX 57.1 FCF_M Engine No. 1, End-of-Year Basis, No Growth

APPENDIX 57.2 FCF_M Engine No. 2, Midyear Basis, No Growth

APPENDIX 57.3 FCF_M Engine No. 3, End-of-Year Basis with Growth

APPENDIX 57.4 FCF_M Engine No. 4: Derivation of Leading and Lagging Basis g_d

APPENDIX 57.5 FCF_M Engine No. 5: Derivation of Leading and Lagging FCF_M

APPENDIX 57.6 FCF_M Engine No. 6: Determination of g_d and FCF_M and Lagging FCF Valuation

APPENDIX 57.7 FCF_M Engine No. 7: Determination of g_d and FCF_M and Leading FCF Valuation

APPENDIX 57.8 FCF_M Engine No. 8: Determination of g_d and FCF_M and Lagging FCF Valuation

APPENDIX 57.9 Comparative FCF Multiples and Resulting Valuations using g_d and Nominal g_n

APPENDIX 57.10 FCF_M Engine No. 9: Determination of g_d and FCF_M and Lagging FCF Valuation

APPENDIX 57.11 FCF_M Engine No. 10: Determination of g_d and FCF_M and Lagging FCF Valuation

APPENDIX 57.12 FCF_M Engine No. 11: Determination of g_d and FCF_M and Lagging FCF Valuation

APPENDIX 57.13 Derivation of FCF_M, C^*, or g_d from the Other Two Terms

APPENDIX 57.14 Spider Chart Derivation of C^* and FCF_M

APPENDIX 57.15 FCF_M Engine No. 12: Determination of g_d and FCF_M and Lagging FCF Valuation

TOPIC 58
Comparable Multiples

Topic 58 explores the notion of comparable multiples, which often are not comparable at all. Suggested multiples require careful adjustment to render them comparable. Topic 58 describes the adjustments required and demonstrates how to make them more comparable.

The reader is encouraged to take the time to read the text in conjunction with the referenced Appendices to gain the appropriate level of understanding of the subject matter discussed in the narrative. Appendices are either presented at the end of this and each remaining Topic or are available for review and download on this book's companion Web site (see the About the Web Site page for login information).

"COMPARABLE" MULTIPLES ARE NOT COMPARABLE UNTIL THEY ARE ADJUSTED

- Be ready as a buyer to respond to the seller's insistence that "a multiple of x is applicable to value this deal" or to disarm the use of the comparable multiple argument before it is raised by making the necessary adjustments to so-called comparable multiples.
- So-called comparable multiples (of free cash flow [FCF] or earnings) are generally not comparable (between the target and the "comparable" entity) unless they are adjusted for the following issues:
  - Growth potentials, during period T and into perpetuity, of the comparable company versus the target.
  - Size of the comparable company versus the target.
  - Interest rate differences on borrowings available to the firms.
  - Leverage capability (debt-to-cap ratios) of the comparable company versus the target.
  - Systematic risk, or betas, of the comparable company versus the target.
  - Other risk factors of the comparable company versus the target.
- The adjustment exercise is useful to understand the other side's thinking, to effectively communicate and defuse the comparable multiple argument, or to derive a corroborating target value, not to derive a multiple for the sole purpose of valuing the target.
- *A multiple is comparable to a target only after reconciling adjustments* are made, as reflected in the next section.

"COMPARABLE" MULTIPLE ADJUSTMENT PROCESS

- Identify the components of the so-called *comparable public company's* multiple, identify C_U comparable to the target and its size, then forward solve for the *target multiple* and reconcile the comparable company free cash flow multiple (FCF_M) to the target FCF_M component by component. Follow the example presented in Appendix 58.1, Section 1 and as follows: The reader is encouraged to follow the text along with the information flow on the referenced Appendices.
- Step (a) In the example presented in Appendix 58.1, the comparable company has a FCF_M (after conversion from a Ebitda multiple perhaps) of 11.05 (Appendix 58.1, line 1).
  - Using the comparable company's estimated cost of capital drivers (as presented in the component driver example in Appendix 58.2, lines 12 to 22), the capital asset pricing model (CAPM), determines the comparable company's C_U to be 14.203% excluding small-cap size premiums (Appendix 58.2, line 23 and Appendix 58.3, line 18 of the capital asset pricing model).
  - However, the target company is a micro cap company, decile 10y, while the comparable public company is a mid-sized company, decile 5. The levered beta of the comparable company is 1.50 and the unlevered asset beta is 1.1719 (Appendix 58.1, lines 7 and 8). While the unlevered asset beta of the comparable company may appropriately reflect the systematic risk of the target's industry it does not reflect the inverse relationship of size risk as reflected in the beta of securities along the spectrum of the security market line, which demonstrates that beta increases inversely to the size of the market cap of a security (see Topics 23 and 29).
  - It is appropriate to reflect an adjustment for the size differential between the comparable and target company in the derivation of a comparable FCF_M for the target as follows.
  - The unlevered beta of the comparable company of 1.1719 (Appendix 58.1, line 8) requires adjustment for general comparability of size between the comparable company, size decile 5, and the target company, size decile 10y. Using Ibbotson beta data,[1] the comparable company C_U should be multiplied by the ratio of the 10th decile beta to the 5th decile beta as follows:

unlevered beta	of comparable public co			1.17188
unlevered beta size adjustment	decile	5	10y	
unlevered beta size adjustment	decile beta	1.16	1.40	1.2069
size adjusted unlevered beta	of comparable & target cos			1.41433

  - The beta for the 5th decile is 1.16. The beta for the 10y decile is 1.40. The 10th decile beta is 20.7% higher than the 5th decile.

[1] Ibbotson Associates, *2010 Valuation Yearbook, Market Results for Stocks, Bonds, Bills and Inflation 1926–2009* (222 W. Washington, Chicago, Illinois: Morningstar, Inc., 2010), p. 92.

  - The resulting adjustment to the comparable company unlevered beta based on the difference in decile betas is 1.2069, resulting in a unlevered beta comparable to the size of the target of 1.414 (1.17188 times 1.2069). See Appendix 58.1 lines 8 to 11.
  - Without the size adjustment, the unlevered beta for the target company does not appropriately reflect the general size risk of the micro cap company consistent with CAPM.
  - It should be noted that had the size adjustment been applied first to the comparable company levered beta of 1.5 and then de-levered, the resulting unlevered beta adjusted for size would also be 1.4133.
 - Using the comparable company's estimated cost of capital drivers including the size adjusted unlevered beta as determined above, the capital asset pricing model (CAPM) determines the comparable company's adjusted C_U to be 15.9% excluding the small-cap size premium (Appendix 58.1, line 15 and Appendix 58.4, line 18 of the capital asset pricing model).
- Step (b) *Next, forward-solve for the target's FCF_M.*
 - Re-lever C_U of 15.9% using the anticipated debt to capital mix, resulting size adjusted levered beta, borrowing rate, and tax rate of the target following the direct approach principle set forth in Topic 37 to derive a levered C* for the target without a size premium of 15.017% as below (Appendix 58.1, line 22).

$$C^* = [(C_U)(1 - ((D/C)(t)))] + [((i - RF)(1 - t))(D/C)]$$
$$C^* \text{ Target} = [(.159)(1 - ((.1987)(.36)))] + [((.08 - .06)(1 - .36))(.1987)]$$
$$C^* \text{ Target} = .14763 + .002544$$
$$C^* \text{ Target} = .15017 = 15.017\%$$

 - The equivalent C* value for the target excluding small cap premiums may also be derived using the weighted average approach of CAPM to *derive a levered C* for the target without a size premium as presented in* Appendix 58.4, line 32.
- Step (c). *Next, add the size risk premium for the target of 9%, adjusted for the target's D/C ratio, to derive C* for the target, Appendix 58.1, line 26.*

Target C^* without size premium	15.017%	(Appendix 58.1, **line 22**)
Plus target size premium	7.212%	(Appendix 58.1, **line 24**)
C^* incl size premium	22.230%	(Appendix 58.1, **line 26**)

 - The same C* value including the size premium is derived using the weighted average approach of CAPM (see Appendix 58.5, line 32).
 - The adjustment to the comparable company size premium of 9% resulting from multiplying by (1 – .1987, the D/C ratio of the target company,

Appendix 58.1, line 20,) is to reflect the net amount of the size premium included in C* of the target. It should be remembered that of the 9% that is included in C_L, only (1 − .1987) or .8013 is included in C* calculation due to the D/C effect in the weighted average calculation of C*. (07212 = (9%(1 − .1987)).

- Step (d). If other target risk premiums such as key man risk, single product risk, country risk, thin management, and so forth are appropriate and they have not been quantified in the target FCF (which is the preferable treatment), they may be added to the targets C* computation (Appendix 58.1, line 25) after adjustment for the targets D/C ratio. This adjustment is the same as was done for the size premium, in the determination of C* for the target (see Topic 48).
- Step (e). Next, the expected long-term compound average growth rate for the target, g_d, should be determined. Employing the method set forward in Topic 57, g_d is found to equal 10.675%, utilizing the target's expected nominal growth rates during period T of 13% (Appendix 58.1, line 28) and after T of 4% into perpetuity (Appendix 58.1, line 30). (See Appendix 58.6 pages 1, 2 for the computation of g_d.)
- Step (f). Next, the equivalent to the reciprocal of the target's adjusted free cash flow multiple is derived by deducting the target's discount weighted growth rate, g_d, (g) above, Appendix 58.1, line 31, from target C* as shown:

Target C^* incl size premium	22.230%	(Appendix 58.1, **line 26**)
Less target g_d	10.675%	(Appendix 58.1, **line 31**)
Reciprocal of target's FCF_M	11.555%	(Appendix 58.1, **line 32**)

- Step (g). **Lastly, the adjusted FCF multiple comparable to the target is determined** to be 8.65, equal to the reciprocal of the target's FCF_M (equal to $C^* - g_d$) as determined in (h) above, Appendix 58.1, line 31, as follows:

$$FCF_M = \frac{1}{.115551} = 8.6542 \qquad \text{(Appendix, 58.1, Line 33)}$$

DEVELOP COMPONENT RECONCILIATION OF COMPARABLE COMPANY TO TARGET FCF_M

- The comparable company's FCF_M multiple is reconciled to the company's FCF_M by deriving the reconciling components as follows. The reconciling items are included on Appendix 58.1 in Section 2 where noted.
- Step (h) The first reconciling step is to lever the adjusted C_U of the comparable company from (step a) above to derive C* of the comparable company without any size premium.
  - C* for the comparable company may be derived directly from C_U excluding the size premium of 15.9% utilizing the direct method principle set

forth in Topic 37 (excluding the size premium factor in the direct approach presented in Topic 37 as the size premium has already been removed) to derive a comparable levered cost of capital, C* of 14.737% excluding the size premium as follows (Appendix 58.1, line 41).

$$C^* = [(C_U)(1 - ((D/C)(t)))] + [((i - RF)(1 - t))(D/C)]$$
$$C^* = [(.159)(1 - ((.2857)(.30)))] + [((.07 - .06)(1 - .30))(.2857)]$$
$$C^* = .14537 + .001999$$
$$C^* = .14737 = 14.737\% \quad \text{(Appendix 58.1, line 41)}$$

- This approach yields the same C* value as would result from the CAPM method. In Appendix 58.7, line 32, C* for the comparable company is equal to 14.737%, excluding the 1.69% size premium. Including the size premium, C* for the comparable company equals 15.94%.

- Step (i) The next step is to *derive* g_d, the discounted weighted growth rate of the comparable company, by starting with the derived C* without the size premium from (h) above, add the estimated size premium effect, then subtract the reciprocal of the FCF_M.

C^*	**14.737%**	(**C^* not including size premium**), from above
(Plus)adj size premium	1.207%	(1.69%(1 − .2857)) Appendix 58.1, line 40
Equals est. C^*	15.945%	(including size premium), Appendix 58.1 line 39
Less 1/FCF_M of 11.054 =	9.047%	(1/11.054 = .09047 or 9.047%), Appendix 58.1 **line 37**
Equals g_d	6.898%	(derived g_d in FCF_M), Appendix 58.1, line 38

- The adjustment to the 1.69% comparable company size premium (Appendix 58.1, line 24) results from multiplying 1.69% by (1 − .2857, where .2857 is *the D/C ratio of the comparable company*). This adjustment is to reflect the net amount of the size premium included in C* remembering that of the 1.69% that is included in C_U and C_L, only (1 − .2857) or .7143 is included in the weighted average cost of capital C* calculation due to the D/C effect in the weighted average calculation of C* (1.207 = 1.69%(1 − .2857)).

- The component-by-component reconciliation of the comparable company FCF_M to the target FCF_M is presented on Section 2 of Appendix 58.1, lines 35 to 68. The reconciliation provides the basis to present to the other side why the proposed comparable FCF_M of 11.06 (line 36) is not appropriate to the target and why the adjusted reconstructed FCF_M of 8.65 (line 68) is comparable to the target.

CONCLUSION

- The adjusted target FCF_M of 8.65 (Appendix 58.1 lines 33 and 68) results in an enterprise value that is 22% lower than the unadjusted proposed comparable company multiple of 11.06.
- The component-by-component reconciliation is a useful tool with a rigouous approach to present to the other side to logically defuse the "comparable multiple" argument.
- It is worth noting the component amounts of the adjusted target multiple versus the originally proposed comparable FCF_M deriving from growth versus C* (see Appendices 58.1, lines 26 to 31 for the target components and Appendix 58.2, lines 30 to 34 for the comparable company components, which are summarized below). While the growth component of the multiple is comparable, the cost of capital component for the micro-cap target is as expected lower (a higher reconstructed C*) than the mid-cap comparable.

	Comparable FCF Multiple Appendix 58.2	Adjusted Target FCF Multiple Appendix 58.1
C*	6.9 (line 30)	4.5 (line 26)
g_d	4.1 (line 34)	4.2 (line 31)
FCF_M	11.05 (line 36)	8.65 (line 36)

USE OF THE ADJUSTED FCF_M

- The adjusted comparable FCF_M should not be used as the primary basis to value the target, although it may be used to corroborate the valuation.
- The adjusted target FCF_M should be used to defuse or counter an inappropriate unadjusted FCF multiple.
- Do not get trapped arguing against a noncomparable "multiple valuation" proposition.
- Reconcile the so-called comparable FCF multiple by tearing it open and then rebuilding it.
- Guide the valuation discussions away from inappropriate conclusions to the meaningful discussions about C*, growth opportunities, risk management, and risk allocation pertinent to completing the deal.
- Once the target FCF_M is determined, it may be converted if necessary to other multiples of the target's financial results.
- See Topic 59 for methods of converting FCF multiples to earnings multiples and vice versa.
- See Topic 59 for the methods of converting FCF_M to other multiples and vice versa.

FCFM RECONCILIATION ENGINE no 1

	SECTION 1	ENGINE TO BUILD TARGET FCFM FROM DERIVED COMPARABLE COMPANY C U						Target	Comparable Co
1	**FCFm of comparable public company**			**tie to comp co data = 1 , 0= no**	**0**	11.05387		**11.0539**	**11.0539**
2	reciprocal of FCF m	of comparable public co							
3			**COMP CO DRIVER**	**COMP CO DRIVER**					
4	risk free rate	of comparable public co	6.00%	6.00%	6.00%				
5	interest rate		7.00%	7.00%	7.00%				
6	large co equity risk premium	of comparable public co	7.00%	7.00%	7.00%				
7	levered beta	of comparable public co	1.500	1.500	1.500				
8	unlevered beta	of comparable public co			1.17188				
9	unlevered beta size adjustment	decile	5	**10b**					
10	unlevered beta size adjustment	decile beta	1.16	1.40	1.20690				
11	**size adjusted unlevered beta**	**of comparable & target cos**			**1.41433**				
12	tax rate	of comparable public co	30.0%	30.00%	30.00%				
13	Dm/Em	of comparable public co	40.00%	40.00%	40.00%				
14	Dm/Cm	of comparable public co			28.57%				
15	**unlevered CU of comparable public co w/o small cap + other premium**					**0.15900**	**a**	**6.2892**	
16			**COMP CO DRIVER**	**TARGET CO DRIVERS**					
17	interest rate	of target co	7.00%	8.0%	8.00%				
18	tax rate	of target co	30.0%	36.0%	36.00%				
19	Dm/Em	of target co	40.00%	24.79%	24.79%			0.3697	
20	Dm/Cm	of target co			19.87%				
21	**size adjusted levered beta**	of target co			1.639				
22	**relevered C* comparable to target w/o small cap +other premium**					**0.15017**	**b**	**6.6589**	
23			**COMP CO DRIVER**	**TARGET CO DRIVERS**					
24	small cap risk premium	of comparable & target cos	1.69%	9.00%	9.00%	0.07212	**c**	-2.1604	
25	other risk premiums	of comparable & target cos	0.00%	0.00%	0.00%	0.00000		0.0000	
26	**relevered C* comparable to target with small cap +other premium**					**0.22230**	**d**	**4.4985**	
27			**COMP CO DRIVER**	**TARGET CO DRIVERS**					
28	estimated cagrd during period T	of comparable & target cos	9.00%	13.0%	13.00%			3.2549	
29	period T in years	of comparable & target cos	4.0	5	5				
30	estimated cagrd beyond T	of comparable & target cos	2.00%	4.0%	4.00%			0.9008	
31	**discount weighted cagr gd**	of target co				**0.10675**	**e**	**4.1557**	
32	**C*-dwcagr (reciprocal of the targets FCFm)**					**0.11555**	**f**		
33	**FCF m comparable to the target**			1/28			**g**	**8.6542**	**11.0539**
34									

APPENDIX 58.1, Section 1 FCF_M Reconciliation Engine No. 1

The following Appendices, as well as those presented earlier, are available for viewing or download on the Web site for this book at: www.wiley.com/go/emott. Please see the About the Web Site page at the back of this book for login information.

APPENDIX 58.1, Section 2 FCF_M Reconciliation Engine No. 1

APPENDIX 58.2 FCF_M Reconciliation Engine No. 2: Impact of Each PE Component Driver on Comparable Company FCF_M

APPENDIX 58.3 Cost of Capital Engine: Cost of Capital of Comparable Company without Size Premium with Unadjusted Beta

APPENDIX 58.4 Cost of Capital Engine: Cost of Capital of Target Company without Size Premium with Adjusted Beta

APPENDIX 58.5 Cost of Capital Engine: Cost of Capital of Target Company with Size Premium with Adjusted Beta

APPENDIX 58.6 FCF_M Engine No. 3: Determination of Target g_d and FCF_M

APPENDIX 58.7 Cost of Capital Engine: Cost of Capital of Comparable Company without Size Premium with Adjusted Beta

TOPIC 59

Converting FCF_M to P/Es and Other Valuation Multiples and Deriving Slot Multiples for Public Companies

Topic 59 explores the methodology to convert free cash flow multiples to other valuation multiples and vice versa and presents the price/earnings (P/E) eviscerator as a means to evaluate public company P/Es and valuations.

The reader is encouraged to take the time to read the text in conjunction with the referenced Appendices to gain the appropriate level of understanding of the subject matter discussed in the narrative. Appendices are either presented at the end of this and each remaining Topic or are available for review and download on this book's companion Web site (see the About the Web Site page for login information).

UNDERSTAND THE SUSTAINABLE RELATIONSHIPS BETWEEN FCF AND OTHER EARNINGS FUNDAMENTALS

- Adjusted free cash flow (FCF) multiples (FCF_M) are used to corroborate discounted cash flow (DCF) enterprise basis valuations.
- Sales multiples (Sales M), earnings before interest and tax (EBIT) multiples ($EBIT_M$), and earnings before interest, tax, depreciation, and amortization (EBITDA) multiples ($EBITDA_M$) derive corroborating enterprise basis valuations.
- Price-to-earnings (P/E) multiples derive corroborating equity basis valuations.
- Sales, P/E, EBIT, and EBITDA multiples may be derived from FCF_M and from one another by following the derivation formulas in the next section. These formulas capture the effect of *sustainable relationships* between the target's FCF, earnings, and financing fundamentals to derive the related multiples.
- Analysts must understand these likely sustainable relationships to derive meaningful related multiples from FCF_M and vice versa. Historical financial relationships provide a guide to the sustainable relationships for this purpose.

DERIVATION FORMULA TO CONVERT FROM FCF_M TO OTHER VALUATION MULTIPLES AND VICE VERSA

- To derive a P/E multiple *from an FCF multiple*:

$$P/E = \left[\frac{FCF_M}{\left[\frac{NI\%}{FCF\%}\right]}\right] \times [1 - DC\%]$$

- To derive an FCF multiple *from a P/E multiple*:

$$FCF_M = \frac{PE}{1 - DC\%} \times \frac{NI\%}{FCF\%}$$

- To derive an EBIT multiple *from an FCF multiple*:

$$EBIT_M = \left[\frac{FCF_M}{\left[\frac{EBIT\%}{FCF\%}\right]}\right]$$

- To derive an FCF multiple *from an EBIT multiple*:

$$FCF_M = EBIT_M \frac{EBIT\%}{FCF\%}$$

- To derive an EBITDA multiple *from a FCF multiple*:

$$EBITDA_M = \left[\frac{FCF_M}{\left[\frac{EBITDA\%}{FCF\%}\right]}\right]$$

- To derive an FCF multiple *from an EBITDA multiple*:

$$FCF_M = \left[\frac{EBITDA_M}{\left[\frac{EBIT\%}{EBITDA\%}\right]}\right] \times \frac{EBIT\%}{FCF\%}$$

- To derive an EBIT multiple *from a P/E multiple*:

$$EBIT_M = \frac{[PE]}{1 - DC\%} \times \frac{NI\%}{EBIT\%}$$

- To derive an EBIT multiple *from a P/E multiple*:

$$EBIT_M = \frac{[PE]}{1 - DC\%} \times \frac{1}{\left[\left[DE\% \times i \times \frac{1}{ROE_{MV}\%}\right] + \frac{1}{1-t}\right]}$$

- To derive an EBITDA multiple *from a P/E multiple*:

$$EBITDA_M = \frac{PE}{1 - DC\%} \times \frac{NI\%}{EBITDA\%}$$

- To derive a P/E multiple *from an EBITDA multiple*:

$$P/E = \frac{\frac{EBIT\%}{FCF\%} \times \left[\frac{EBITDA_M}{\frac{EBIT\%}{EBITDA\%}}\right]}{\frac{NI\%}{FCF\%}}$$

- To derive a P/E multiple *from an EBITDA multiple*:

$$P/E = \left[\frac{EBITDA_M}{\frac{NI\%}{EBITDA\%}}\right] \times 1 - DC\%$$

- To derive an EBITDA multiple *from an EBIT multiple*:

$$EBITDA_M = EBIT_M \times \frac{EBIT\%}{EBITDA\%}$$

- To derive an EBITDA multiple *from an EBIT multiple*:

$$EBITDA_M = EBIT_M \times \frac{EBIT\%}{EBIT\% + DEPR\%}$$

- To derive a sales multiple *from a P/E multiple*:

$$SALES_M = \frac{PE}{NI\%}$$

- To derive a sales multiple *from an FCF multiple*:

$$\text{SALES}_M = \frac{\text{FCF}_M}{\text{FCF\%}}$$

- To derive a sales multiple *from an EBIT multiple*:

$$\text{SALES}_M = \frac{\text{EBIT}_M}{\text{EBIT\%}}$$

- To derive a sales multiple *from an EBITDA multiple*:

$$\text{SALES}_M = \frac{\text{EBITDA}_M}{\text{EBITDA\%}}$$

where T = tax rate
$ROE_{Mv}\%$ = return on equity market value
NI% = sustainable net income as a percentage to sales
EBIT% = sustainable EBIT as a percentage to sales
EBITDA% = sustainable EBITDA as a percentage to sales
FCF% = sustainable FCF as a percentage to sales
i = interest rate on debt
DC% = percentage that debt is to market value of capital (debt plus equity)
DE% = percentage that debt is to market value of equity capital
DEPR% = sustainable depreciation expense as a percentage to sales

- Appendix 59.1 presents the derivation of related multiples using the methods just presented based on the *sustainable relationships* among the target's FCF, earnings, and financing assumptions as reflected in the example presented in Topic 60.

VISUAL CONVERSION OF FCF_M TO $EBITDA_M$

- Appendix 59.2 presents a method of approximating EBITDA multiples directly from FCF_M using a graphical visual format based on the example presented in Topic 60.
  - On the illustration in Appendix 59.2, the FCF_M of 10.1598 (point (1) on Appendix 59.2) on the y axis results from the example in Topic 60 .
  - The FCF_M on the x axis is found at any point of intersection of an FCF_M with any of the selected arcs where the arcs represent the ratio of EBITDA as a percent of sales to FCF as a percent of sales.
  - The intersection of the FCF_M of 10.1598 with the illustrated ratio of 1.91 (2) on Appendix 59.2, results in an $EBITDA_M$ of 5.31 (3) on Appendix 59.2.
  - Appendix 59.3 presents a clean illustration of Appendix 59.2 for the reader's use.

USE THE P/E EVISCERATOR TO VALIDATE P/E TRADING MULTIPLES OF PUBLIC COMPANIES

- The *P/E Eviscerator and Slot Multiple Engine* apply the principles presented in Topics 57, 58, and 59 to the evaluation of the P/E multiples of two public companies and illustrates the process of *dissecting the P/E ratios and converting the P/E data into FCF_M and the elements of C* and g_d.*
- The P/E Eviscerator and Slot Multiple Engine enable the user to evaluate the *market P/E multiple* of a traded security; determine the multiple effect of C*, g_d, and market exuberance, *u*, and contrast the results of the analysis with a derived *slot multiple* and slot value, *versus the market trading multiples and share price valuation and answer: Is the quoted market value of the security over or under the slot value derived from analysts expectations?*
- The sustainable financial relationships for the public companies selected were drawn from historical relationships as synthesized from the companies' current financial statements as reported on the MSN Money financial statement database on the reference date.
  - *The user is able to evaluate the g_d effect on the current valuation: Is the implicit g_d (in the P/E) realistic versus a g_d derived from fundamental market growth drivers as available from market analysts?*
- *Slot multiples are the derived (likely?) multiples (or range of multiples) resulting from the combined effects of the likely ranges of:*
  - C* component values and resulting C*.
  - The consensus market analysts' earnings growth estimates (assuming such consensus g_d are also appropriate for FCF growth).
  - Appropriate estimates of the other sustainable valuation drivers noted in this topic's appendices.

P/E EVISCERATOR APPLIED TO THE ILLUSTRATION IN TOPIC 60

- Appendix 59.4 presents the P/E Eviscerator and Slot Multiple Engine, which utilizes the data presented in Topic 60 and in Appendix 59.1. The P/E Eviscerator and Slot Multiple Engine begin with the P/E of 7.9 and derives the C* and g_d multiple of FCF (10.158) utilizing the P/E-to-FCF_M conversion expression in Equation 59.1.

$$FCF_M = \frac{P/E}{1 - DC\%} \times \frac{NI\%}{FCF\%} \tag{59.1}$$

P/E EVISCERATOR APPLIED TO COCA-COLA COMPANY AS OF OCTOBER 31, 2007

- Appendix 59.5 presents a component analysis of the P/E of *Coca-Cola Company (ticker KO)* as of October 31, 2007, utilizing the P/E eviscerator.

- The implicit fundamental P/E of Coca-Cola as of October 31, 2007, of 26.4, is composed of a C* multiple of 7.5 times net income (Appendix 59.6, line 29, Section 1) and a implicit g_d multiple of 20.7 times net income (line 30) resulting in a *fundamental P/E* of 28.2 times net income (line 31). (The fundamental PE excludes the effect of cash, debt, and other long-term liabilities that *are* captured in the market valuation and the market P/E of KO.)
  - Cash net of debt and other long-term liabilities represent –1.8 times net income (lines 32 plus 33) resulting in the market P/E of 26.4 at the measurement date (line 34).
- C* for KO is estimated to be 9.99% (line 23) and reflects an estimated debt at capacity to market capital ratio of 25.3% (line 17), or six times EBITDA (author assumed capacity). The input data presented result from synthesis of current and the long-term (5-year) relationships reflected in the financial data available for KO from MSN Money as of October 31, 2007.

IMPLICIT PE, FCF_M VERSUS DERIVED SLOT P/E, FCF_M, AND g_d

- *The estimated implicit fundamental FCF_M* derived from the market PE per equation 591 above, is approximately 37.8 times FCF (line 37 and line 7, Section 2), of which the C* component is 10.0 times FCF (line 35) and the g_d component is 27.8 times FCF (line 36), resulting in a implicit fundamental FCF_M of 37.8 times free cash flow (line 37).
- The implicit fundamental FCF_M excludes the effect of cash, debt, and other long-term liabilities that *are* captured in the market FCF_M.
  - Cash net of debt and other long-term liabilities represent –2.4 times FCF (lines 38 plus 39), resulting in the estimated market FCF_M of 35.4 (line 40).
- The annual discounted weighted earnings growth rate (g_d) implicit in the market P/E is approximately 9.9% (line 30) or 7.4% in the FCF_M (line 36). The *computed consensus* FCF_M *Slot* g_d is 5.6% ((line 41), which is below the implicit FCF_M gd of 7.4% (line 36) and was derived by utilizing the analyst's consensus forecast (as published in MSN Money) for the next five years of annual growth of 9% (line 9) and assuming that annual FCF growth into perpetuity is equivalent to GNP growth of 4% (author assumed GNP growth).
  - This assumes that the consensus earnings g_d are also appropriate for FCF growth. The g_d factor was derived utilizing the method presented in Topic 57.
- *The derived consensus fundamental Slot FCF_M* (excluding the effect of cash, debt and other long term liabilities) is 22.5 times FCF (line 7, Section 3) or an equivalent fundamental Slot P/E of 16.8 times net income (line 3, Section 3) versus the market fundamental P/E of 28.2 (also excluding the effect of cash, debt and other long term liabilities) (line 3, Section 2). *The implicit FCF_M (37.8) is 67% over the indicated Slot FCF_M (22.5). Why?*
- The implicit $EBITDA_M$ derived from the FCF_M is 24.1 times EBITDA (line 11, Section 2) versus the calculated consensus Slot $EBITDA_M$ of 14.4 times (line 11, Section 3).

- The difference between the implicit fundamental FCF_M of 37.8 (line 7, Section 2) and the consensus Slot FCF_M of 22.5 (line 7, Section 3) is 15.3 times FCF. The difference between the implicit fundamental P/E of 28.2 and the consensus Slot P/E of 16.8 is 11.4 times net income. *Why?*

VARIANCE IN SLOT RESULTS IF ASSUMPTIONS ARE SENSITIZED

- Either a 2.5% point increase in the GNP growth assumption to 6.5% beyond year five (a 60% increase), or a 11.5% point increase in the analyst's next five years, annual growth assumption to 20.5% annual growth (versus 9% per analyst's consensus estimates, a 130% increase) would close this FCF_M gap. Are the analysts that far off? Not likely.
- If the GNP expansion rate is assumed to be 3%, the calculated Slot FCF_M is 19.7 times FCF versus the implicit fundamental FCF_M of 37.8 times FCF (assuming the analyst's consensus forecast for the next five years of annual growth of 9%).
- If the C* for KO was 8.8% versus 10.0%, reflecting a lower marginal borrowing cost of 6% versus 7% and a lower risk free rate of 4.5% versus 6.0%, the derived Hi Slot FCF_M is 28.7 versus the implicit FCF_M of 37.8 and the Hi Slot P/E is 21.4 versus the implicit fundamental P/E of 28.2.

CONCLUSION ON KO P/E

- *The implicit fundamental P/E of 28.2 (line 31, Section 1) appears to be on the high side of reasonable* as supported by the fundamentals analysis range of the P/E Eviscerator and Slot Multiple Engine indicating a Slot P/E of 16.8 (line 3, Section 3) and a Hi Slot P/E of 21.4 at the date of multiple evaluation.
- The derived Slot value per share is $35.04 per share (line 45, Section 4), versus the market value of $61.76 (line 44, Section 4), or 43% below the market price at October 31, 2007.
- If the Slot FCF_M and Slot P/E appear to be the more likely multiple levels versus the higher implicit fundamental multiples, then growth rate perceptions and *u*, other overall market exuberance or the real option value of other opportunities must account for the difference. Almost 47% of the implicit fundamental FCF_M of 37.8, or about 17.7 times FCF (line 49, Section 4), would result from something, *u*, other than the consensus growth forecasts.

THE VALUE-CREATION POTENTIAL INDEX FOR KO

- *The value-creation potential of KO of 20.3% is strong as measured by the value-creation potential index (VCPI) (line 19, Section 5).* The strength index is a composite measure of the spread between r, the Nopat return on operating assets (line 27, Section 1) and cost of capital, C* (line 23) and the analysts' growth forecast, gT over period T (line 12, Section 1).

- The value creation strength potential presented on the graph presents the fundamental drivers of the VCPI index of 20.3%:
  - On the y axis, r (23.2%) is more than twice C* (10%).
  - On the x axis, the growth during T, gT, (9%) is less than r and the sustainable long term growth rate, gs (14.2%).
  - Along arc *r, gs' (the intersection of r and the sustainable growth rate, gs)* cash requirements for growth and dividends (at the target payout ratio) are sourced from internal cash generation plus new debt finance (at the target debt to capital ratio).
  - The closer the point of intersection of r and gT lies to the left of and approaches arc *r, gs'*, and the further out the intersection lies along arc *r, gs'*, the larger the market value and the faster will be the increase in the growth of market value. Also, the level of excess cash accumulation in the business will be minimized.
  - Intersections of r and gT which lay to the right and below of arc *r, gs'* indicate an unsustainable growth rate gT and a need for cash in excess of that available from the target debt to capital ratio.
  - The point of intersection of r and gT for KO lies above and to the left of the arc *r, gs'*, indicating that if the fundamentals of the recent past are indicative of the future, KO will continue to generate cash in excess of its growth reinvestment and dividend requirements. Also, excess debt finance remains available for additional growth and expansion opportunities (see Topic 55).

P/E EVISCERATOR APPLIED TO GOOGLE INC. AS OF NOVEMBER 1, 2007

- Appendix 59.6 presents component analysis of the P/E of Google Inc. (ticker GOOG) as of November 1, 2007, utilizing the P/E eviscerator.
- The implicit fundamental P/E of Google as of November 1, 2007, of 54.3 is composed of a C* multiple of 6.3 times net income a (line 29, Section 1) and an implicit g_d multiple of 44.9 times net income (line 30) resulting in a *fundamental P/E* of 51.2 times net income (line 31). (The fundamental P/E excludes the effect of cash, debt and other long-term liabilities that are captured in the market valuation and the market PE of GOOG.)
  - Cash net of debt and other long-term liabilities represent +3.2 times net income (line 32 plus line 33) resulting in the market P/E of 54.3 at the measurement date (line 34).
- C* for GOOG is estimated to be 13.8% (line 23) and reflects a estimated debt at capacity to market capital ratio of 13.9% (line 17), or six times EBITDA (author assumed capacity). The input data presented result from synthesis of current and the long-term (5-year) relationships reflected in the financial data available for KO from MSN Money as of November 1, 2007.

IMPLICIT P/E, FCF_M VERSUS DERIVED SLOT P/E, FCF_M, AND g_d

- The estimated *implicit fundamental* FCF_M derived from the market P/E per equation 59.1 above, is approximately 59.4 times FCF (line 37 and line 7, Section 2) of which the C* component is 7.3 times FCF (line 35) and the g_d component is 52.2 times FCF (line 36) resulting in the fundamental FCF_M of 59.4 times free cash flow (line 37).
- The implicit fundamental FCF_M excludes the effect of cash, debt, and other long-term liabilities that *are* captured in the market FCF_M.
  - Cash net of debt and other long-term liabilities represent +3.6 times FCF (line 38 plus line 39), resulting in the estimated market FCF_M of 63.0 (line 40).
- The annual discounted weighted earnings growth rate *(g_d)* implicit in the market P/E is approximately 14.0% (line 30) or 12.1% in the FCF_M (line 36). The *computed consensus* FCF_M *Slot g_d* is 10.7% (line 41), which is below the implicit FCF gd of 12.1% (line 36), and was derived by utilizing the analyst's consensus forecast for the next five years of annual growth of 32% (line 9) and assuming that annual FCF growth into perpetuity is equivalent to GNP growth of 4%.
  - This assumes that the consensus earnings g_d are also appropriate for FCF growth. The g_d factor was derived utilizing the method presented in Topic 57.
- The *derived consensus fundamental Slot* FCF_M (excluding the effect of cash, debt, and other long-term liabilities) is 32.4 times FCF (line 7, Section 3) or an equivalent fundamental Slot P/E of 27.9 times net income (line 3, Section 3) versus the market fundamental P/E of 51.2 (also excluding the effect of cash, debt and other long term liabilities) (line 3, Section 2). The implicit FCF_M is 84% over the indicated Slot FCF_M.
- The implicit $EBITDA_M$ derived from the FCF_M is 34.8 times EBITDA (line 11, Section 2), versus the calculated consensus Slot $EBITDA_M$ of 18.9 times (line 11, Section 3).
- The difference between the implicit fundamental FCF_M of 59.4 (line 7, Section 2) and the consensus Slot FCF_M of 32.4 (line 7, Section 3) is 27.0 times FCF. The difference between the implicit fundamental P/E of 51.2 (line 3, Section 2) and the consensus Slot P/E of 27.9 (line 3, Section 3) is 23.3 times net income. *Why?*

VARIANCE IN SLOT RESULTS IF ASSUMPTIONS ARE SENSITIZED

- Either a 5% point increase in the GNP growth assumption to 9% beyond year five (a 125% increase) or a 19% point increase in the analyst's next five years annual growth assumption to 51% annual growth (versus 32% per analyst's consensus estimates, a 60% increase) would close this FCF_M gap. Are the analysts that far off? Not likely.

- If the GNP expansion rate is assumed to be 3%, the calculated Slot FCF_M is 29.9 times FCF versus the implicit fundamental FCF_M of 59.4 times FCF (assuming the analyst's consensus forecast for the next five years of annual growth of 9%).
- If the C* for Google was 12.4% versus 13.8% reflecting a lower marginal borrowing cost of 6% versus 7% and a lower risk-free rate of 4.5% versus 6.0%, the derived Hi Slot FCF_M is 38.2 versus a Slot FCF_M of 32.4 and the Hi Slot P/E is 32.9 versus the Slot P/E of 27.9.

CONCLUSION ON GOOG P/E

- *The implicit fundamental P/E of 51.2 (line 31, Section 1) appears to be on the high side of reasonable* as supported by the fundamentals analysis range of the P/E Eviscerator and Slot Multiple Engine indicating a Slot P/E of 27.9 (line 3, Section 3) and a Hi Slot P/E of 32.9 at the date of multiple evaluation.
- The derived Slot value per share is $403.42 per share (line 45, Section 4) versus the market value of $707.00 per share (line 44, Section 4), 43% below the market price at November 1, 2007.
- If the Slot FCF_M and Slot P/E appear to be the more likely multiple levels versus the higher implicit fundamental multiples, then growth rate perceptions and *u*, other market exuberance, or the real option value of other opportunities must account for the difference. Almost 40% of the implicit fundamental FCF_M of 59.4, or about 24 times FCF (line 49, Section 4), would result from something, *u*, other than the consensus growth forecasts.
- The implicit fundamental P/E of 51.2 reflects more than the underlying range of C* fundamentals and market growth assumptions versus a Slot P/E in the 30s unless the analyst's growth estimates are very understated. The market P/E possibly reflects the exuberance effect of Google announcing its entry into the smart phone software market, which surged the P/E by approximately 40% in September 2007. Prior to the surge, the market P/E was close to 39.
- One has to wonder if a company the size of Google can grow its FCF at a rate necessary to sustain such a multiple. However, such a multiple is justified by any holder if there is a buyer with the same exuberance regardless of indicated value arising from fundamentals; everyone is right.

THE VALUE CREATION STRENGTH INDEX FOR GOOG

- *The value creation strength potential of GOOG of 98.9%, is very strong as measured by the strength index (VCPI) (line 16, Section 5).* The strength index is a composite measure of the spread between r, the Nopat return on operating assets (line 27, Section 1), and cost of capital, C* (line 23) and the analysts, growth forecast, gT over period T (line 9, Section 1).

- The value creation strength potential presented on the graph presents the fundamental drivers of the VCPI index of 98.9%:
  - On the y axis, r (38.4%) is more than twice C* (13.8%).
  - On the x axis, the growth during T, gT, (32%) is less than r and the sustainable long term growth rate, gs (44.6%).
  - Along arc *r, gs', (the intersection of r and the sustainable growth rate, gs)* cash requirements for growth and dividends (at the target payout ratio) are sourced from internal cash generation plus new debt finance (at the target debt to capital ratio).
  - The closer the point of intersection of r and gT lies to the left of and approaches arc *r, gs'*, and the further out the intersection lies along arc *r, gs'*, the larger the market value will be and the faster will be the increase in the growth of market value. Also, the level of excess cash accumulation in the business will be minimized.
  - Intersections of r and gT that lay to the right and below of arc *r, gs'* indicate an unsustainable growth rate and a need for cash in excess of that available from the target debt to capital ratio.
  - The point of intersection of r and gT for GOOG lies above and to the left of the arc *r, gs'* indicating that if the fundamentals of the recent past are indicative of the future, GOOG will continue to generate cash in excess of its growth reinvestment and dividend requirements. Also, excess debt finance remains available for additional growth, expansion opportunities, or dividend payout (see Topic 55).

CONCLUSION: P/E EVISCERATOR

- The P/E Eviscerator and Slot Multiple Engine can be used effectively by a buyer as a preparatory or reaction tool to counter a pricing P/E put forward by a seller or by a seller to support a P/E position put forward to a buyer.
  - A buyer would evaluate the seller's financial data, input the information drivers into the P/E Eviscerator and Slot Multiple Engine, and present a range of evidence supporting the buyer's offer position (or challenging the seller's P/E position).
  - A seller would likewise evaluate the seller's and potentially comparable public company financial data and analyst assumptions, input the information drivers into the P/E Eviscerator and Slot Multiple Engine, and present a range of evidence supporting the seller's P/E position.

GRAPHS OF APPROXIMATE SMALL- AND LARGE-COMPANY FREE CASH FLOW AND EBITDA MULTIPLES OVER A RANGE OF GROWTH

- Graphs in Appendices 59.7, 59.8, 59.9, and 59.10 present representative fundamental EBITDA and Free Cash Flow lagging midyear basis multiples for "Small" (C* of 15.1%) and "Large" (C* of 8.2%) companies assuming a range of five-year T period FCF *annual* growth rates and the following representative assumptions: 3% perpetuity FCF growth rates (0% to 3% when T period growth rates are 0% to 3%), EBITDA to sales ratios of 40%, combined 38% federal and state income tax rates, depreciation to sales of 1.5%, and assuming incremental investment in plant and equipment and working capital investment to incremental sales equals 20% over the growth range.

- The charts provide a view of the interrelationships of the key value drivers on and a representative indication of the resulting FCF and EBITDA multiples along the entire growth range indicated for small and large cap companies.
- The charts also present the C* multiple and Growth g_d components of the FCF and EBITDA multiples demonstrating the dramatic effect of the accelerator, growth, and the dramatic multiple differences between large and small companies along the entire growth range indicated.

APPENDIX 59.1 Multiple Conversion Table Target Company Valuation

FCFM= 10.1598	1/[1/	C* 0.2097	gd] 0.1113					
P/E= 7.9040	FCFM / 10.1598	[NI% / 0.2069	FCF%]* 0.1949	1-D/C% 0.8260				
FCMM= 10.1598	[P/E / 7.9040	1-D/C%]* 0.8260	[NI% / 0.2069	FCF%] 0.1949				
EBITM= 5.6431	FCFM / 10.1598	[EBIT% / 0.3509	FCF%] 0.1949					
FCMM= 10.1598	EBITM* 5.6431	[EBIT% / 0.3509	FCF%] 0.1949					
EBITDAM= 5.3102	FCFM / 10.1598	[EBITDA% / 0.3729	FCF%] 0.1949					
FCMM= 10.1598	[EBITDAM / 5.3102	[EBIT% / 0.3509	EBITDA%]] 0.3729	* [EBIT% / 0.3509	FCF%] 0.1949			
EBITM= 5.6431	[P/E / 7.9040	1-D/C%)* 0.8260	[NI% / 0.2069	EBIT%] 0.3509				
EBITM= 5.6431	[P/E / 7.9040	1-D/C%]* 0.8260	1 / 1 /	[[D /E%* 0.2107	i]* 0.0800	[1/ROEMV%]+ 0.1265	[1 / 1 /	1-T]] 0.6400
EBITDAM= 5.3102	[P/E / 7.9040	1-D/C%]* 0.8260	[NI% / 0.2069					
P/E= 7.9040	[EBITDAM / 5.3102	[NI% / 0.2069	EBITDA%]]* 0.3729	EBITDA%] 0.3729				
EBITDAM = 5.3102	EBITM* 5.6431	[EBIT% / 0.3509	EBITDA%] 0.3729	1-D/C% 0.826				
EBITDAM= 5.3102	EBITM* 5.6431	[EBIT% / 0.3509	[EBIT% + 0.3509	DEPR%]] 0.0220				

Small Company

Lagging Ebitda Multiple Drivers

C*= 15.1% Ebitda%= 40.0% depr % = 1.5% 10th Q Levered beta= 1.40

gd perp= 0% to 3.0% Tax rate = 38.0% ^I /^ sales%= 20.00% Mid Year Rate

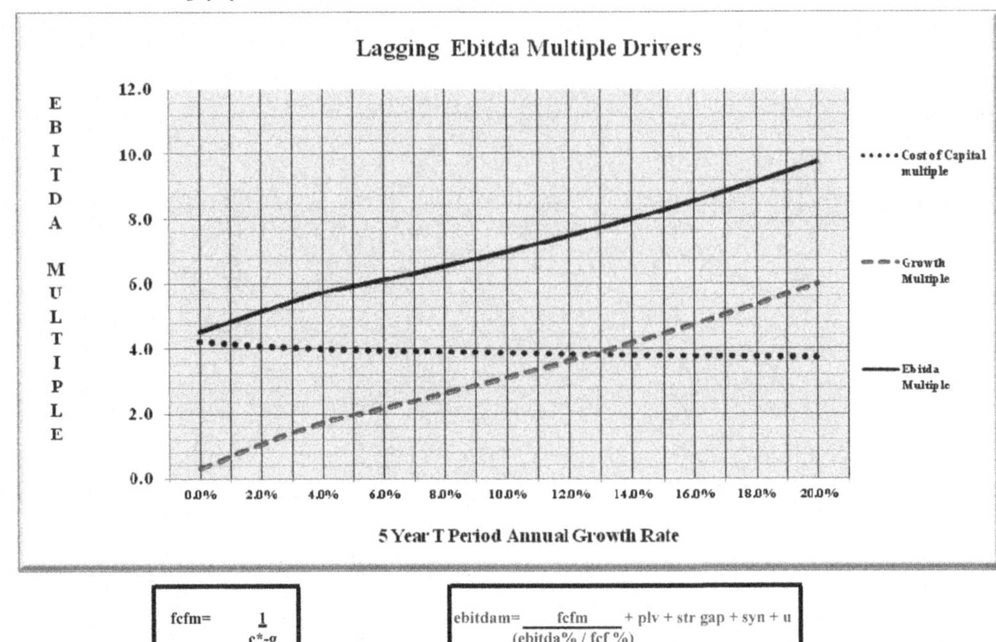

APPENDIX 59.7 Lagging EBIDTA Multiple, Small Company

Large Company
Lagging Ebitda Multiple Drivers

C*= 8.2% Ebitda%= 40.0% depr % = 1.5% 1st Q Levered beta= .91
gd perp= 0% to 3.0% Tax rate = 38.0% ^I /^ sales%= 20.00% Mid Year Rate

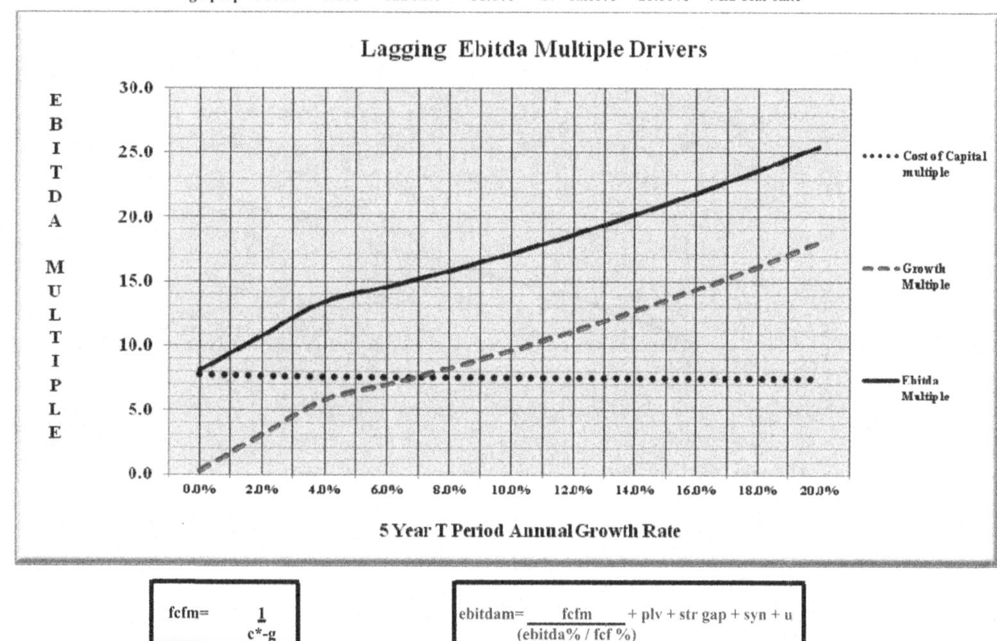

fcfm= $\frac{1}{c^*-g}$

ebitdam= $\frac{\text{fcfm}}{(\text{ebitda\% / fcf \%})}$ + plv + str gap + syn + u

APPENDIX 59.8 Lagging EBITDA Multiple, Large Company

Small Company

Lagging FCF Multiple Drivers

C*= 15.1% Average FCF%= 24.20% depr % = 1.5% 10th Q Levered beta= 1.40

gd perp= 0% to 3.0% Tax rate = 38.0% ^I /^ sales%= 20.00% Mid Year Rate

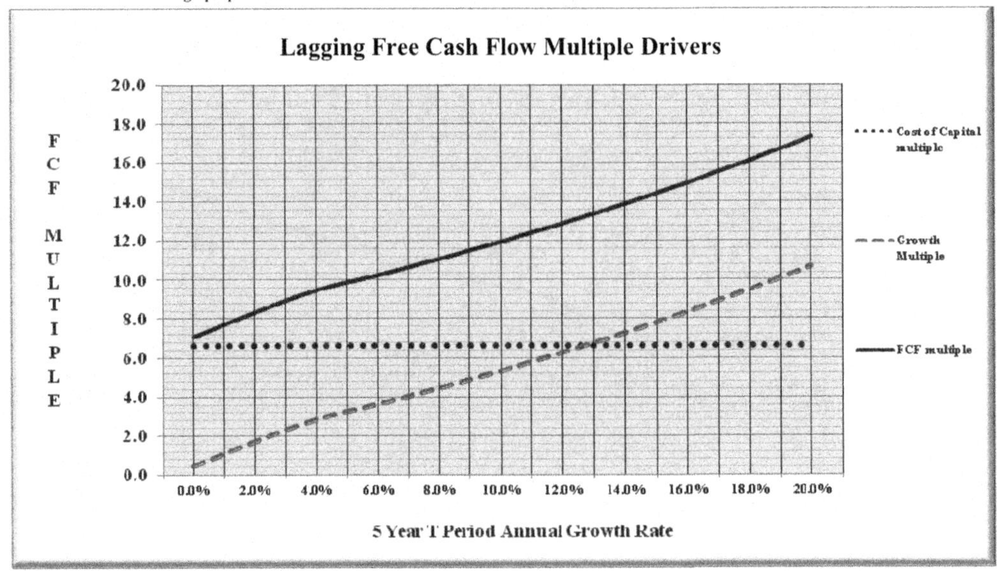

$$fcfm = \frac{1}{c^* - g}$$

APPENDIX 59.9 Lagging FCF_M, Small Company

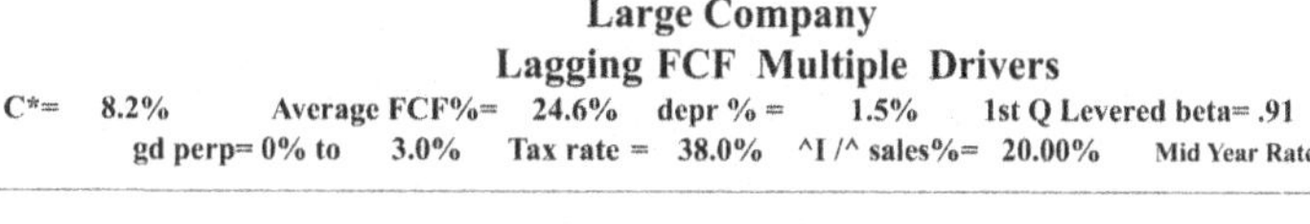

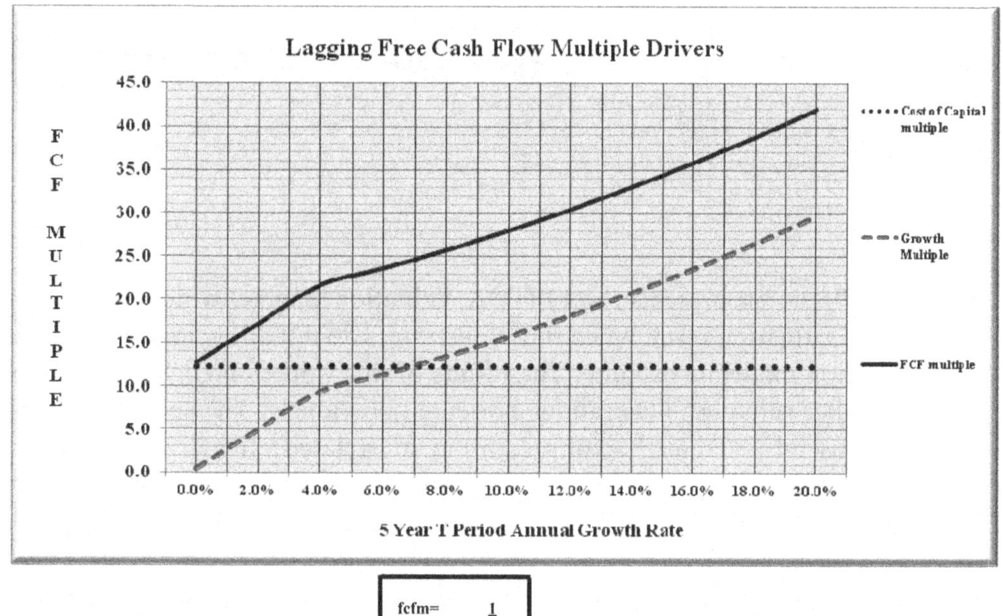

fcfm= $\frac{1}{c^*-g}$

APPENDIX 59.10 Lagging FCF_M, Large Company

The following Appendices, as well as those presented earlier, are available for viewing or download on the Web site for this book at: www.wiley.com/go/emott. Please see the About the Web Site page at the back of this book for login information.

APPENDIX 59.2 $EBITDA_M$ Engine No. 1: To Derive $EBITDA_M$ from FCF_M or Derive FCF_M from $EBITDA_M$

APPENDIX 59.3 $EBITDA_M$ Engine No. 2: To Derive $EBITDA_M$ from FCF_M or Derive FCF_M from $EBITDA_M$

APPENDIX 59.4 P/E Eviscerator and Slot Multiple Engine

APPENDIX 59.5 P/E Eviscerator and Slot Multiple Engine B: Coca-Cola, October 31, 2007

APPENDIX 59.6 P/E Eviscerator and Slot Multiple Engine: Google, November 1, 2007

TOPIC 60

EBITDA Valuation Engine

Topic 60 presents the EBITDA Valuation Engine, which provides an accurate valuation result when time constraints do not allow for a more extensive valuation modeling exercise. The results of this valuation engine are compared to the other valuation illustrations presented previously. The spider chart illustration is a useful visual method of presenting interrelated value drivers of volume, variable margin, fixed costs, fixed and variable capital efficiency, tax rates, cost of capital and their impact on economic value added (EVA^{TM})[1] and enterprise value over time period T.

The reader is encouraged to take the time to read the text in conjunction with the referenced Appendices to gain the appropriate level of understanding of the subject matter discussed in the narrative. Appendices are either presented at the end of this and each remaining Topic or are available for review and download on this book's companion Web site (see the About the Web Site page for login information).

EBITDA ENGINE OVERVIEW—A SHORTHAND VALUATION METHOD

- Early in the deal evaluation exercise or when time is short, data on the target are limited in quantity and quality. Precise modeling is not yet needed, or sometimes, in place of a more rigorous computerized discounted cash flow (DCF) exercise, shorthand approximations of value will suffice.
- The shorthand valuation method, driven by the EBITDA (earnings before interest, tax, depreciation, and amortization) Valuation Engine, will result in reasonable approximations of enterprise value (excluding the net value of cash or other assets or liabilities) quickly versus more extensive DCF valuation exercises.
- EBITDA Valuation Engine results are generally a few percentage points different from DCF valuations.
- The EBITDA Valuation Engine drivers (EBITDA, growth rates, tax rates, investment rates, franchise time period) are well known and very familiar to

[1] EVA is a trademark of Stern Stewart.

business people. Therefore, they enable fast translation to a free cash flow (FCF) approached valuation.

- While the arithmetic appears imposing, it reduces itself to a growing FCF valuation method similar to the one first presented in Topic 20 and easily translates to spreadsheet applications.

$V_L =$	V_F	+	V_P
FCF Value (V_L) =	Target Value created during period T including growth (V_F)	+	Target Value created after franchise period franchise T into perpetuity – the Terminal Value (V_P)

$$\text{FCF Value } (V_L) = \frac{\text{Average Annual FCF during period T}}{\text{Mid period T Cap rate}} + \frac{\left[\dfrac{\text{FCF in period T + 1}}{\text{Cap rate less perp growth rate into perpetuity}}\right]}{\text{Cap rate at end of T}}$$

EBITDA ENGINE EXPLAINED

- The EBITDA Valuation Engine valuation approach, *utilizing EBITDA as the value driver,* is as shown for an *end-of-year discount rate basis* valuation.

$$V_L = V_F + V_P$$

$$V_F = \frac{\left[(E_0(1+g_{dT}))\left(1-(t\%-((td\%/E_0\%)t\%))\right)(1-I_T)\left[(1+g_{dT})^T\right]^{0.5}\right]}{(1/(T/((1+C^*)^{(T+1)0.5})))}$$

$$V_P = \frac{\left[\dfrac{[E_0\,(1+g_{dT})^{(T)}\,(1+g_{dp})(1-(t\%))(1-I_p)]}{(C^*-g_{dp})}\right]}{(1+C^*)^T}$$

where

V_L = levered enterprise value of the target = $V_F + V_P$
V_F = target value created during franchise period T
V_P = target value created after franchise period T into perpetuity
E_0 = EBITDA of base year 0
$E_0\%$ = EBITDA at base year 0, as a percentage of sales at base year 0
T = number of years of the franchise period where superior returns and growth can be realized from the capability base
td% = tax depreciation expense as a percentage of sales
t% = marginal income tax rate

g_{dT} = annual (nominal) discount rate weighted growth rate in EBITDA during franchise period T determined on a midyear discount rate basis or an end-of-year discount rate basis

g_{dp} = discount weighted compound average rate of growth in EBITDA expected into perpetuity after period T

- The nominal growth rate beyond period T to determine g_P should generally not exceed the expected long-term served market growth rate plus the net effect of inflation on EBITDA beyond period T.
- g_{dp} may be determined on a midyear discount rate basis (g_{dpm}) or an end-of-year discount rate basis (g_{dpe}).

C^* = long-term weighted average cost of capital from the capital asset pricing model, CAPM

I_T = *incremental investment rate during T* = amount of EBITDA that will be reinvested for working capital or new plant and equipment or other operating assets during period T to grow the business at rate g_T, *expressed as a percentage of EBITDA after cash tax during period T*

- I_T may be approximated by evaluating the past (say the last five years) as a guide to the T period (and perpetuity period) investment rate where:

$$I_T = \frac{\Delta\,CCE}{\Delta\,EBITDA\text{ after tax}}$$

Δ CCE = $CE_0 - CE_{-6}$ (change in capital employed level over the last five years)

CE_0 = capital employed (net property, plant, and equipment plus working capital) most recent year (Year 0)

CE_{-6} = Capital employed six years ago

Δ EBITDA = $EBITDA_0 - EBITDA_{-6}$ (change in EBITDA level over the last five years)

$EBITDA_0$ = EBITDA earned most recent year (Year 0) after cash tax

$EBITDA_{-6}$ = EBITDA earned six years ago after cash tax

I_p = *incremental investment rate during perpetuity* = amount of EBITDA that will be reinvested for working capital or new plant and equipment or other operating assets during the perpetuity period to grow the business at rate g_p (adjusted for the lower perpetuity period growth rate), *expressed as a percentage of EBITDA after cash tax during perpetuity period P.*

- *The first term,* V_F, determines the present value (end-of-year basis) of the posttax free cash flow (EBITDA posttax at the marginal cash tax rate including the tax shield on tax depreciation less investment required for growth) during T, by deriving an *annual* value of the FCF *expected at the midway point* of the T period (including growth during T to the midway point), then capitalizes it using an *end-of-year basis discount rate* calculated at the *midway point* of period T.

- This is roughly equivalent to the value resulting from discounting annual growing FCF amounts by end-of-year basis discount rates for each year during T.
- This results in an end-of-year discount rate basis present value of the FCF arising during period T.
- To determine a midyear discount rate basis enterprise value of the average annual free cash flow *expected at the midway point* of the T period, a *midyear basis discount factor* is used in the denominator of V_F, determined as:

$$(1/(T/((1 + C^*)^{(T)0.5})))$$

- *The second term,* V_P, estimates the present value (end-of-year basis) of the posttax free cash flow occurring *after* T into perpetuity by estimating the *annual* perpetuity FCF value *following period* T. This equals EBITDA at period T after cash tax including the tax shield of depreciation [assuming book and tax depreciation will be equal after the T period] less investment required in the period following period T, plus one post-T year of perpetuity growth. This amount is then capitalized as at the end of period T using the perpetuity growth method by dividing the FCF value by C* less the growth factor g_{dp}, *where* g_{dpe} *is an end-of-year basis discount weighted growth rate into perpetuity.* (See Topics 54 and 57.)
  - The resulting perpetuity value at the end of year T is then discounted to time 0 by dividing the perpetuity value at the end of T by the *end-of-year basis discount factor* as at the end of year T: $(1 + C^*)^T$.
  - This results in an end-of-year discount rate basis terminal value of the FCF arising after period T at time 0.
- *To estimate a midyear discount rate basis terminal value for the second term,* V_P, determine the annual perpetuity FCF value following period T as described above, then capitalize it as at the end of period T using the perpetuity growth method by dividing the free cash flow value by C* less the growth factor g_{dpm} *determined as a midyear basis discount weighted growth rate into perpetuity.* (See Topics 54 and 57.)
  - The resulting perpetuity value at the end of year T (whether on an end-of-year or midyear basis) is then discounted to time 0 by dividing the perpetuity value at the end of T by the *end-of-year basis discount factor* as at the end of year T: $(1 + C^*)^T$.
  - This results in an end-of-year discount rate basis terminal value of the FCF arising after period T at time 0.
- V_L, the levered fully distributable enterprise value of the target, equals the sum of $V_F + V_P$.
- V_{LE}, the levered equity value of the target, equals V_L less the amount of debt employed in the target capital structure.

- Substituting C_U in place of C^* (in V_F and V_P) will result in an approximate *unlevered value* (V_U).

  where $V_U = V_{FU} + V_{PU}$ (when C_U replaces C^*)

  To obtain the levered value V_L, add Dt to V_U:

$$V_L = V_U + Dt$$

  where Dt = value of leverage in the target's capital structure
  t = target's marginal tax rate
  D = fixed amount of debt in place over the life of the investment

- If the amount of debt is not a fixed amount and is expected to be paid off or paid down from the initial level incurred at the date of acquisition, the value of leverage should be determined using the discounted cash flow method described in Topic 42.

VALUE OF GROWTH DURING T

- The approximate value created by growth (V_g) during the franchise period T and its effect in the perpetuity period are estimated as shown next.

$$V_g = V_L - \frac{FCF_0}{C^*} \quad \text{when using } C^* \text{ as the discount rate}$$

$$V_g = V_U + Dt - \frac{FCF_0}{CU} \quad \text{when using } C_U \text{ as the discount rate}$$

where $\frac{FCF_0}{C^*}$ or $\frac{FCF_0}{C_U}$ = simple perpetuity value of a no-growth FCF stream
FCF_0 = free cash flow in the base period
V_g = amount of value included in V_L attributable to execution of growth strategies

EBITDA ENGINE VALUATION EXAMPLE

- Appendix 60.1 presents a summary of the EBITDA Valuation Engine, drivers (highlighted cells, columns 3 and 5), and the valuation results on an end-of-year and midyear discount rate basis (columns 8 and 11), using the same business drivers as presented in the leveraged buyout (LBO) valuation example in Appendix 44.2.
- Appendix 60.2 (pages 1–3) presents the results of the BITDA Valuation Engine computations (V_F and V_P). The approximate value created by growth is presented on page 3.
- Appendices 60.3 and 60.4 present for comparative purposes a discounted cash flow valuation using midyear and end-of-year basis discount rates and the same financial driver assumptions as used in the EBITDA Valuation Engine.

- Appendices 60.5 and 60.6 present for comparative purposes a comparable multiple method valuation using the method presented in Topic 58, using end-of-year and midyear basis discount rates and the same financial drivers as used in the EBITDA Valuation Engine as presented in Appendix 60.1. See Appendix 60.5(a), (b), and (c) for end-of-year valuations and Appendix 60.6(a), (b), and (c) for midyear valuations.

COMPARISON OF EBITDA ENGINE VALUATION RESULTS WITH OTHER METHODS

- Illustration 60.1 presents the comparative enterprise valuations resulting from the approaches and examples as noted, assuming the same value driver assumptions.

ILLUSTRATION 60.1 COMPARISON OF ENTERPRISE VALUATION RESULTS FROM FOUR VALUATION APPROACHES

	End-of-year Basis Discount Rate $000	Midyear Basis Discount Rate $000	Topic and Appendix
EBITDA engine valuation	14,983	16,538	60.1
DCF valuation	14,591	16,048	60.3, 60.4
Comparable multiple method	14,591	16,048	60.5, 60.6
LBO valuation	14,621	16,133	44.2

SPIDER CHART PRESENTATION OF THE EBITDA ENGINE ILLUSTRATION OF APPENDIX 60.2

- Appendix 60.7(a) and (b) present the *Spider Chart Illustration* of the EBITDA Engine Valuation in Appendix 60.2 for the midyear discount rate basis valuation.
- The chart displays the interrelated value drivers of volume, variable margin, fixed costs, fixed and variable capital efficiency, tax rates, cost of capital and their impact on economic value added (EVA) and enterprise value creation in a clear graphical format for the base year (year 0) and year 5 of the EBITDA Engine Valuation example. The year 5 chart (the fifth year of the T period) compares the growth result through year 5 with year 0, illustrating the expansion expected from the growth and other valuation drivers and the resulting increase in EVA and valuation.

- Break-even volume is presented as well as the enterprise value for each year, assuming the declining EBITDA g_d growth outlook profile for each succeeding year during the T period.
  - The g_d growth outlook profile for each year during the T period forecast declines. At the beginning of T there are T years (in the example, 5) of high growth ahead followed by perpetuity growth in the future. After two years in period T there are three high-growth years ahead, followed by perpetuity growth in the future. After five years in period T there are zero growth years ahead and only perpetuity growth in the future.
  - As a result, g_d and the EBITDA multiple outlook for each succeeding year after the beginning of T decline. The enterprise value and EVA increase somewhat.
- The sensitivity impacts of changes to any of the drivers of EVA can be visually approximated quickly on any one of the charts during the T period by using the plus and minus bands around the baseline drivers.
- The spider chart is a helpful visual tool to present and depict the interplay of assumed valuation drivers on EVA and enterprise valuation. It allows fast visual sensitivity and insight into the ultimate questions: Does this valuation make sense, and can we live with it?

A FINAL NOTE ON VALUATIONS

- Although $V_L = V_F + V_P$, as discussed earlier (and $V_U + TS_{PV}$ and D + E per Topic 44), in reality, V_{LP}, the levered value *paid* in auction and sometimes privately negotiated deals, often equals $V_F + V_P + s + o + u$

where s = amount of buyer integration and control *synergies shared with the seller* during the negotiation process to close the deal
o = buyer's perception of the other real option values provided by the platform acquired
u = "buyer lust" premium over $V_F + V_P$ often resulting from a case of buyer deal fever

- When buyer desire runs high, the normally expected negotiating range of V_L can be significantly exceeded by the almost indeterminable value, u.
- Whether s and o are grounded, as they should be, in real option analysis and hard integration and deal structuring synergies arising from control, and not from a case of deal fever, u, often remains to be seen.

1					EBITDA ENGINE VALUATION SUMMARY							
2												
3					input data							
4	1	2	3	4	5	6	7	8	9	10	11	12
5	EBITDA ENGINE VALUATION DRIVERS				Illustration			Illustration			Illustration	
6	discount rate convention for interest tax shield debt: End yr = 0, Mid yr = 1				1	FX Rate		Mid Year rate	FX fc to USD		End of Year rate	FX fc to USD
7			base year:	% to	currency	FC to USD		priced at C*	1		priced at C*	1
8			usd	sales	usd	1		US $ mils	US $ mils		US $ mils	US $ mils
9	sales		7,369				pv of fcf in period T	8,034	8,034		7,304	7,304
10	ebitda		2,748	37.3%	37.3%		pv of perpty fcf after T	8,504	8,504		7,678	7,678
11	working capital employed		1,282	17.404%	17.4%		levered fcf enterprise value	16,538	16,538		14,983	14,983
12	net ppe + other op assets employed		1,179	15.999%	16.0%		value of debt; est or tD if Cu used	0	0		0	0
13	indication:	yr 1 new ppe	216	yr 0 incr ppe %	12.0%		levered fcf enterprise value	16,538	16,538		14,983	14,983
14	tax depn expense for year 0		162	2.200%	2.2%		plus cash/investments	0	0		0	0
15	indication:	yr 1 tax depn exp	192	yr 1 ppe / sales	2.93%		less other Lterm liabilities	0	0		0	0
16	book deprec expense for year 0		162	2.200%	2.2%		less begin'g debt-existing plus new	2,878	2,878		2,878	2,878
17	indication:	yr 1 book depn exp	192	yr 1 ppe / sales	2.93%		equity market value	13,660	13,660		12,105	12,105
18	number of franchise years " T Period"				5							
19					5		pre tax irr to equity investor	17.2%				
20	nominal marginal tax rate on ebit during T period " t "				36.00%							
21	nominal marginal tax rate on ebit during Perpetuity period " tp "				36.00%							
22	nominal effective tax rate on ebit over deal life-for C*				36.00%		ebitda period 1	3,251				
23	input cagr during T Period				18.30%		cash tax expense	1,101	debt to lagging ebitda		1.05	
24	cagr during T Period				18.30%		ebida post tax period 1	2,149	debt to leading ebitda		0.89	
25	calculated incr w/c & nppe investment as % of ebida after cash tax expense in yr 1 of T Period				20.96%		investment in period 1	450	lagging ebitda to interest		11.9	
26	input default investment rate % as % ebitda atax in period T if w/c and ppe % = 0=				15.00%		fcf in period 1	1,699	leading ebitda to interest		14.1	
27	cost of capital:	company long term marginal debt cost			8.00%		fcf in period 0	1,436	d/cap period 1		0.0%	
28		c cap - specific risk premium			0.00%		ebitda post tax first yr of prpty **		d/cap period 5		0.0%	
29		c cap - country risk premium (30 yr local versus 30 yr us treas)			0.00%		fcf in first yr of prpty		enterprise value to sales		2.24	
30		c cap - small cap equity risk premium			9.00%		enterprise value to ebitda yr 1	5.09			4.61	
31		c cap - long term risk free rate			6.00%		enterprise value to ebitda yr 0	6.02			5.45	
32		c cap - large cap equity risk premium			7.00%		enterprise value to fcf yr 1	9.73				
33		c cap - ulnevered business risk beta			1.1719		enterprise value to fcf yr 0	11.52				
34	enter 1 for LBO valuation using Cu or, 0 for WACC valuation using C*				0		reciprocal of fcfm	8.684%				
35			C*, T & perp	Cu Period T	C*		derived gd-C* - reciprocal of fcfm	12.286%				
36	calculated Cu or C*		20.9701%	23.203%	20.9701%		C*	20.970%				
37	C*				20.97007%							
38	enter levered C* beyond T if using Cu to drive LBO value				20.97%	<<<<<<<<<<<enter CU amount		20.970%	to drive pre tax irr %			
39	input debt to unlevered value of mkt cap ratio if pricing using C*				17.401%	<<<<< for C* based valuation , enter D / C ratio (and iterate) to determine max ebitda d / cap ratio						
40	input default debt/market cap ratio:				15.0%							
41	optional input investment rate after T into perpty if T >0				0.00%							
42	expressed as % of ebitda after cash tax expense.											
43	optional input % decline in investment after T		(perp cagr% /Tcagr%)	73.62%	0%	use indicated adjustment or other to adjust calculated investment % in perpetuity						
44	calculated incr w/c & nppe investment as % of ebitda after cash tax expense in yr 1 of Perpetuity				20.9568%							
45	calculated incr w/c & nppe investment as % of ebitda or input % after cash tax expense in yr 1 of Perpetuity				20.9568%							
46	cagr after T in stage one of perpetuity period		5	periods	4.00%							
47	cagr after stage one into perpetuity				4.00%							
48	proxy for mid year discount weighted cagr after T into perpty			LAGGING	5.541%							
49	proxy for end of year year discount weighted cagr after T into perpty			LAGGING	4.113%							
50	actual amount of cash or investments assumed at closing				0							
51	actual amount of other L Term liabilities assumed at closing				0							
52	actual amount of debt D in place at valuation date				0							
53	actual book debt to levered enterprise value ratio				0.00%							
54	optional input enter targeted debt capacity as multiple of ebitda if Cu used				4.00	0.89	debt to leading ebitda at input level of debt to enterprise value level					
55	calculated amount of debt based on ebitda multiple if Cu used				0							
56	pay debt off with free cash flo? If Cu used		1=yes , 0=no		0							
57	fcf cash dividend take out during T if debt pay down is to be < fcf available				0	iterate amount of dividend takeout to target ending D/Cmkt employed (enhances equity holder irr)						
58	beginning debt to enterprise value ratio of targeted debt at yr 1 of T period				0.00%		and to drive pre tax irr%					
59	ending debt to enterprise value ratio of targeted debt at yr 5 of T period				0.00%							
60	enter the average debt to enterprise value ratio during the terminal value period if valued as LBO				31%							
61	average debt to enterprise value ratio during T of targeted debt				0.00%							
62	tax depn as % ebitda				5.9%							

APPENDIX 60.1 EBITDA Engine Valuation Summary

Illustration of EBITDA Engine Valuation

End of Year discount rate basis Valuation

			% to sales
	sales	$7,369	
E0	ebitda at base year 0	$2,748	37.288%
	operating profit at base year 0	$2,586	35.088%
	working capital	$1,282	17.404%
	gross plant and equipment and other operating assets	$1,179	15.999%
td %	tax depreciationn	$162	2.200%
bd %	book depreciation	$162	2.200%
T	number of franchise years " T Period"- 5 max		5
t%	nominal marginal tax rate on ebit during T period " t "		36.0%
tp%	nominal marginal tax rate on ebit during Perpetuity period " tp "		36.0%
gdT	cagr during T Period		18.3%
C* or Cu	levered fcf entreprise value discount rate C*		20.97007%
IT	incremental working cap & net ppe expressed as % of ebitda after cash tax expense during T		20.95678%
Ip	incremental working cap & net ppe expressed as % of ebitda after cash tax expense during p		20.95678%
gdpe	end of year year discount weighted cagr after T into perpty		4.11278%
VL	Levered Enterprise Value		7304
VF	Enterprise Value created during Franchise period T		7678
Vp	Enterprise Value created after Franchise period T into perpetuity		14983
FCF0			1436

VL = VF + VP

End of Year discount rate basis present value in T

VF = [(EBITDA in yr 1) (1-(effective cash tax rate in T)) (1- Investment rate in T) ((T period cagr)^T)^.5] / Capitalization rate at mid period T

$$VF = \frac{\left[\left(E_0(1+g_{dT})\right)\left(1-\left(t\%-\left((td\%/E_0\%)t\%\right)\right)\right)(1-I_r)\left[(1+g_{dT})^T\right]^{\wedge.5}\right]}{(1/(T/((1+C^*)^{\wedge(T+1)\wedge 0.5})))}$$

VF = [(2748 * (1+.183)) * (1-(.36 - ((.022/.37288) *.36))) * (1-.2095678) * [(1+.183)^5]^0.5]] / (1 / (5 / ((1.2097007) ^(5+1) ^ 0.5)))

VF = [* 3250.594752 * 0.66124 * 0.790432 * 1.52217] / 0.35405

VF = [2,586] / 0.3540

End of Year discount rate basis present value in T

VF = **7,304**

Mid Year discount rate basis Valuation

			% to sales
	sales	$7,369	
E0	ebitda at time 0	$2,748	37.288%
	operating profit at time 0	$2,586	35.088%
	w/c	$1,282	17.404%
	g ppe	$1,179	15.999%
td %	tax depn	$162	2.200%
bd %	book deprec	$162	2.200%
T	number of franchise years " T Period"- 5 max		5
t%	nominal marginal tax rate on ebit during T period " t "		36.0%
tp%	nominal marginal tax rate on ebit during Perpetuity period " tp "		36.0%
gdT	cagr during T Period		18.3%
C* or Cu	levered fcf entreprise value discount rate C*		20.97007%
IT	incremental working cap & net ppe expressed as % of ebitda after cash tax expense during T		20.95678%
Ip	incremental working cap & net ppe expressed as % of ebitda after cash tax expense during p		20.95678%
gdpm	mid year year discount weighted cagr after T into perpty		5.54082%
VL	Levered Enterprise Value		8034
VF	Enterprise Value created during Franchise period T		8504
Vp	Enterprise Value created after Franchise period T into perpetuity		16538
FCF0			1436

VL = VF + VP

Mid Year discount rate basis present value in T

VF = [(EBITDA in yr 1) (1-(effective cash tax rate)) (1- Investment rate in T) ((T period cagr)^T)^.5] / Capitalization rate at mid period T

$$VF = \frac{\left[\left(E_0(1+gd_T)\right)\left(1-\left(t\%-\left((td\%/E_0\%)t\%\right)\right)\right)(1-I_r)\left[(1+gd_T)^T\right]^{\wedge.5}\right]}{(1/(T/((1+C^*)^{\wedge(T)\wedge 0.5})))}$$

VF = [(2748 * (1+.183)) * (1-(.36 - ((.022/.37288) *.36))) * (1-.2095678) * [(1+.183)^5]^0.5]] / (1 / (5 / ((1.2097007) ^5) ^ 0.5)))

VF = [3250.594752 * 0.66124 * 0.79043 * 1.52217] / 0.32190

VF = [2586 *] / 0.3219

Mid Year discount rate basis present value in T

VF = **8,034**

APPENDIX 60.2 EBITDA Engine Valuation Computations Example

Illustration of EBITDA Engine Valuation

End of Year discount rate basis Valuation

			% to sales
	sales	$7,369	
E0	ebitda at base year 0	$2,748	37.288%
	operating profit at base year 0	$2,586	35.088%
	working capital	$1,282	17.404%
	gross plant and equipment and other operating assets	$1,179	15.999%
td %	tax depreciationn	$162	2.200%
bd %	book depreciation	$162	2.200%
T	number of franchise years " T Period"- 5 max		5
t%	nominal marginal tax rate on ebit during T period " t "		36.0%
tp%	nominal marginal tax rate on ebit during Perpetuity period " tp "		36.0%
gdT	cagr during T Period		18.3%
C* or Cu	levered fcf entreprise value discount rate C*		20.97007%
IT	incremental working cap & net ppe expressed as % of ebitda after cash tax expense during T		20.95678%
Ip	incremental working cap & net ppe expressed as % of ebitda after cash tax expense during p		20.95678%
gdpe	end of year year discount weighted cagr after T into perpty		4.11278%
VL	Levered Enterprise Value		7304
VF	Enterprise Value created during Franchise period T		7678
Vp	Enterprise Value created after Franchise period T into perpetuity		14983
FCF0			1436

End of Year discount rate basis present value in p

Vp = [((EBITDA in yr T *(1+perp period gd) * (1-(effective cash tax rate in p)))* (1-invest rate as % of ebitda in P))] / Capitalization rate less growth rate in perpetuity as if flows are at end of T period / End of year discount rate at end of T

$$Vp = \frac{\left[\frac{[E_0(1+g_{dT})^{(T)}(1+g_{dpe})(1-(tp\%))(1-I_p)]}{(C^*-g_{dpe})}\right]}{(1+C^*)^T}$$

Vp = [2748 * ((1+.183)^5) (1+.0410735) * (1- 36.0%) * (1- 20.95678%)] / 20.97007% - 4.11278% / (1 + 20.97007%)^ 5

Vp = [2748 * 2.41228 * 0.64000 * 0.79043)] / [0.168573] / 2.590535708

Vp = [3353] / [0.168573] / 2.59053571

Vp = 19891 / 2.590535708

End of Year discount rate basis present value in p

Vp = 7678

End of Year discount rate basis present value

VL = VF + VP

levered fcf entreprise value

VL = 7304 7678 = **14983**

Mid Year discount rate basis Valuation

			% to sales
	sales	$7,369	
E0	ebitda at time 0	$2,748	37.288%
	operating profit at time 0	$2,586	35.088%
	w/c	$1,282	17.404%
	g ppe	$1,179	15.999%
td %	tax depn	$162	2.200%
bd %	book deprec	$162	2.200%
T	number of franchise years " T Period"- 5 max		5
t%	nominal marginal tax rate on ebit during T period " t "		36.0%
tp%	nominal marginal tax rate on ebit during Perpetuity period " tp "		36.0%
gdT	cagr during T Period		18.3%
C* or Cu	levered fcf entreprise value discount rate C*		20.97007%
IT	incremental working cap & net ppe expressed as % of ebitda after cash tax expense during T		20.95678%
Ip	incremental working cap & net ppe expressed as % of ebitda after cash tax expense during p		20.95678%
gdpm	mid year year discount weighted cagr after T into perpty		5.54082%
VL	Levered Enterprise Value		8034
VF	Enterprise Value created during Franchise period T		8504
Vp	Enterprise Value created after Franchise period T into perpetuity		16538
FCF0			1436

Mid Year discount rate basis present value in p

Vp = [((EBITDA in yr T *(1+perp period gd) * (1-(effective cash tax rate in p))) * (1-invest rate as % of ebitda in P))] / Capitalization rate less growth rate in perpetuity as if flows are at end of T period / End of year discount rate at end of T

$$Vp = \frac{\left[\frac{[E_0(1+gd_T)^{(T)}(1+g_{dpm})(1-(tp\%))(1-I_p)]}{(C^*-g_{dpm})}\right]}{(1+C^*)^T}$$

Vp = [2748 * ((1+.183)^5) (1+.052814 * (1- 36.0%) * (1- 20.95678%)] / 20.97007% - 5.54082% / (1 + 20.97007%)^ 5

Vp = [2748 * 2.44537 * 0.64000 * 0.79043] / [15.42924%] / 2.590535708

Vp = [3399] / [15.42924%] / 2.590535708

Vp = 22030 / 2.590535708

Mid Year discount rate basis present value in p

Vp = 8504

Mid Year discount rate basis present value

VL = VF + VP

levered fcf entreprise value

VL = 8034 8504 = **16538**

APPENDIX 60.2 *(Continued)*

Illustration of EBITDA Engine Valuation

End of Year discount rate basis Valuation

				% to sales
	sales		$7,369	
E0	ebitda at base year 0		$2,748	37.288%
	operating profit at base year 0		$2,586	35.088%
	working capital		$1,282	17.404%
	gross plant and equipment and other operating assets		$1,179	15.999%
td %	tax depreciationn		$162	2.200%
bd %	book depreciation		$162	2.200%
T	number of franchise years " T Period"- 5 max			5
t%	nominal marginal tax rate on ebit during T period " t "			36.0%
tp%	nominal marginal tax rate on ebit during Perpetuity period " tp "			36.0%
gdT	cagr during T Period			18.3%
C* or Cu	levered fcf entreprise value discount rate	C*		20.97007%
IT	incremental working cap & net ppe expressed as % of ebitda after cash tax expense during T			20.95678%
Ip	incremental working cap & net ppe expressed as % of ebitda after cash tax expense during p			20.95678%
gdpe	end of year year discount weighted cagr after T into perpty			4.11278%
VL	Levered Enterprise Value			7304
VF	Enterprise Value created during Franchise period T			7678
Vp	Enterprise Value created after Franchise period T into perpetuity			14983
FCF0				1436

Value created by growth

end of year discount rate basis present value

$$V_g = V_L - \frac{FCF_0}{C^*}$$

	VL		value with no growth
Vg =	14983	-	1436 / 0.2097007
Vg =	14983	-	6849
Vg =			**8134**

Mid Year discount rate basis Valuation

				% to sales
	sales		$7,369	
E0	ebitda at time 0		$2,748	37.288%
	operating profit at time 0		$2,586	35.088%
	w/c		$1,282	17.404%
	g ppe		$1,179	15.999%
td %	tax depn		$162	2.200%
bd %	book deprec		$162	2.200%
T	number of franchise years " T Period"- 5 max			5
t%	nominal marginal tax rate on ebit during T period " t "			36.0%
tp%	nominal marginal tax rate on ebit during Perpetuity period " tp "			36.0%
gdT	cagr during T Period			18.3%
C* or Cu	levered fcf entreprise value discount rate	C*		20.97007%
IT	incremental working cap & net ppe expressed as % of ebitda after cash tax expense during T			20.95678%
Ip	incremental working cap & net ppe expressed as % of ebitda after cash tax expense during p			20.95678%
gdpm	mid year year discount weighted cagr after T into perpty			5.54082%
VL	Levered Enterprise Value			8034
VF	Enterprise Value created during Franchise period T			8504
Vp	Enterprise Value created after Franchise period T into perpetuity			16538
FCF0				1436

Value created by growth

mid year discount rate basis present value

$$V_g = V_L - \frac{FCF_0}{C^*}$$

	VL		value with no growth	
Vg =	16538	-	1436 / 20.97007%	
Vg =	16538	-	6849	value with no growth
Vg =			**9689**	

APPENDIX 60.2 *(Continued)*

The following Appendices, as well as those presented earlier, are available for viewing or download on the Web site for this book at: www.wiley.com/go/emott. Please see the About the Web Site page at the back of this book for login information.

APPENDIX 60.3 FCF_M Engine DCF Valuation End-of-Year Basis

APPENDIX 60.4 FCF_M Engine DCF Valuation Midyear Basis

APPENDIX 60.5 Comparable Multiple Valuation Method End-of-Year Basis: (a) Impact of Component Driver on FCF Multiple, (b) Summary of Multiple Derivations, and (c) Summary of Multiple Derived Valuations

APPENDIX 60.6 Comparable Multiple Valuation Method Midyear Basis: (a) Impact of Component Driver on FCF Multiple, (b) Summary of Multiple Derivations, and (c) Summary of Multiple Derived Valuations

APPENDIX 60.7 Spider Chart Example: (a) Year 0: Effect of Volume, Variable Margin, EBITDA, Capital, Return, and Cost of Capital Drivers on EVA and Enterprise Value; (b) Year 5 and Year 0: Effect of Volume, Variable Margin, EBITDA, Capital, Return, and Cost of Capital Drivers on EVA and Enterprise Value

TOPIC 61

Free Cash Flow Equivalent Impacts for Arbitrary Adjustments to Discount Rates

Topic 61 provides insight into the negotiation process drawbacks and valuation impacts of making arbitrary "risk" adjustments to discount rates.

The reader is encouraged to take the time to read the text in conjunction with the referenced Appendices to gain the appropriate level of understanding of the subject matter discussed in the narrative. Appendices are either presented at the end of this and each remaining Topic or are available for review and download on this book's companion Web site (see the About the Web Site page for login information).

ARBITRARY ADJUSTMENTS DISCUSSION

- Although not the preferred or most informative method to compensate for unsystematic risk when valuing a business, arbitrary adjustments to discount rates are often made in an attempt to "adjust" for certain perceived unsystematic risks inherent in the free cash flow (FCF) rather than quantifying the risks and making the adjustments directly to the FCF element.
- In some cases, the FCF forecast is judged to be overstated or to have such volatility that the discount rate is adjusted in an attempt to dampen the volatility or to correct the forecast overstatement, thereby resulting in a value that has a higher confidence level of realization (as if it resulted from a lower-level FCF forecast with less volatility risk and an unadjusted discount rate).
- In other cases, investors simply want a higher return. Therefore, they price investment opportunities accordingly with a discount rate premium reflecting their return targets.
- In other cases, adjustments to discount rates often are made to capture the adverse impact of these types of risks, among others:
  - Market position risk
  - Key man or sole owner risk

- Size or dominance risk versus competition
- Foreign exchange risk
- Industry concentration risk
- Appendices 61.1, 61.2, and 61.3 present the percentage decrease in enterprise value associated with a 1%, 2%, and 3% increase in the weighted average cost of capital, C* ranging from 8% to 20% for FCF projections with growth rates of from 0% to 12% (6% average) during a T period of five years and growth into perpetuity of 0% to 10%.
- The valuation impacts from arbitrary adjustments are quite substantial; generally they are not less than 10% to 15% (and in most cases significantly exceed these levels) of what the valuations would have been without the arbitrary adjustment.
- The obvious question is whether the result of a gross discount rate adjustment is as meaningful or as useful as could be derived if the range of impact of the risk was quantified based on modeled business conditions.
- In addition, one needs to assess whether the negotiation process and the negotiators' credibility is enhanced if a gross risk adjustment is made to a discount rate to determine the value of a seller's business. A thoughtful adjustment to FCF, the impact of which could be incrementally modified during the negotiation process, is a more reasonable position to be in during a negotiation. Negotiating from a place that can be interpreted as having no foundation does not enhance the negotiation process.

The following Appendices are available for viewing or download on the Web site for this book at: www.wiley.com/go/emott. Please see the About the Web Site page at the back of this book for login information.

APPENDIX 61.1 Impact on Enterprise Valuations from a 1% Increase in C* Example

APPENDIX 61.2 Impact on Enterprise Valuations from a 2% Increase in C* Example

APPENDIX 61.3 Impact on Enterprise Valuations from a 3% Increase in C* Example

TOPIC 62

Transferring Defined Benefit Pension Plan Liability Issues

Topic 62 explores some of the complexities and issues associated with the valuation and transfer of defined pension plan liabilities in M&A transactions.

INTRODUCTION

- M&A transactions can require the transfer of pension plan liabilities and assets along with the transferred employees.
- The main issues arising in the transfer of pension plan obligations are valuation of the liability transferred and any related assets and the new benefit levels for the transferred employees versus the benefits previously provided.

BUYER'S VALUATION OF PENSION LIABILITY

- In valuation negotiations, buyers—the transferees—utilize valuation methods that result in a high value of the target's pension plan liability, thereby reducing the target's value.
- In the United States, buyers often start negotiations by stating that the plan liabilities for the transferred employees must be valued using financial statement basis valuation methods (per Financial Accounting Standard (FAS) 87) including either the projected benefit obligation method (PBO) or the accumulated benefit obligation method (ABO).
- Financial statement basis liability valuations ABO or PBO are designed to:
  - Present a conservative settlement basis liability level where it is not clear whether the plan will be ongoing.
  - Require conservative consistency across financial reporting entities, not liability transfer in a deal context.

PROJECTED BENEFIT OBLIGATION BASIS FOR LIABILITY VALUATION

- The PBO method values the liabilities assuming the next points, which results in a high pension liability:
  - The financial statement settlement basis discount rate is based on the long-term AAA bond rate. This is a very conservative rate that leads to a high pension liability value.
  - Future salary increases are assumed to continue at a given percentage.
  - Years of service are assumed by the buyer.
- FS PBO basis liabilities stretch the limits of credibility in a liability transfer context, as the use of a future salary increase assumption with a conservative settlement basis discount rate is not consistent.

ACCUMULATED BENEFIT OBLIGATION BASIS FOR LIABILITY VALUATION

- A somewhat less conservative FAS 87 FS basis liability valuation method is the ABO, basis where the conservative settlement discount rate is used but future salary increases are not assumed, thus resulting in a lower liability than the PBO approach.

PROJECTED TERMINATION BASIS FOR LIABILITY VALUATION

- The plan termination (PT) or windup liability method approximates the FS PBO basis liability.
- The PT liability reflects a discount rate dictated by the Internal Revenue Service (IRS) (it is lower than the FS PBO or ABO discount rate) but without a salary increase assumption.
- The PT liability is an estimate of what actual plan termination liability would be, based on actual liability monetization resulting from purchased annuities.
- From a seller's perspective, the PT liability is not an appropriate valuation method in the context of a liability and plan transfer as the plan usually continues when its members are transferred.

SELLER'S VALUATION OF PENSION LIABILITY

- In valuation negotiations, sellers—the transferors—utilize valuation methods resulting in a low value of the plan liabilities, thereby increasing the value of the target.

GOING-CONCERN BASIS FOR LIABILITY VALUATION

- Sellers start negotiations by proposing that plan liabilities be valued using a going-concern ABO basis, which values the liabilities assuming:
  - A discount rate equal to the expected long-term return on blended plan assets, with the rate being higher than the FS PBO or FS ABO basis discount rate.
  - Future salary increases will not continue.
  - The buyer takes over years of service to date.
- The arguments for the going-concern ABO basis are listed next.
  - It anticipates continuation of the plan, not settlement, as in the FS PBO method.
  - The discount rate reflects a long-term asset allocation mix (debt and equity).
  - It reflects benefits actually earned to date.
  - Future salary increases under a new owner are unknown and uncertain—salary benefits may change, so they are not reflected in the going-concern ABO model.

NEGOTIATED VALUATION OF PENSION LIABILITY

- In negotiations, in an attempt to reach agreement on liability valuation, it is not unusual for buyers and sellers to agree on a limited salary increase assumption and a discount rate equal to or slightly less than the asset earnings rate.
- As the value of the pension liability transferred is a reduction in the consideration received for the business, sellers often attempt to negotiate that there will be no changes in plan provisions for a period of time to ensure that the value transferred is not diminished but, more important, to mitigate employee uncertainty.
- This negotiating position can be used as a trade-off, depending on the agreements reached regarding salary increase and discount rate assumptions.

PENSION ASSET TRANSFER ISSUES

- In the United States, the transfer of pension assets associated with transferred liabilities is dictated by IRS guideline spin-off rules.
- Where sellers retain retired employee liabilities, that liability is determined first, followed by the liability for transferred employees pursuant to valuation rules established by the IRS.
- The seller retains pension plan assets equal to the liabilities for the retained retired employees.
- The remaining pension plan assets are available for transfer associated with the liability of the transferred employees, depending on the overall deal consideration agreed.

- Pension assets and liabilities do not have to be transferred.
- Pension assets and liabilities can remain with the transferor if so negotiated.
- In such cases, the seller will participate in the payment of future pension benefits made by the target when transferred employees retire.
- The seller will manage the plan assets for the benefit of the transferred employees.
- The payment obligation by the transferor at the time of employee retirement should be agreed as part of the deal.
- The rate of future salary increase and discount rate assumption obligations of the transferor requires agreement between the parties to determine the transferor's participation payment amount when transferred employees retire.
- The cost of desired plan benefit equalization can be settled as part of overall deal consideration.

BENEFIT TRANSFER ISSUES

- The key issue for employees is whether they will be worse off, equal, or better off under the new owner's pension plans versus the old owner's plans.
- A demotivated workforce benefits no one in making a deal work.
- As pension benefits are one of many benefits provided, pension benefits should be put in context with the overall benefit package rather than considered alone.
- The total employee benefit package under the new versus old owner should be compared to evaluate the net benefit change to transferred employees.

TOPIC 63

Environmental Remediation Expenses

Topic 63 provides an overview of the tax treatment of postclosing environmental remediation expenses incurred by the buyer.

OVERVIEW

- Generally, the expenses incurred by a buyer associated with the cleanup of a transferred environmental condition existing at the closing, either assumed or purchased by the buyer, are not tax deductible by the buyer as incurred.
- Such incurred expenses increase the tax basis of the property (as an improvement) and are deductible only when the property eventually is sold (or abandoned).
- The present value of the cash flow required to clean up a transferred existing environmental condition is often the subject of considerable negotiation. Eventually an agreed amount is offset against the pre-environmental total deal consideration.
- Generally, expenses incurred associated with the cleanup of an environmental condition caused by the buyer after the closing are tax deductible, as shown:
  - The expenses are capitalized into inventory and are deducted as part of cost of goods sold as inventory turns over.
  - Such expenses maintain the value of the acquired property.
  - Fixed assets employed in remediation of buyer-incurred pollution follow fixed asset accounting treatment, resulting in tax-deductible depreciation expense.

TOPIC 64

Environmental Insurance

Insurance is generally available to buyers to deal with cost overruns incurred in resolving postclosing environmental issues. Topic 64 explores the essential issues of such insurance and what such insurance is and is not.

GENERAL TERMS OF ENVIRONMENTAL INSURANCE

- Certain underwriters have made available insurance to cover costs overruns in excess of state-approved remediation plan spending estimates. A general description follows.
- Underwriters preview or perform their own environmental cost assessment of the approved plan to determine the cumulative spending level after which insurance will take over.
- One-time, up-front premiums approximate 2.5% of the agreed insured amount (the amount in excess of the spending plan).
- A deductible amount of approximately $250,00 to $500,000 is typically offered by the insurer.
- Terms of up to ten years are generally available.
- Coverage is also available for newly identified site contamination of the same contaminants discovered in the course of performing the site remedial plan.
- Coverage does not cover new contamination conditions that arise that are outside of the scope of known contaminants specified in the remedial plan.
- Coverage is provided for cleanup overruns at a covered location or beyond the boundaries of the covered location that is included in the remediation plan.
- Cost overruns associated with off-site (from the property being remediated under the plan) cleanup costs for pollutant originating from the covered location included in the remedial plan are covered.
- Change orders to the plan required by government authorities are covered.
- The cost overrun insurance is triggered only if the agreed spending limit is exceeded before the term of the policy expires.
- If the term of the policy expires before the plan spending limit is exceeded, the obligor is not covered for cost overruns beyond the cumulative spending limit of the remediation plan.
- Automatic term extension coverage is available if the spending limit is less than an agreed percentage of completion at the time the term of the policy is reached.

POLLUTION LEGAL LIABILITY INSURANCE

- Pollution legal liability insurance is available for properties with known or unknown records of pollution liability conditions.
- Such insurance covers new unknown contamination conditions that may arise and includes third-party claims for bodily injury, legal expenses, property damage, and cleanup costs (both on- and off-site).
  - Covers punitive damages, fines, and penalties.
  - Covers sudden and gradual pollution conditions.
  - Terms are typically for five (perhaps up to 10) years.
  - Premiums and policies are individually underwritten, depending on the site, history, term, and underwriter's evaluation (environmental work documentation must be complete and in excellent order).

IF BUYER ACQUIRES AN ACTIVE KNOWN ENVIRONMENTAL ISSUE

- Negotiate a solid indemnification that affords financial protection if the buyer was not fully satisfied by the consideration setoff value.
- Depending on the seller, obtain security to back the indemnity up in the form of a cash escrow, letter of credit, or equivalent.
- If warranted by the situation, obtain a state-approved remediation plan covering the detailed remediation actions required, timetable for completion. and cost estimate.
- Buyers should attempt to require sellers to install facilities, systems, and procedures that will assure zero release of contaminants prior to closing. Costs may be shared.
- Buyers must establish a baseline of site pollution existing as at the closing.
- Buyers must operate the site after the closing with zero pollution as documented by buyers' records and site inspections pursuant to the new operating procedures. This will ensure that buyers will not be held responsible for on-site contamination caused by seller claims that arise after the closing (e.g., any pollution that arises post losing can be due only to preclosing contamination).
- Buyers often require the sellers to contractually assume responsibility for existing contamination and to enter into cleanup operations to the satisfaction of regulatory authorities.
- Buyers and sellers sometimes negotiate a year-by-year transfer of the site liability on a percentage basis (e.g., 5% per year over 20 years).
- The cost of completing the remediation plan cannot be insured.
- The site owner must pay for the remediation pursuant to the remediation plan.

TOPIC 65

Management Warrant Incentive Plans

Equity manager investors of leveraged buyouts often employ management incentive plans to allow management to participate in the equity value of an acquired business that ultimately will be sold or go public after the investors' holding period. Topic 65 explores the fundaments of a management warrant plan often implemented to align the interests of management with the equity investor.

MANAGEMENT WARRANT INCENTIVE PLAN DESCRIPTION

- Leveraged buyout (LBO) deals often contain management incentive warrant plans provided by the primary equity holder. Such plans entitle key operating management to additional equity in the acquired firm if targeted results are achieved over given time frames.
- A management incentive warrant is a right to purchase shares in the firm at a future price at a future date under certain defined conditions.
- Operating management is either allowed or required by the primary equity holder to purchase initial equity in the acquired firm at the closing.
- The purchase of initial shares ensures that management has skin in the game and entitles them to participate in the warrant program.
- The buy-in price is often subject to a slight discount from the fair market value of the shares at the time of purchase.
- Management is entitled to receive a specified number of warrants per owned share, depending on the level of achievement of targeted results up to the time of the exit event.
  - The warrants are usually exercisable on an exit event undertaken by the primary equity holder.
  - The warrants are redeemable for shares upon the exit event.
  - The shares issued to management pursuant to the warrants dilute the primary equity holder.

  - The shares issued to management pursuant to the warrants are eligible for participation in the exit event.
  - The issuance of the shares pursuant to the warrant exercise is a taxable event for management shareholders, but the sale of shares at the exit event provides cash flow to meet the tax obligation.
- The actual versus target results measurement often is based on the actual internal rate of return (IRR) realized on the primary equity holder's per share investment value measured at the time of exit (sale or IPO).
  - The IRR is that discount rate that discounts the actual exit value per share to equilibrium with the primary equity holder's per share investment value.
  - The number of warrants awarded is a function of an award matrix specifying the warrants awarded to each level of management for a given range of actual IRR realized.
  - If the actual IRR is below a minimum target IRR, no warrants will issue; the warrants are under water.
  - Warrants are in the money if the actual IRR exceeds the minimum target IRR.

WARRANT PLAN ILLUSTRATION

- Appendix 65.1 illustrates a management warrant incentive plan and warrant valuation.
  - The deemed exercise price of the management warrants usually is determined at the exit date by multiplying the primary equity holder's investment price per share by a target cost of capital return expected for the elapsed period from the initial investment date to the actual exit date (see Appendix 65.1, Section I).
  - If the equity holder's target cost of capital is 12%, the actual elapsed period from purchase to exit is 4.5 years, and the primary equity holders' investment price per share is $100, the exercise price at exit is determined to be $\$100.00((1.12)^{4.5}) = \$166.53$ (see Appendix 65.1, Section II).
  - Per Appendix 65.1, Section II, if after 4.5 years of elapsed time from the original investment date the actual exit value per share is $244.69, resulting in an actual IRR of 22% on the equity holders' original investment price of $100 per share, versus the equity investor's target minimum IRR of 15%, each management share issued on warrant exercise will result in a yield of $78.16 ($244.69 – $166.53).
    - As this gain is generally deemed taxable income, a certain number of the management shares issued under the warrant or initially acquired usually are sold to provide cash flow equal to the tax liability.
  - Alternatively, as presented in Appendix 65.1, Section II, if after four years of elapsed time from the original investment date to exit the actual exit value per share is $153.56, resulting in an actual IRR of 10.0%, versus the target

minimum IRR of 15%, no warrants will issue as the warrants are under water.

  - Appendix 65.1, Section II, also presents the in-the-money and underwater results for a five-year holding period from the original investment date to exit.
- Such performance-based plans are designed to completely align the interests of management and the LBO investor.

Section I Illustration of a Management Warrant Incentive Plan

Warrant Exercise Price Determination								
Elapsed number of years from investment to exit date					4.5	5.0	5.5	6.0
Primary shareholder investment price per share					$100.00	$100.00	$100.00	$100.00
Cost of capital					12%	12%	12%	12%
Manage warrant exercise price					$166.53	$176.23	$186.51	$197.38

Warrant Award Matrix

Actual IRR Achieved			Warrant Awards	Cumulative Warrant Awards	Years to Exit 4.5 Exit Price	Years to Exit 5.0 Exit Price	Years to Exit 5.5 Exit Price	Years to Exit 6.0 Exit Price
15.000%	to	16.999%	0.5	0.5	$188	$201	$216	$231
17.000%	to	18.999%	0.5	1.0	$203	$219	$237	$257
19.000%	to	20.999%	0.5	1.5	$219	$239	$260	$284
21.000%	to	22.999%	0.5	2.0	$236	$259	$285	$314
23.000%	to	24.999%	0.5	2.5	$254	$282	$312	$346
25.000%	to	26.999%	0.5	3.0	$273	$305	$341	$381
27.000%	to	28.999%	0.5	3.5	$293	$330	$372	$420
29.000%	to	30.999%	0.5	4.0	$315	$357	$406	$461
31.000%	to	and above	0.5	4.5	$337	$386	$442	$505

Section II Illustration of Management Warrant Valuation at Exit under the Plan Design

	"In the Money" Warrant	"Underwater" Warrant	"Underwater" Warrant	"In the Money" Warrant
Elapsed number of years from investment to exit	4.5	4.5	5.0	5.0
Primary shareholder investment price per share	$100.00	$100.00	$100.00	$100.00
Actual Price per Share at Exit Date	244.69	153.56	196.80	343.60
Actual IRR	22.000%	10.000%	14.500%	28.000%
Target Minumum IRR	**15.000%**	**15.000%**	**15.000%**	**15.000%**
Warrants Earned per Share of Equity Owned	2.0	0	0	3.5
Actual Price per Share at Exit Date	244.69			343.60
Exercise Price	$166.53			$197.38
Per Share Gain on Exercise of Warrant	$78.17			$146.22

APPENDIX 65.1 Management Warrant Incentive Plan

TOPIC 66

Negotiation: Introduction and Overview

Topic 66 provides an overview of the process of negotiation, which is fully developed over the course of the next 16 topics.

OVERVIEW OF NEGOTIATION CONSIDERATIONS AND CONDUCT GUIDELINES

- Negotiation starts as you make the first phone contact or enter the first face-to-face meeting to discuss how to proceed, deal value, risk allocation, and so forth, all of which, it is hoped, leads to a deal.
  - Knowing what to expect and that the unexpected will occur is a unique thrill.
  - Be prepared—homework wins (see Topic 10).
- Consider how, and in what order, you want to present your position (see Topics 9, 68, 84, and 85).
- What do the facts of the target business today tell you about tomorrow (see Topics 1, 4, 10, and 56)?
- What are tomorrow's likely scenarios, risks, and why (see Topics 1, 4, and 10)?
  - How can the apparent risk impacts be managed—controllable versus not controllable (see Topics 3 and 26)?
  - Why are your views different/same as those of the other side?
  - How do the scenarios play out in terms of valuation levels (see Topics 58 and 59)?
- What is your position on key valuation and consideration issues and assumptions (see Topic 67)?
  - How did you value and weigh the probability of occurrence of the business scenarios, and why?
  - Valuation methods employed (discounted cash flow [DCF], corroborating comparables and multiples, transaction).
  - Use of leverage in the financing mix (see Topics 40 to 44).
  - All key assumptions, and why.
  - Applied discounts and explanation (see Topic 48).

- Consider initial offer and deal structures (see Topics 11, 62 to 68, 73 to 76, 84, and 85).
- Consider the seller's expected or desired price levels (see Topic 16).
  - Expected counteroffers and re-counters (see Topics 72, 73, 75, and 78).
  - Why and how justified.
  - Seller's tax implications arising from the deal and expected cash takeaway position (see Topics 16, 84, and 85).
- What are your walk-away offer levels, and why (see Topics 16 and 67)?
- Present your position as a risk manager, not a gambler.
  - "Show me where I can manage away the risks so I can approach your requirements."
  - "Tell me more about this so I can understand the risks and my ability to manage them."
  - "The more I understand the opportunities and risks, the more I can sharpen my pencil."
- Speak slowly, directly, explain, listen.
- Decorum always—do not sink to a "baited," lesser level.
- Have key support and expert staff available or at the table.
- Appoint an empowered negotiator and decision maker to present, and coordinate your side.
- Do more listening than talking. Listen hard.
- Keep the total head count at meetings to four to six people—two or three to a side.
  - This limits input overload and allows the negotiator and final decision maker to size up the major issues and potential risk trade-offs and engage in a series of redirects to close the gap.
- Agree only to what you can at the time.
- If you cannot agree, then say so with a commitment to consider and revisit the issue.
- If you do agree, live up to it.
- The goal throughout negotiations is to build one thing: *trust* (see Topic 81).
  - You will complete and close only if you are respected and trusted.
- Negotiations proceed based on incremental agreements along the way. It is difficult to go back if you previously agreed to a point based on an error in judgment, data, or misinterpretation. Because you may be given only one chance to back up without significant damage to the mutual respect and trust established, which keeps the rails greased, proceed carefully.
- The structure, agreements, and terms of a deal should in the end reflect the risk trade-offs made during negotiation and not be an elegant end in itself.
- Excellent, experienced deal lawyers and tax advisors are a must on both sides to make a deal work.
  - Good attorneys and tax advisors understand the issues and risks and find innovative ways to create trade-offs and find compromise.
  - You get what you pay for so do not skimp on fees or quality.

TOPIC 67

Negotiation: Values, Offers, Prices, and Risk Assumption

It is important to keep the relationships among valuation, structure, prices, offers, and assumed risk (elements of total consideration) in mind as you initiate and proceed through a transaction. Topic 67 explores these relationships along the buyer's desired total consideration frontier versus the acceptable total consideration and the actual total consideration frontier.

The reader is encouraged to take the time to read the text in conjunction with the referenced Appendices to gain the appropriate level of understanding of the subject matter discussed in the narrative. Appendices are either presented at the end of this and each remaining Topic or are available for review and download on this book's companion Web site (see the About the Web Site page for login information).

DRIVERS OF THE DESIRED AND ACCEPTABLE TOTAL CONSIDERATION FRONTIER

- It is critical to understand the relationships among values and value determination, offers, target and final prices, and total consideration paid when going into and proceeding through a transaction.
- Appendices 67.1 through 67.4 illustrate the relationships between a buyer's total target consideration, composed of target value and risk assumption, offer price, negotiated purchase price, and ultimately realized actual total consideration including risk assumption.
- Appendix 67.1 shows the "*desired* total consideration frontier" along line DG and "*acceptable* total consideration frontier" along line EH.
- The closer both elements of the consideration frontier are to the apex of the chart, the smaller the area below the frontier, the better off is the buyer's position. The negotiation process will lead to a trade-off between risk and price that will change the slope of the frontier.
- The buyer's initial offer price, A, should be somewhat above the buyer's estimate of the seller's walk-away price, B (see Topic 16); should approximate fair

market value, C (see Topic 47); and should leave plenty of target negotiation space, AD, up to the buyer's target price, D.

- The buyer's target price, D, should be well below the buyer's estimated investment value for the target, F (see Topic 47), leaving a value gap, DF, to improve the buyer's return.
- The target price, D, should also be well below the buyer's walk-away price, E, to allow a margin for valuation and execution error.
- The buyer's walk-away price, E (subject to the level of risk assumption), above the target price, D, is well below target full value, F, as the probability of value creation opportunity diminishes above E.
- The buyer's assumed risk issues might include, for example, environmental, intellectual property encroachment, tax, pension valuation, permits and consents required postclosing, customer contract warranty claims, representation and warranty breaches, and a multitude of other risk factors the impact of which may exceed indemnity caps. (See Topics 26, 83, and 84 regarding risk assumption considerations and Topic 92 regarding papering the deal.)
- The buyer's acceptable target total consideration frontier is measured along EH (see Topics 26, 83, and 84 regarding risk assumption considerations).

DRIVERS OF THE ACTUAL TOTAL CONSIDERATION FRONTIER

- Appendix 67.2 shows a possible actual total consideration frontier, IJ (in contrast to the desired and target frontiers), where, following negotiations, the actual price, I, exceeds the target price, D (the actual price approaches the buyer's walk-away price, E, which is not an unexpected negotiation result), and somewhat more risk, J, was assumed by the buyer than was originally acceptable, H.
- If the actual price, I, remains below the target full value, F, a value gap potential exists, IF, to improve the buyer's return and allow a margin for valuation and execution error.
- Appendix 67.3 shows the situation where, in retrospect, after a number of years of results, the actual realized value, K (sum of dividends plus potential realizable equity value), is less than the actual final price, I, and overall shareholder value is lost, IK, due principally to significantly less realized synergy value as shown along the left axis under the column Buyer's Actual Value. The actual (ultimately expected) value frontier is found along KJ.
- This a bad place to be, one that should be avoided but must be learned from if encountered.
- A postdeal audit must be done following all deals to capture the learning.
- Appendix 67.4 shows the situation where, in retrospect, following a number of years of results, the actual realized value, K, exceeds the actual final price, I, and overall shareholder value is gained principally due to realization of more

synergy value, as shown along the left axis. The actual (ultimately expected) value frontier is found along KJ.

- This is a desirable place to end, which also must be learned from.

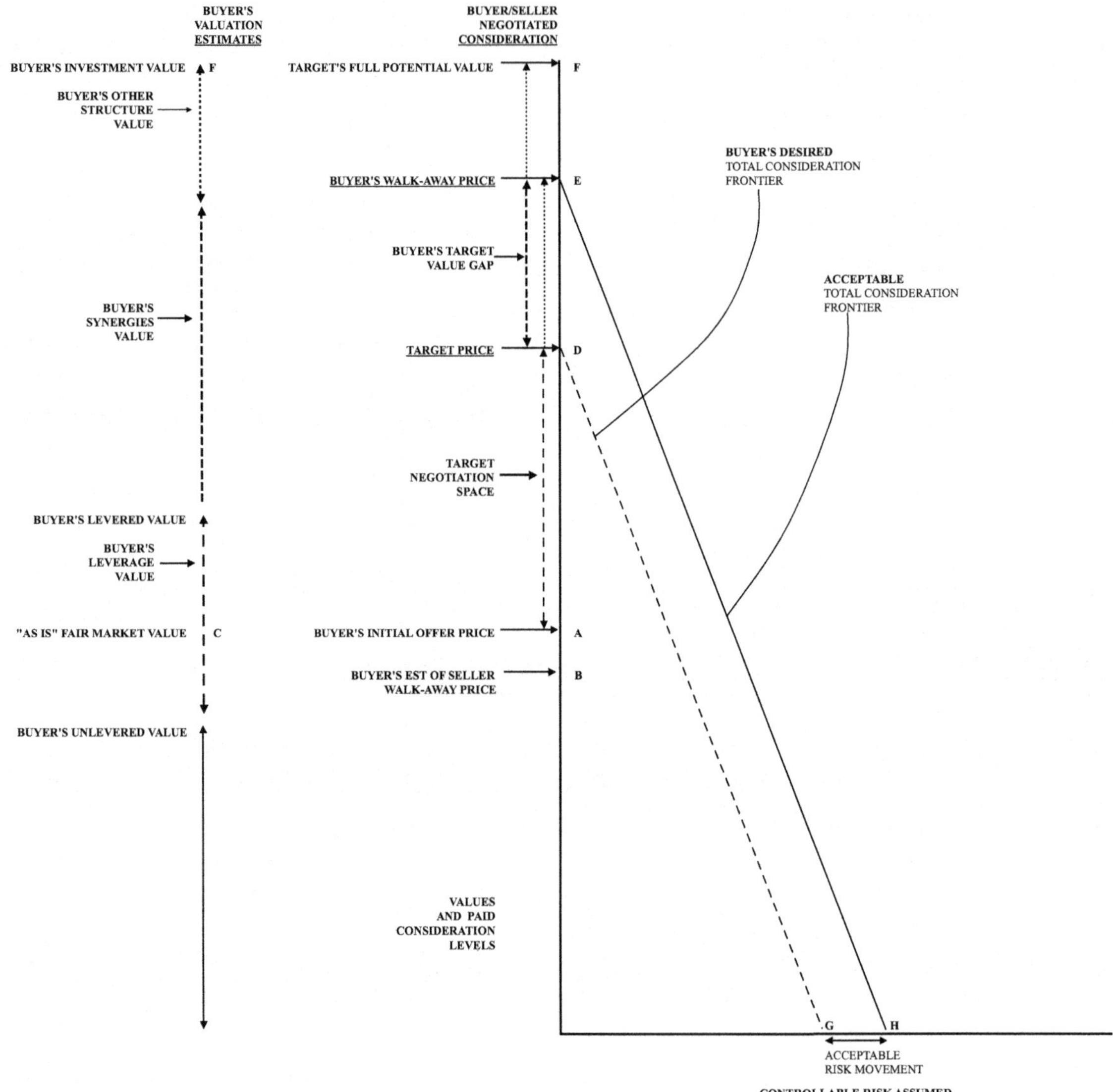

APPENDIX 67.1 Relationships among Value Estimation, Offers, Negotiated Target Prices, and Risk Assumption Example

The following Appendices, as well as those presented earlier, are available for viewing or download on the Web site for this book at: www.wiley.com/go/emott. Please see the About the Web Site page at the back of this book for login information.

APPENDIX 67.2 Relationships among Value Estimation, Offers, Negotiated Target Prices, Risk Assumption, and Finally Negotiated Prices and Risks Assumed Example

APPENDIX 67.3 Relationships among Value Estimation, Offers, Negotiated Target Prices, Risk Assumption Where Actually Realized Value Is Below Actual Price Paid and Value Is Lost and More Risk Was Assumed Example

APPENDIX 67.4 Relationships among Value Estimation, Offers, Negotiated Target Prices, Risk Assumption, and Finally Negotiated Prices and Risks Assumed Where Actually Realized Value Exceeds Actual Price Paid and Value Is Created but More Risk Was Assumed Example

TOPIC 68

Negotiation: Offer Content

Topic 68 discusses the need to make a complete offer that presents all of the key elements concisely and understandably. A complete offer will provide the baseline for the negotiation process and the backbone of a deal.

THE COMPLETE OFFER: KNOW WHERE YOU WANT TO END UP BEFORE YOU GET STARTED

- *The content of the offer* put on the table by a buyer should include and be clear on the next items and should preferably be *written down* (see also the list in Topic 77).
- *The offer should include:*
  - Legal and tax structure of the deal
    - What is being purchased—assets, stock (see Topic 84).
    - Taxable, tax deferred; merger, acquisition
    - What is transferred from what entity to what entity, how, when
    - If a merger, description of which entity merges into which entity
  - What assets and liabilities are being purchased and/or assumed or not assumed; be as specific as necessary.
    - Working capital level expectation at closing and method of determination, in units if appropriate or dollars or appropriate currency.
    - Plant and equipment.
    - Intellectual property, including business know-how, technology, trademarks, patents, licenses, customer list, and so forth.
    - Assets to be leased from seller lessor or other lessor and terms (include price per period, square footage, facility, duration, etc.).
    - Key liabilities assumed—list them.
    - Environmental liabilities assumed, if any, or not assumed; escrow requirements; insurance requirements; baseline or Phase I requirements and key terms and conditions thereto (see Topic 62).
    - Pension plan liabilities assumed net of any assets assumed.
    - Other assets and liabilities assumed by buyer, if any, and key terms.
    - Describe, list the assets not purchased and liabilities not assumed—be specific.
  - Transfer taxes if any, who pays, (see Topic 84).

- Agreed consideration and form and timing of payment.
  - Cash, currency, denomination
  - Notes, terms, interest rate, duration
  - Acquirer's shares
  - Number, assumed share price value
  - Share price collars at closing and number of shares adjustment mechanism
- Deferred payments and triggers for payment.
- Contingent payments, methods of determination, and triggers for payment.
- Terms of earn-out (if any) or contingent payments and triggers—time or events.
- Postclosing purchase price adjustments (see Topic 92).
  - Working capital or capital employed adjustments and key terms of method of determination
  - Target working capital determination method
  - Working capital collars, floors
  - Accounts receivable guarantees
  - Working capital level required of the target at closing
  - Working capital floors, collars, if applicable
- Key closing agreements required and who drafts them, by when.
  - Buyers usually control drafting of agreements and announcements other than in an auction, where sellers usually will have provided initial drafts as part of the auction process. Follow your attorney's lead here.
- Key employee issues and how they are to be handled.
  - Pension plan obligation and asset disposition and transfers (see Topic 62).
  - Employee benefit continuance understanding.
  - Employee severance conditions and who pays.
- Key seller and buyer indemnity issues: baskets, caps, carve-outs, durations matrix (see Topic 98).
- Key seller and buyer representations required (see Topics 93 and 94).
- Seller noncompete terms (see Topic 76).
- Consulting stay-on terms, duration, fees.
- Escrow duration, amounts.
- Environmental due diligence plan remaining, baseline or Phase I requirements.
- Customer due diligence remaining and completion plan.
- Employee due diligence remaining and completion plan.
- Technical due diligence plan remaining.
- Legal and regulatory approvals required, timing for preparation and filing, filing preparation attorney, cost sharing agreement.
- Open tax issues, buyer, seller.
- Deal breakup arrangements and obligation.

TOPIC 69

Negotiation: Create Space in Your Ideas

If you cannot create some space in your ideas for the other side's concerns, needs, and ideas, you will have a hard time finding the meeting place where a deal can be reached.

OVERVIEW

- See the issues and your ideas from the other side's perspective as you proceed.
  - Frame options and solutions that work for both parties.
- Test out alternative responses through mock negotiations with your team.
  - What will the other side want, need, be concerned with?
  - What is reasonable and unreasonable about these positions?
  - What risks are involved?
- What are reasonable responses to these positions, risks, and why?
- Emphasize that you are a risk manager, not a gambler. If the other side can help you see how to manage its risks, you are willing to listen and learn.
- Deals are like puzzles and require similar skills:
  - Patience
  - Innovative thinking
  - Willingness to try and fail
  - Inquisitiveness

TOPIC 70

Negotiation: Beware of the Emotions of Private Sellers

Topic 70 discusses the need for buyers to be very aware of the sensitivity of the owners of privately held target companies (private sellers) to buyers' observations of business weakness or divergent views of the business's prospects and suggested approaches to avoid an emotional reaction from the seller.

OVERVIEW

- Buyers need to be aware of the emotional reaction private sellers may have in response to their observations of the seller's business.
- Private entrepreneurial sellers are often emotional about selling the businesses they raised and built. They can easily take comments about businesses, weaknesses or divergent views as to prospects very personally. A root cause of this reaction may be that sellers are simply concerned how a buyer will treat the business after it is sold if a buyer has disparaging views of it during negotiation.
- Additionally, private sellers may be so invested in all elements of the business that they do not or are unable to separate the business personality from their own.
- This emotional reaction often makes the process of connecting during negotiations, building a sense of trust, and finding compromise over complicated issues very difficult.
- Buyers should precede negotiations with private sellers with their recognition of the personal sacrifice and investment in time and effort that was made by the sellers to seed and develop a going concern over many years.
- Buyers should tangentially present (avoid a head-on approach) potentially divergent (from the seller's perspective) views of the business that could arouse a cold response if not handled well. Present such concerns by building on the base seller has created or in terms of the goal the seller's approach is going after. Pose fact-based issues as questions and solicit seller's ideas, for example:
  - "While you might be correct continuing along that path, we think there may be other approaches to get to the same answer and avoid some of the potholes along the way such as... What do you think?"

- "The manufacturing approach you have implemented will provide an excellent platform for us to implement certain improvements to ensure the gross margin forecast is achievable, such as... There will, of course, be a certain investment on our part to achieve this."
- "Our due diligence of your intellectual property has identified certain areas we think we can and should improve on to further protect the patent estate you have created, such as... There will, of course, be a certain investment on our part to achieve this to avoid certain risks."
- "What do you think is the customer's concern or experience that is leading to the increasing percentage of product returns over the last few years? What would you suggest should be the area of focus to build on the reputation you have built with your customers? We could use your input here because we do see an issue."
- "You may be right about the sales growth prospects of the company, although our due diligence points toward alternative scenarios. We are, however, willing to pay you if you are right in the form of an earn-out as follows...."
  - Buyers must not be disingenuous in approaching sellers regarding potentially sensitive issues. They must find the approach that avoids negative reactions but shows genuine concern for the well-being of the business and its prospects and how it may best be run to continue to prosper once it is in the hands of the buyer.
  - Buyers should work to ensure that, during the negotiation process, sellers come to view them as genuinely concerned with the well-being of the business in the future, not indifferent buyers.

TOPIC 71

Negotiation: Imprint; Do Not Lecture

Topic 71 explores the need to imprint your message as negotiations proceed, as opposed to lecturing in an attempt to convince the opposing party and gain a change of mind. If you imprint valid positions carefully and slowly, this approach will lead to the sense of trust needed to get to the finish line.

IMPRINT, CAREFULLY

- During the negotiation process, it is important to present the critical assumptions and elements supporting observations, offer valuations and risk assumption positions with friendly passion and concern for what you know and feel to be true, respecting the other side at all times.
  - Do not lecture; say only what is necessary on each point, no more.
  - Discuss and present your thinking clearly and crisply.
  - Do not create an enemy by attempting to ramrod the other side.
- Carefully imprint your message in the other side's mind by explanation and example. Do not try to convince or prevail or seek gratification from a brilliant or pointedly intimidating lecture.
- The other side will never agree with your brilliant value determination or risk assumption position in open discussions. Do not expect the other side to tell you how smart you are.
- Your role is to see that the other side in the negotiation hears and understands the compelling logic of your arguments and feel your passion for its correctness.
- When making your point, speak politely, slowly, and clearly and look directly into the eyes of the other side's negotiating party. Do not attempt to be intimidating. Pace your delivery to the rate of reception registering on their faces.
- Once the point is made and received, leave it and move on.
  - Only if necessary, repeat your position and use simple examples to make the point.

- Keep your demeanor friendly, smile if it is genuine, and use a little humor.
  - The author often placed a few small electronic toy toilets on the negotiation table for either side to use during negotiations. If either party went too far in an explanation or asked for too much or offered too little, the other party was allowed to press the toilet handle. The gurgling sound of a flushing toilet in the middle of a negotiation always loosened the place up to laughter and made the sender's point: Please, you have to do better than that!
  - The deal attorney the author employed most often used a noteworthy line to defuse the reaction to a strong position: "It's just rough justice, but it's fair."
- If you know your subject and did your homework, you will make your point successfully.
- If you imprinted well, the effect should be evident later as you close the gap between bid and ask.

TOPIC 72

Negotiation: Handling Tight Spots

Topic 72 explores how to handle the tight spots that always arise in negotiations.

A PRIMER ON HANDLING TIGHT SPOTS

- The seller's or buyer's response is beyond unrealistic: What now?
  - Remember, in negotiations, an outlandish offer or response or position is some progress.
  - The offeror is doing what you want: talking, posturing, negotiating—looking for your reaction.
  - You must now look for the offeror's reaction to your reply.
  - Do not say "That is absurd" or something more clever.
- Ask for a full explanation of the offer or counteroffer and of the opposing parties' thinking.
  - Explain that you are extremely interested and need to understand their thinking, how they got to where they are.
  - Listen very hard, look at their faces, take notes, acknowledge points made, nod your head as you understand.
  - Find and rank the weakest, most vulnerable, and consequential elements in the offeror's position—they probably include:
    - Assumptions as to risk impact and occurrence
    - Understated environmental issues
    - Likelihood of scenario occurrences
    - Multiple applied
    - Discount rate construction and application
    - Served market growth rate and forces
    - Served market size
    - Market segmentation
    - Market share capture rate
    - Market pricing prospects
    - Impact of competitive forces
    - Growth effects of as-yet-nonexistent franchise capability
    - Success of soon-to-be released products or technologies

- Inflation in costs
- Variable contribution margins and gross margins
- Period cost and operating leverage
- Capital spending plan requirements
- Working capital requirements
- Terminal values and methods of determination

- Develop a response to each critical issue with a redirection spin, not a confrontational assault.
  - "I see this point a bit differently. . . ."
  - "You might consider the merits of the following. . . ."
  - "I see the merits of your thinking but feel it may have a lower [or higher] likelihood of occurrence versus the following scenario for these reasons."
  - "Imagine, if you will, the following situation. . . ."
- Listen, redirect, keep the other side in the negotiation talking about risk, impact, control, alternative views and scenarios, inconsistencies, judgments made, and so forth.
  - Remember, the other side is probing and seeking your reaction. They are "telling" you their needs and where they are going without doing so directly.
- When you are at a point of saying "not acceptable," clearly state your reasons why and give two alternatives that would be acceptable to you and move on to further issues, giving the other side time to consider your feelings.
  - The alternatives should show some flexibility on your part and ask for some flexibility on their part in exchange.
  - Innovation, reasonableness, and creative thinking must prevail here.
  - An alternative is to put the issue on a side list of open items that must be revisited as a package later in the negotiation process.
- Barring a situation of unusual buyer advantage, sellers, particularly of privately held companies, will not sell until they are emotionally ready.
- The buyer's job is to find out what combination of solutions meet the seller's motivated needs, perhaps without ever having those needs fully explained.

TOPIC 73

Negotiation: Closing the Bid-Ask Negotiating Gap

Topic 73 explores the approaches required to work through a final bid-ask gap that always exists between buyers and sellers.

MANAGING AND WORKING THROUGH THE GAP

- After initial offers and risk allocation positions have been put on the table and thoroughly discussed, a bid-ask gap will exist.
- Explore the basis for the other side's valuation, risk perception, and positions. Gain an understanding of the other side's perception of the fundamental drivers of value and risk allocation and how they differ from yours. See Topic 72 for some of the issues to expect.
- A useful place to revisit is a side list of unresolved open issues maintained during the negotiation.
  - Ask the other side if that is everything that needs to be on the list.
  - With your team, divide the list between seller wants and buyer wants. Identify trade-off positions and global or bundled asks and concessions as a package: "We would consider giving on point one and point two in favor of the other side if the other side will give us point three."
  - Present the trade-off positions to the other side.
  - Narrow the list as concessions are made.
- Discuss, assess, and revise positions to show flexibility.
  - Expect flexibility from the other side, and ask for it: "I can see my way to revise my thinking or accept greater risk if you can recognize the following. . . ."
- Have logical positions regarding revised assumptions and risks undertaken.
  - Unsupported or illogical positions or outright demands regarding valuations or risk assumption will harm your credibility.
  - It is far preferable to modify a logical position (e.g., accept more risk or relax an assumption) to offer a concession than to retreat from a mindless proposition.
  - Gives must be in the form of trades.

- Continue to exchange ideas and discuss each other's views. Know your limit on value and risk tolerance. Know your estimate of the other side's limits.
- Make concessions very sparingly, asking for a quid pro quo or conditions from the other side.
- Write down and keep a numbered list of your and their concessions. Revisit the open issues list as it shortens and repackage bundled trade off requests.
- Take your time.
- Remember, if you do not ask for something you want, you will almost certainly not be offered it. So ask for it!

WALK OUT IF NECESSARY, BUT KEEP TALKING

- If necessary, walk out to indicate your concerns and your need to rethink where you are and where you are going.
  - Urge the other side to do likewise.
- Remember, a bad deal is worse than a deal that is stalemated or terminated because you just could not get there.
- Have resolve and project it.
- The deeper your homework, diligence, knowledge, and prior imprinting of the soundness and fairness of your positions, the better off you will be at this critical stage.
- This is where the hard work pays off—keep the other side talking.

CONTRACTUAL CONDITIONS APPORTION FINAL RISK POSITIONS—WORK THEM HARD DURING NEGOTIATIONS

- Negotiation surrounding virtually any issue is about distributing the consequences of owning or having rights to the benefits of owning assets or of undertaking or potentially assuming liabilities. The rules governing the distribution of such consequences for each party are captured in carefully worded conditions.
- *Conditions* are defined along three interrelated negotiating dimensions surrounding almost any business contract issue or tight spot: value, time, and scope. All must be exercised simultaneously and often woven together in reaching solutions and closing negotiating gaps, particularly in closing consideration differences.
- The *values* (ultimately cash) associated with most issues (e.g., the amount of an indemnification or an escrow) can be increased, decreased, stepped, floored, or capped.
- The *timeline* associated with most issues (e.g., the survival period of an indemnification, the trigger date for the release of an escrow) can be lengthened, shortened, gapped, start delayed, capped, or date certain defined.
- The *scope* of the breadth and depth of events surrounding, included in, or excluded from an issue (e.g., an indemnified environmental liability) can be

narrowed or widened by defining what is excluded or by defining only what is included in the definition. Another clarifying method is to add "with the exception of items listed" in the definition.

- As you work through the side list of issues noted above, you can make small but creative meaningful concessions using the multifaceted dimensions of conditions: shorten a time frame but broaden the scope; narrow the scope but increase a cap; cap the value but lengthen the time, and so forth.

TOPIC 74

Negotiation: Be Aware of Leverage and Deal Momentum Shift

Topic 74 explores the notion of leverage, an advantage held by one party versus the other party in a deal negotiation setting. In addition, this Topic explores deal momentum and how it tends to change sides as a deal progresses to conclusion.

LEVERAGE: IF YOU HAVE IT, USE IT (APPROPRIATELY)

- Leverage in negotiations is a known advantage held by one party versus the other party. It emanates from a tangible or intangible possession held by the first party that the encumbered party desperately needs to possess or eliminate and can obtain such satisfaction only from the first party.
  - For example, such leverage can be in the form of intellectual property advantages or customer or contractual advantages enjoyed by one party that the other party deeply desires.
- Leverage is also knowledge of something the encumbered party does not want revealed to others; if so revealed, the information may inure to the encumbered party's detriment if action is not taken to eliminate the knowledge encumbrance.
  - For example, such leverage can be in the form of knowledge that a third party is about to enter a market with new technology that will impair the encumbered party unless the encumbered party joins with the knowledgeable party.
- Either way, the holder is in a position to extract a certain value from the other party in exchange for elimination of the leverage overhang. It must do so legally, without causing ill will or embarrassment.
- The value extracted may be in the form of increased or decreased consideration, specific performance, assumption of liability, elimination of demands, timing of events, or a combination of the foregoing.
- The value extracted may not be identified with the point of leverage; it simply may be a factor used in the process of determining consideration or contractual terms. The holder of the leverage must assess the value exchange.

- The possessor of the leverage must, at the appropriate time, enlighten the encumbered party of the leverage possessed and possible impact if it is not eliminated for the advantage of the encumbered party.
- This must be carefully communicated during transaction negotiations between the parties to assure that the maximum value is received in exchange for eliminating the point of leverage: "We think the 'possession of our intellectual property estate that will effectively bar new entrants' has exceptional value to you [and/or others], and we hope and expect to realize this value [or eliminate the impact on you] from our transaction with you."
  - Such an approach avoids the unstated threat: "If you don't compensate us, we will exploit it on our own or sell it to others, resulting in harm to you."

BEWARE OF EXTORTION

- Knowledge of something about the encumbered party or another party legally obtained and possessed by one party that may affect the encumbered party if revealed to a third party should not be communicated during negotiations if the form of the communication, or the statement that such knowledge is possessed, amounts to extortion: "I know A and unless you do B, I will use A to harm you."
  - Leverage in the form of such knowledge possessed may be communicated only by a tangential reference to the knowledge, if at all. Such knowledge should have been legally obtained.
  - Generally the encumbered party is aware of the possessed knowledge.
  - The party possessing the knowledge must consult legal counsel and follow counsel's lead as to how to present the possession of such knowledge to leverage the other party during negotiations but avoid the possibility of extortion.

DEAL MOMENTUM SHIFTS AS A DEAL PROGRESSES

- Deal momentum shifts throughout the progress of a deal.
- The first stage is the chase, the second is the walk-along, and the third is the catch.
- The *chase* takes place in the early stage of an auction or a privately negotiated deal.
  - During the chase, deal momentum favors the seller, particularly in an auction. Buyers respond to the prospectus and the demands of the auction boss. Offers reflect the tension of the auction. During buyer selection, risk allocation and contract terms favor the seller, particularly where a bidder indicates a desire to make a preemptive offer.
  - During this phase, sellers must set out their primary risk allocation terms that a bidder must comply with to be selected. The terms must be set out in an exclusivity letter reciting the terms agreed and the period of exclusivity (see Topic 12).

  - Seller risk allocation terms may include these items, which should be negotiated during this phase when the momentum favors the seller: escrows, indemnification caps and baskets, product return warranty claim look-back periods, primary seller representations and warranties, employment agreement terms, and closing conditions (see Topics 90 to 98).
- The *walk-along* stage takes place after the bidder selection in an auction or term sheet agreement in a privately negotiated deal.
  - During the walk-along, deal momentum swings somewhat to the buyer. Contracts and related documents are in preparation, and the buyer wants to gain ground on the lesser representation and consents required in the risk allocation phase of the contract negotiation process.
  - Buyer due diligence often results in findings that lead to additional seller representations or in attempts to retrade key agreement points based on previously unknown information.
  - Sellers have a deal in play and do not want to lose it.
- The *catch* stage takes place as the momentum of the walk-along wanes and signing and closing approach. It is an almost imperceptible shift that is critical for the seller to recognize.
- During the catch, deal momentum shifts back to the seller. If the due diligence process has presented the buyer with certain seller issues and all of them have been successfully negotiated away to the buyer's reasonable satisfaction, the buyer will have become inflamed with the desire to close the deal. The buyer is committed. Sellers will sense this.
- At this inflection point of full commitment to the deal, final negotiating points will start to fall to the seller, including potentially significant money issues such as:
  - Outstanding indemnity issues.
  - Outstanding consulting and employment agreement issues.
  - Outstanding escrow issues.
  - Outstanding assumed liability issues.
  - Target working capital. This amount often is determined late in the process, based on the most current operating run rate times; historical working capital–to–sales ratio; and actual working capital element definitions, procedures, and rules for determination.
- During this phase, sellers may become very aggressive in gaining ground. However, sellers must be careful in the process of winning negotiating points not to push buyers into a downward spiral of self-confidence where, upon reflection, they feel they have been cumulatively steamrolled into an unfair risk allocation position and have lost control of their direction.
- This can be a dangerous time for the deal and the seller. If buyers, particularly the primary buyer negotiator, feel this way, they can enter a cycle of anger, embarrassment, and a great need to regain control.
- This spiral can lead to harsh reaction to any remaining deal points, outright grabs, and retrades of previously agreed points.
- During the catch, sellers should be careful and aware not to overreach.

TOPIC 75

Negotiation in the Final Stages

Topic 75 explores the typical events experienced during the final stages of a negotiation and how to prepare for them. This is when lobbed offers and counteroffers start to fly.

THE LOBBED OFFER STAGE

- Often, in the final stages, when each side has tested the other side and the offers are fairly close yet a reasonable gap still exists, one side or the other will put the negotiation into a "lob stage," where a round number is put on the table.
- The logic of the risk assessments positioning, valuations, and negotiated conditions will be abandoned and a final, "this-is-what-we-can-live-with" offer will be presented.
  - Intuitive instinct will be critical in this stage.
  - The "lobbor." The first to act must be ready, as must the "lobbee," the second to act response.
  - *The "final" lobbed offer is not the final one!* It is a test to see how much the other side wants it.
    - *Do not accept it.* You will do better!
- The lobbee must step back and be ready to toss out one or more counteroffers designed to test the lobbor—how much does that party want it?
  - Counteroffers and responses must show movement toward the other side, but not too much.
  - Show movement by conditional acceptance of some or part of the offer if the other party can meet one or more conditions of the counteroffer.
  - Show movement by improving on the position that resulted from the previously presented logic and valuations; do it slowly, however.
  - Movement must show you want it, not *how much* you want it.
- The role of lobbor and lobbee will reverse as cross-counters are tossed onto the table.
  - If each side shows movement, the gap will close.

- The creative lob and cross-counter lob will show small movement but will cause the other side to grapple with the alternatives and conditions proposed (see Topic 73).
  - An immaterial (.5% to 1% or so) final gap in dollar offers on total purchase price or point of consideration can and should be closed with a "You cut and I'll choose" gesture.
  - The art is to get the gap to this level.
  - Do not jump to large concessions to close the gap.

STEP BACK WHEN YOU ARE READY TO SHAKE HANDS

- When you are ready to shake hands, step back (mentally) with your team.
  - Review all the concessions made, one by one.
  - Review the risks accepted and liabilities assumed.
  - Ask yourself: Given all this, can we make this deal work?
  - Perform a deep soul search.
  - Do not jump to shake hands if there are any major risks whose cumulative impact your team cannot control and that would cut the heart out of the deal benefits, free cash flow, and value creation path (see Topic 79).
  - Shake hands if you can see your way to gaining control over risks (see Topic 80).

TOPIC 76

Negotiation: Use Earn-Outs or Noncompete Agreements to Close a Bid-Ask Gap

When a bid-ask gap exists arising from a disagreement between buyer and seller over valuation due to expected target forecast results, consider an earn-out to bridge the gap. It is not easy to make earn-outs work postclosing.

The reader is encouraged to take the time to read the text in conjunction with the referenced Appendices to gain the appropriate level of understanding of the subject matter discussed in the narrative. Appendices are either presented at the end of this and each remaining Topic or are available for review and download on this book's companion Web site (see the About the Web Site page for login information).

WHY DO AN EARN-OUT?

- Earn-outs are postclosing contingent purchase price payment mechanisms whereby the seller is paid additional purchase price amounts based on the performance of the target entity after the closing over specific time frames.
- Earn-outs are difficult to:
  - Sell to the other side
  - Structure
  - Make work after the deal
- Earn-outs are prospective methods of settling perceived differences in risk of achievement of the sellers business forecast leading to variations in expected business performance and business valuation.
- *Buyers propose earn-outs* to avoid assuming all the business performance risk at the closing.
  - The advantage is that the buyer pays less up front but assumes the obligation, in the purchase and sale agreement or as part of an individual consulting agreement, to pay more if certain events happen over certain time frames.
- *Sellers accept earn-outs* to avoid losing the sale. With earn-outs, the prospect of getting more later exists if, as sellers have argued, future performance exceeds the buyer's expectation.

- The risk to sellers is that the operations are no longer in their control. Postclosing results may not reflect the underlying capability that would have been achieved had the business remained under the seller's control.
  - For this reason, sellers prefer to use simple performance measurements, such as units sold, dollar sales, or gross profits, as opposed to levels of operating profits (earnings before interest and tax; earnings before interest, tax, depreciation, and amortization; net operating profit after tax, and so forth).
  - In any event, sellers will seek language in earn-out agreements whereby the buyer undertakes to operate the business (or allow sellers to have a hand in doing so) postclosing in ways that will give sellers comfort that performance results will not be curtailed by the buyer by, for example, intercompany sales and profit transfer methods during the earn-out performance period.

EARN-OUT PERFORMANCE PAYMENTS

- Performance payments may include fixed and variable interim payments and final period end payments, depending on threshold levels of results and earn-out design.
  - Typically, earn-out structures cap total payments payable in any one year following the closing, and cumulatively over the term of the earn-out. Houlihan Lokey reports that the median earn-out as a percentage of the purchase price paid was 11% in 2008 with a maximum level of 75%.[1]
  - In addition, earn-out structures typically include cumulative performance thresholds. Below threshold performance requirements in any period have to be made up in future periods before contingent payments are earned or paid.
  - Earn-out structures may reflect deferred payment requirements for any period in which payments are earned.
    - Such payout deferrals are in place to prevent payments for front-loaded performance without consistent performance over the term of the earn-out period.
- Buyers must carefully construct earn-out offers to ensure that incremental earn-out payments are value justified by running numerous valuation scenario exercises.
  - The additional cash flow and value creation from improved performance must exceed the earn-out payment to ensure they are justified. The earn-out payments are therefore paid out of improved performance results.

TAX CONSIDERATIONS OF EARN-OUTS

- Buyers and sellers must carefully consider the tax impact of earn-out arrangements (see Topics 84 and 85).

[1] See Houlihan and Lokey Mergers and Acquisitions Group, Purchase Agreement Study, May 2009 at http://www.hlhz.com/pressdetail.aspx?id=1695.

- For tax purposes, earn-outs structured as contingent additional purchase price on *asset purchases* generally are recorded on the buyer's books as excess purchase price. This sum is allocated to assets acquired or to goodwill and is deductible for tax purposes over the asset life, per the asset class tax rules. For goodwill, the tax deduction in the United States is over 15 years. Sellers are taxed as proceeds are received as additional purchase price on the deal at the rates prevailing at the time of sale of the business.
- For tax purposes, earn-outs structured as contingent additional purchase price on *stock purchases* are attributed to the basis in the stock acquired and are deductible when the stock is sold. Sellers are taxed as proceeds are received as additional purchase price on the deal at the rates prevailing at the time of sale of the business.
- Earn-outs structured as *personal performance bonuses* are deductible as paid by the buyer. Sellers are taxed at ordinary income tax rates. The amount of the earn-out payments must be viewed by the tax authorities as being reasonable pursuant to tax regulations governing compensation for services rendered.

AN EARN-OUT EXAMPLE

- An earn-out example, based on the leveraged buyout (LBO) example in Appendix 44.2, is presented in Appendix 76.1.
  - The circled number references in Appendix 76.1 follow the LBO valuation description in Appendix 44.2.
  - Seller seeks a closing price of $16,133 ($ in millions) based on achievement of seller's forecast. Buyer estimates this to be equivalent to $12,096 after state and federal capital gains tax of 20% (excluding the effect of seller's basis for clarity and simplicity in the example). See Appendix 44.2(b), line 8.
  - Buyer informs seller that seller's future growth expectation is too optimistic and counters with a contingent earn-out bonus arrangement.
  - After negotiation, seller seeks no less than $12 million up front to consider the proposed earn-out.
  - The illustrated earn-out is structured to provide for an annual sharing of all gross margin earned above a baseline amount equal to the last year's actual gross margin of $4,200 plus a deferred earn-out payable in year 5 equal to 25% of the cumulative growth in gross margin over the five-year period versus no growth in gross margin (actual gross margin over the next five years less five times the last year's actual amount prior to the closing). (See Appendix 76.1(b), lines 4 and 5, and Appendix 76.1(l) for the earn-out computation.)
  - The earn-out payment shown in Appendix 76.1(l) is predicated on achievement of the seller's forecast, per Appendix 76.1(h), the risk of which the buyer is willing to accept and pay for if realized.
  - The example assumes that the earn-out payments are currently deductible for the buyer, because the earn-out was structured as a personal performance

bonus, not as contingent purchase price. Seller is willing in this case to accept personal income tax consequences.

- In Appendix 76.1(b), the present value to seller (at the seller-provided cost of capital of 20%) of the up-front posttax consideration at the closing of $9,600 (purchase price of $12,000 after a 20% capital gain tax excluding seller's basis for clarity and simplicity (lines 5–8), plus the earn-out payments (line 4 and 5) after tax at an ordinary income rate of 35%, amounts to a present value of $13,221 (line 10) and exceeds the total after-tax consideration of an all-up-front deal desired by the seller in Appendix 44.2(b), line 8 ($12,096, purchase price of $16.1 million after a 20% capital gain tax).
- If the growth forecast is achieved, the buyer's internal rate of return (IRR) on a midyear rate basis on the earn-out deal is 38.6% (see Appendix 76.1(a), line 6); on the equity investment in the earn-out proposal of $4,704 (see Appendix 76.1(a), line 22; ($12,000 up front of which $7,296 is debt); versus a 35.4% IRR on the no earn-out deal if $16.1 million was paid up front and the growth forecast is achieved per Appendix 44.2(a), line 6). (The all-up-front deal of 16.1 million had an equity investment of $6,324 up front and debt of $9,809 per Appendix 44.2(a), lines 22, 23.)
- If sales growth is flat during the T period and the growth forecast is not realized, the value of the earn-out deal to buyer in the T period is $10,266 (see Appendix 76.2(a), line 20). The buyer's IRR on the buyer's equity investment of $4,704 (Appendix 76.1(a), line 22) with a $12,000 up-front payment is 25.8% on a midyear basis (Appendix 76.2(a), line 6), which is approximately equal to the buyer's cost of levered equity, CL, of 25.7% (Appendix 76.2(a), line 4), an acceptable risk to buyer.
- The earn-out payment shown in Appendix 76.2(d) was predicated on achievement of the seller's forecast per Appendix 76.1(h). As it was not achieved, the result is a diminished earn-out.

EARN-OUT CONCLUSION

- In the earn-out deal example, seller receives the desired after-tax value over time if seller's forecast is realized; buyer pays less up front; buyer's return to equity at risk is improved if the earn-out forecast is achieved and is acceptable if the forecast is not achieved; and buyer's investment risk is minimized versus an all-up-front deal. The buyer's risk of paying more than fair value with the earn-out is acceptable.

NONCOMPETE AND CONSULTING AGREEMENTS

- Noncompete and consulting agreements with the seller also can be employed to bridge a price gap. The tax effect of such agreements generally do not materially alter the present value of the buyer's after-tax transaction cost from a long-term status (acquisition of depreciable assets and amortizable goodwill, for example) to a nearer-term current expense deduction stream (see Topic 86).

- Noncompete agreements generally require that sellers of the target (or the target if the corporation is not transferred to the buyer) shall not compete in the target's product field, market, and geographic sector with existing target customers for a period of time (generally three to five years) in exchange for a stream of payments, which are taxed at personal income tax rates as received.
- Generally, buyers receive a tax deduction for the payments under such noncompete agreements over a 15 year period regardless of the term of the noncompete agreement. Generally, where the IRS views such payments as not distinct from or to assure the benefit of goodwill acquired, the contractual obligation is treated as an intangible amortizable over 15 years.
- In very limited circumstances, payments under noncompete agreements generally not in connection with an acquisition, can be tax deductable as paid.
- The present value cost of the noncompete or consulting payment stream is valued as demonstrated in Topic 85.

The following Appendices are available for viewing or download on the Web site for this book at: www.wiley.com/go/emott. Please see the About the Web Site page at the back of this book for login information.

APPENDIX 76.1 Leveraged Buyout Example with Earn-Out, Earn-Out Growth Forecast Realized, A to K

APPENDIX 76.2 Leveraged Buyout Example with Earn-Out, No Growth, A to D

TOPIC 77

Negotiation: After the Deal Is Agreed

At last the time comes in all deals where the parties have finally agreed on all the major points and shake hands. Topic 77 explores the necessity of fully documenting the terms of the business agreements in a text that will form the backbone for drafting the legal agreements.

When agreement has been reached and the parties shake hands, be sure to take the time to orally review and document your business agreements on all the points discussed before anyone leaves. The points of agreement should be circulated shortly thereafter to all parties to the deal.

HEADS OF AGREEMENT AND WHAT TO INCLUDE IN IT

- Prepare as long or short a document as needed to capture all the points of agreement. Initial it, date it.
- Such document is often referred to as:
  - Heads of agreement
  - A term sheet
  - Memorandum of understanding
  - Letter of intent (binding or nonbinding) (see Topic 89)
- Such document should include:
  - Signing date anticipated
  - Closing date anticipated
  - Legal and tax structure of the deal
    - Taxable, tax deferred; merger, acquisition
    - What is being purchased—assets, stock (see Topic 84)
    - What is transferred from what entity to what entity, how, when
    - New acquiring entities to be formed, limited liability corporation, C corporation, partnership, and so on
    - If a merger, plan of merger key terms; description of which entity merges into which entity
  - What assets and liabilities are being purchased and/or assumed or not assumed
    - Working capital level expectation at closing and method of determination, in units if appropriate or dollars or appropriate currency

  - Plant and equipment
  - Intellectual property including business know-how, technology, trademarks, patents, licenses, customer list, and so forth
  - Assets to be leased from seller lessor or other lessor and terms (price per period, square footage, facility, duration, etc.)
  - Key liabilities assumed (list them)
  - Environmental liabilities assumed, if any, or not assumed; escrow requirements; insurance requirements; baseline or Phase I, II, or III requirements and key terms and conditions thereto (see Topic 62)
  - Pension plan liabilities assumed net of any assets assumed
  - Other assets and liabilities assumed by buyer, if any, and key terms
  - List of the specific assets not purchased and liabilities not assumed
- Transfer taxes if any, who pays (see Topic 84)
- Agreed consideration and form and timing of payment
  - Cash, currency, denomination
  - Notes, terms, interest rate, duration
  - Acquirer's shares
    - Number, assumed share price value
    - Share price collars at closing and number of shares adjustment mechanism
- Deferred payments and triggers for payment
- Contingent payments, methods of determination, and triggers for payment
- Terms of earn-out (if any) or contingent payments and triggers—time or events
- Postclosing purchase price adjustments (see Topic 92)
  - Working capital or capital employed adjustments and key terms of method of determination
  - Target working capital determination method
  - Working capital collars, floors
  - Accounts receivable guarantees
  - Working capital level required of the target at closing
  - Working capital floors, collars, if applicable
- Key closing agreements required and who drafts them, by when
  - Buyers usually control drafting of agreements and announcements other than in an auction, where sellers usually will have provided initial drafts as part of the auction process. Follow your attorney's lead here.
  - Stock purchase or asset purchase or plan of merger agreements
  - Terms of other key agreements: technology exchange, licensing, management, employment, and so forth
  - Seller noncompete agreements (see Topic 76)
  - Consulting stay-on agreements
  - Escrow agreements
- Key employee issues and how they are to be handled
  - Pension plan obligation and asset disposition and transfers (see Topic 62)
  - Employee offer letters/contracts
  - Employee retention (stay on) agreements and who pays for it

  - Employee benefit continuance understanding
  - Employee terms of employment
  - Employee severance conditions and who pays
  - Employee 401 (k) asset disposition and transfers (roll-over program)
  - Key employee transfer conditions
    - "Must-have" people to be delivered by seller
    - Employee contracts and key terms
  - Key seller and buyer indemnity issues: baskets, caps, carve-outs, durations matrix (see Topic 98)
  - Key seller and buyer representations required (see Topics 93 and 94)
  - Seller noncompete terms (see Topic 76)
  - Consulting stay-on terms, duration, fees
  - Escrow agreement terms duration, amounts, triggers for release
  - Key seller and buyer permits, consents required
  - Limitations on preclosing payments, disbursements, and commitments until closing (dividends, bonuses, salary increases, capital equipment, leaseholds, etc.)
  - Key seller and buyer consents and closing conditions required (see Topics 92, 94, and 96)
  - Environmental due diligence plan remaining, baseline or Phase I requirements
  - Customer due diligence remaining and completion plan
  - Employee due diligence remaining and completion plan
  - Technical due diligence plan remaining
  - Legal and regulatory approvals required, timing for preparation and filing, filing preparation attorney, cost sharing agreement
  - Open tax issues, buyer, seller
  - Announcement restrictions and agreements
  - Termination provisions (see Topic 96)
  - Deal breakup arrangements and obligation
- Such document should be as binding as may be appropriate (not usual) and contain all material points of business agreement as are needed to allow drafting of documentation by the attorneys.

TOPIC 78

Negotiation: Bluffing and How to Handle It

At the conclusion of negotiations, do not be surprised if the other side calls your bluff and changes the deal. Topic 78 provides some guidance on how to deal with this situation.

The reader is encouraged to take the time to read the text in conjunction with the referenced Appendices to gain the appropriate level of understanding of the subject matter discussed in the narrative. Appendices are either presented at the end of this and each remaining Topic or are available for review and download on this book's companion Web site (see the About the Web Site page for login information).

THE FOUR COURSES OF ACTION WHEN YOUR BLUFF IS CALLED

- When you are at the end of the negotiations, about to close, and the other side calls your bluff and changes the negotiated price (or risk assumptions) with the threat of walking from the deal if not accepted, what do you do?
- Initially, keep your emotions in check. Do not do anything other than ask why.
- The reasons for and the amount of the change matter here.
  - Do the reasons resonate with you? Was something overlooked?
  - Is there substance and validity behind the facts presented?
  - Does the change emanate from material change in a critical value or risk driver.
  - Do you have counterarguments that are equal in substance that meet the test of validity?
  - Is a price reduction demand out of line, or is it reasonable given the circumstances?
- There are basically four courses of action:

ROLL OVER

- Agree to the amount proposed and get on with it if:
  - The reasons proposed are substantially correct.

- The reduction is reasonable.
- You have no valid counterpositions or leverage to argue otherwise.
- You do not have any other likely buyers at the proposed price level.
- The deal still makes sense at the revised price versus what may be achievable with another party.

NO WAY, BUT

- Protest and offer a counter proposal if:
  - You have counter arguments that meet the test of validity.
  - Your counter arguments are equal in substance to that offered, but a valid difference of opinion prevails in the other side's favor.
  - You still can justify the deal at a different price than was originally agreed.
  - You feel the other side wants the deal but at a slightly better price.

YOU TALKING TO ME?

- Protest and flatly reject the proposal and be ready to walk away if:
  - You are convinced that the initially agreed pricing and terms are fair and correct.
  - There are alternative parties in the wings you can complete your deal with quickly at the same pricing and terms.
  - Inform the other side of these positions in no uncertain terms but be sure you are right.
  - Tell them to accept the original deal as agreed in the next thirty minutes or you must go elsewhere.

BLUFF AND TURN

- Protest and reject the proposal and insist that the negotiated price prevails (call their bluff but be ready to go back if they walk) if:
  - You feel they are searching to test your mettle based on reasons that are not particularly compelling and can be argued or reasoned away.
  - You do not have a number of alternative parties readily accessible.
  - You feel the negotiating advantage at this stage of the proceedings has shifted to your side and you want to test their stamina.
  - If you bluff and reject, the rejection must clearly put the other side on the boil and give them only two choices: walk or agree with the previously negotiated price.
  - Do not waffle in presenting this response position.
  - Your goal is to stress and test the other side.
  - If they walk, you can always go back; read on.
  - If you bluff and reject but you want the deal to happen with this party, you must have an option plan ready if the other side sticks to their guns and walks on the deal after your initial rejection.

- Wait a few days for parties to cool off and to see what happens.
- If the other party calls back first, you have gained an advantage.
- If there is no call back within a short period of time, place the call, recognizing that you are giving a slight advantage.
- Do not cave in to the original demand—you may not have to.
- Explain that you have had time to think about it (so have they).
- Ask them where they are in their thinking before declaring where you are.
- If they offer no change and you still want to do the deal, present a counter position with a very small amount of give and the reasons for the counter positions validity.
  - Differences of opinion on value drivers are fruitful ground to give on to bridge a price gap: "We have rerun the numbers and can see some give toward your position; we can make it work at..."
  - Be creative in presenting the option.
  - Reach out to the other side and give some ground.

- If the bluff and turn does not work and they hold out again for their terms, you must be prepared to:
  - Agree to their new price and terms indicating your disappointment.
  - Indicate that you have other options, but you are willing to go forward quickly and will do so but only at the revised terms, and that any other change in terms or new terms will kill the deal.
  - Ask for and gain their assurance that there are no other terms to be considered. This is important at this stage.
  - Have good reasons that *you* and your team can live with for going forward at revised terms (such as you do not have good alternatives at hand and do not want to invest the time and energy to go through search and negotiations again).
  - Or, walk away (if the offered terms just do not work for you and you have some alternatives and are willing to invest the time and energy to go through search and negotiations again; see Topic 79).
- Appendix 78.1 is an example of a last-minute bluff and rebluff response. Appendix 78.2 has been modified to protect the parties involved. What do you think the outcome was?

The following Appendices are available for viewing or download on the Web site for this book at: www.wiley.com/go/emott. Please see the About the Web Site page at the back of this book for login information.

APPENDIX 78.1 Buyer Letter to Seller Requesting Price Reduction

APPENDIX 78.2 Seller Letter in Response to Bluffing Buyer Letter

TOPIC 79

Negotiation: When Do You Step Away?

Topic 79 offers some guidance on when to step away from a deal. Remember, stepping away from a deal is better than doing and struggling with a bad deal.

FOR BUYERS

- When you are satisfied that:
  - Your due diligence has uncovered untenable risks that you do not have the capability to manage and for which you cannot satisfactorily (or do not want to) transfer the financial risk via insurance or some other contractual vehicle: step away!
  - You do not have the management capability or depth of staff to manage complex integration plan programs associated with this deal with reasonable certainty: step away!
  - The critical criteria fit evaluations just cannot get near the acceptable target levels (see Topic 4). As a result, you will be left with just an okay situation that will never really meet your expectations: step away!
  - When you reflect on your negotiations and find you are satisfied that you have pressed the other side to the point where they have dug in to final positions that:
    - Are unreasonable to you, and you in a sense of balanced fairness would never ask the other side to live with: step away!
    - Leave you with unmanageable risk, where you cannot conceive of a way at any reasonable cost to manage the impacts of the composite risks you are asked to take, and the impacts could be significant or fatal to a successful deal: step away!
    - May likely leave you with risk-adjusted returns below your targets, and you cannot conceive of any way to improve your position: step away!
    - If you step away from a negotiation, leave alternatives on the table that you can live with, should the other side wish to reconsider.
- As a general rule, a good deal will be seen as a good deal fairly quickly in the discovery and investigative process. If you have to struggle and dig through problem after problem to find the goodness, it probably is not there. This is a real red light.

FOR SELLERS

- When you are satisfied that:
  - When you reflect on your negotiations and find you are satisfied you have pressed the other side to the point where they have dug in to final positions which:
    - Are unreasonable to you, and you in a sense of balanced fairness would never ask the other side to live with: step away!
    - Leave you with unmanageable postclosing risk, where you cannot conceive of a way at any reasonable cost to manage the impacts of the composite postclosing indemnification risks you are asked to take, and the impacts could lead to untenable postclosing claims that exceed your expected present value thresholds: step away!
    - Most likely leave you with return expectations well below your targets, and you cannot conceive of any way to improve your position with this buyer and you do have options with other buyers providing likely better results: step away!
- Stepping away is not easy to do, particularly after you have invested a reasonable amount of time.
  - The key is to keep your mind open to where fairness and reality meet and to not get lost in the fever of doing a deal because "closing is winning."
  - Winning is doing the right thing.
  - We are defined in the deal journey life not by whether we close deals but by how we conduct ourselves in getting to the finish line.
  - Closing or stepping away should only be a reflection of the quality and excellence of our conduct.

TOPIC 80

Negotiation: When Do You Proceed?

Topic 80 provides some guidance for buyers and sellers as you reach the point of full commitment to proceeding with a deal.

FOR BUYERS

- When you are confident that:
  - You can manage the risks you have agreed (among your team) to assume in the deal; market, competitive, regulatory, contingent liability, and so on (see Topic 10) . . .
  - You have thoroughly thought out the integration and synergy extraction plan and have a team that can execute and realize the attractive returns expected . . .
  - You feel good about your judgment of the quality, character, and capability of the management team you are buying with the target . . .
  - You have made a proper integrated assessment of market attractiveness, criteria fit, and overlap fit . . .
  - You have made a thorough due diligence effort . . .
  - You have not been overly rushed in the process, resulting in errors in judgment . . .
  - You have a fair price and postclosing indemnification structure that will yield a reasonable return on equity and provide fair protection against preclosing breaches by sellers . . .
  - You do not have a significant question or issue that has not been addressed . . .
  - Then go for it!
- As a general rule, a good deal will be seen as a good deal fairly quickly in the discovery and investigative process. If your learning process keeps hitting "green lights" early on in the discovery effort and the facts support what you are being told about the goodness of this deal, it probably is a good deal.

FOR SELLERS

- For sellers, when you are confident that:
  - You have realized a fair selling price consistent with reasonable market expectations...
  - You have negotiated postclosing indemnity obligations and claim potentials (from breaches of representations and covenants in the durations negotiated) that are fair, and their expected present value is acceptable and in the event of occurrence would not unfairly dilute your return...
  - Your overall after-tax return after all postclosing adjustments is consistent with reasonable expectations...
  - Then go for it!

TOPIC 81

Negotiation: Do a Time Capsule

Deals are about hard work and often drudgery as the process of discovery takes place and the stress of negotiations unfolds. Everyone likes to be a winner so before your deal starts, have your team members prepare a time capsule of how each feels the deal will turn out.

THE TIME CAPSULE

- Put some humor in your life!
- Prior to commencing with negotiations on a deal, have all your team members put up some cash and secretly write down their guess of where the deal will finally settle out in terms of:
  - Cash up front
  - Major terms of the deal
  - Dollar earn-out, and terms, if any
  - Working capital thresholds
  - Other key risk allocations positions taken
  - Or whether it will crater and not complete
- Put the cash and secret positions in a jar.
- Do not open the time capsule until the deed is done one way or the other.
- Winner takes all!

TOPIC **82**

Negotiation: Build Trust to Get Closed

The road to a closing need not be unpleasant. If your negotiating style is based on creating a space resonating with trust the journey can be fulfilling for both parties to a deal. Topic 82 explores how to get there and how to handle the bully whose style is the antithesis of creating trust.

HOW TO CREATE TRUST

- The road to negotiating a deal to closure is usually long and stressful, but it need not be unpleasant.
- Negotiating is an intense, personal, high-stakes, sometimes confrontational, sometimes humorous journey—kind of like life.
- The trick to getting to closure is to find answers that suit each party—hence the existence of different deal risk frontiers (see Topics 26, 73 and 84).
- *You get to the finish line of closing the deal by creating a successful negotiating space.* This is a place of discovery characterized by:
  - Intense communication
  - Fact finding
  - Opinions and conclusions
  - Open dialogue
  - Honest assessment of positions: yours, theirs
  - Fair and prudent asking and giving
  - Sharing
  - Understanding of:
    - Facts
    - Feelings
    - History
    - Legacy
    - Association
    - Assumptions
    - Strengths
    - Weaknesses

- *Above all, trust*
- The best path to this space is rooted in behavior that leads to a deepening *sense of trust* between the players.

LET YOUR NEGOTIATING BEHAVIOR BE GUIDED BY YOUR DAILY SPIRITUAL NEEDS

- Consider that if you *let your behavior be guided by a desire to find fulfillment of your own daily spiritual needs,* you can create resonance with the other side to behave similarly. In so doing, you can find the path to a working negotiating space where answers that work for both sides can be found.
- Illustration 82.1 provides examples of daily spiritual needs that can be fulfilled by our negotiating behavior. Our behavior also should resonate with and fulfill the daily spiritual needs of those with whom we negotiate. These needs are highly personal characteristics or principles that characterize who we are, fulfill us, govern how we conduct our lives, give life meaning when they are fulfilled, and are a barometer of our days.
- The negotiating process is as much about giving as it is about taking and is one of *influencing, not telling.*

ILLUSTRATION 82.1 LET NEGOTIATING BEHAVIOR BE DICTATED BY DAILY SPIRITUAL NEEDS TO CREATE TRUST

Daily Spiritual Needs	Lead to	Resonating Negotiating Behavior
Be treated fairly		Seek reasonableness, give as you take
Have feelings felt		Ask, "How would you feel if . . ."
Tell my story		Seek out others' ideas
Be needed		Give constructive input on others' ideas
Contribute		Ask for constructive input on your ideas
Be appreciated		Acknowledge, congratulate
Be heard		Listen
Be respected		Say only what you can deliver
Be understood		Ask why, talk straight
Be forgiven		Forgive take-backs, forgive errors
Be not abused		Be firm, speak up, handle bullies appropriately
Be considered		Be considerate
Be reflective		Engage mind before mouth
Be accepting		Deflect, do not confront; imprint, do not tell

- Abusive, authoritative, confrontational negotiating styles encountered often can be defused and disarmed with a consistent negotiating style based on a spiritually fulfilling approach.
  - Negative behavior is not reinforced.
  - The other side quickly learns that neither party will be abused or taken advantage of.
  - A consistent negotiating style enables constructive, controlled deliberation of differences in views.
  - A consistent negotiating style displays fairness and firmness.
  - A consistent negotiating style enables negotiators to be the best they are, not what they think the other side thinks they should be.
- Take the risk to extend your negotiating behavior from your spiritual base.

HOW TO HANDLE THE BULLY

- *If you encounter a bully*—a negotiator who has chosen to adopt a bully style or really is a bully, who runs over you or your side at every turn, agrees controversial points for both of you in his or her favor then moves on, or makes outlandish, intimidating statements or demands designed to gain an upper hand and has no interest in creating a negotiation space centered on trust—*handle the bully the old-fashioned way* shortly after the bully style gets in the way: *Punch the bully in the mouth* (well, not literally).
  - Give bullies the time-out sign (T), look them straight in the eye, and verbally deliver your own form of a heavy-handed corrective interview:
    - "Cut the bully-boy behavior now because if it continues, it's lights out on this deal until you get it right.
    - I would never behave that way toward anyone and will not tolerate anyone who behaves that way toward me or my people.
    - We are here to work a deal acceptable to both sides—give-and-take. If you can't deal with that, let me know.
    - That clear enough?" Tell them everyone will take a five-minute break, and walk out. (This usually works.)
  - Upon return, take up the last point and see if the message has sunk in.
  - If the bullying approach continues, repeat the message and ask what the other side wants to do because a good deal cannot be reached with its negotiating approach.
  - If the bully is the owner and decision maker, you may have a problem to get to a close.
  - Take the person aside and see if a civil conversation is possible.
  - If the bully is an assigned negotiator, take the owner aside or call and say that meaningful progress is unlikely unless a change is made in the negotiator and/or his or her style.
- *If you encounter a hard-headed wing-nut* who takes outright firm positions on every point *way* too early in the negotiation process simply to intimidate and gain a continuing upper hand or to close off discussion (e.g., "We have

never provided an indemnity on such a matter in any deal"), counter with the diametrically opposed view (e.g., "We have never *not* received a fair indemnity on such a matter in any deal, and this one will not be an exception").

- Propose your fair and reasonable position and suggest that you all move on while the opposing party considers it. Revisit the point later. (This also usually works.)
- A negotiating style that is based on a spiritually fulfilling approach will always wear well, regardless of the people you are dealing with.

TOPIC 83

Exits under Duress: Have a Plan if the Deal Does Not Work

Deals often do not work, no matter how hard you try or how diligent you were. Before you close a deal, be sure to have at least considered what you might do if the deal you choose does not work.

HAVE AN EXIT PLAN

- Be sure there is a bolt-hole on every deal before you close it.
  - A bolt-hole is a place through which one can exit on short notice to escape peril.
- Have a few practical bolt-hole options in mind regarding how a deal, once done, can be "undone" if it does not perform or fit, or needs to be liquidated in a way to mitigate the damage of a mistake:
  - Sale to competitor
  - Sale to customer
  - Sale to investor group
  - Sale to management
  - Initial public offering
- Be sure you have some options.

TOPIC 84

Structuring the Deal: An Overview

Topic 84 presents an overview of many of the essential legal and tax issues associated with the primary taxable and tax-deferred deal structures and the often-conflicting desires of buyers and sellers.

The reader is encouraged to take the time to read the text in conjunction with the referenced Appendices to gain the appropriate level of understanding of the subject matter discussed in the narrative. Appendices are either presented at the end of this and each remaining Topic or are available for review and download on this book's companion Web site (see the About the Web site page for login information).

DEAL STRUCTURES AND LEGAL AND TAX IMPLICATIONS

- Deal structuring is concerned with the legal form and tax consequences of a transaction to best satisfy the desires and goals of sellers and buyers—goals that are, many times, at odds:
  - Sellers often prefer to limit or defer tax liability on a transaction structure (receive shares). This is often at odds with buyer goals of fast investment basis write-off (pay cash for assets).
  - Buyers often prefer to obtain as much of a new, short-lived tax basis as possible for their investment. Often this leads to a taxable seller transaction structure that sellers do not desire.
  - On taxable deals, buyers often prefer to maximize the allocation of the purchase price to inventory, depreciable assets, and faster turnover assets to exploit the postclosing current tax deduction and reduce postclosing taxes.
- Deal structuring is a highly complex, sometimes highly charged, area in putting deals together. Both parties need expert tax and legal advice in arriving at the economic trade-offs and ultimate structure and terms adopted that work for both sides of a deal.
- Appendix 84.1 introduces the primary taxable and tax-deferred deal structures and the major considerations and implications of structuring U.S. tax-based transactions.

- Appendix 84.2, pages 1 to 3, presents an affinity matrix for each of the deal structures listed. The matrix summarizes many of the primary legal and tax implications related to that deal structure and the conditions that may be sought by or may motivate sellers seeking taxable or tax-deferred deals.
  - The highlighted intersections on the matrix in Appendix 84.2 present the points of affinity (intersecting resonance) between each deal structure and the indicated legal or tax implication listed (to the left of the listed deal structures). The affinity between each deal structure with certain conditions (to the right of the listed deal structures) is also presented.
  - Sellers preferring immediate liquidity and acceptable tax consequences proceed along the solid line to the right-hand vertical section of Appendix 84.2 (which presents conditions relevant to such a liquidity preference) and proceed down the chart to the points of intersection with the different taxable deal structures.
  - Sellers preferring tax deferral without immediate liquidity proceed along the dotted line to the right-hand vertical section of Appendix 84.2 (which presents conditions relevant to such a tax-deferred preference) and proceed down the chart to the points of intersection with the different tax-deferred deal structures.
  - The affinity matrix may also be entered and interrogated for answers by selecting a deal structure (in the center, for example, taxable deals-cash for stock) and by moving left to identify the legal and tax implications of the selected structure or move to the right to identify other general consequences of the selected structure.
  - The affinity matrix may also be entered and interrogated for answers by identifying a legal and tax implication (along the left side, for example asset step-ups) and dropping down to identify the deal structures that resonates with that implication.
  - The affinity matrix may also be entered and interrogated for answers by identifying other consequences of interest (along the right side, for example, seller shareholder approval is required) and dropping down to identify the deal structures that resonates with that implication.
- The remaining pages of Appendix 84.2 present a more in-depth explanation of the issues pertinent to the taxable and tax-deferred deal structures as well as charts demonstrating the transaction mechanics. The issues presented for each deal structure include:
  - What the buyer acquires
  - Who the seller is (target or shareholder)
  - What the buyer pays the seller with (cash, shares, etc.) and limitations on each payment method
  - Seller tax impact and consequences
  - Buyer tax impact and consequences
  - Legal form and attributes
  - Valuation issues for buyer and seller
  - Buyer pros and cons

- Seller pros and cons
- Other issues
- Book accounting treatment

FRONTIERS OF TRANSACTION ACCEPTANCE

- The essence of reaching agreement on a transaction is to find enough overlap between the frontiers of acceptance for both parties. Deal frontiers are the composite space existing between interrelated factors of deal consideration: purchase price paid, contractual risk assumption, and tax risk sharing.
- Sellers and buyers will each have a different view of the consideration frontier that can lead to an acceptable deal as presented in Appendix 84.3.
- The seller's consideration frontier in Appendix 84.3 is bounded by points A, H, and G. That frontier lies below the buyer's consideration frontier, which is bounded by points B, E, and F, beyond points C and D where the buyer and sellers frontiers meet and cross one another.
- The frontiers represent the composite total consideration frontier of each side to a deal. For the seller, a lower price must often be accompanied by more favorable transaction and postclosing risk and tax consequences (generally less favorable for the buyer). For the buyer, a higher price must often be accompanied with less transaction and postclosing risk and tax consequences (generally less favorable for the seller).
- The deal maker's job is to bring the deal frontiers together through the process of trading off price against risk against tax consequence and find the point where the deal frontiers meet, point CD in Appendix 84.3.
- Because the tax ramifications of opposing deal structures usually are quantifiable, economic consequences often can be satisfied by selling-price adjustment trade-offs by both parties.

DEAL-STRUCTURING CONSIDERATIONS AND TRADE-OFF OPTIONS

- The deal-structuring considerations and trade-off options available to both parties are almost endless but may include, particularly in private, nonpublic deals, a mix of options as presented in Appendix 84.4. The appendix illustrates many of the typical benefits and trade-off tensions considered by buyers and sellers in reaching agreement.
- The essential buyer-seller tensions revolve around the premise that:
  - Sellers seek as high a purchase price as possible and to receive it as early as possible, to pay as little tax as possible, to limit purchase price allocation to fast-turnover assets, and to eliminate postclosing recovery avenues for the buyer.
  - Buyers seek to pay as little as possible as late as possible, obtain a high tax basis in fast-turnover assets, and have access to many postclosing recovery

avenues to the seller resulting from a breach of representations that survive the closing.

- Appendix 84.4 lists the primary monetary and contractual trade-offs (vertical axis) and the buyer and seller advantages sought (horizontal axis).

GENERAL TAX CONSEQUENCES ASSOCIATED WITH DEAL-RELATED EXPENSES

- Acquirers' deal fees (bankers, legal consulting, and accounting) on completed *asset acquisition* deals (for tax) generally are allocated to the basis of the assets acquired and provide a tax deduction as the assets are amortized for tax purposes.
- Acquirers' deal fees (bankers, legal consulting, and accounting) on completed *stock acquisition* or legal reorganization deals (for tax) generally are allocated to the basis of the stock acquired and provide a deduction only upon disposition of the shares.
- Target deal fees (bankers, legal consulting, and accounting) on completed asset acquisition deals (for tax) generally are deductible as incurred.
- Target deal fees on completed stock acquisition or legal reorganization deals (for tax) incurred up to the date of a final binding decision (board resolution) to go forward with the deal generally are deductible as incurred. Those incurred after such date generally are capitalized and deductible upon disposition of the shares or the merged entity.
- Acquirer's due diligence expenses on completed deals generally are deductible over five years.
- Acquirer's due diligence expenses on failed deals, are deductible immediately. Fees associated with obtaining debt financing generally are deductible over the term of the debt.
- Deal fees (bankers, legal consulting, and accounting) paid on failed deals are deductible immediately. The basic tax premise of taking a current deduction or not is whether future benefits are or are not associated with the fee expense. On failed deals there is no future benefit associated with the expense.
- Deal fees (bankers, legal consulting, and accounting) on closed deals usually are capitalized into goodwill for book accounting. Recent accounting statements in the United States and Europe call for immediate expensing to book income.

CONTRACTUAL CONDITIONS LIMIT AND APPORTION FINAL RISK ASSUMPTION POSITIONS—WORK THEM

- As first discussed in Topic 73 and restated here for emphasis, negotiation about essentially any issue is about the distribution of the consequences of owning or having rights to the benefits of owning assets or the consequences of undertaking or potentially assuming liabilities. The rules governing the distribution of such consequences for each party are captured in carefully worded conditions.

- Conditions are defined along three interrelated negotiating dimensions surrounding almost any business contract issue or tight spot: value, time, and scope. All must be exercised simultaneously, and often they are woven together in reaching solutions and closing negotiating gaps, particularly in the area of deal and tax structuring.
- The values (ultimately cash) associated with most issues (e.g., the amount of an indemnification cap, basket, or escrow) can be increased, decreased, stepped, floored, or capped.
- The timeline associated with most issues (e.g., the survival period of an indemnification, the trigger date for the release of an escrow) can be lengthened, shortened, gapped, start delayed, capped, or date certain defined.
- The scope of the breadth and depth surrounding, included in, or excluded from an issue (e.g., an indemnified environmental liability) can be narrowed or widened by defining what is excluded from or only what is included in the definition. Another clarifying method is to add "with the exception of items listed" to the definition.
- As you work through the side list of issues maintained as the deal negotiation proceeds, you can make small but creative meaningful concessions using the multi faceted dimensions of conditions: shorten a time frame but broaden the scope; narrow the scope but increase a cap; cap the value but lengthen the time, and so forth.

BASIC DEAL STRUCTURES SUMMARY "TAXABLE" AND "TAX DEFERRED"

84.2:	TAXABLE DEALS FOR SELLER	SELLER AND OR SELLER SHAREHOLDER GETS OR KEEPS	BUYER AND BUYER SHAREHOLDER GETS OR KEEPS	ATTRIBUTES AND LIKELY FORM WHERE
A	**CASH (PLUS OTHER; NOTES, STOCK) FOR ASSETS** (ASSETS AND SELECT BAL SHEET LIABILITIES SOLD TO BUYER)	DOUBLE TAX POTENTIAL, TARGET KEEP NOLS AND CONTINGENT LIABILITIES	TARGET ASSETS; ASSET STEP UPS; GOODWILL DEDUCTIBLE SELECTED LIABILITIES ASSUMED SUBJECT TO INDEMNITIES	SELLER WANTS CASH, NOLS AVAILABLE; CONTRACTS, IP AND LICENSES ARE TRANSFERRABLE; SELLER SHAREHOLDER APPROVAL REQUIRED BUYER SHAREHOLDER APPROVAL GENERALLY NOT REQUIRED
A1	**FORWARD CASH MERGER (DEEMED ASSET SALE)** (TARGET MERGES INTO BUYER) (USE OF A BUYER SUB IS MORE LIKELY FORM, SEE A2)	DOUBLE TAX POTENTIAL, TARGET KEEP NOLS; TARGET LIABILITIES INHERITED BY BUYER SUBJECT TO SHAREHOLDER INDEMNITIES	TARGET ASSETS; ASSET STEP UPS; GOODWILL DEDUCTIBLE ALL TARGET LIABILITIES INHERITED BY BUYER SUBJECT TO SHAREHOLDER INDEMNITIES	SELLER WANTS CASH, NOLS AVAILABLE; CONTRACTS, IP AND LICENSES ARE NOT TRANSFERRABLE W/OUT CONSENT; TARGET SHAREHOLDER APPROVAL REQUIRED TARGET DISSOLVES; MINORITY OUT; BUYER SHAREHOLDER APPROVAL REQUIRED
A2	**FORWARD TRIANGULAR CASH MERGER (DEEMED ASSET SALE)** (TARGET MERGES INTO BUYER SUB)	DOUBLE TAX POTENTIAL, TARGET KEEP NOLS, TARGET LIABILITIES INHERITED BY BUYER SUB SUBJECT TO SHAREHOLDER INDEMNITIES LARGE STOCK SELLER MAY HAVE FIDUCIARY DUTY TO MINORITY HOLDER	TARGET ASSETS; ASSET STEP UPS; GOODWILL DEDUCTIBLE ALL TARGET LIABILITIES INHERITED BY BUYER SUB SO PARENT SHIELDED SUBJECT TO SHAREHOLDER INDEMNITIES	SELLER WANTS CASH, NOLS AVAILABLE; CONTRACTS, IP AND LICENSES ARE NOT TRANSFERRABLE W/OUT CONSENT; TARGET SHAREHOLDER APPROVAL REQUIRED; TARGET DISSOLVES; MINORITY OUT; BUYER SHAREHOLDER APPROVAL MAY BE RE
B	**CASH FOR STOCK** (TARGET BECOMES SUBSIDIARY OF BUYER)	SINGLE TAX ON STOCK SALE, TARGET RETAINS ALL LIABILITIES SUBJECT TO SHAREHOLDER INDEMNITIES	TARGET STOCK AND NOLS, NO ASSET STEP UPS, CARRY OVER BASIS ALL TARGET LIABILITIES STAY IN SUB; GOODWILL NOT DEDUCTIBLE NOLS RESTRICTED IN FUTURE USE AGAINST INCOME	TARGET MUST CONTINUE; CONTRACTS, IP, AND LICENSES NOT TRANSFERRABLE W/OUT CONSENT; SELLER WANTS TO AVOID DOUBLE TAX SELLER WANTS CASH, TARGET SHAREHOLDERS MUST SIGN AGREEMENTS
B1	**REVERSE CASH MERGER (FOR STOCK)** (BUYER MERGES INTO TARGET) (USE OF A BUYER SUB IS MORE LIKELY FORM, SEE B2)	SINGLE TAX ON STOCK SALE, TARGET RETAINS ALL LIABILITIES SUBJECT TO SELLER OR SHAREHOLDER INDEMNITIES	TARGET NOLS, NO ASSET STEP UPS, CARRY OVER BASIS ALL TARGET LIABILITIES STAY IN SUB; GOODWILL NOT DEDUCTIBLE NOLS RESTRICTED IN FUTURE USE AGAINST INCOME	SELLER WANTS CASH; NOLS AVAILABLE; IP AND LICENSES NOT TRANSFERRABLE W/OUT CONSENT; TARGET MUST SURVIVE; TARGET SHAREHOLDER VOTE REQUIRED BUYER SHAREHOLDER APPROVAL REQUIRED
B2	**REVERSE TRIANGULAR CASH MERGER (FOR STOCK)** (BUYER SUB MERGES INTO TARGET)	SINGLE TAX ON STOCK SALE, TARGET RETAINS ALL LIABILITIES SUBJECT TO SHAREHOLDER INDEMNITIES	TARGET NOLS, NO ASSET STEP UPS, CARRY OVER BASIS ALL TARGET LIABILITIES STAY IN SUB; GOODWILL NOT DEDUCTIBLE NOLS RESTRICTED IN FUTURE USE AGAINST INCOME	SELLER WANTS CASH; NOLS AVAILABLE; IP AND LICENSES NOT TRANSFERRABLE W/OUT CONSENT; TARGET MUST SURVIVE; TARGET SHAREHOLDER VOTE REQUIRED BUYER SHAREHOLDER APPROVAL MAY BE REQUIRED
C	**CASH (PLUS SOME STOCK) FOR STOCK SEC 338** (TREATED AS DEEMED ASSET SALE FOR TAX PURPOSES)	SINGLE TAX ON STOCK SALE, TARGET RETAINS ALL LIABILITIES SUBJECT TO SHAREHOLDER INDEMNITIES	TAX LIABILTIY ON DEEMED TARGET ASSET SALE; NOLS AVAILABLE TO OFFSET TAX ON ASSET SALE GAIN ONLY; ASSET STEP UPS; GOODWILL IS DEDUCTIBLE; ALL TARGET LIABILITIES INCL PRIOR YEARS TAX, STAY IN ACQUIRED SUB	TARGET HAS LARGE NOLS TO OFFSET TARGET DEEMED ASSET SALE GAIN ASSUMED BY BUYER; IP AND LICENSES ARE NOT TRANSFERRABLE W/OUT CONSENT TARGET MUST SURVIVE; BUYER WANTS LIABILITY SHIELD; SELLER WANTS STOCK SALE AND CASH; TARGET SHAREHOLDERS SIGN AGREEMEM
D	**CASH (PLUS SOME STOCK) FOR STOCK SEC 338 (h) (10)** (TREATED AS DEEMED ASSET SALE FOR TAX PURPOSES)	SINGLE TAX TARGET ON DEEMED ASSETS SALE, TARGET USES NOLS AND RETAINS ALL LIABILITIES SUBJECT TO SHAREHOLDER INDEMNITIES; POSSIBLE "BIG" TAX ISSUES FOR SELLER AND OR SHAREHOLDER	ASSET STEP UPS, ALL TARGET LIABILITIES STAY IN ACQ'RD SUB GOODWILL IS DEDUCTIBLE; ALL TARGET LIABILITIES INCL PRIOR YEARS TAX, STAY IN ACQUIRED SUB	TARGET IS AN "S" OR MEMBER OF A CONSOLIDATED GROUP TO MAKE ELECTION; SELLER GROUP HAS LARGE NOLS TO OFFSET ASSET SALE GAIN; TARGET MUST SURVIVE; USE GOODWILL TAX SHIELD TO STRETCH OFFER; SELLER WANTS STOCK SALE AND CASH; TARGET SHAREHOLDERS SIGN AGREEMEM

84.2:	TAX DEFERRED DEALS FOR SELLER **	SELLER AND SELLER SHAREHOLDER GETS OR KEEPS	BUYER AND BUYER SHAREHOLDER GETS OR KEEPS	LIKELY FORM WHERE
E	**"A" REORG - STATUTORY MERGER (A, B,)** (TARGET MERGES INTO BUYER) (USE OF A BUYER SUB IS MORE LIKELY FORM, SEE E2)	BUYER STOCK AND CASH(<50% CASH), DEFERED TAX GAIN ON STOCK, ANY CASH RECEIVED (BOOT) IS TAXABLE; BASIS IN BUYER STOCK EQUAL TO BASIS IN TARGET; STEP UP IN BASIS UPON DEATH OF SELLING SHAREHOLDER FOR INHERITORS	NO STEP UPS, CARRY OVER BASIS IN TARGET ASSETS ALL TARGET LIABILITIES INHERITED BY BUYER PRIVATELY HELD SELLERS REPS SURVIVE CLOSING	LARGE (PRIVATELY HELD) SELLER WANTS TAX DEFERRAL SOME CASH; WANT MINORITY OUT; CONTRACTS, IP AND LICENSES MUST BE TRANSFERRABLE; TARGET DISSOLVES BUYER AND TARGET SHAREHOLDER APPROVAL REQUIRED
E1	**"A" REORG - STATUTORY CONSOLIDATION (A, B)** (BUYER AND SELLER MERGE INTO NEWCO)	BUYER STOCK AND CASH(<50% CASH), DEFERED TAX GAIN ON STOCK, ANY CASH RECEIVED (BOOT) IS TAXABLE; BASIS IN BUYER STOCK EQUAL TO BASIS IN TARGET; STEP UP IN BASIS UPON DEATH OF SELLING SHAREHOLDER FOR INHERITORS	NEWCO STOCK AND CASH, DEFERED TAX , CASH TAXABLE ALL TARGET LIABILITIES INHERITED BY NEWCO PRIVATELY HELD SELLERS REPS SURVIVE CLOSING	WHERE A MERGER OF EQUALS IS THE PRERVAILING SENTIMENT; PARTIES WANT STOCK AND SOME CASH; WANT MINORITY OUT; CONTRACTS, IP AND LICENSES MUST BE TRANSFERRABLE; PARTIES DISSOLVE; BUYER AND TARGET SHAREHOLDER APPROVAL REQUIRED
E2	**"A" REORG - FORWARD TRIANGULAR MERGER (A, B)** (TARGET MERGES INTO BUYER SUB)	BUYER STOCK AND CASH (<50% CASH , DEFERED TAX GAIN ON STOCK, CASH, TAXABLE ANY CASH RECEIVED (BOOT) IS TAXABLE; BASIS IN BUYER STOCK EQUAL TO BASIS IN TARGET; STEP UP IN BASIS UPON DEATH OF SELLING SHAREHOLDER FOR INHERITORS	NO STEP UPS, CARRY OVER BASIS IN TARGET ASSETS ALL TARGET LIABILITIES INHERITED BY BUYER PRIVATELY HELD SELLERS REPS SURVIVE CLOSING	LARGE (PRIVATELY HELD) SELLER WANTS TAX DEFERRAL SOME CASH, CONTRACTS, IP AND LICENSES MUST BE TRANSFERRABLE; TARGET DISSOLVES TARGET SHAREHOLDER APPROVAL REQUIRED BUYER SHAREHOLDER APPROVAL MAY BE REQUIRED
E3	**"A" REORG - REVERSE TRIANGULAR MERGER (A, B)** (BUYER SUB MERGES INTO TARGET)	BUYER STOCK AND CASH (<20% CASH), DEFERED TAX GAIN ON STOCK; ANY CASH RECEIVED (BOOT) IS TAXABLE; BASIS IN BUYER STOCK EQUAL TO BASIS IN TARGET; STEP UP IN BASIS UPON DEATH OF SELLING SHAREHOLDER FOR INHERITORS	NO STEP UPS, CARRY OVER BASIS IN TARGET ASSETS ALL TARGET LIABILITIES INHERITED BY BUYER PRIVATELY HELD SELLERS REPS SURVIVE CLOSING	LARGE (PRIVATELY HELD) SELLER WANTS TAX DEFERRAL, SOME CASH; IP AND LICENSES NOT TRANSFERRABLE SO TARGET MUST SURVIVE; TARGET SHAREHOLDER APPROVAL REQUIRED BUYER SHAREHOLDER APPROVAL MAY BE REQUIRED
F	**"B" REORG - STOCK FOR STOCK EXCHANGE (A,B)** (TARGET ACQUIRED BY AND BECOMES SUB OF BUYER)	BUYER VOTING STOCK ONLY, NO CASH ALLOWED, DEFERED TAX GAIN, BASIS IN BUYER STOCK EQUAL TO BASIS IN TARGET; STEP UP IN BASIS UPON DEATH OF SELLING SHAREHOLDER FOR INHERITORS	NO STEP UPS, CARRY OVER BASIS IN TARGET ASSETS ALL TARGET LIABILITIES STAY IN ACQUIRED TARGET SUB PRIVATELY HELD SELLERS REPS SURVIVE CLOSING	BUYER WANTS STOCK OF ANOTHER COMPANY SUBSIDIARY; IP AND LICENSES NOT TRANSFERRABLE SO TARGET MUST SURVIVE; TARGET CONTINUES MINORITY REMAIN, CREEPING TAKEOVER ALLOWED; BUYER SHAREHOLDER APPROVAL MAY BE REQUIRED, TARGET REQUIRED
F1	**"B" REORG - SUB STOCK FOR STOCK EXCHANGE (A,B)** (TARGET ACQUIRED BY AND BECOMES SUB OF BUYER SUB)	100% BUYER OR SUBSIDIARY VOTING STOCK ONLY, NO CASH ALLOWED , DEFERED TAX GAIN; BASIS IN BUYER STOCK EQUAL TO BASIS IN TARGET; STEP UP IN BASIS UPON DEATH OF SELLING SHAREHOLDER FOR INHERITORS	NO STEP UPS, CARRY OVER BASIS IN TARGET ASSETS ALL TARGET LIABILITIES STAY IN ACQUIRED TARGET SUB PRIVATELY HELD SELLERS REPS SURVIVE CLOSING	LARGE (PRIVATELY HELD) SELLER WANTS TAX DEFERRAL IP AND LICENSES NOT TRANSFERRABLE SO TARGET MUST SURVIVE; TARGET CONTINUES MINORITY REMAIN, CREEPING TAKEOVER ALLOWED; BUYER SHAREHOLDER APPROVAL MAY BE REQUIRED, TARGET REQUIRED
G	**"C" REORG - STOCK FOR ASSETS* EXCHANGE (A)** * SUBSTANTIALLY ALL	BUYER STOCK AND CASH (<20% CASH), DEFERED TAX GAIN ON STOCK; ANY CASH RECEIVED (BOOT) IS TAXABLE; BASIS IN BUYER STOCK EQUAL TO BASIS IN TARGET; STEP UP IN BASIS UPON DEATH OF SELLING SHAREHOLDER FOR INHERITORS	NO STEP UPS, CARRY OVER BASIS IN TARGET ASSETS SELECTED TARGET LIABILITIES PRIVATELY HELD SELLERS REPS SURVIVE CLOSING	LARGE (PRIVATELY HELD) SELLER WANTS TAX DEFERRAL SOME CASH, TARGET DISSOLVES, MINORITY OUT, CONTRACTS, IP AND LICENSES MUST BE TRANSFERRABLE; BUYER SHAREHOLDER APPROVAL MAY BE REQUIRED, TARGET REQUIRED
G1	**"C" REORG - SUB STOCK FOR ASSETS* EXCHANGE (A)** * SUBSTANTIALLY ALL	BUYER STOCK AND CASH (<20% CASH), DEFERED TAX GAIN ON STOCK; ANY CASH RECEIVED (BOOT) IS TAXABLE; BASIS IN BUYER STOCK EQUAL TO BASIS IN TARGET; STEP UP IN BASIS UPON DEATH OF SELLING SHAREHOLDER FOR INHERITORS	NO STEP UPS, CARRY OVER BASIS IN TARGET ASSETS SELECTED TARGET LIABILITIES IN SUB PRIVATELY HELD SELLERS REPS SURVIVE CLOSING	LARGE (PRIVATELY HELD) SELLER WANTS TAX DEFERRAL SOME CASH, TARGET DISSOLVES, MINORITY OUT, CONTRACTS, IP AND LICENSES MUST BE TRANSFERRABLE; BUYER SHAREHOLDER APPROVAL MAY BE REQUIRED, TARGET REQUIRED

** TAX DEFERRED DEALS RESULT IN DEFERED TAX OBLIGATIONS NOT ELIMINATION OF TAX LIABILITY
SEE ALSO DEAL STRUCTURE EXPLANATIONS AND CONSEQUENSES PRESENTED ON THE FOLLOWING MATRICES A THROUGH G

See Also:
** For Tax Deferred Deals , Internal Revenue Code Section 368 (a)

APPENDIX 84.1 Basic Deal Structures: Summary: "Taxable" and "Tax Deferred"

The following Appendices, as well as those presented earlier, are available for viewing or download on the Web site for this book at: www.wiley.com/go/emott. Please see the About the Web Site page at the back of this book for login information.

APPENDIX 84.2 Deal-Structuring Engine

APPENDIX 84.2 A P1-2 Cash for Assets

APPENDIX 84.2 A1 P1-2 Forward Cash Merger for Assets

APPENDIX 84.2 A2 P1-2 Forward Triangular Cash Merger for Assets

APPENDIX 84.2 B P1-2 Cash for Stock

APPENDIX 84.2 B1 P1-2 Reverse Cash Merger (for Stock)

APPENDIX 84.2 B2 P1-2 Reverse Triangular Cash Merger (for Stock)

APPENDIX 84.2 C P1-2 Sec 338 Cash for Stock

APPENDIX 84.2 D P1-2 Deal Structures, Sec 338(H)(10) Cash for Stock

APPENDIX 84.2 E P1-2 'A Reorganization' Statutory Forward Merger

APPENDIX 84.2 E1 P1-2 'A Reorganization' Statutory Consolidation

APPENDIX 84.2 E2 P1-2 'A Reorganization' Forward Triangular Merger

APPENDIX 84.2 F P1-2 'B Reorganization' Stock for Stock Exchange

APPENDIX 84.2 F1 P1-2 'B Reorganization' Stock for Stock Exchange

APPENDIX 84.2 G P1-2 'C Reorganization' Subsidiary Stock for Assets Exchange

APPENDIX 84.2 G1 P1-2 'C Reorganization' Stock for Assets Exchange

APPENDIX 84.3 Acceptable Deal Structure Frontier Example

APPENDIX 84.4 Deal-Structuring Considerations and General Trade-Off Issues Example

TOPIC 85

Structuring the Deal: Asset Step-Ups, Noncompete, and Synergy Valuation Engines

The negotiated interests of the parties to the deal will provide the rationale for the deal structures utilized (taxable, tax deferred, and so forth, see Topic 84). The structures employed can lead to asset step-ups in tax basis and the use of noncompete arrangements, each of which requires appropriate valuation. In addition, synergy estimates also require valuation. Topic 85 explores these issues and how to value them in the context of determining total deal value.

The reader is encouraged to take the time to read the text in conjunction with the referenced Appendices to gain the appropriate level of understanding of the subject matter discussed in the narrative. Appendices are either presented at the end of this and each remaining Topic or are available for review and download on this book's companion Web site (see the About the Web Site page for login information).

VALUATION OF ASSET TAX BASIS STEP-UPS

- Buyers prefer to realize as large a tax deduction for the amount of their investment in a deal as early as possible.
- To do so, buyers must obtain as high a tax basis as possible in the most short-lived tax deductible assets acquired. One way to accomplish this is through structuring deals as asset or deemed asset purchases for tax purposes (see Topic 84), thus increasing the tax basis of assets acquired.
- Asset or deemed asset purchase structures allow the buyer to allocate the total of the purchase price paid to the assets acquired at a value equal to the fair market value of the asset at the date of purchase; such value usually exceeds the book value of the seller, hence the step-up in value (see Topic 84). The remaining unallocated portion of the purchase price is attributed to goodwill.
- Step-ups in asset values limit the amount of purchase price attributable to goodwill. Goodwill is tax deductible, but over a longer time period (generally 15 years) than depreciation expense on fixed assets or on inventory turnover.

- The deal value impact of the early tax deduction is the present value (PV) of the difference between the tax expense of accelerated tax deductions resulting from the asset step-up amount versus later realization of a tax deduction (without a step-up) from goodwill amortization of the asset step-up amount.

FIXED ASSET STEP-UP VALUATION

- The mechanics of determining the deal value impact of a buyer's fixed asset step-ups are illustrated in Appendices 85.1, 85.2, and 85.3.
  - The purchase price allocated to fixed assets at the fair market value of the asset of $75 million (Appendix 85.1, column 2,) creates a step-up amount of $25 million (column 4) over the book value of $50 million (column 3), which generates a tax deduction of $5 million per year for five years, assuming five-year straight-line depreciation (used for simplicity in the illustration; tax depreciation on fixed assets generally is determined using accelerated depreciation methods). At a 36% tax rate, this deduction has a PV of taxes not paid resulting from the step-up of $6.8 million (at a 12.5% midyear discount rate) (column 10).
  - If the same $25 million excess purchase price amount were allocated to goodwill in a non–step-up basis transaction (Appendix 85.2, column 5), this would result in a tax deduction of $1.7 million per year over 15 years, assuming a 15-year amortization period for tax at a 36% tax rate, resulting in a PV of $4.2 million (column 10).
  - The net benefit of the fixed asset step-up allocation versus goodwill allocation is therefore $2.6 million (Appendix 85.3, column 10), $6.8 – $4.2.

INVENTORY STEP-UP VALUATION

- Appendix 85.4 shows the mechanics of determining the deal value impact of buyer's finished goods inventory step-ups.
  - Deals structured as asset or deemed asset purchases for tax, allow purchase price allocation to finished goods inventory at the fair market value of the inventory. Finished goods inventory is essentially acquired at market price in an asset purchase transaction.
  - In Appendix 85.4 column 2, the inventory is valued at $100 million and creates a step-up amount of $40 million (column 4) over the book value at cost of $60 (column 3). The deduction of the stepped up inventory basis of $40 million inventory generates a tax savings of $14.4. Assuming that the acquired inventory turnover is in year 1, this deduction has a PV of $13.6 (at a 12.5% midyear discount rate).
  - If the same $40 excess purchase price were allocated to goodwill in a non–step-up basis transaction (Appendix 85.5, column 5) resulting in a

tax deduction of $2.7 million per year, assuming a 15-year amortization period for tax at a 36% tax rate, this deduction would generate a PV of $6.8 million (column 10).
- The net benefit of the inventory step-up versus goodwill is therefore $6.8 ($13.6 – $6.8) (Appendix 85.6, column 10).

NONCOMPETE VALUATION

- Appendices 85.7–85.9 show the mechanics of determining the buyer's deal value impact of noncompete contracts.
  - Noncompete contracts calling for tax-deductible payments to the sellers to refrain from competing in the target's markets and products for a period of time are sometimes utilized in connection with the acquisition of a business. (See Topic 76).
  - The free cash flow (FCF) impact of noncompete payments of $25 million (Appendix 85.7, column 2) paid evenly over five years net a tax credit of $0.6 million per year for 15 years resulting from the amortization of the noncompete obligation over 15 years at a 36% tax rate ($25/15*.36) is a net outflow as indicated in Appendix 85.7, column 7, which results in a net outflow PV of $14.7 million at a 12.5% midyear discount rate (Appendix 85.7, column 10).
  - If the $25 was paid as purchase price at the closing and was allocated to goodwill (Appendix 85.8, column 4) resulting in a 15-year amortization of $1.7 million per year, this deduction would result in a tax credit of $0.6 million per year (Appendix 85.8, column 6) or net outflow PV of $20.8 million ($25 million purchase price paid less the tax not paid arising from the goodwill deduction; Appendix 85.8, column 10).
  - The net benefit of the noncompete payments versus higher purchase price and resulting goodwill is therefore a net PV of $6.1 million (($14.7 outflow of the noncompete) – ($20.8 net outflow if the noncompete was goodwill)) (Appendix 85.9, column 10).

SYNERGY VALUATION

- Appendix 85.10 shows the mechanics of determining the buyer's deal value impact of net synergy advantages.
  - The after-tax synergies of $5.1 million for five years (Appendix 85.10, column 6), less the capital expense of $10 million (column 2) for facilities, equipment, and so forth, to achieve the synergy benefits, net of the tax savings of $0.7 million resulting from a five-year straight-line depreciation shield (column 3) result in a net PV of $12.1 (column 10) (at a 12.5% midyear discount rate).

SYNERGY VALUATION USING THE REAL OPTION MODEL

- The buyer needs six months after the closing to be satisfied that the initial assumptions about the synergy benefits are correct.
- What is the maximum amount the buyer should consider paying to the seller as part of the deal consideration (essentially for the right to evaluate the synergy value)? The answers to this synergy-sharing example lend themselves to evaluation as a real option.
- Under a real option valuation, the question to be addressed is: What is the maximum amount the buyer should consider paying (as a partial or full payment to the seller) as part of the overall deal consideration for the right to an option to verify that the synergy economics will pay off as estimated before actually making the synergy investment in time, effort, and the $10 million in capital?
- The real option synergy valuation approach attempts to answer this question by evaluating the fact set as a delay call option (see Topics 45 and 46). Illustration 85.1 summarizes the essential input to the modified Black-Scholes real option model and the resulting real option value of $4.1 million. See Appendix 85.11 for the real option solution.

ILLUSTRATION 85.1 SUMMARY OF REAL OPTION VALUATION OF SYNERGY EXPECTATION

Value of underlying asset FCF	$23.0
Value of investment required to realize FCF	$10.0
Time frame to realize benefits	5 years
Volatility of FCF (illustration estimate)	80%
FCF forgone as a percentage of asset value due to delay ($5.8/$22.1)	26%
Risk-free rate	5%
Option value	$4.1

- The value of the underlying asset FCF of $23.0 (first line of input to the model) is the present value of the FCF from the synergy of $8.0 per year for 5 years at a risk-free rate of 5%. The $23.0 million value of the underlying asset FCF is therefore the gross benefit of the synergy expectations excluding the investment of $10 million, which is a separate input to the modified Black-Scholes real option model.
- The conceptual way to interpret entering into this real option structure is this: If all the upside option assumptions made prior to the closing prove to be accurate, the buyer should be willing to pay as much as $4.1 million to the seller for the option to evaluate and satisfy him- or herself that the upside FCF valuation can in fact be realized before investing the $10 million. It will become clear by waiting that, as a result of management's decision to prove the case, the present value of the returns is going to be $23.0 million. Not bad

for a $14.1 million investment ($10 million capital plus $4.1 million option value paid).

- The corollary to this view if the preclosing assumptions are not validated is that while $4.1 million (pre tax) has been spent, $10 million (pretax investment) and considerable management time and effort is saved.
- In justifying the deal, $4.1 million is also a conservative estimate of the buyer's deal value impact of synergy advantages.

The following Appendices are available for viewing or download on the Web site for this book at: www.wiley.com/go/emott. Please see the About the Web site page at the back of this book for login information.

APPENDIX 85.1 Fixed Asset Step-Up Valuation Engine

APPENDIX 85.2 Fixed Asset Step-Up Valuation Engine if Step-Up Amount Was Goodwill

APPENDIX 85.3 Net of Fixed Asset Step-Up versus Goodwill Valuation Engine

APPENDIX 85.4 Inventory Step-Up Valuation Engine

APPENDIX 85.5 Inventory Step-Up Valuation Engine if Step-Up Amount Was Goodwill

APPENDIX 85.6 Net of Inventory Step-Up versus Goodwill Valuation Engine

APPENDIX 85.7 Noncompete Valuation Engine

APPENDIX 85.8 Noncompete Valuation Engine if Noncompete Amount Was Goodwill

APPENDIX 85.9 Net of Noncompete versus Goodwill Valuation Engine

APPENDIX 85.10 Synergy Valuation Engine

APPENDIX 85.11 Synergy Example Call Option Engine Modified Black-Scholes

TOPIC 86

Total Shareholder Return

Topic 86 explores the calculation of the return that really matters to equity investors in M&A deals: total shareholder return (TSR).

TOTAL SHAREHOLDER RETURN DEFINED

- *Actual total shareholder return (TSR)* measures actual return on investment performance to the equity investor from a current valuation date back to the time of the original investment.
- *Prospective TSR* measures projected return performance from the future back to the present.
- *TSR measures* the results of the amount returned to the equity investor during the measurement period in the form of realized or unrealized gains from distributions, dividends, or returns of capital from recapitalizations, loan repayments or exit proceeds, versus the equity amount invested.
- TSR is expressed as an annual average return since inception, the internal rate of return (IRR).
- The business acquirer should track the TSR since inception on an acquired business using the methods to be described.
- TSR for the acquired business presumes the existence of a market value measure of equity value, I_E, at the time of measurement or a reasonable surrogate for privately held business (a valuation).
- TSR is expressed on a pretax basis to the equity investor. (The returns of the business being valued are measured after tax.)
- The TSR realized from an acquired business is comparable to the anticipated forward-looking returns on which the acquisition was justified by the equity investor: C_L, the equity investor's levered opportunity cost (see Topic 23).
- TSR should be greater than or equal to C_L.

CALCULATION OF TSR

- Average annual TSR equals that rate (r) that discounts realized and unrealized returns from an investment to a value equal to the beginning initial investment, I_B.

- Average annual TSR is the time-weighted rate of return r (equivalent to the IRR) that *satisfies* the next equality (where the present value of the returns at discount rate r (equivalent to TSR), equal the initial investment and is comparable to C_L:

$$I_B = \left[\left(\sum_{i=1}^{n} \frac{D_i}{(1+r)^i} - \frac{NI_i}{(1+r)^i}\right) + \frac{I_{En}}{(1+r)^n}\right]$$

where I_B = initial equity investment = \$1 million
D = dividends or other proceeds (e.g., recapitalization proceeds) paid in period n (see illustration)
r = return rate, TSR, that satisfies the equality
i = each annual period n since inception
I_{En} = market value of the equity investment (enterprise value less debt and exit fees) at the n measurement date = \$1,800,000
n = number of annual periods since inception = 5
NI_i = new cash investments made in each period since inception = \$0

- Illustration 86.1 presents the data set required to calculate TSR. Illustration 86.2 presents the calculation of TSR per the data set in Illustration 86.1.

ILLUSTRATION 86.1 AVERAGE ANNUAL TSR SINCE INCEPTION

The TSR on an equity investment of \$1 million (I_B) made five years ago with returns received at the end of each year following the year of investment (time 0) is as shown:

Year after Investment	Dividends	I_E
1	0	1,100,000
2	10,000	1,200,000
3	20,000	1,400,000
4	10,000	1,500,000
5	40,000	1,800,000

ILLUSTRATION 86.2 AVERAGE ANNUAL TSR SINCE INCEPTION

I_B	Year 1	Year 2	Year 3	Year 4	Year 5	Year 5
1,000,000 =	$\frac{0}{(1.136)}$ +	$\frac{10,000}{(1.136)^2}$ +	$\frac{20,000}{(1.136)^3}$ +	$\frac{10,000}{(1.136)^4}$ +	$\frac{40,000}{(1.136)^5}$ +	$\frac{1,800,000}{(1.136)^5}$
1,000,000 =	0 +	7,749 +	13,643 +	6,005 +	21,143 +	951,460
1,000,000 = 1,000,00						

- By iteration, TSR in Illustration 86.2 is found to equal 13.5995%:
  - For ease of illustration, no new cash investments are shown.
  - That is, over the five years of the investment, the IRR on the shareholders' equity investment has equaled 13.5995% before tax (end-of-year basis).
  - TSR is comparable to C_L (see Topic 37). The greater the spread between TSR and C_L, the greater the increase in the equity investor's wealth.

TOPIC 87

Stakeholder Value Creation

Topic 87 explores the notion that successful M&A deals rest on stakeholder value creation: for the shareholder, customer, and employees.

The reader is encouraged to take the time to read the text in conjunction with the referenced Appendices to gain the appropriate level of understanding of the subject matter discussed in the narrative. Appendices are either presented at the end of this and each remaining Topic or are available for review and download on this book's companion Web site (see the About the Web site page for login information).

SATISFY THE CUSTOMER AND EMPLOYEES

- *Satisfy the customer's product and service needs reflecting the stated values of the enterprise* (see Topic 52).
  - *Measure customer satisfaction*—use customer surveys and determine why the customer values you and keeps coming back to you or does not, so you can improve on doing the right things that keep them coming back tomorrow. Measure where you stand on those factors of most importance to the customer:
    - Product returns due to quality issues
    - Product delay lead time versus expectations versus competition
    - Product order fill rates versus expectations versus competition
    - Product on-time delivery rate versus expectations versus competition
    - Product service complaints versus competition
    - Product failures versus competition
    - Product price versus competition
    - Money for value delivered
- Treat *employees* in a manner that reflects the stated values of the enterprise (see Topic 52).
  - Measure employee satisfaction.
    - Use employee surveys.
    - Do competitive wage, salary, incentives, and benefit analysis.
    - Employ an effective employee review and skill development process.
    - Empower your employees to own their process and feel vested in the business.

SATISFY THE SHAREHOLDER THROUGH VALUE CREATION

- Satisfy the *shareholder* through value creation.
  - *Shareholder value creation* occurs when return on net operating capital employed for the business (r) is greater than the levered weighted average cost of capital, C*, and total shareholder return, TSR (see Topic 86) for the shareholder is greater than C_L.
  - The critical interdependent factors are:
    - Rate of return on operating capital, r > C* leads to economic value added (EVA™)[1]
    - EVA is the amount of operating earnings after tax in excess of a capital charge equal to C* times net operating capital employed.
    - EVA captures the impact of profitability, rate of return to operating capital, r, and growth in one economic measure.
    - TSR results from dividend flow (d) and/or increasing investment equity value and is comparable to C_L.
    - TSR ≥ C_L creates value added for the equity investor.
    - Growth (g) in the enterprise, free cash flow (FCF), earnings, and EVA are made available from (or limited by) the level of r (adjusted for dividend payout (d) and leverage (debt to market value of capital ratio, D/Cm); See Topic 56.)
    - Dividends (d) (if paid) are the result of positive r.
    - C* is a function of the cost of unlevered capital, C_U, tax rate (t), risk-free rate (RF), and the level of debt (D) employed.
    - C_U is a function of equity risk premium (ERP), unlevered beta (b), and risk-free rate (RF).
- These key dependencies are shown in Appendix 87.1 with the arrows indicating the driving forces on each other.
- *Equity investor value creation* exists when the cumulative value of all returns as at an n measurement date is in excess of the *opportunity value* of the original equity investment at the n measurement date.
- *Equity investor value erosion* exists when the cumulative value of all returns as at a measurement date, n, is *below* the opportunity value of the equity investment at any point in time.
- It is, therefore, possible to have earnings, even increasing earnings, and book value with simultaneous destruction of real shareholder value.
  - This situation can occur for the business when r < C* but > 0 and g = < r but > 0 (growth occurring but with poor-performing investment results).
  - This situation can occur for the equity investor when TSR < C_L but > 0.
- At the heart of shareholder value creation and growth is EVA and preferably growing EVA.
  - It is possible to realize shareholder value without growing EVA if r > C* and growth = 0%, resulting in positive but flat EVA and I_E, the current market value of the equity investment.

[1] EVA is a trademark of Stern Stewart.

   - Free cash flow (FCF) essentially will equal net income (no reinvestment needs for incremental working capital and property, plant, and equipment, investments ≈ depreciation), and all net increases in cash will be available for dividends or share repatriation proceeds; in that case, TSR will be driven entirely by dividend flow, and enterprise value remains flat into the future.
- The primary factors affecting growth in value are:
   - r of the enterprise
      - Long-term sustainable growth, g_s, barring new equity, will be equal to r adjusted for dividend payout and debt level (see Topic 56).
   - Projects or investments where r is less than C*
      - Do not invest in such projects. Accumulate cash, pay it out to the shareholders or find projects where r > C*.
- The maxim for M&A deals is: Paying more than the value indicated by an analysis based on C* will, even if all actual equals forecast results, cause value destruction, not creation.

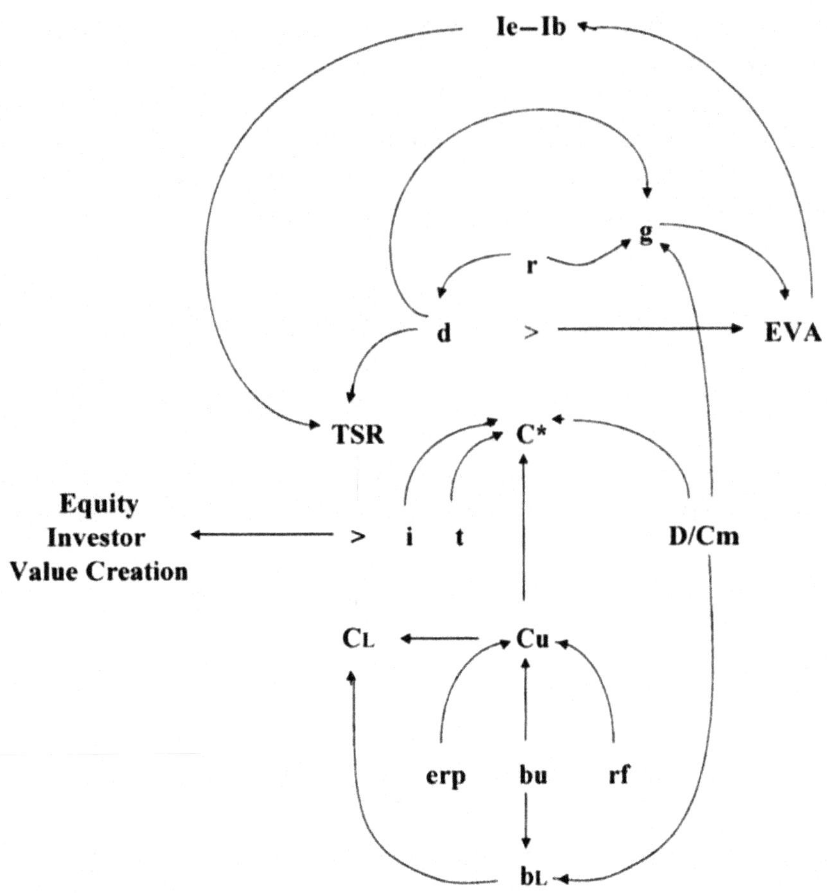

where:

r = operating profit after tax return on net operating capital employed
C* = weighted average cost of capital
C_L = levered cost of equity
Cu = unlevered cost of equity
D/Cm = debt to market capital ratio
g = growth rate
d = dividend flow
t = cash tax rate
EVA = economic value added
TSR = total shareholder return
Ib = initial equity investment
Ie = period end equity market value (enterprise value less debt)
i = interest rate
erp = equity risk premium
bu = unlevered beta
b_L = unlevered beta
rf = risk-free rate

APPENDIX 87.1 Interrelationships among Growth, r, C*, TSR, and Value Creation

TOPIC 88

EVAquity: Align Shareholder and Management Interests

Topic 88 explores the use of a form of tax-effecient shadow equity, EVAquity, to align the interests of the equity investor and management of an acquired (or otherwise) business.

The reader is encouraged to take the time to read the text in conjunction with the referenced Appendices to gain the appropriate level of understanding of the subject matter discussed in the narrative. Appendices are either presented at the end of this and each remaining Topic or are available for review and download on this book's companion Web site (see the About the Web Site page for login information).

EVAQUITY INCENTIVE PLAN OVERVIEW

- You have closed the deal and want to be sure that management interests are closely aligned with the equity investor's goal of creating value.
- Align those long-term shareholder value creation goals with a management incentive plan, "EVAquity," that provides a tax-efficient equity equivalent to management, without the issues associated with issuing transfer-restricted or marketable common share equity.
- The EVAquity incentive plan captures the effect of the value drivers' growth (g), return on capital (r) (net operating profit after tax [NOPAT]/operating capital), and C* and rewards management to effectively manage the drivers and allows management to share in the growth in value of the business as measured by growth in the composite result of the drivers, EVA™ (EVA is a trademark of Stern Stewart).
- EVA is equal to operating profit after tax (NOPAT) less a capital charge (equal to C* times net operating capital employed). Operating capital employed is operating working capital plus net property, plant, and equipment plus other operating capital. See *Quest for Value*[1] for a full discussion.
- The EVAquity incentive plan is essentially self-funding as payments are made only from realized EVA. Management's equity equivalent has value only if EVA grows.

[1] G. Bennett Stewart III, *The Quest for Value* (New York: HarperBusiness, 1991).

EVAQUITY PLAN TERMS

- The EVAquity incentive plan terms are described next.
  - EVAquity units are awardable to management annually at the beginning of each year; the number of units awarded is a function of management position and EVAquity unit share value growth.
  - The value to the management participant is based on the increase in the EVAquity unit value from year to year times the number of units held for each annual award.
  - The per-unit value of the units upon issue is equal to a three-year moving average of the annual EVA per share; the number of shares can be the number of issued shares outstanding for the business or a fixed arbitrary number to establish a per-unit value.
  - The number (and value) of the EVAquity units potentially issued annually to each manager class may be associated with a market compensation survey that establishes a maximum expected value award schedule (expected award payoff value if held to maturity as a percentage of salary) for each manager position based on the long-term expected annual payoff value of the awards and competitive market conditions.
    - The unit award schedule can be calibrated to various EVA achievement or growth levels (lesser or slower growth in EVA, the lower the scheduled unit awards). This approach could provide for a plan without a maximum expected value award cap.
  - The number of EVAquity units awarded each year is based on growth in the EVAquity unit share value over the prior year versus a target minimum growth threshold percentage.
  - If the EVAquity unit share value growth is 0% or less over the prior year, the EVAquity units awarded in the next year would be zero; if the EVAquity unit share value growth over the prior year is greater than 0% but less than a target minimum value growth threshold percentage, the EVAquity units awarded in the next year would also be zero.
  - If the EVAquity unit share value growth over the prior year exceeds the minimum value growth threshold percentage established by the principal equity shareholder, the number of EVAquity units awarded is equal to the maximum manager position schedule amount allowed.
    - The awards for performance below the threshold could be prorated between greater than 0% growth up to the growth performance threshold. (The example presented in the next section does not reflect proration of awards between zero and the threshold growth percentage.)
    - Here again, the unit awards for EVA growth performance above the minimum EVA growth threshold can be based on a calibrated unit award schedule. (The example presented in the next section does not reflect a calibrated award schedule above the threshold growth percentage.)
  - Each EVAquity unit award would vest in three years (or other period) from date of award. After that time it would be redeemable at the participant's option up to a maximum holding period of six years (or other period) at an

amount equal to the number of units redeemed times the unit value at the redemption date less the unit value at the date of award.

- The redemption value would be paid in cash to the recipient as W-2 compensation and would be tax deductible to the company as compensation.
- Other plan terms to be considered would include:
  - Upon the death or disability of the participant, all vested awards are redeemed and all unvested awards become vested and are redeemed; eligibility for future awards ceases.
  - Upon employee termination for cause, all vested awards are redeemed and all unvested awards are canceled; eligibility for future awards ceases.
  - Upon employee retirement, all vested awards are redeemed and all unvested awards vest per plan terms and are redeemed on the vesting date; eligibility for future awards ceases.
  - Award redemption shall be for all award units; no partial award redemptions are possible.

EVAQUITY PLAN EXAMPLE: PROSPECTIVE PLAN

- Appendix 88.1 presents an example of a prospective EVAquity plan.
  - Section 1, the EVA Computation section, presents the shareholder's prospective view of the business EVA potential expressed in terms of EVA (Appendix 88.1, page 1, lines 7–12); moving average EVA per share (line 18); and expected enterprise value (EV) of the firm (line 23), which is expected to grow at 8.5% per year for 12 years (line 25) and establishes the target number of units that may be issued.
  - Section 2, the Cumulative Increase in Value per Unit throughout the Potential Holding Period of an EVAquity award, illustrates the prospective cumulative increase in each year's EVAquity award value, through the vesting date (highlighted) and at the final redemption date (highlighted) (lines 35–to 44).
  - Section 3, the EVAquity Management Position Nominal Unit Award Schedule, presents the nominal number of EVAquity units that would be awarded each year, assuming that the prospective EVA values are realized (lines 60–64).
    - The present value of the future award payoff at redemption as a percentage of the plan inception salary is commensurate with the market compensation survey. The example in Appendix 88.1 assumes that the first grant of EVAquity units awarded takes place on the first day of the year of plan start-up to ensure alignment from inception. The number granted is based on the prior three years' actual results.
    - A 4% annual inflation in salary levels is anticipated over the prospective period (lines 60–64).
    - The number of units prospectively awarded decreases annually as the prospective EVA and EVA per share increase over time, ensuring the same award present value as a percentage of salary per the compensation survey.

- Section 4, the Pro Rata Award Schedule based on the prior year EVAquity unit price growth, presents the pro rata award factor applied to the number of EVAquity units potentially awarded each year depending on the achievement of growth in the prior year's EVAquity unit price below the threshold EVA growth target of 10% per year (see line 68). This prorated award assumption is not reflected in the example. Performance below the 10% threshold does not result in any award units.
- Section 5, the EVAquity Payout as a Percentage of Increase in Enterprise Value, summarizes the program's prospective award payout value for all managers, if all awards are held to maturity.
  - The cumulative payout value of incentive payments if all units were held to maturity of $4.4 million in year 10 is 8.1% of total EV of $55.2 million in year 10 (Appendix 88.1, page 2, lines 95–97).
  - The cumulative payout value of incentive payments if all units are held to maturity of $4.4 million is 17.5% of the increase in EV from inception to the end of year 10 of $25.5 million (lines 100–102).
  - The maximum payout liability that could take place in any one year if all vested shares outstanding were tendered as a percentage of the increase in EV is 10.9% in year 6 (line 107).
  - The maximum payout liability that could take place in any one year if all vested shares outstanding were tendered is $2.6 million in year 10 or 10.4% of the increase in EV from inception to the end of year 10 of $25.5 million (line 107).
- Section 6, the Prospective Total Value of Manager Awards, presents for each of the ten years of the example the prospective award value for all managers (lines 117–129) if the awards are held from the vesting date to the maximum term allowed by the program (highlighted).
  - The cumulative value of the potential payout is highlighted if all the awards are held from the vesting date to the maximum term allowed by the program ($4.4 million by the end of year 10) (line 120).
- Section 7, the Prospective Value of Each Manager's Awards, presents the prospective award value for each manager for each of the ten years of the example if the awards are held to the maximum term allowed by the program (highlighted).

- The question for the shareholder is whether the percentage of EV and EV growth shared with management in the form of the targeted payout is appropriate and whether the growth in EV is attributable to the incentive plan and EVA performance or whether it would take place in any event. Setting an aggressive benchmark for the EVA growth threshold can ameliorate payout levels until the shareholder target is attained. The plan should be designed to align interests and award payout if stretch performance is achieved.
- *Underlying all of the payout results of the program as explained above is the shareholder's belief that the business value (and shareholder's wealth) is in fact increasing along with, attributable to, and a function of the increase in EVA.*

EVAQUITY PLAN EXAMPLE: AFTER TWO YEARS' ACTUAL RESULTS

- Appendix 88.2 presents an example of the EVAquity awards and payouts assuming an actual growth in EVA below that assumed in the prospective plan design, Appendix 88.1, for the first two years of the plan. Plan results per the shareholder's forecast follow.
  - Because EVA growth in the first two years is below the target growth of 10% (Appendix 88.2, page 1, lines 13–14), zero award factors are imposed on the number of units awarded in years 2 and 3 of the program.
  - The total award values are below those expected in the prospective plan resulting from the plan design.
    - The cumulative payout value of incentive payments (after the first two years of actual results) if all units were held to maturity of $2.6 million through year 10 is 4.9% of total enterprise value of $52.1 million in year 10 (Appendix 88.2, page 2, lines 95–97) versus 8.1% of the planned prospective payments of $4.4 million through year 10 (Appendix 88.1, page 2, line 97).
    - The cumulative payout value of incentive payments (after the first two years of actual results) if all units are held to maturity of $2.5 million through year 10 is 10.5% of the increase in enterprise value from inception to the end of year 10 of $24.5 million (Appendix 88.2, page 2, lines 101–102) versus 17.5% of the increase in EV from inception to the end of year 10 of $25.5 million (Appendix 88.1, page 2, lines 100–102).

The following Appendices are available for viewing or download on the Web site for this book at: www.wiley.com/go/emott. Please see the About the Web Site page at the back of this book for login information.

APPENDIX 88.1 EVAquity Incentive Plan: Prospective Results, pages 1–4

APPENDIX 88.2 EVAquity Incentive Plan, Actual Results for Two Years, pages 1–4

TOPIC 89

Letter of Intent

The letter of intent (LOI) is finalized upon conclusion of deal negotiations. Topic 89 explores the necessity for an LOI.

INTRODUCTION TO THE LOI

- *Draft LOIs* often are presented as part of the offer process to capture the essential offering positions and to form the basis of ensuing negotiations. As negotiations proceed, the documents are altered (see Topic 68).
- *Final/letters of intent* (or term sheets) should result from the deal negotiation process and present the final list of agreed points and understandings between the parties (see Topic 77).
- The final LOI forms the basis of the essential terms of the purchase and sale agreement and clarifies final negotiating positions that can be difficult to change during purchase and sale agreement negotiations.
  - Do not attempt to negotiate every issue in the final LOI.
  - Negotiate only the key economic, risk allocation, and human resource issues.
  - Final LOIs are typically nonbinding on the parties except with respect to:
    - How each party's expenses are to be paid.
    - No-shop exclusivity provisions during the specified term of the LOI and penalties related thereto.
    - Conditions for withdrawal for each party.
    - Continuing confidentiality provisions and possibly breakup fees if a buyer that has been granted "no-shop" or "exclusivity" or walks away from the deal.
  - The buyer typically drafts the LOI, but sellers may undertake this effort, particularly in auction transactions.
- Ultimately, the essence of the valuation, structuring, and negotiation effort is captured in the legal agreements.
- Although a merger, joint venture, or other more complex transaction requires extensive documentation, all deal agreements will include these documents:
  - LOI
  - Purchase and sale agreement (see Topic 90)
- A typical LOI generally includes the items presented in Topic 77.

TOPIC 90

Purchase and Sale Agreement

Topic 90 introduces the purchase and sale agreement (PSA). This topic summarizes the contents, with Topic 91 exploring them in more detail.

INTRODUCTION TO THE PSA

- The PSA (as typically referred to in asset purchase agreements) captures all the commercial and financial implications of the deal in a legally binding and enforceable framework. In a purchase of stock transaction the governing agreement is commonly referred to as the stock purchase agreement (SPA).
- The buyer typically controls the drafting of the PSA, except in an auction, where the seller's investment bank presents a draft PSA for comment as part of the auction process.
- The PSA is the definitive legally binding and enforceable agreement that:
  - Captures all the elements of the deal as agreed in the letter of intent (LOI) and as negotiated otherwise in the preparation of the PSA.
  - Obligates each party to do certain things and behave in certain ways up to (and possibly after) the closing.
  - Allocates the economic impact of certain known or unknown risks associated with the seller's business.
  - Governs what happens up to and after the closing, depending on certain conditions that may arise before or after the closing.
- The PSA captures the result of the price negotiation as well as the rest of the consideration terms in a deal (e.g., the allocation of risk).
  - The risk allocations reflected in the terms of the PSA capture the same risk parameters discussed in Topic 26: time, impact, breadth of scope, and control over the events giving rise to the impact.
  - These risk allocations are captured in the carefully worded conditions associated with each issue contained in the document.
- The essential elements of the PSA are generally (contents vary from deal to deal) as listed next and are discussed in Topics 91 to 93.
  - Parties
  - Definitions
  - The purchase and sale
  - Purchase price and adjustments
  - Covenants prior to closing

- Representations and warranties of the seller
- Representations and warranties of the buyer
- Conditions to closing
- Closing and deliveries at the closing
- Postclosing covenants
- Survival of representations and warranties
- Other provisions:
  - Public announcements
  - Dispute resolution procedures
  - Process to amend the agreement
  - Waiver of compliance agreement and understanding
  - Expenses paid by incurring party
  - Giving notice procedures
  - Assignment not be permitted without other party's consent
  - Governing law
  - Termination procedure

TOPIC 91

Purchase and Sale Agreement: Explanation by Section

Topic 91 presents a summary of the contents generally presented (contents vary deal to deal) in the body of the purchase and sale agreement (PSA) that a party to an M&A deal can expect to encounter. Italic paragraphs present commentary relevant to buyer and seller preferences. The PSA governs the conduct of the parties with respect to completing the deal and for periods of time following the closing and provides the basis for dispute settlements under contract law.

PARTIES, DEFINITIONS, PURCHASE, AND SALE

- *The parties to the agreement section* recites the interests of the parties to enter the deal and includes:
  - *Precise legal name*, corporate form and domicile of seller and buyer
  - *Seller's business definition* and location
    - The business definition generally focuses on the products, markets, and customer group served, technologies utilized, and territory or field of use.
    - *This section usually receives considerable attention. The definitions often are utilized in defining the noncompete provisions in the postclosing conditions and /or in noncompete agreements.*
- *The recitals section* presents the statement of buyer's desire to purchase and seller's desire to sell and the parties agreement to the terms of the (PSA).
- *The definitions section* sets forth a glossary of key defined terms used in the PSA.
- *This section also receives considerable attention as the defined terms are referred to throughout the PSA and in other agreements to the deal.*
- *The purchase and sale section* sets forth specifically what is being sold and purchased, including, for example:
  - *Assets sold:* Inventory, machinery, automobiles, intellectual property (IP), books and records, trade secrets, rights under leases and contracts, receivables, property, tools, Web sites, software and computer equipment used

exclusively in the business, all as listed on schedules attached to and part of the agreement

- *Assets excluded:* Cash, insurance policies, certain IP, prepaid items, certain software and computer equipment not used exclusively in the business, e-mail servers, certain leases, all as listed on schedules attached to the agreement
- *Assumed obligations:* Assigned contracts and leases, obligations under certain contracts or bonds, all as listed on attached schedules to the PSA.
- *Excluded obligations:* All, other than assumed obligations.

PURCHASE PRICE AND ADJUSTMENTS, COVENANTS PRIOR TO CLOSING

- *The purchase price, adjustments, and allocations sections* set forth the financial considerations of the transaction, including, for example:
  - *The purchase price* shall be a cash payment of $X plus or minus the purchase price adjustments.
  - *At closing,* buyer shall wire immediately available funds $X to seller's bank.
  - *Within X days of closing seller shall provide a closing balance* sheet and statement of working capital pursuant to an audit conducted by seller's auditors within X days of the closing, which shall provide the basis of post closing purchase price adjustments.
  - *Within X days of closing, the purchase price adjustment* shall be wired to seller by buyer if in seller's favor, or to buyer by seller if in buyer's favor.
  - *Post-closing purchase price adjustments*, such as (see Topic 96):
    - A working capital adjustment shall be paid to seller by buyer if closing working capital exceeds $X (the target working capital amount).
    - A working capital adjustment shall be paid to buyer by seller if closing working capital is less than $X.
- *Covenants prior to closing* of seller and buyer set forth the obligations of the parties regarding conduct between the signing of the PSA through the closing, including, for example:
  - *Covenants of seller*: Except as otherwise consented to by buyer:
    - Seller shall conduct the business in the ordinary course as done prior to signing until the closing.
    - Seller agrees not to alter the condition of the business as stated in the representations and warranties, other than in the ordinary course except as consented to by the buyer.
      - *This covenant is referred to in the conditions to closing as being true as at the closing date, so is a significant obligation of the seller if breached.*
    - Seller shall consult with buyer prior to making inventory, capital expenditure, or other commitments in excess of $X.
    - Seller shall not alter obligations or benefits under benefit plans.

    - Seller shall not enter into employment agreements or increase employee compensation.
    - Seller shall use best efforts to cause transaction to close.
    - Seller shall not conduct sale negotiations with anyone other than buyer.
    - Seller shall provide information to enable buyer to verify performance of seller obligations.
    - Seller shall obtain required consents to enable buyer to verify that acquired assets, contracts, and other are transferrable.
    - Seller shall provide information to enable buyer to verify performance of seller obligations.
- *Covenants of buyer*: Except as otherwise consented to by seller:
    - Buyer shall use best (or all reasonable) efforts to cause the transaction to close.

REPRESENTATIONS AND WARRANTIES OF THE SELLER, INTRODUCTION

- This section sets forth statements about the financial and legal status of the business, the condition of the property sold, and certain general information about the business and the ability of the seller to close as at the date of signing of the PSA.
- Representations and warranties provide Buyers with the basis to exit a deal under the provisions of the closing conditions that refer to the representations and warranties, if a seller representation or warranty is untrue as at the closing date.
- Additionally, representations and warranties provide the basis for seller indemnification of buyers for seller breaches of representations and warranties after the closing during the survival period.
- Insurance (representation and warranty insurance [RWI]) is generally available to buyers regarding breaches of representations and warranties by seller to protect against damage collection default by sellers.
- RWI insurance is generally available to sellers to minimize future liability obligations regarding breaches of certain representations and warranties by seller or for unintentional nondisclosure.
- RWI insurance is priced at approximately 4% to 8% of the coverage purchased, depending on the scope of the covered representations and warranties, type of business, quality of the due diligence, policy deductible, and term period.
- Sellers have a strong desire to limit the number and scope of the representations and warranties which can be done by:
    - Not making representations and warranties except to material issues.
    - Making the representation and warranties *to the best of sellers' knowledge* (presumes due inquiry by the sellers) or to the sellers' *actual knowledge* (precludes due inquiry).

- Qualifying the representation and warranties with a materiality provision.
- Making affirmative representation with respect to certain matters with the exception of certain listed matters on a disclosure schedule.
  - *If buyer closes over such excepted disclosures the disclosed matters may not be used as a basis for a post-closing claim.*
- Sellers must be wary of making any representation relating to the future performance of the business.
- Seller representation and warranties relating to the condition of inventory and fixed assets, financial statements, undisclosed liabilities, intellectual property, notice of customer business discontinuance, warranty and repair obligations, and environmental condition of the business often receive the most attention in negotiations.

REPRESENTATIONS AND WARRANTIES OF THE SELLER

- *Representation and warranties of seller include, for example*:
  - *Seller is in good standing* and duly organized and qualified in its legal jurisdiction to conduct business.
  - *Seller has requisite power* to do the deal.
  - By doing the deal, seller will not be in violation of its corporate governing documents and will not cause any liens or defaults, except as scheduled.
  - *Seller has no finders' or brokers fees'* except as scheduled.
  - *Seller financial statements* are prepared per generally accepted accounting principles (GAAP), are complete, and fairly present in all material respects the financial position of the business.
    - *Buyers look for as many assurances (hooks) as possible to provide for recourse to the seller if the deal does not work out.*
    - *Buyers look for assurances as to the quality of the financial statements as a basis of their reliance that all reserves are appropriate and that the financial statements are accurate, true, and complete and have been prepared in accordance with GAAP consistently applied.*
    - *Sellers, particularly sellers of business divisions, seek to limit the hooks available to buyers by narrowing the financial statement representation away from quality assurances to assurances that the financial statements have been "consistently prepared on an internal basis" or have been "maintained in conformity with reasonable business practice."*
  - *Tangible assets* are in good working order, ordinary wear and tear excepted, except as scheduled.
    - *Buyers seek "quality of condition statements, free from defects and fit-for-purpose" assurances.*
    - *Sellers prefer "as-is" assurances.*
  - *Inventories* are of a type and quality salable in the ordinary course and are valued at lower of cost or market on a first-in, first-out (FIFO) basis net of appropriate reserves for obsolescence, except as scheduled.

- *Buyers seek "quality and fit-for-purpose" assurances.*
- *Sellers prefer "as-is" assurances.*
- *There has not been any material adverse change* in the business or financial condition of the business as a whole since a certain date, except as scheduled.
- *Seller has good title* to all assets.
- *Seller is not aware of, has not been informed of pending claims and has no current claims* against the ownership or use of IP.
- *Seller is not in default* under any contract assigned to buyer.
- *Seller has not received any written notice* from its largest customers of intention to discontinue or substantially reduce business except as scheduled.
  - *Buyers sometimes seek assurances related to the future of the business and the business forecast provided by the seller. Sellers generally refuse to make any representation with respect to the future of the business and the business forecast provided to the buyer.*
  - *Buyers seek statements that seller has no knowledge of buyers' dissatisfaction that may lead to a reduction in sales.*
  - *Sellers seek to limit the hooks available to buyers by narrowing the customer representation away from any knowledge to a factual written notice basis statement.*
  - *Sellers must be wary of making any representation that can be interpreted to relate to the future performance of the business.*
  - *Sellers often solicit their key employees in writing, requesting a written reply as a basis for making the customer representation provided.*
- *There is no union strike pending* or under way or charges pending before Equal Employment Opportunity Commission (EEOC).
- *There are no actions before any court* that involve the assets of seller or that would prevent the transaction except as scheduled.
- *No approval or notice is required* to do the deal except as scheduled.
- *Seller has complied and is in compliance* with all laws in all material respects except as scheduled.
- *Seller has all material approvals* and permits for conduct of the business, and all are in full force and effect.
- *There is no action or suit* or governmental investigation to the knowledge of seller pending or threatened with respect to the business that may affect the deal except as scheduled.
- *Seller has timely paid all taxes* due.
- *Neither seller nor its officers*, directors, employees, or agents has received or made any unlawful payments, gifts, or expenditures.
- *Intellectual property (IP)* of seller does not infringe the IP of others. No outstanding claims against the company for infringing the IP of others exist preclosing nor do infringements of seller's IP exist preclosing except as scheduled.
  - *Depending on the business and the seriousness of the postclosing issue that may arise for the seller, sellers often attempt to insert a knowledge or actual knowledge proviso into IP representations (and other potentially troublesome representation areas, such as environmental).*

  - *The "knowledge proviso" removes the seller from the postclosing liability associated with a preclosing breach arising postclosing unless the seller is proven to have known about the potential breach but does presume a certain level of due diligence on the seller's part.*
  - *An "actual knowledge" does not presume such due diligence requirement on the part of seller.*
  - *Buyers resist such a proviso as they are acquiring the ability to practice the acquired IP and do not want to suffer the cost of defending or settling a claim or proving the seller had knowledge.*
  - *Sellers however, do not want to have to pay for such claims, many of which can prove to be frivolous and often expensive.*
  - *Claims for infringement that occurs and are made postclosing fall to the buyer and are not captured in the scope of seller's IP representations as of the closing.*
  - *The conflicting postclosing concerns arising over IP (and other areas) often are reflected in the risk-sharing exercise of a specific indemnity cap, basket, and term for IP (and other) representations.*
- *Seller is in compliance with all environmental laws* and regulations and seller's operating sites are free of any environmental contamination, or order to remediate, or penalty from any authority. Seller has all environmental permits required to operate its sites except as scheduled.
  - *Depending on the business, this representation is probably the most troublesome in many transactions today. It can be the cause of deal breakdown or lead to difficult, time-consuming establishment of baseline conditions, escrows, and indemnity provisions.*
- *There are no undisclosed liabilities* for which seller is liable.
  - *Sellers often prefer to provide that there are no undisclosed liabilities that require disclosure on the financial statement per GAAP.*

REPRESENTATIONS AND WARRANTIES OF THE BUYER

- Representation and warranties of buyers generally are limited to provide certain assurances to sellers and include, for example:
  - *Buyer is in good standing* and duly organized and qualified in its legal jurisdiction to conduct business.
  - *Buyer has requisite power* to do the deal.
  - *By doing the deal, buyer is not in violation* of its corporate governing documents and will not cause any liens or defaults, except as scheduled.
  - *Buyer has no finders' or brokers' fees except* as scheduled.
    - *Sellers often require a buyer representation that financing has or will be secured by buyer before or at the closing to minimize seller closing risk.*
    - *By requiring a financing representation from the buyer, sellers bear a slight risk regarding the limitations they may seek in their representations and warranties in the PSA that are disclosed to the buyer's lender. As a result, the seller representations and warranties may not meet lender approval.*

CONDITIONS TO CLOSING, CLOSING AND DELIVERIES AT THE CLOSING

- The conditions to closing section sets forth conditions of each party to be met at the closing that, if not satisfied (or waived), shall give the other side the right to terminate the agreement without liability. Such conditions include those listed.
- *Conditions to Sellers' Obligation to Close*
  - Buyer shall have performed all acts and covenants and deliveries required.
  - All buyer representations and warranties are true as at the closing date.
  - All approvals and consents and closing documents required are delivered to seller.
- *Conditions to Buyers' Obligation to Close*
  - Seller shall have performed all acts and covenants and deliveries required.
  - All seller representations and warranties are true as at the closing date.
  - All seller approvals and consents required are delivered to buyer.
  - All seller actions have been taken to convey intellectual property.
  - No adverse change exists in the business of seller since a reference date.
  - No liens on seller assets exist.
    - *The conditions to closing hinge directly on the full statement of covenants, representations and warranties, and delivery of closing documents. The bring-down condition "true as at the closing date" gives the buyer (and seller) the right to terminate the deal if any covenant or representation and warranty is not true at the closing, even if the PSA is signed prior to the closing.*
    - *On occasion, buyers seek an exception to their obligation to close the deal if they cannot obtain financing. This is a high-risk condition for the seller that should be rejected or countered with the need for the buyer to provide a financing commitment prior to the signing of the PSA or by a date shortly after the signing, or to pay a breakup fee if the financing is not obtained by the closing date and the deal craters as a result.*
    - *Closing recitals* include when and where the closing shall take place and what must be delivered at the closing by the seller and the buyer, for example:
- *Deliveries by the seller* will include:
  - *Consents* under leases and assigned contracts, bill of sale, titles to automobiles
  - *Copies of all consents, permits,* waivers, approvals required of the seller
  - *Documents of assignment of intellectual property*
  - *Copies of board of directors minutes* authorizing the execution of seller's obligations to perform
  - *Legal opinion* as to seller's legal status, power to perform, and so on
  - *Sellers escrow agreements*
  - *Seller consulting agreements*
  - *Seller noncompetition agreements*
  - *Payoff letters of indebtedness*
  - *Other agreements* related to the transaction

- *Deliveries by the buyer* will include:
  - *The consideration*
  - *Agreement to pay* all assumed obligations
  - *Agreement to assume* IP rights
  - *Copies of board of directors' authorization* for the execution of buyers obligations to perform
  - *Certificate of legal existence* of the buyer
  - *Legal opinion* as to buyer's legal status, power to perform, and so forth
  - *Other agreements* related to the transaction

POSTCLOSING COVENANTS, INDEMNIFICATION, SURVIVAL OF REPRESENTATIONS, AND WARRANTIES

- The *postclosing covenants* section sets forth the parties' undertakings to take further actions to perfect the transaction contemplated and make available information contemplated by the agreement to perfect the transaction, including, for example:
  - *Buyer agrees to remit collections of others payments.*
  - *Parties agree to give reasonable access to records* related to the sold business.
  - *Buyer shall offer employment* and provide buyer benefits to employees of seller as listed on schedule.
  - *Seller guarantees collection of accounts receivable* transferred to buyer for a guaranty period and agrees to take uncollected receivables back after such period.
  - *Seller agrees not to compete* with buyer for x years.
- *Indemnification by seller and survival of representations and warranties* include for example:
  - *Survival* of representations and warranties (see Topic 93).
  - *Seller agrees to indemnify* and hold harmless buyer from losses, costs, obligations, liabilities, judgments, fines, penalties asserted or imposed against buyer arising out of breach of seller's representations and warranties and covenants for the period of time stated (see Topic 93).
    - *Buyers often define losses on claims from seller breaches to include "multiples of earnings and diminution of value" to allow effective partial repricing of the deal post-closing.*
    - *Sellers prefer to define losses to "the actual incremental documented cost of the realized losses incurred" and resist the notion of future diminution of value lost in such a definition. A middle ground is the null case where "claims shall be for losses," without the inclusion or exclusion of future value concepts in the definition. In such cases, a judge or jury will decide the loss amount if a claim is disputed.*
  - RWI is available to sellers for claims above the negotiated buyer indemnity limits.
  - *Seller's basket:* Seller shall not have to indemnify buyer until the aggregate amount of all indemnity claims against buyer exceeds $X amount, the seller's basket (see Topic 93).

- *Seller's basket is typically 3/4% (plus or minus) of the purchase price for deductible baskets for strategic buyers of smaller companies.*
- *Baskets often are deductibles: The basket amount is not repaid if buyer claims exceed the basket limit. Tipping baskets require the seller to make the buyer whole from dollar 1 of buyer claims if the amount of claims against the seller's basket amount is exceeded (see Topic 93).*

- *Indemnification by buyer and survival of representations and warranties* include, for example:
  - *Survival* of representations and warranties (see Topic 93).
  - *Buyer agrees to indemnify* and hold harmless seller from losses, costs, obligations, liabilities, judgments, fines, penalties asserted or imposed against seller arising out of breach of buyer's representations and warranties and covenants for the period of time stated (see Topic 93).
  - *Buyer's basket:* Buyer shall not have to indemnify seller until the aggregate amount of all third-party claims against seller exceeds $X amount, the buyer's basket (see Topic 93).
    - *Buyer's basket is typically 3/4% (plus or minus) of the purchase price.*

INDEMNIFICATION PROCEDURE

- This procedure states the process of notice, who shall control defense, access to information, and rights of subrogation of the indemnified party.
- *Successors:* The merger, liquidation, or winding up of an indemnifying party shall not affect the obligations of such party.
- *Nonconsequential damages*: No party shall be liable for consequential or other damages outside of those remedies specified in the agreement that may arise for any reason.

OTHER PROVISIONS

- *Other provisions* include:
  - Public announcements
  - Dispute resolution procedures
  - Process to amend the agreement
  - Waiver of compliance agreement and understanding
  - Expenses incurred by each party shall be paid by such party
  - Giving notice procedures
  - Assignment shall not be permitted without other party's consent
  - Governing law
  - Termination procedures

TOPIC 92

Purchase Price Adjustments for Working Capital

Topic 92 explores the issues relative to the closing adjustment to the purchase price for working capital to be delivered at the closing by the seller. This topic also explores methods for establishing the appropriate level of working capital to be delivered by the seller at the closing. The purchase price agreement, particularly in asset deals but also in stock purchase deals, ordinarily sets forth an expected target dollar value of working capital (sometimes but not usually net operating capital) to be acquired as of the closing date.

TARGET AND ACTUAL WORKING CAPITAL DETERMINATION

- Buyers and sellers should carefully analyze the target's operating working capital employed (as defined in the letter of intent [LOI] or term sheet and generally excluding cash in such definition) over rolling annual periods to determine the historical ratio of the rolling average working capital to the annualized run rate of sales to assess how much working capital was employed to support the activity level of the business at any point in time.
  - The historical ratio is then multiplied by the annualized run rate of sales expected as of the closing date to determine the *target working capital* level to be delivered by the seller at the closing.
  - The significance of this target value is that any ongoing business requires a normal underlying level of working capital to support the activity level of operations at any point in time.
- The goal for a seller is to determine a reasonable *target* dollar amount of working capital employed at the closing that the buyer will accept and include such an amount in the term sheet or letter of intent (LOI) and purchase and sale agreement (PSA).
- The *actual* closing working capital amount will not be known until the closing audit of the seller's balance sheet is completed, sometime after the closing (typically 60 to 90 days postclosing).

THE CLOSING WORKING CAPITAL ADJUSTMENT—A ZERO-SUM EVENT

- To the extent the actual working capital conveyed at closing is greater than the target amount, the buyer reimburses the seller for the difference. The purchase price is therefore effectively increased in the form of this post-closing cash payment by the buyer to the seller, but more working capital than is "normal" is obtained.
- To the extent the actual working capital employed is less than the target amount, the seller reimburses the buyer for the difference. The purchase price is effectively reduced in the form of this post-closing cash payment by the seller to the buyer, but less working capital is conveyed.
- This reimbursement event is actually done in two steps. There is an adjustment at closing based on the target's *estimated* actual working capital at the closing versus the *target* working capital as described above, the "estimated closing adjustment."
- After the actual audited balance sheet is delivered and the actual audited working capital is known, the actual closing working capital adjustment is determined as described above, the "actual closing adjustment" and the difference between the "estimated closing adjustment" amount and the "actual closing adjustment" amount is made in the favor of the buyer or seller.
  - Sometimes no adjustment is made unless the actual working capital employed exceeds or is less than the target amount by a fixed dollar or percentage amount—a so-called working capital collar.
  - Sometimes one-sided working capital collars, ceilings, or floors are employed.
- In an economic and valuation sense, an adjustment required to equalize an actual working capital amount at closing to a realistic and appropriate working capital target should be a zero-sum event for both parties regarding adjustments around the target level.
  - *If there is less working capital at closing* than the target amount, the seller's closing reimbursement payment to the buyer merely compensates the buyer for the cash investment needed to fund the working capital addition required shortly after the closing to bring the working capital up to the target level required to support the business.
    - Although the seller is out of pocket at the closing by a cash amount equal to the amount of working capital shortfall and the selling price is effectively reduced, the seller in fact accumulated this same excess amount of cash prior to the closing via the working capital liquidation to cash that took place and resulted in the lower working capital, hence a zero sum event.
    - The seller either receives credit equal to the working capital shortfall for the excess cash remaining in the target company at the closing (if the buyer receives the seller's cash account—which account includes the excess cash accumulated) or the seller will have distributed the excess cash to himself prior to the closing thus offsetting the reduced purchase consideration paid—hence, a zero-sum event.

- *If there is more working capital at closing* than the target amount, the buyer's postclosing payment to the seller is simply a cash trade.
  - The buyer receives more working capital than is needed to support the business, an amount that, when liquidated as working capital returns to the target level, will be available to the buyer as cash, and thus provides the cash needed for paying back the buyer for the payment made to the seller at the closing.
  - The seller who receives cash at the closing in the form of the working capital adjustment, is simply being reimbursed for the cash invested buy the seller prior to closing that increased the working capital (e.g., more inventory for example) beyond the target level.
- In either case, payments to or from the buyer are booked by the buyer as adjustments to the purchase price for the business and by the seller as adjustments to the net gain (or loss) on the sale via adjustments to the purchase price.

SOMETIMES THE WORKING CAPITAL ADJUSTMENT IS NOT A ZERO-SUM EVENT

- The target working level amount, however, does matter in an economic sense for both parties.
  - If the target working capital was set at a level too low to sustain the business, the buyer will have to inject more capital into the business (or curtail free cash flow disbursements), thus increasing the actual net investment (purchase price) in the business.
  - If the target working capital was more than was required to sustain the business, the buyer will be able to extract this excess capital from the business (in the form of free cash flow disbursements) as working capital declines to the appropriate target level required to support the business, thus decreasing the net investment in the business.
  - The seller will have conveyed more capital to the buyer than was necessary, thereby reducing his or her economic gain.
- The rolling historical average determination method just described incentivizes business operation behavior consistent with preclosing covenants. If prepared carefully, this method provides a symmetrical zero-sum issue at closing for both buyer and seller.
- The rolling historical average determination method is preferable to pegging the target level based on the actual working capital employed just prior to the closing.
  - Pegging the working capital at the closing can lead to seller behavior that favors the seller at closing, potentially to the buyer's detriment (sellers may be tempted to minimize investments in working capital that they would otherwise make in the normal course of operations to accumulate cash).

WORKING CAPITAL COLLARS

- For all the reasons stated here, working capital collars are often employed in the mechanics of the closing working capital adjustment.
  - Closing adjustments to the purchase price are not made if the differences in actual versus target working capital fall within the collar.
  - The rationale for this is that the actual working capital level required to support the business (as a ratio to sales or production) probably falls within a normal distribution range rather than a point amount.

TOPIC 93

Indemnification and Survival Provisions

Topic 93 explores the provisions associated with sellers' indemnifications as stated in the purchase and sale agreement (PSA) with regard to sellers' representations, warranties, and covenants. This topic also provides guidance of what to expect in the establishment of indemnification provisions.

INTRODUCTION

- Sellers represent many things to be true during the due diligence, selling, and negotiation process to compel buyer interest.
- Buyers look to sellers to present those representations and others in the PSAs and look for protection by sellers in the form of indemnity provisions, should the buyer be impaired because the representations and warranties relied on prove to be untrue or sellers fail to abide by the covenants and undertakings in the PSA.
- The indemnity provisions provide for specific damages, depending on the seller breach. These damages generally are preferable to settlements under legal suits brought in court.
- The negotiations concerning the terms of indemnification provisions often seem complex and confusing to the business participants involved in negotiating the terms.

INDEMNITY PROVISIONS, CAPS, BASKETS, DURATIONS

- Indemnity provisions are concerned with:
  - *Indemnified issues.* These issues may include product liability, environmental, taxes, receivables, returns and allowances, nonassumed obligations, intellectual property (IP), and so forth.
  - *Caps.* Caps determine the maximum (aggregate or nonaggregate) amount of damages payable for all or a group of indemnified issues for a specific breach of representations, warranties, or covenants during the period of indemnification.

  - Total seller caps (for all issues) generally are set between 10% and 15% of selling price.
  - Certain caps for fundamental representations, such as IP, employees/Employee Retirement Income Security Act (ERISA), and environmental issues can be higher, 20%+, and usually are different in amount for each fundamental representation, depending on the problems and uncertainties surrounding an issue for which a representation is provided.
  - Caps on other indemnified representations issues, such as organization, title, and tax matters, usually are capped at the purchase price.
- *Baskets.* Baskets set the minimum amount of loss a party must realize before recovery under the indemnity provisions. Seller baskets typically average plus or minus 3/4% of the purchase price.
  - Such amount can be a deductible, a so-called nontipping basket, in which case only amounts in excess of the amount of the basket can be recovered under the indemnity provisions.
  - Such amount can be nondeductible, a so-called tipping basket, in which case after claims against the basket amount are reached, amounts in excess of the amount of the basket plus the basket amount can be recovered under the indemnity provisions.
  - Other general representations and certain fundamental representations, such as IP, employees/ERISA, and environmental usually are subject to the basket.
  - Others, such as organization, title, and tax matters, usually are not subject to the basket.
- *Duration of survivability of an indemnified issue.* This duration sets the length of time an issue remains indemnified under the indemnity provisions.
  - Average survival for nonfundamental representations usually are plus or minus 18 months.
  - Survival for certain fundamental representations, such as IP, employees/ERISA, and environmental, are often plus or minus 36 months.
  - Survival for other representations, such as organization, title, and tax matters, often are unlimited in survival.
- Often broad business judgment and legal advice is required to sort through and break deadlocks over arranging and documenting these complex issues.
- The judgments needed to make risk trade-offs require a clear understanding of the issues, problems, and terms involved.

USE A MATRIX TO SORT OUT INDEMNITY PROVISIONS

- The use of a matrix to isolate and sort out the terms and issues associated with indemnification provisions enables the deal maker to make choices and trade-offs.
  - Illustration 93.1 presents typically encountered issues for which a buyer seeks indemnification from the seller, with not untypical terms.

  - Illustration 93.2 presents a summary of general market-level guidelines for representations and the generally expected survival periods, cap size, and basket size and applicability.
- A useful way to move indemnification negotiations forward is to prepare the format of the matrix presented in Illustration 93.1 jointly, then have each side complete the detail terms as they see them for each issue.
  - Trade the results and separately evaluate the other side's positions and your concerns.
  - Next, meet and discuss the evaluations, seeking common understanding.
  - Consider trading cap or floor amounts for time and duration (see Topic 73).

ILLUSTRATION 93.1 INDEMNITY PROVISIONS MATRIX FOR TYPICALLY ENCOUNTERED DEAL ISSUES

Representations or Issue	Duration of Survival	$ Amount of Cap	Basket Applicable	Scope Limitations
Environmental representations	Unlimited	Aggregate = to 20% of PP[a]	Yes: $500 aggregate 3/4% of PP	
All other representations other than the following fundamental representations	18 months	Aggregate = to 15% of PP	Yes: $500 aggregate 3/4% of PP	
Correction of existing environmental damage representation	10 years	Aggregate = to 20% of PP[a]	No	
Product liability, ERISA, IP	3 years	Aggregate = 15% of PP	Yes: $500 aggregate 3/4% of PP	
Income taxes, title, organization	Unlimited	Aggregate = PP	No	
Accounts receivable	1 year	Aggregate = receivable amount	No	Right to put back to seller
Returns and allowances	2 years	Aggregate = 15% of PP	Yes: $500 aggregate 3/4% of PP	
Nonassumed obligations	Forever	Aggregate = PP	No	

[a]PP: Purchase price.

ILLUSTRATION 93.2 GUIDELINE OF GENERALLY EXPECTED INDEMNITY PROVISIONS: CAPS, DURATIONS, BASKETS

Summary of Representations and the Generally Expected Caps Size, Survival Periods, Basket Size and General Applicability

Representations or Issue	Duration of Survival	$Amount of Cap	Basket Applicability
All other representations	18 months+/−	15% of PP[a] average+/−	yes 3/4% of PP+/−
Fundamental representations IP, employee/ERISA General environmental	24–36 months+/−	15% of PP average+/−	yes 3/4% of PP+/−
Fundamental representations title, taxes, organization	statute of limitations or unlimited	PP	NA[b]
Escrows	18 months+/−	8% of PP average+/−	NA[b]

[1]See Houlihan and Lokey Mergers and Acquisitions Group, Purchase Agreement Study, May 2009 at http://www.hlhz.com/pressdetail.aspx?id=1695.
[a]PP: Purchase price.
[b]NA: Not applicable.

CONTRACTUAL CONDITIONS APPORTION FINAL RISK POSITIONS—WORK THEM HARD DURING NEGOTIATIONS

- As discussed in Topic 73 and restated here for emphasis, negotiation about essentially any issue is about the distribution of the consequences of owning or having rights to the benefits of owning assets or the consequences of undertaking or potentially assuming liabilities. The rules governing the distribution of such consequences for each party are captured in carefully worded *conditions*.
  - *Conditions* are defined along three interrelated negotiating dimensions surrounding almost any business contract issue or tight spot: *value*, *time*, and *scope*. All must be exercised simultaneously and often woven together in reaching solutions and closing negotiating gaps, particularly in the area of indemnification issues.
  - The *values* (ultimately cash) associated with most issues (e.g., the amount of an indemnification or escrow) can be increased, decreased, stepped, floored, or capped.

- The *time* associated with most issues (e.g., the survival period of an indemnification, the trigger date for the release of an escrow) can be lengthened, shortened, gapped, start delayed, capped, or date certain defined.
- The *scope* of the breadth and depth of events surrounding, included in, or excluded from an issue (e.g., an indemnified environmental liability) can be narrowed or widened by defining what is excluded from the definition or by defining only what is included in the definition. Another clarifying method is to add the phrase "with the exception of items listed" in the definition.
- As you work through the side list of issues noted above, you can make small but creative meaningful concessions using the multifaceted dimensions of conditions: shorten a time frame but broaden the scope; narrow the scope but increase a cap; cap the value but lengthen the time, and so forth.

TOPIC 94
Escrows

Topic 94 defines and explores the use, applicability, and terms of escrows in the purchase and sale agreement.

INTRODUCTION

- Escrows are amounts of the purchase price that are retained at the closing. The scheduled release and payment of escrows are subject to postclosing events, including purchase price adjustments (Topic 92), claims under indemnity provisions (Topic 93), satisfactory completion of consulting agreement terms, and possibly others, which, by the terms of the escrow agreement, may be paid from the escrowed amount.
- Escrows are usually demanded by the buyer as a form of protection during the term should a event take place requiring reimbursement by the seller.
- The parties usually enter into an escrow agreement that specifies the terms of release of the escrow funds and the types of claims that may be paid from the escrowed amounts.
- An escrow agent, typically a bank, usually is retained to administer the escrowed funds.
- Escrows generally are approximately 5% to 8% of the purchase price (at market) but can run to 10% or slightly more. Escrow duration terms generally parallel the indemnity provisions and are approximately 15 to 18 months, covering at least one buyer's audit cycle.
- Escrows can be set to release over time (evenly at each quarter, evenly at each year-end, or at completion of the duration period).
- Claims against an escrow that releases over time will freeze further releases from it, generally in an amount equal to the total claim amount plus future unreleased amounts until the claim is fully satisfied. If the claim satisfaction period extends beyond the escrow period, unreleased amounts generally are frozen until claim satisfaction.
- If claim satisfaction occurs prior to the end of the term, previously frozen escrow amounts net of the actual claim usually are available for release on the original terms of the escrow, thus putting the escrow back on the agreed original release schedule.

- Generally, amounts placed in escrow do not represent taxable proceeds for the seller until the escrow funds are released and paid to the seller. The tax basis of the assets or stock sold in a taxable transaction are prorated to cash and stock received by the seller at the closing and to amounts placed in escrow at the closing.
- Claims paid from escrow to the buyer reduce the total deal consideration for the seller. In such case, the tax basis allocated to the escrow is reallocated to the other consideration paid to the seller.

TOPIC 95

Joint Venture Transaction: Valuation and Structuring Overview

Topic 95 discusses the need for joint reliance between the partners to a joint venture, the reasons to form a joint venture, and how to structure and value the partner share interests in a joint venture. The elements to the key agreements to a joint venture are also presented.

The reader is encouraged to take the time to read the text in conjunction with the referenced Appendices to gain the appropriate level of understanding of the subject matter discussed in the narrative. Appendices are either presented at the end of this and each remaining Topic or are available for review and download on this book's companion Web site (see the About the Wed Site page for login information).

WHY DO A JOINT VENTURE

- Joint ventures (JVs) usually are formed when two separate entities find the JV structure to be the most efficient and generally risk-averse way (less investment, highly market focused, and separate from the parent investor entity issues) to capture the economic benefits associated with an investment in a target market (as opposed to either entity going it alone).
- The key word is *joint*:
  - Each partner must have a generally equal (in terms of recognition and urgency) need for and joint reliance on what the partner shareholder brings to the venture.
  - Each partner must recognize that on its own, it has a close-to-unsolvable strategic void (generally not a financial void) in the operating capabilities required to capture an opportunity that the other partner possesses and is willing to bring to a JV.
  - Each partner must share the same view of the significance of the economic opportunity and the urgency associated with going after it in the same way (customer needs, product and services, new technology applications, market size, pricing, customer capture programs, etc.).

- Each partner must share the same view of what it will take to capture the opportunity in terms of business capabilities required (technology, staffing, location, production, marketing and distribution, etc.), investment levels required, and partner contributions.
- Without such joint reliance on complementary operating capabilities, a JV is probably not a good structural approach for ether party.
- The partners to a potential JV should work through the integration templates presented in Topic 52 to ensure there is the appropriate level of joint reliance between the partners and operators of the JV with a focus on "Do we share the same view?" and "Who will bring what to fill out the capabilities required?"
- The results of having worked through the integration templates together will form the backbone of the JV business plan.

WHO CONTROLS THE JOINT VENTURE

- A key issue requiring early resolution in the potential formation of a JV is which (or neither) party shall have the controlling equity interest in the JV entity.
  - Equity control (the controlling partner) can be a function of strategic leverage (due to location, capabilities on the ground, relative need, speed, cash availability, technology, expediency).
  - Equity control can simply rest on who puts up the most cash or makes the greatest contribution to the formation of the joint venture.
  - It needs to be agreed between the parties early in discussions.
  - 50/50 joint ventures are certainly workable, particularly when there is real joint reliance on one another's capabilities that will be brought to the JV. Such structure will require 100% approval of key decisions and preclude the need for supermajority control provisions to protect the interests of minority partners.
- Legal agreements associated with a JV can be more extensive than an acquisition and generally include these documents and their key issue provisions:

LETTER OF INTENT AND PARTNERSHIP AGREEMENT

- *A letter of intent* or memorandum of understanding (see Topic 89) will capture the key business points that eventually must be documented in the fundamental agreements shown.
- *Partnership agreement includes*
  - Location and jurisdiction
  - Corporate form: C corporation, partnership, limited liability corporation (LLC)
  - Name
  - Equity ownership; rights to increase participation
  - Initial equity capitalization: Cash, property, services, method (tax issues)

- Initial loan capitalization: Type, amount, target debt to capital ceiling
- Subsequent capitalization: Rights or obligations to increase, failure to contribute consequences (dilution, buy-out, dissolution, new party)
- Dividend policy: Target payout percentage, determination, timing
- Business scope: Mission, product field, geographic field, organization design, term of duration of the JV
- Shareholder governance: Voting, issues calling for vote, approval by simple majority, supermajority approval percentage, shareholder meeting location and frequency, quorum, notice, written consent action
- Supermajority approval issues (generally in place to protect the minority partner):
  - Annual business plan, management bonus, capital expenditure over certain amount, incurring debt, extending credit, making guarantees, sale of assets, settlement of litigation
  - Transactions with shareholders, changing business mission and objectives of venture, issuing added shares, payment of dividends other than per approved policy
  - Appointment or removal of general manager, appointment or removal of auditors, changing accounting standards
  - Sale, liquidation or merger of the partner's venture shares or the business, liquidation of the JV
  - Acquisition of technology, contract research for a shareholder, transfer of technology, acquisition of a business or product line
  - Amendment to the charter, bylaws, and memorandum of association
- Board of directors and governance:
  - Number, term, and appointment of directors from each shareholder
  - Appointment of chairman and duties, how removed, filling vacancies, board action approval vote percentage requirements
  - Supermajority issue approval percentage, directors' meeting location and frequency
  - Meeting quorum, notice, written consent action allowed, board deadlock resolution procedure
- Officers: duties, appointment power, removal, filling vacancy, term
- Transfer of equity:
  - Permitted methods: minimum holding period
  - Advance notice to other party—approval not required, approval by other party required for any action
  - First refusal right to other party at offer price or formula price, tag-along right for other party, drag-along right for seller
  - Third-party valuation, put right to other party at formula value after specified period or upon change of control of either party, call right if breach by other party, prohibition "black hat" list of third parties as possible buyers
- Termination or dissolution trigger events:
  - Deadlock, breach of agreement, term completed, failure of party to meet obligations, failure to meet targets

    - Change of control of either party, valuation of business/assets for sale by formula value or other
    - Distribution advantage to nonbreaching party, survival of claims following termination
  - Dispute resolution:
    - If deadlock or dispute: First by chief executive officer negotiation with parties within set period of time
    - Mediation by third party (one or more) within set period of time
    - Mediator selection at time or at formation within set period of time
    - Arbitration (binding or nonbinding) within set period of time
    - Judicial resolution if prior fails, right to trial jury or waived, notice procedure, representation by counsel
  - Documents: Who drafts, governing law, timelines
  - General management issues:
    - Key management positions and how they will be filled, roles, and duties
    - Employment agreements, employee secondment agreements
    - Human resource issues: Pension benefit transfer (service, assets, liabilities), medical and other benefits alignment
    - Environmental liability, valuation, and responsibility apportionment
    - Intellectual property transfer or availability from each partner
    - Supply or distribution agreements between venture and shareholders

JV FORMATION AGREEMENT

- *Joint venture formation agreement* (see Topic 91, as the components of the JV formation agreement are similar those in a purchase and sale agreement):
  - Parties
  - Definitions
  - Purchase and sale or contribution
  - Covenants prior to closing of each party
  - Representations and warranties of the seller
  - Representations and warranties of the buyer
  - Conditions to closing
  - Closing
  - Post-closing covenants
  - Survival of representations and warranties
  - Other provisions such as:
    - Public announcements
    - Dispute resolution procedures
    - Process to amend the agreement
    - Waiver of compliance agreement and understanding
    - Expenses paid by incurring party
    - Giving notice procedures
    - Assignment not be permitted without other party's consent
    - Governing law
    - Termination procedure

TECHNOLOGY LICENSE AGREEMENTS

- *Technology license agreements include*
  - What technology or products are needed from each party or third parties
  - Product field, geographic field
  - Exclusive or nonexclusive for product field, geographic field
  - Royalty-free or royalty basis: method of determination
  - Restrictions on use and application
  - Term of license
  - Ability to assign
  - Patents transferred, list
  - How each technology is conveyed: drawings, lab books, consulting time, payments required
  - Improvements in technology by venture become owned by contributor of base technology or both parties
  - Termination rights: who gets technology practice rights
  - Dispute resolution
  - Confidentiality

SUPPLY AGREEMENTS

- *Supply agreements include*
  - What will be supplied to the venture from each party exclusively or nonexclusively
  - Quantity, price, currency, payment terms
  - Shipment, delivery method
  - Annual price adjustment basis
  - Specifications, inspection, quality failure demonstration, returns liability and cure, alternate supplier
  - Who pays freight terms, title passage border, insurance, import duties, tariffs, taxes
  - Trademark usage
  - Requirements forecast annually, lead time planning and monthly update
  - Term
  - Termination rights
  - Dispute resolution
  - Confidentiality

DISTRIBUTION AGREEMENTS

- *Distribution agreements include*
  - Distribution services provided: Sales, marketing, advertising, pickup, distribution and delivery, customer invoicing and collection, product support, field service, tech support

- What products will be distributed by which party on behalf of the venture
- Venture product selling price to distributor, currency, payment terms
- Product field, geographic field/territory of distributor
- Exclusive or nonexclusive for product field, geographic field
- Annual price adjustment basis
- Specifications, inspection, quality failure demonstration, returns liability and cure, alternate supplier
- Who pays freight terms, title passage border, insurance, import duties, tariffs, taxes
- Trademark usage by distributor
- Requirements forecast annually, lead time planning and monthly update
- Term
- Permits and licenses
- Termination rights
- Dispute resolution
- Confidentiality

OTHER AGREEMENTS

- *Other agreements* can include shareholder buy-sell agreements, management agreements)

JV VALUATION AND SHAREHOLDER EQUITY CONTRIBUTION TO THE JV

- The shareholder's equity in and contributions to the JV follows the JV valuation process and the negotiation between the parties regarding control.
  - Appendix 95.1 shows an example of a JV valuation, formation, and the resulting partner contribution determination process.
  - Generally, the enterprise and equity valuation of a JV follows the joint development of the JV business plan and from formative discussions that capture each party's contributions to the JV including transfer pricing, licensing fees, and other economic drivers, and the impact on the prospective economic results (lower cost, market penetration, new product, new technology, etc.) and the amount of debt capital to be utilized by the JV (Appendix 95.1, section 1).
  - In the example, the partners have agreed to a 60% partner A; 40% partner B split.
  - Each side generally will have its own view of the impact of the economic results of the other party's contributions and therefore the JV results, which ultimately are expressed by each party as JV free cash flow (FCF) forecasts (section 2). Partner A views the value of the JV to be $17.8 million. Partner B views the value of the JV to be $16.0 million.

- Negotiations over the valuation of the free cash flow of the contributed components to the JV and the discount rates appropriate to each component are not unusual (e.g., FCF arising from old versus new product or market, timing of new facility investment and results, contributed tax-loss carry-forward utilization, cost reduction and timing, etc.) (sections 2 and 3).
- The partners agree a value of the FCF flow of the joint venture to be worth $18.5 million (section 3).
- In addition, partners will want to ensure that the initial transaction is tax free to each contributing partner; the impact of taxes often guides partner contribution mechanics (section 4).
  - For example, partner contributions of technology or know-how in exchange for JV equity in cross-border deals can create taxable transactions for the asset contributor. In such case, clarity on the value or the tax basis of assets contributed for equity can be left up to negotiation with the taxing jurisdiction, which can lead to adverse unexpected tax consequences.
  - An alternate and often better form is for the partners to contribute cash to the JV and for the JV to purchase the asset from the partners at company-established, negotiated arm's length pricing (section 4).
- A final negotiated JV valuation in the amount of $18.5 million (section 3) is critical to determining the cash contribution required (section 4) (net of the value of other contributions) of the party whose contributed asset value is lower than the party's desired equity position in the JV.
- The JV capitalization and the party contributions for JV equity (section 5) will reflect the agreed equity splits of the negotiated total JV valuation. The payments required of the JV to acquire the operating capacity from each party will reflect the negotiated asset valuations of each party's contributions (section 4).
  - As shown in sections 4 and 5 in Appendix 95.1, Partner B will make available to the JV technology, markets, and process improvement undertakings jointly valued at $6 million. Partner B will pay $7.4 million to the JV at the closing for 40% of the agreed value of $18.5 million.
  - The JV will purchase from or enter into consulting agreements with Partner B with an aggregate value of $6 million, thus leaving $1.4 million in the JV.
  - According to sections 4 and 5, Partner A will make available to the JV a business with an agreed value of $12 million. Partner A will pay $11.1 million to the JV at the closing for 60% of the agreed value of $18.5 million.
  - The JV will purchase from Partner A the business of partner A for $12 million funded from the equity contribution of Partner A plus the $1.4 million excess proceeds available from Partner B.
- Partner equity splits are closely related to the partnership agreements, where the minority partner seeks certain supermajority approval, other blocking rights, and termination rights to ensure protection of its minority position.

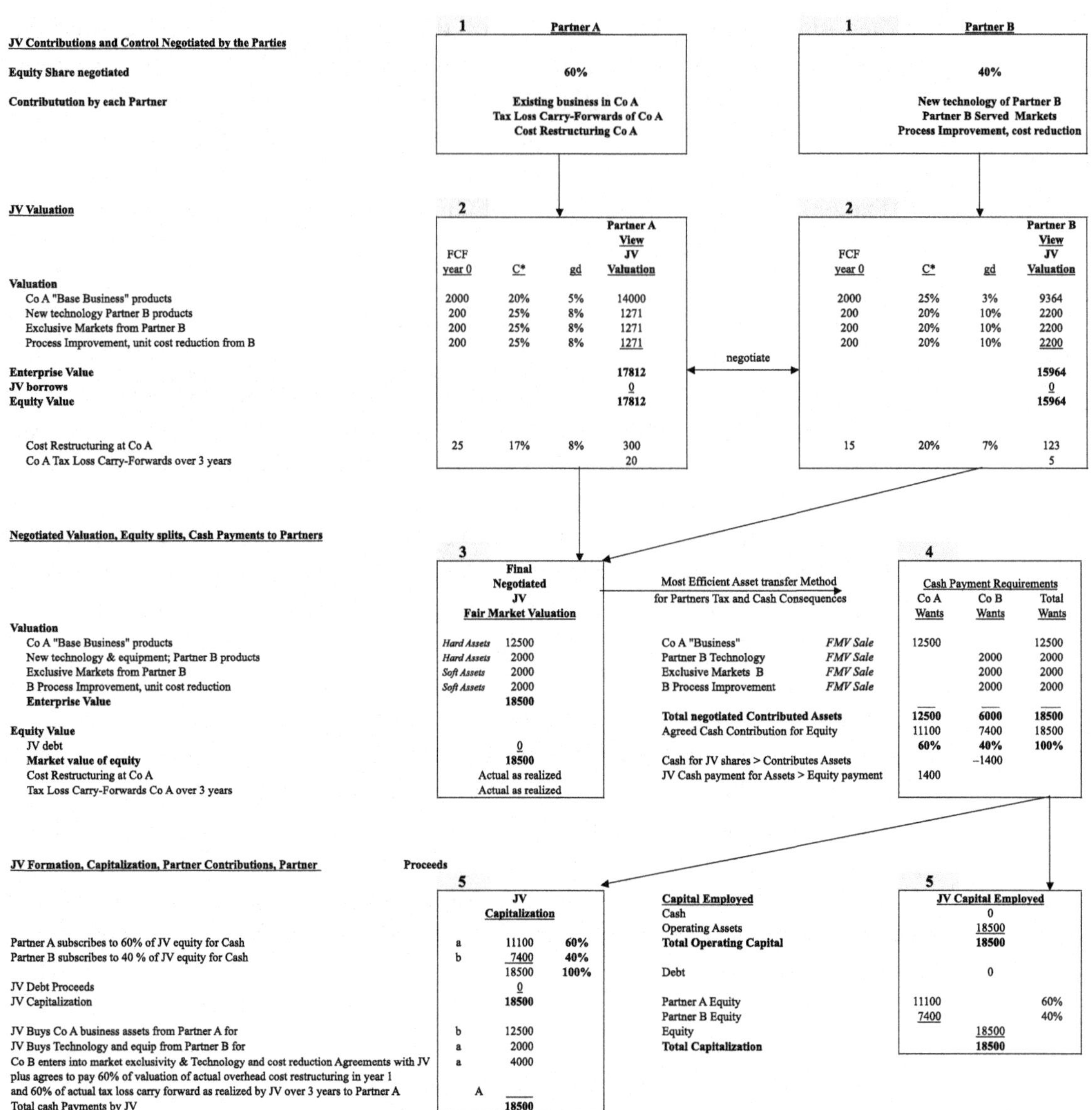

APPENDIX 95.1 Joint Venture Formation Engine

TOPIC 96

Why Deals Go Bad

Topic 96 explores why M&A deals often go bad and do not provide the expected economic results.

WHY DEALS GO BAD OR DO NOT WORK OUT

- Many M&A transactions do not realize their goals, for a number of reasons:
  - Goals and priorities of the postmerger new company are unclear or not well communicated.
  - Operating philosophies are not reconciled; differences persist between the views of the buyer and the target employees or management: "My way is better than yours."
  - Participants from the acquired target do not feel a vested ownership in a new vision, mission, and goal-setting process.
  - A participatory, empowered culture is not encouraged, defined, or allowed to flourish; a top-down hierarchical model prevails; morale and productivity plummet.
  - Integration and synergy-achieving activities are not well planned and therefore not well executed.
  - Human resource planning is poor, and the employees of the acquired business feel left out or mistreated due to noncomparable medical and retirement benefits and pay levels.
  - Employees of the acquired business do not feel involved in the operating decisions they feel they were involved in previously.
  - Information technology enablers do not work well or early enough.
  - The transition, integration, and synergy development process takes too long.
  - Risk events occur with material impact on the business without adequate insurance or risk management capabilities to control and mitigate the impact.
  - Buyers overestimated the value of the business and as a result, overpaid for it. The economic returns do not meet debt repayment, dividend return, and market valuation growth expectations.

WHAT HAS TO HAPPEN TO AVOID BAD DEALS

- Essentials to succeed:
  - Speed. The transition teams must move quickly at the expense of mistakes (see Topics 51 and 52).
    - Progress matters most.
    - Fix the mistakes later.
    - Identify the tree huggers (who cannot make the change from the past—the way they did it) and get rid of them early.
  - Make the tough decisions quickly regarding people and facilities and move on.
  - Conduct meaningful strategic and integration planning development sessions for the key players in the new company and execute the integration plan fast and hard (see Topics 51 and 52).
  - Create an empowered culture to get results.
  - Realize benefits through effective buy-in of the achievability of the synergy plans in each area.
    - Allow management participants to redo the synergy estimates and thereby own them.
  - Create meaningful incentive plans, including equity-building plans, for the key players in the new organization.
  - Carefully track and measure the benefits of cost restructuring and integration initiatives.
  - Get the information technology systems working; make system and organization choices and move on.
  - Conduct a realistic, meaningful risk assessment for the business in the owner's hands.
  - Realistically value the deal.

TOPIC 97

After the Deal: Do a Deal Bible

The deal bible provides the background of the value proposition as to why a deal was done and the backbone for assessing progress toward achieving the value proposition.

DEAL BIBLE DEFINED

- The deal bible captures the business thinking, rationale, justification, key terms, follow-ups, and integration plans for the deal.
- The deal bible should contain the acquisition and execution teams' commitment sign-up sheet.
- The deal bible is a working document setting forth why the deal was done, when integration milestones are to be achieved, what the integration plan is and how it is to be achieved, how much was invested, and what the value creation goals are and who is on the line to realize them.
- The deal bible provides the background document for all postdeal audits (see Topic 98).
- Typical sections of the deal bible include:
  - Memorandum, reports, and summaries setting forth the business plan and rationale as to why the deal makes sense.
  - Final acquisition criteria rating analysis and risk assessment.
  - Final due diligence report findings.
  - Documents and reports on the business risk and mitigation strategies.
  - Documents and reports relating to opportunity explanations and value creation strategies and implementation plans, assignments and timetables, goals, and targets—the business plan and value proposition.
  - Strength, weakness, opportunity, and threat (SWOT) assessment summaries.
  - The integration plan summary presenting what, when, how, who, expense and capital plans, timetables, and synergy value creation targets.
  - The key elements of the business valuations justifying the offer and final consideration (target returns, cost of capital, leverage assumed, free cash flow).
  - Key negotiating and deal structuring memoranda.
  - Postclosing adjustments, memoranda, or summaries.
    - Working capital true-ups
    - Earn-out or other deferred payment mechanisms
    - Escrows, amounts, holders, terms of release, timing

  - Deferred payments, amounts, timing conditions
  - Noncompete payments
  - License payments
  - Tax step-up valuation
- The deal bible must be reviewed carefully by tax departments for consistent disclosure relative to tax positions taken with respect to the transaction.

TOPIC 98

Do the Audits of the Integration and Deal Value Creation Plan

The integration plan and the value creation plan should be subjected to post-closing audits to determine progress toward successful achievement of the investment made and to determine what the organization can learn to enhance the deal-making capabilities of the acquirer in the future.

AUDIT THE INTEGRATION PLAN: ARE YOU GETTING THERE?

- Hold regular check-point meetings to manage the integration plan closely.
- Persons from the integration team responsible for each integration plan element should report:
  - Element status versus plan
  - Gaps and issues
  - Gap closure plans
  - Revised timetables and goals
- Identify human resource, organizational, and culture clash issues, and make people adjustments as early as possible.
- See Topic 52.

AUDIT THE DEAL VALUE CREATION: WHAT DID YOU LEARN?

- Annually, at least, review the deal's actual value creation versus the integration and synergy value creation plan (see Topic 51).
- Compare key plan assumptions, as captured in the deal bible, including:
  - Market size and growth rates
  - Target customer development
  - Competitive responses and conditions
  - Served market shares
  - Served market development
  - New product development

    - Product pricing levels and gross margins
    - Key financial performance metrics
    - Key operating performance metrics
- Compare plan versus actual cumulative economic value added (EVA) to date and isolate causes of material differences.
- Compare actual cumulative total shareholder return (TSR) versus the plan TSR.
- Determine the revised deal valuation based on the latest set of value driver assumptions.
- Assess the deal with a critical eye to these questions:
    - Is the deal providing what was expected? How do we get on track?
    - Can the value creation gaps be managed and closed?
    - Is reasonable value being created for the shareholder?
    - Is it reasonable to expect value creation for this deal in the future—should you stick with it?
    - Will prospective cumulative TSR including prior underperformance (sunk costs) be acceptable?
    - What do we need to do better on our next deal?
    - Where are our deal-making gaps, and what do we need to do to close them?

About the Web Site

As a purchaser of this book, *Practitioner's Complete Guide to M&As: An All-Inclusive Reference,* you have access to the supporting Web site:

www.wiley.com/go/emott

This Web site contains files for the appendices that appear in this book. These appendices are provided in Word/Excel format.

The password for this site is: Emott.

Index

A
'A reorganization'
forward triangular merger, Appendix 84.2E2 p1-2, 340
statutory consolidation, Appendix 84.2E1 p1-2, 340
statutory forward merger, Appendix 84.2E p1-2, 340
Acquisition criteria illustration, 19–21
Acquisition criteria rating engine, Appendix 4.1, 25
Acquisition criteria rating engine, example, 22–24
Acquisition premiums, 183
Asset step ups, valuation, 341–343
Auction
bid instruction letter example, Appendix 12.3, 61
bid solocitation letter example, Appendix 12.2, 61
conditional offer letter example, Appendix 12.4, 61
exclusivity letter example, Appendix 12.6, 61
preemptive offer letter example, Appendix 12.5, 61
timeline, Appendix 12.1, 60
Auction bidding strategy, 58
Auction exclusivity, 57
Auctions process, 55–57
Auctions, fear is compelling, 54, 55

B
'B reorganization'
stock for stock exchange, Appendix 84.2F p1-2, 340
stock for stock exchange, Appendix 84.2F1 p1-2, 340
Banker engagement letter example, Appendix 6.2, 35
Beta
debate over, 114
definition, 113
deleverage beta, 121
inverse relationship to size of market cap, 114
levered, 119, 120–122
releverage beta, 121–122
systematic risk, 96–99, 113, 114, 116, 117
unlevered, 118, 120–122
Beta application to C_U, 123–124
Bluffing, how to handle it, 321–323
Business development options, 1
Business driver assessment engine, 46–47
Business driver assessment engine, Appendix 10.4, 52
Business risk in M&A
deal risk frontier, Appendix 26.1, 109
defined, 106, 107
knowledge overlaps provide control, 107, 108
Buy side fee chart, Appendix 6.4, 35
Buy side fee example, Appendix 6.3, 35
Buy side investment banker fees, 32, 33

C
'C reorganization'
stock for assets exchange, Appendix 84.2G1 p1-2, 340
subsidiary stock for assets exchange, Appendix 84.2G p1-2, 340
Capability overlaps to balance acquisition risk, 18
Capital asset pricing model, CAPM, 95, 96
Capitalization of benefits approach, valuation, 82–83
CAPM calculation, 99–100
CAPM, the problems with, 96
Caps, baskets, survival duration, 374–377

Cash for assets, Appendix 84.2A p1-2, 340
Cash for stock, Appendix 84.2B p1-2, 340
Close the bid ask gap, 305–307
Competitive continuum
  Appendix 4.2, 24
  where does target fall in it, 23
Compounding, 86, 87
Confidentiality agreements, 39, 41–43
Conglomerant discounts, 189–190
Contractual conditions, work them to come to terms, 306–307, 338, 341, 377–378
Control premiums, 183
Control value, 179–180
Corporate mission, 2
Corporate strategies, 2
Corporate vision, 2
Cost of capital
  direct approach to weighted average, C*, 133
  weighted avearge, C*, 96, 130–132
Cost of capital example, Appendix 37.1, 136
Cost of debt capital, i, interest rate, 96
Cost of equity capital
  CAPM, 95
  international, 101–103
  levered, C_L, 96
  unlevered, C_U, 96

D
Deal bible, 391–392
Deal fees illustration, Appendix 6.1, 34
Deal fees tax consequences, 337
Deal momentum
  the catch, 310
  the chase, 309
  shifts in as deals progress, 309–310
  walk along, 310
Deal sources, 26–27
Deal structures
  'A reorganization' forward triangular merger, Appendix 84.2E2 p1-2, 340
  'A reorganization' statutory consolidation, Appendix 84.2E1 p1-2, 340
  'A reorganization' statutory forward merger, Appendix 84.2E p1-2, 340
  'B reorganization' stock for stock exchange, Appendix 84.2F p1-2, 340
  'B reorganization' stock for stock exchange, Appendix 84.2F1 p1-2, 340
  'C reorganization' subsidiary stock for assets exchange, Appendix 84.2G p1-2, 340
  'C reorganization' stock for assets exchange, Appendix 84.2G1 p1-2, 340
  cash for assets, Appendix 84.2A p1-2, 340
  cash for stock, Appendix 84.2B p1-2, 340
  forward cash merger for assets, Appendix 84.2A1 p1-2, 340
  forward triangular cash merger for assets, Appendix 84.2A2 p1-2, 340
  reverse cash merger (for stock), Appendix 84.2B1 p1-2, 340
  reverse triangular cash merger (for stock), Appendix 84.2B2 p1-2, 340
  sec 338 cash for stock, Appendix 84.2C p1-2, 340
  sec 338(h)(10) cash for stock, Appendix 84.2D p1-2, 340
Deal structuring engine, Appendix 84.2 p1–3, 340
Debt
  negative covenants, positive covenants, 149
  the discounted cash flow derivation of the benefit of debt, appendices 42.1–42.2, 154
  the practical limits, 149–150
  use leverage to increase deal value, 147–148
  the valuation and tax benefit of debt in M&A, Dt, 151–154
Deleverage beta, 121
Department of justice, 39
Detail due diligence, 44–46

Discount rate engine, Appendix 54.1, 221
Discount rates
  beginning of year, 213–214
  continuous, 219–220
  end of year, 211–212
  mid year, 214–215
  monthly, 218–219
  quarterly, 215–218
Discounted cash flow approach, valuation, 86–89
Discounting, 87–88
Discounts and valuation levels
  fuzzy logic, 191
  fuzzy logic example, Appendix 48.1, 191
Do a time capsule, 328
Due diligence business driver assessment engine, Appendix 10.4, 52
Due diligence overview, Appendix 10.1, 50
Due diligence preliminary due diligence information request list, Appendix 10.2, 51
Due diligence process, 44–52
Due diligence threshold issues, Appendix 10.6, 52
Due diligence valuation driver assessment engine, Appendix 10.5, 52
Due diligence work plan formats
  accounting, financial results and forecast, Appendix 10.3K p1-2, 51
  acquisition criteria rating, Appendix 10.3B p1-2, 51
  business drivers rating, Appendix 10.3A p1–3, 51
  business strategy, Appendix 10.3E, 51
  competition, Appendix 10.3H, 51
  corporate governance, Appendix 10.3X, 52
  customers, channels, markets, Appendix 10.3G, 51
  environmental, Appendix 10.3O, 52
  financial policy driver rating, Appendix 10.3C, 51
  information technology, Appendix 10.3P, 52
  intellectual property, Appendix 10.3N, 52
  internal control, Appendix 10.3V, 52
  inventory, cost accounting, Appendix 10.3L, 51
  legal, litigation, Appendix 10.3T, 52
  manufacturing facilities and property, Appendix 10.3J, 51
  marketing/sales/products, Appendix 10.3F p1-2, 51
  material contracts, Appendix 10.3R, 52
  operation effectiveness Appendix 10.3I, 51
  organization, human resources and labor, Appendix 10.3Q, 52
  procurement, Appendix 10.3S, 52
  research and development, Appendix 10.3M, 52
  risk management and insurance, Appendix 10.3U, 52
  target company culture, Appendix 10.3D, 51
  tax matters, Appendix 10.3W, 52
Due diligence working capital issues, Appendix 10.7, 52

E
Earnout example, 315–316
Earnout tax considerations, 314–315
Earnouts, 313–317
EBITDA valuation example, appendices 60.1, 60.2, 268
EBITDA valuation, engine, short hand method, 264–272
Enterprise value, 178
Entropy in M&A, 110–111
Environmental insurance, 283–284
Environmental remediation, tax treatment, 282
Equity investor risk, 112
Equity risk premium, 96, 105
Equity value, 180
Escrows, 379
EVA, 350–352

EVAquity incentive plan, align management and shareholder interests, 353–357
Extortion and leverage, beware, 309

F
Failed auctions, 58
Fair market value, 180
Fair return on a deal, 95
Federal trade commission, 39
Financial buyers, 36–37
Firewall, in mergers between competitors, 40
Forward cash merger for assets, Appendix 84.2A1 p1-2, 340
Forward triangular cash merger for assets, Appendix 84.2A2 p1-2, 340
Franchise capabilities
  evolution, Appendix 14.1, 67
  inherent, 65–67
Free cash flow, 90–93
Frontiers of deal acceptance, 336

G
Goals, 2
Growth
  deferred tax advantage result, 223
  ROI and cost of capital interdependencies, 222
  ROI and cost of capital interdependencies, Appendix 55.1, 224
  sustainable level, 225–226

H
Handling tight spots, 303–304
Have an exit plan, 333
Heads of agreement, 318–320
How to avoid bad deals, 389
How to handle the bully, 331–332

I
Imprint message, do not lecture, 301
Indemnification and survival, 374–378
Inflation in DCF valuations, 194
Initiatives, 2
Integration
  business mission work sheets, Appendix 52.2, 206
  business support function design, 203–204
  business vision and values work sheets, Appendix 52.1, 206
  communication, 201
  culture gaps work sheets, Appendix 52.8–52.10, 207
  information technology alignment, 204–206
  information technology alignment work sheets, Appendix 52.15–52.17, 207
  initiatives drive deal value, 73–74
  key planning areas to consider, 198
  key strengths, capabilities, gaps work sheets, Appendix 52.4–52.6, 207
  management capabilities work sheets, Appendix 52.11–52.13, 207
  market and customer based synergies, 204
  mission critical issues work sheets, Appendix 52.3, 207
  organizational design, culture, and policy alignment, 200–201
  planning and synergy evaluation, 197
  plant and facility closure work sheets, Appendix 52.18–52.21, 207
  policy initiatives work sheets, Appendix 52.14, 207
  research and development and facility selection, 202–203
  steps to develop the plan, 195–196
  strategic initiatives work sheets, Appendix 52.7, 207
  strategy alignment, 198
  technology, IP and R&D project alignment, 205
Investment banker fees
  buy side arrangements to align seller and banker interests, 32
  illustration, 32–33
Investment value, 179

J
Joint ventures
distribution agreement content, 385–386
formation agreement, 384
partnership agreement content, 382–384
supply agreement content, 385
technology license agreement content, 385
valuation and equity contribution, 386–387

K
Kanbans, pull signals, 79–80
Key man discounts, 189
Key performance indicators, KPIs, 2

L
LBO
defined, 155
recaps and equity investors end game, 156–157
LBO valuation
sponsor entry/exit sensitivity, Appendix 44.4, 168
valuing the leveraged buyout, 160–168
LBO valuation benefit of using debt, Appendix 44.3, 168
LBO valuation engine, Appendix 44.1, 167
LBO valuation example, Appendix 44.2, 168
LBO, characteristics and capital structure, 157–159
Lean enterprise
identify non value added activities, 78–79
to unlock hidden value, 75–77
Lean value pyramid, Appendix 19.1, 81
Letter of intent, 318–320, 358
Leverage, use it if you have it, 308–309
Levered beta increases with debt to equity, 125–126
Liquidity discounts, 187–189

M
M&A process, 13–16
activity and contact, 13
activity and stages map, Appendix 2.1, 15
close it, 14
come to terms, 13
matrix of responsibility and authority, Appendix 2.2, 16
preparation, 13
Market approach, valuation, 83–84
Marketability discounts, 187–189
Matters not allowed to be discussed between merging competitors, 39
Matters permitted to be discussed between merging competitors, 40
Metrics, 2
Minority discounts, 185–186
Minority value, 181
Multiple conversion table, FCF_M to other multiples, 259
Multiples
comparable, adjustments required, 239–244
derivation of gd, 231–233
derivation of PE and other multiples from FCF_M, 236–237, 248–250
discount rate adjusted growth rate, gd, method of derivation, 230
factor to convert end of year to midyear basis, 228–229
FCF_M reconciliation example, Appendix 58.1, 245
of cash flow, 227–230
of cash flow, lagging, leading, no growth, 227–228
of cash flow, lagging, leading, with growth, 230
of EBITDA, large company illustration, Appendix 59.8, 261
of EBITDA, small company illustration, Appendix 59.7, 260
of free cash flow, large company illustration, Appendix 59.10, 263
of free cash flow, small company illustration, Appendix 59.9, 262

N

Negotiation
- be sensitive to private sellers, 299–300
- bluffing, how to handle it, 321–323
- build trust to close it, 329–332
- close the bid ask gap, 305–307
- contractual conditions, 306–307
- create space in your ideas, 298
- deal momentum shifts, 309–310
- earnouts, 313–316
- earnout example, 315–316
- earnout tax considerations, 314–315
- extortion, beware, 309
- handling tight spots, 303–304
- heads of agreement, 318–320
- how to handle the bully, 331–332
- imprint message, do not lecture, 301
- introduction, 290–291
- letter of intent, 318
- leverage, use it, 308–309
- noncompete agreements, 316–317
- rank offer weak spots, 303–304
- side list of open items, 304, 305
- term sheet, 318
- the catch, 309–310
- the chase, 309
- the complete offer, 296–297
- the lobbed offer stage, 311–312
- the walk along, 310
- when to proceed, buyers, 326
- when to proceed, sellers, 327
- when to step away, buyers, 324
- when to step away, sellers, 325
- values offers, price and risk assumption, 292–293
- values offers, price and risk assumption, appendices 67.1–67.4, 294–295

Net realized seller value, 182
Non value added activities, 78–80
Noncompete agreements, 313–317
Noncompete, valuation, 343

O

Offer determination and negotiation process, Appendix 16.1, 72
Offer value, 181
One piece flow, pull production, 79–80

P

PE eviscerator
- Appendix 59.4, 263
- applied to Coca-Cola Co., slot multiples, 251–252
- applied to Google, slot multiples, 254
- Coca-Cola Co., Appendix 59.5, 263
- Google, Appendix 59.6, 263
- to validate public trading multiples, 251

Pension liability valuation
- ABO method, 278–280
- PBO method, 278–280

Pension liability valuation issues, 278–280
Platform value, 68–69
Platform value, real option valuation approach, 69
Postdeal audits, 393–394
Preemptive offers in auctions, 57
Prelimnary due diligence, 45–46, 50
Preliminary due diligence information request list, Appendix 10.2, 51
Prospectus, 62–64
Purchase and sale agreement
- conditions to closing, 367–368
- other provisions, 369
- parties, definitions, 361–362
- post closing covenants, indemnification, 368
- price adjustment, covenants to closing, 362–363
- representations and warranties of buyer, 366
- representations and warranties of seller, 363–366

Purchase price adjustments for working capital, 370–373

R

Rank offer tight spots during negotiation, 303–304
Real option black scholes valuation illustration, appendices 46.2, 46.4, 46.6, 178
Real option valuation approach to platform value, 69

Real option valuation illustration, 174–178
Real option valuation illustration, appendices 46.1, 46.3, 46.5, 178
Real option valaution in M&A, 172
Real option valuation methodology overview, 169–172
Releverage beta, 121–122
Results, 3
Reverse cash merger (for stock), Appendix 84.2B1 p1-2, 340
Reverse triangular cash merger (for stock), Appendix 84.2B2 p1-2, 340
Risk free return, 96, 104

S
Search mandate example, 28
Sec 338 cash for stock, Appendix 84.2C p1-2, 340
Sec 338(h)(10) cash for stock, Appendix 84.2D p1-2, 340
Security market line, 97
Security market line illustration, Appendix 23.1, 103
Shareholder value creation, 349–351
Side list of open items, 304, 305
Size risk premium, Ibbotson Associates, 96, 127–129
Spider chart
  Appendix 57.14, 236–237, 238
  EBITDA valuation engine example, Appendix 60.7, 275
Stages in the strategic planning process, 2
Stakeholder value creation, customers and employees, 349
Strategic buyers, 36–37
Strategic planning process engine, Appendix 1.1, 10
Strategy development, 1–11
  activity/capability analysis, Appendix 1.3–1.4, 12
  attractive market composition, Appendix 1.7, 12
  capabilities versus market requirements, Appendix 1.5–1.6, 12
  competence alignment of targets, Appendix 1.9, 12
  SWOT analysis, Appendix 1.8, 12
  where and how to create value, 3
  where and how to create value, Appendix 1.2, 11
Synergy, valuation, 344
Systematic risk, beta, 96, 113–115, 116–117

T
Tax deferred and taxable deals, 334–337
Term sheet, 318–320
Terminal value, 137–139
Terminal value determination methods, 138–139
Terminal value, illustration, appendices 38.1–38.4, 141
The lobbed offer stage, 311
The role of M&A, 17
The value creation potential index, VCPI for Coca-Cola Co., 253
The value creation potential index, VCPI for Google, 256
Time required to complete deals, 38
Total shareholder return, TSR, 346–348
Transaction value, 182
Trust, build it to close it, 329–332

U
Unsystematic risk, 100–101, 118
Unsystematic risk, treatment in valuation, 100–101

V
Valuation
  discounted cash flow approach, 85–89, 142–144
  discounted cash flow example, Appendix 39.2–39.3, 146
  discounted cash flow valuation and offer process engine, Appendix 39.1, 145
  Fama French Method, 98
  market approach, 83–84
  of terminal value, 137–139

Valuation (*Continued*)
real option methodology overview, 169–172
terminal value determination methods, 138–141
unsystematic risk, 98
valuing the leveraged buyout, LBO, 160–166
venture capital approach, 208–210
Valuation considerations and methods, 82–83
Valuation driver assessment engine, 47–48
Valuation driver assessment engine, Appendix 10.5, 52
Valuation impacts from adjustments to discount rates, appendices 61.1–61.3, 277
Valuation, arbitrage pricing method, APT, 98–99
Valuation, build up method, 98
Valuation, capitalization of benefits approach, 84–85
Valuation, discounted cash flow, minority or control, 192–193
Value perspectives of buyers and sellers, 70–72
Venture capital valuation, 208–210

W
Warrant incentive plans, 285–287
Warrant incentive plan illustration, Appendix 65.1, 288–289
What to do when deals leak out, 53
When to proceed
buyers, 326
sellers, 327
When to step away
buyers, 324
sellers, 325
Why deals go bad, 389

Printed in the United States
By Bookmasters